Reprints of Economic Classics

OUTLINES
OF
ECONOMIC THEORY

Also Published In

<u>Reprints of Economic Classics</u>

By HERBERT J. DAVENPORT

Value and Distribution [1908]

The Economics of Alfred Marshall [1935]

OUTLINES

OF

ECONOMIC THEORY

BY

HERBERT JOSEPH DAVENPORT

[1896]

REPRINTS OF ECONOMIC CLASSICS

AUGUSTUS M. KELLEY · PUBLISHERS
NEW YORK 1968

First Edition, 1896

(New York: The Macmillan Company, 1896)

Reprinted 1968 by
AUGUSTUS M. KELLEY · PUBLISHERS
New York New York 10010

Library of Congress Catalogue Card Number
67-29500

PRINTED IN THE UNITED STATES OF AMERICA
by SENTRY PRESS, NEW YORK, N. Y. 10019

OUTLINES

OF

ECONOMIC THEORY

BY

HERBERT JOSEPH DAVENPORT

New York
THE MACMILLAN COMPANY
LONDON: MACMILLAN & CO., Ltd.
1896

PREFACE

This book was not originally projected as a text-book, nor is it now directed primarily to teachers. In attempting, however, to make it serviceable in his own work in the class-room, the writer has found it advisable to adopt the plan of suggestive questions as introductory to the various topics, and to follow the discussions with a wide selection of questions, serving in part as a review of the text and in part to indicate the bearing of the theoretical discussions upon subjects of current and practical interest. In so far as this method is well adapted to pedagogical needs, it can hardly fail to prove helpful to the independent reader. It has therefore seemed desirable to retain the text-book manner of presentation.

For such teachers as shall make use of the book for class-room purposes, it is advised that the student be required to bring to the recitation-room written answers to both the suggestive and the review questions. Answers to the introductory questions should be attempted before the text is appointed for study.

HERBERT J. DAVENPORT.

SUMMARY

(References are to Sections)

	PAGE

INTRODUCTION, 1–7 1
   Scope of the science, 1.
   Character of economic laws, 2.
   Economics a study of two terms, (1) *man;* (2) *environment.*
      Man the centre of the science, 5, 6.
   Law and *freewill*, 7.

WEALTH, 8–23 14
   Desires and *utility*, 8.
   Utilities external and internal, 10.
   Only external are wealth, 10.
   Moral questions irrelevant for this purpose, 9.
   Utilities exist (1) in superfluity ; (2) in scarcity.
      Only (2) are wealth, 11.
   Is *material existence* essential ? 12–17.
   Wealth *socially* a sacrifice-commanding utility exterior to mankind.
      Individually . . . exterior to individual, 12–21.
      A question of *correspondence,* 22 ; not necessarily a product of labour, 23.

ECONOMIC MOTIVE, 24–28 29
   Selfishness is not the first postulate, 25.
   The *minimizing* of *sacrifice* is the formula, 25–28.

VALUE 35
   Desires are each satiable, 29, 30.
   Individual economics underlies social, 31, 32.
   Antagonism between utility and value, 33, 34.
   Value, how fixed — sacrifice for sacrifice, 35, 36.
   Method of fixation, 38.
   Value. Personal — the measure of sacrifice involved in obtaining or retaining utility, 39, 40. *Market* — this sacrifice as fixed in the market by marginal adjustments, 41.
   Value measures marginal *relative* utility = sacrifice, 41–43.

	PAGE
COST OF PRODUCTION	50

Restated as *marginal producers' sacrifice* (*a*) possibly in *effort;* (*b*) commonly in possible *products.*

Values exist apart from labour, but tend roughly to correspond, 46.

Product measures value of labour, rather than labour, product, 47–48.

In what sense has labour value ? 49.

Question how important, 50.

Usual statement, 52 ; criticised, 53, 54.

    Criticism applied to (*a*) wages, 52 ; (*b*) interest, 59 ; (*c*) labour cost, 53.

All economic forces resolved finally into demand, 54.

WAGES AND PROFITS DEFINED, 61–66	68

Man and *nature* are factors, 61.

Profits and *wages* identical, 64, 65.

Risk, 66.

RENT, 67–91	75

What produces the crop ? 67.

Ricardian theory (1) *stated,* 68.

    (2) *Modified* — Enlarged conception of products, 72 ; margin of usefulness, 73 ; origins irrelevant, 73 ; *rent, wages,* and *interest* are results — distributive shares — not causes, 82–91.

Law of diminishing returns, 68.

Rent and price, 69, 82–91.

    Monopoly aspects, 77.

Law of rent is restatement of law of value, 78.

Rent and population, 79 ; urban land, 80 ; single tax, 81.

POPULATION, 92–99	106

Does cost of production apply to men ? 92.

Evidence of Malthusian statement, 94, 95 ; *contra,* 96.

Is there a law, 97, 98.

CAPITAL AND INTEREST	119

Capital in two aspects — (1) individual ; (2) social.

Some ambiguities, 101 ; credits and fiats, 102–104.

Relations between (*a*) credit and savings, (*b*) credit and capital, 105–107.

	PAGE
Capitalization takes place mostly through credit system, 106, 107.	
Capitalization not a question of existing wealth, 108.	
Interest.	
Advantages obtained by borrowers, 109–111.	
Interest is *sacrifice* made for these, marginally determined, 114–117.	
Enlarged conception of *income*, 115.	
Risk, 118, 119.	

WAGES, PROFITS, AND DISTRIBUTION 143
  Wages and profits vary with individuals, 120, 121.
  Relation of labour supply to wages; women's wages, 122.
  What is *starting point* in wages problem? 123–126.
    Imprenditors, 127.
      Their competition, 128; monopoly aspects, 129.
    Distribution, 130, 131.
      Tendencies of interest, 130; of profits, 131; of wages and profits together; President Walker's theory examined, 131.

MINOR MARKET MOVEMENTS. INCREASING RETURNS AND SPECU-
  LATION, 132–136 168

INTERNATIONAL TRADE, 137–146 178
  Division of labour advantageous to nations, 137; a question of least sacrifices, 137; inertia of labour and capital, 140.
  Domestic competition the real danger to struggling industries, 140.
  Protection under monopoly conditions, 142; as method of taxing the foreigner, 144; temporary stimulus, 145; effects on rents and distribution, 146.

COMBINATION AND MONOPOLY, 147–154 201
  Laissez-faire and competition, 147, 148.
  Where is the *evil* in combination? 149.
  Theory of monopoly, 150.
  Limits of monopoly, 151.
  Purchasers' combinations, 152.

TRADES-UNIONS 208
  May they lower interest? remuneration for risk; profits on oppression of employés; on adulteration, etc., 153.
  Conditions of success, 154.

x SUMMARY

	PAGE

TAXATION, 155–161 213
    Different formal rules examined, 155.
    Tax shifts only as demand and supply undergo readjustment.
        Therefore tax on *any form of rent* does not shift, 156; on *incomes* does not shift, 156; on *commodities, capital,* or *interest* shifts in part, 156, 157.
    Shifting ceases when consumer is reached, 159, 160.
    Increasing and decreasing returns, 160.
        Bounties — benefits shift in part, 161.

CURRENCY, 162–212 224
    Fluctuation and inaccuracy inevitable over *long periods*, 162.
    Standard should follow *utility* rather than *value*, 163.
    Must take account of *services*, 164, and if possible of changing *standards of living*, 165, 166.
    Functions of currency, and *necessary qualities*, 167–169.
        All credits are *protracted* cases of *exchange*, 170.
        Need for money results from division of labour and is limited by it, 173.
        Test of sufficiency, 173, 174.

VALUE OF MONEY, HOW FIXED, 175–183 238
    Different kinds of currency — credit, commodity, and fiat, 184, 185.

GRESHAM'S LAW, 187–192 249
    Increased supply *lowers value* of unit, 187.
    Fiat or credit issues therefore increase non-currency demand for commodity elements, 188.
    But *outflow* is unequal to inflow, 189.

INTERNATIONAL TRADE AND CURRENCY 256
    Foreign markets as related to currency movements, 190, 191.
    Futility of *local attempts* at *inflation*, 192.
    Irredeemable currency, 193–202.
        Value of currency a question of *demand* and *supply*, and *not of material*, 193–201. But first issues are always ill-advised, 202.
    Bimetallism, 204–206.
        National, means alternations of monometallism, 204.
        International, could be made to succeed, 205, 206.

	PAGE
COMMERCIAL CRISES, 207–211	273

A collapse in credit, 207, 208; not in fictitious prosperity, 209.
Advantages and dangers of credit, 210, 211.
Expansion of currency *as remedy* considered, 212.

TARIFF TAXES AND PRICES	280

Effects of tariff barriers on commodity and metal production and on prices, 213–217.

ECONOMICS AS ART

THE COMPETITIVE SYSTEM, 218–238	284

The *modern* industrial *era* analyzed, 218–220.
The Economic Harmonies, 221, 222.
Laissez-faire as an *ethical* system, 223.
Tendencies indicated by *history*, 226–228.
Laissez-faire and *socialism* compared economically, 229, 230.
    Competitive production criticised, 231–233.
    Competitive distribution criticised, 234, 235.
    Competitive consumption criticised, 236.
Socialism generally, as remedy, 238–242.

CO-OPERATION AND PROFIT-SHARING, 243–246	315
STATE AND MUNICIPAL OWNERSHIP, 248, 249	319
SOCIAL FUNCTIONS OF THE RICH, 250, 251	320
POPULATION AND NATIONAL SURVIVAL, 252–254	324
BIRTH-RATES, STANDARDS OF LIFE, AND NATURAL SELECTION, 252–254	326
FASHION, 259–274	330

Consumption and *ethical* standards, 259–261.
Expansiveness of *needs* as bearing on *civilization*, 262, 263.
Standards and opinions of others, 264.
Nineteenth century unrest, 265, 266.
The cause, 267–274.

TAXATION, 275–283	344

Applications of theory to income, vice, luxury, land, and inheritance taxes, 275–281.
Land tax, 282, 283.

	PAGE
EIGHT-HOUR DAY, 284, 285	350
APPRENTICES, 286	351
SWEATING SYSTEM, 287–289	351
LABOUR OF WOMEN AND CHILDREN, 290, 291	353
NON-EMPLOYMENT, 292–296	355
CURRENCY	360

    Fluctuation and panics, and different remedial proposals, 296.
    Commodity standard, 297.
    The ultimate evil, 298, 299.
    The imprenditor system and wages, 300–302.
    Bank issues *vs.* government issues, 303–307.
    International free coinage of silver; American free coinage of silver, 308–310.
    Injustice of the change, 311–313.
    Merits of silver as a standard; statistics, 314–317.

" La notion de la valeur est le fondement de toute l'économie politique, et ce n'est pas seulement l'échange, mais la répartition, la consommation et la production elle-même qui se ramènent, tant au point de vue purement scientifique qu'au point de vue pratique, à des questions de valeur. Les traités d'économie politique pure ne sont que des traités sur la valeur."

CHARLES GIDE.

OUTLINES OF ECONOMIC THEORY

CHAPTER I

THE SCOPE OF THE SCIENCE

Ask yourself some unanswerable questions about Electricity. About Light, Ether, a Flower, a Chair, a Dab of Mud. What does Tennyson mean when he says :

> "Flower in the crannied wall,
> I pluck you out of the crannies,
> Hold you here root and all in my hand,
> Little flower, — but if I could understand
> What you are, root and all, and all in all,
> I should know what God and man is."

In what sense is it true that a perfect knowledge of any one fact is a perfect knowledge of all facts ?

Mention some relations of Chemistry to Medicine ; of Geography to Botany ; of Mathematics to Physics ; of Geology to Zoölogy ; of History to Astronomy.

From the point of view of how many sciences can you discuss a stick of wood ?

1. Sociology may be broadly, though perhaps not very precisely, defined as a study of man as a social being. Political Economy is a field of investigation inside sociology, and may be stated to be a study of man in his commercial and industrial activities. This definition will not be found greatly helpful if attempt is made to apply it. The chemistry of farming, or the mechanics of weaving, hardly fall within the field of economic investigation. But it is the murrain of definitions that, in about the

The unity of knowledge.

degree that they get helpful and mentally tangible, they get inaccurate. No science is properly to be regarded as separated by any definite line of demarcation from all others. In some manner, more or less remote, all knowledge is related to all other. The field which any science covers is mostly a question of point of view. Men's commercial and industrial activities are in countless points of contact with questions of social morality and physical health; with questions of pedagogy and jurisprudence; with chemistry, mechanics, and physics; with law, politics, and medicine; with physiology, sanitation, and dietetics; with religion, criminology, and penology. Geography is handmaid to transportation. Geology discloses the gold and silver mines. Astronomy may hide the secret of drouths and famines.

Evidently enough we need a point of view, else Political Economy is not sociology merely, but sociology and a good deal more. *Political Economy treats of the commercial and industrial activities of men from the standpoint of values and markets.* Law and religion have place in Political Economy accordingly as they bear upon the production and distribution of the things which are bought and sold. Medicine, sanitation, and education are economic questions only as they bear upon the productive efficiency of the economic actor, Man. Vice and crime pertain to economic investigation, in so far as they are elements in the productive efficiency of society, and in the terms of security on which production takes place and effort is rewarded. Political Economy is more than the science of trades and values; but its horizon includes only what falls into view from this point of survey.

The economic field.

2. Something also needs be said of the attitude of the economic investigator toward questions of morality and attempts at social amelioration. Is Political Economy concerned with moral questions, or does it merely describe conditions and analyze tendencies? What is its function in the struggle of humanity towards a higher plane of living? Are its processes coldly scientific and un-

Economics as science and as art.

sympathetic, or is there some throb of heart and purpose in it? What of the poor? Can it help? Would it if it could? Is it dismal, or hopeful, or neutral?

Accordingly as one's point of view is theoretical or practical will the value of facts be differently estimated. To the scientific investigator they are valuable in the first instance for the inferences and tentative generalizations which they suggest; in the second instance, for the opportunity of testing by particular applications the correctness of the generalizations formed. Otherwise than as a basis for generalizations, or as a test of generalizations, facts have no value to the scientist.

The attitude of the scientist, however, is a professional one, taking into consideration only one aspect of the value of knowledge, and this aspect not the most important one. Science alone is not fruitful. If for the purposes of science, facts are valueless otherwise than as the raw material for principles and theories and generalizations, it is equally true that the systematizing and generalizing of facts which constitutes science is mere raw material for service to human welfare. Somehow and sometime the scientific law must fit into the business and practice of life in its moral, emotional, or bread-winning activities,— otherwise science has failed to justify itself. It is not its own excuse for being. It is held to a no less rigid account of itself than are harvest fields or orchard trees. "By their fruits ye shall know them." But it is the high peace of science to rest secure in the oneness of knowledge — to know that in the interdependence of all truth with all other, no fact stands dimly out of relation and verily unfertile for the needs of life. To the farmer his plough and to the weaver his shuttle. The scientist rightly pursues his search for truth with an eye single to its scientific import, since, for whatever he starts from cover, by some one and somewhere there will be found a place in the uses of living.

The ultimate purpose of science.

Thus any object may be studied in its laws and principles, or in its applications to the well-being of society. Nor is it necessary that both lines of labour be performed by the same investigator. Economics as a science deals with the general laws and tendencies concerning man as an economic actor. As an art, it deals with the application of these laws to the well-being of society. Science treats mostly of what is or tends to be. It is not greatly concerned to commend or to criticise, but to analyze, describe, and generalize. Art devotes itself to the practical outcome of the scientific laws, to questions of what may be and ought to be, and to the different processes of attainment. In the one aspect evil is treated as a fact to be studied; in the other, as a wrong to be remedied. The bacteriologist best studies bacilli coldly, and the physician diagnoses disease unemotionally, writing no sentiment into his prescriptions. Sympathy has no great place in a hand-book on surgery. Yet the purposes of medicine are philanthropic, and the sick-room has its need of kindness.

Suggestive Questions

Discuss from your present outlook the correctness of the following definitions of Political Economy: —

1. Reflections upon the formation and distribution of wealth.
— Turgot.
2. Researches upon the nature and causes of the wealth of nations.
— Adam Smith.
3. How the wealth which satisfies the needs of societies is created, distributed, and consumed. — J. B. Say.
4. The theory of the basis, the methods, and the laws of development of the prosperity of nations. — Kantz.
5. The science of the production and distribution of wealth. — Mill.
6. A study or inquiry concerned with the production, distribution, and exchange of wealth and services. — Sidgwick.
7. A study of man's action in the ordinary business of life.
— Marshal.
8. The reasoned activity of a people tending towards the satisfaction of its needs. — Conrad.
9. As science has for subject that part of the voluntary activity of men which applies itself to the production, appropriation, and consumption of wealth — As an art was long considered to be limited to a search for the conditions in which a people could most advance its wealth — To-day this purpose is confused with that of sociology viewed as an art.
— Charles Benoist in *Nouveau Dict. d'Économie Politique.*

THE SCOPE OF THE SCIENCE

The change in point of view is worth noticing. The early economists regarded the subject purely from the point of view of the state. Political Economy was one aspect of Kingcraft. The second conception was that of the study of wealth and man's relation to it. The third, the study of man in his relation to wealth.

THE CHARACTER OF ECONOMIC LAWS

What is the distinction between the moral law and the civil law?
Between the civil law and a law in Physics or Chemistry?
Is a law in Chemistry a force or in any sense a cause of things?
What do we mean when we speak of the planets moving in obedience to law?
Tell what you mean when you speak of the law of gravitation.
What do we mean when we speak of nature providing, arranging, etc.?
In what sense is the term law used in relation to statistics, prices, the course of things in history?

3. Too much is sometimes claimed for Political Economy as an accurate science; and on the other hand too little is often allowed it. As the art of conducting affairs in their diversity and complexity, the applications are full of question, and are open to the charge of inexactness. There is a certain truth in the position of the historical school that each age demands its separate system; that political economy is a matter of perpetual flux and change; that there is no one economic science, that there are only economic sciences. This is correct enough if the subject is considered from the point of view of an art; and from the point of view of a science it is also true that Political Economy deals in a considerable measure with mere tendencies, and declares laws which are deduced from hypothetical cases and are true to the exent only that the hypotheses correspond to the facts of life.

But whatever one may judge of the correctness of the laws at present declared by economic investigation, it is not open to doubt that man's relations to wealth, to the creation and distribution of utility, will sometime be found to disclose in some measure constant orders of phenomena. The advance of science is the discovery and proof of regular sequences in nature.

Are there economic laws? The movements of the stars, the alternations of day and night, the succession of the seasons, the currents of the sea and even of the air, have revealed a constancy in their order of occurrence, an invariable following of one fact by another, a fixity of relation between phenomena. It is quite possible that the laws to be observed in human affairs are more obscure — that often tendencies instead of definite measurable facts stand for one side of the constant relation. For example, a tendency of prices to rise after certain occurrences can be scientifically asserted, even though the rise has not taken place, and has perhaps been more than counterbalanced by some other tendency.

4. In some degree prevision and prophecy are possible in human affairs. In this degree there are laws. If it is true that the human will is free, it is none the less true that the manner in which it will manifest its freedom can be predicted because of its regularity. There is no business man and no speculator whose conduct is not based upon the conviction that there is a regularity in social affairs; no statistician who is not daily confronted with the proofs; no historian to whom history is not full of illustrations. Marriages and suicides, as well as births and deaths, incendiary as well as accidental fires, all are capable of accurate prediction in totals; and it would be strange if observation and analysis did not discover other orderly sequences of phenomena in the affairs of industry and trade. It is to a study of these sequences that Political Economy applies itself.

MAN AND ENVIRONMENT

1. Brilliant-plumaged domesticated doves set at liberty on an uninhabited island will revert to sober colours. Why? The cultivated strawberry set in the field changes to the type of the wild berry. Why?

2. Name such different elements or conditions of success in life as you can.

THE SCOPE OF THE SCIENCE

3. On what does the raising of a good crop depend?
4. In what sense, if any, do you believe in luck?
5. Has a good chance in life much to do with success?
6. Why not raise bananas in Canada?
7. Could Shakespeare's plays have been written in the Sioux language? Could they have been thought out in a Sioux civilization?
8. Are there any millionnaires in Patagonia? Why? Where are they found? Why?
9. Mention such necessary conditions as you can to the prosperity of a great silk factory.
10. Is an opportunity to get a good education to be regarded as part of yourself or as part of your surroundings?
11. When you have got the education, which is it?
12. Apportion the different elements in answer nine into two classes: First, those which are human in their character; second, those which are not.
13. Apportion these elements into (1) those elements which pertain to the owner; (2) those which pertain to his surroundings and opportunities.
14. Describe the *social* conditions necessary to the existence of a great silk factory: (*a*) public tastes, (*b*) transportation, (*c*) machinery and mechanical skill, (*d*) motive power, (*e*) social security and morality, (*f*) laws, (*g*) international relations.

5. We have seen that for humanity science means nothing unless it ultimately serves for human welfare. Thus even in those lines of investigation the farthest removed from the direct study of man, man yet remains in some sort their centre and ultimate fact. All sociological studies, however, make him the object of their direct attention. The human race in its relations to its environment, and the individual of the race in his relations to an environment of which the other members of his race are themselves a part, are the subject-matter of all sociological investigation. Man, as one term of the science, is conceived as standing over against an outside world of fact and circumstance. He is neither entirely the master of his destinies, nor yet entirely the puppet of the forces by which he is surrounded. He is himself a force — a centre of energy and activity. He is one of the facts in this complex interplay of human with natural energies. If he receives, he gives. If his environment rains its influences upon him, he puts forth his

The interplay of human and outside forces.

own efforts in adapting self to environment, or environment to self. He strives and resists and reacts. George Eliot has put the case helpfully when in supplement to the half truth, "Our deeds are fetters which we forge ourselves," she adds, "Ay, but I think it is the world that brings the iron." The history of human development is the story of what circumstance has done for man, and man for circumstance — the incidence of outside forces upon him, and his reactions thereupon. There are thus two forces in the problem of history, — man and nature. The resultant is the direction of human development.

This is not a difficult conception. It is one aspect of that which the biologists call the law of adaptation or of correspondence to environment. Life for each one of us is a question of what there is in us plus what is outside — of our powers and energies in face of our surroundings and opportunities. Give Crusoe his island. What will he do with it? This is in part a question of Crusoe, and in part a question of his island. Likewise for races the question is one, on one side of character and propensity, on the other, of surroundings and opportunity.

6. It is unnecessary for the purposes of Political Economy to push the question into an inquiry as to which of these two forces of human development, if either, is the primary fact, and which the derivative. We may, for example, regard coral polyps as a product of the sea. It is none the less true that, once existing, they not merely suffer but work the processes of sea change. It constantly occurs that that which is result becomes in turn a cause — as for example, in chemistry, where a product of combination or decomposition itself furnishes the basis for a new series of chemical changes — or in physics, where in a row of blocks one falls as the result of an impact received, and by delivering its impact causes the next to fall — or where combustion liberates gases which themselves furnish material for further combustion.

Man as cause and man as result.

Economic science is not greatly concerned with the history of human development. So far as seems necessary the economist borrows his postulates in this regard from others of the social sciences without undertaking in his own behalf the labour of investigation. The main purpose of our immediate discussion is to fix clearly and definitely the first and perhaps the most important distinction in economic theory — the division of its subject-matter into the two terms, Man and Environment — the human and the non-human elements in the problem. Taking man as he is in relation to his environment as it exists, Political Economy treats of him in his commercial and industrial activities as viewed from the standpoint of markets and values.

7. Regarding Man as the centre of economic science, Political Economy becomes in one of its aspects a system of special psychology, — a generalization of the influences which bear upon human volitions in certain orders of phenomena. Preference and choice and desire are the very raw material of the science.

<small>Are economic laws consistent with freedom of the human will?</small>

Man's relations to his surroundings can then be rightly known only when he, the most important term, is rightly known. How comes it, then, that Man with his whims and hates, his antagonisms, his desires and his fears, his weakness and his strength, should furnish the basis of a rational science? Are men not free? How, then, can their activities be reduced to law and made the subject of orderly prevision? How can the adequacy of causes and the inviolability of law be made consistent with freedom of choice and the self-determined character of human actions? If men are mere results, each thought and act the necessary outcome of preceding states, where, then, is human freedom? And if human freedom holds, where is the place for law in human affairs, the room for generalization, the basis for science? It is idle to deny that for some purposes and in some lines of investigation the case presents a difficulty. But just as Political Economy is not concerned with the courses of human development, but only with men as they are, so it is not concerned with the origin and derivation of choice. Men do choose. To this extent at least they are free, that they can and do follow their choices, — in truth, they cannot do otherwise as long as choice governs act. It may be that the sheerest sort of fatalism lies back of choice. It may be that motives are causeless, undetermined, facts of sheer hazard. But they *are*. Our freedom lies in our ability to follow them. If fatalism holds, character is one term of fate. We are concerned with human character as it is, — with the simple fact that men follow their choices, and with the influences which bear upon these determinations.

Suggestive Questions

Do you like peaches? How came you to like them?
How came you to have two hands instead of three?
What can you do about these facts?
Can you do all things which you choose to do?
Can you try? Can you get anything in the way of results?
Can you deliberately act contrary to your choice?
Are you master of your preferences and choices?
Whence come they?
Are you free to follow them?
To what zones is civilization mostly confined? Why?
Where did it originate? Why?
In what direction, north or south, has it moved? Why?
What physical reasons can you find for the lead which Western Europe has taken in civilization?
What is the trouble with the poles in this regard? With the tropics? In (*a*) human needs, (*b*) ease of satisfaction?
Will the human race ever come to do well where the snow never falls? Why? Buckle's History of Civilization, Vol. 1, Chap. 2, is suggestive on these questions.
In what sense are there economic laws? What are economic laws?

NOTES

The influence of soil and climate is often preëminent. With regard to silver or copper, for example, Chili has a productive power infinitely greater than that of France or England. But as to porcelain, France has the advantage; and likewise each country has certain products which it could obtain, supposing equality in skill and energy, with less of effort than the others. But often again the superiority in productive

power depends upon superiority in skill or in energy in a particular place. If, for example, North America has larger productive power as to cotton than have other countries, such as India, Brazil, Algeria, or Peru, it is only because America has applied, and does daily apply, to the culture of cotton as raw material more skill and energy than this or that other people.
— COURCELLE-SENEUIL, France, translated from *Traite d'Economie Politique*, 3me Edition, Tome 1, p. 120.

Notice that all social progress is attended by an increase in the confidence of men in their neighbours, which, as we have already remarked, is the ultimate fact in coöperation. Every decrease in social progress manifests itself in diminution of this confidence. Note, likewise, that observance of moral precepts relative to the duties of man towards himself, favours the growth of his muscular powers, and that observance of moral precepts relative to the duties of each man towards his fellows, concurs in increasing productive forces, and in consequence increases the wealth of society by a better application and wider extension of progress. This is a fact which suggests a multitude of reflections. . . . Customs and institutions are more favourable to production as they distract men less from productive labour, either to insure the safety or the preservation of the riches which labour produces, or to devote themselves to idleness, vanity, and ostentation; they are less favourable as they demand a larger expenditure of force in those quarrels and contests, whether warlike, judicial or otherwise, which make up, so to speak, the general expenses of society.
— COURCELLE-SENEUIL, France, *Traité d'Ec. Pol.*, T. 1, p. 115.

We must first distinguish labour which is put forth only on terms of continued effort from art (industrial knowledge), the product of an earlier effort, thereafter furnishing to man a gratuitous help; labour, limited by the purely material conditions in which it acts; art, whose limitations no one knows; labour subjected to the law of numbers, from which no part can be taken without decrease of the aggregate; art which escapes from the law of numbers, and is not at all decreased by the uses and applications to which it is put; in a word, the material element and the spiritual element in the productive powers which man has in himself. . . . Analysis shows us clearly the nature of that which is sometimes wrongly termed immaterial or moral or personal riches like health, virtue, intelligence, etc., generative forces — causes of wealth, but not wealth themselves. — COURCELLE-SENEUIL, *Traité d'Ec. Pol.*, T. 1, p. 117.

Suppose two societies equal in all respects with one exception : in one industrial effort is respected, in the other despised; in one social institutions encourage industrial education by honouring those who give or receive it ; where families are energetic in procuring for children this education, and where government fosters it ; in the other no attention is given to this instruction, no thought devoted to the manner in which it is given or received ; where the young, sinking into natural slothfulness, make no endeavour to learn, and receive no stimulus from either the state or their families, where they are brought up in disdain of industrial effort. Is it not evident that the first society will manifest larger productive power than the second ?

Suppose, again, two societies equal in all respects with one exception : in one the laws and customs which support the ownership of wealth are generally respected ; in the other they are not. In the first, for example, each man honours the obligations which he has undertaken, fulfils them in good faith without deceit or fraud — the seller delivers exactly that which he has sold, and the buyer pays the price punctually ; the wage-earner makes no attempt to deprive the employer of some share of his due, the employer none to cheat his employé of a part of his wages ; the laws, the courts, and the system of administration favour these excellent characteristics ; in the second society, obligations are undertaken carelessly without great thought for their fulfilment, and when the time comes to meet them, there are found in public opinion, and in the laws, and through the courts, a thousand opportunities to escape their consequences — where all sorts of frauds are practised to escape from obligations and to profit at the expense of another. It is clear that this second society will possess less productive effectiveness than the first.

Suppose two societies equal in all respects with one exception : in one, men unite willingly in interests and efforts ; they attempt to render their coöperation in production ever closer through well-managed associations, since each appreciates the tie which binds his own interest to the general interest. In the other society, on the contrary, the general opinion is antagonistic to association ; there are wanting confidence and esteem for one's fellows, and human relations fail in necessary tolerance ; personal interests are harsh, impatient, and blind, vanity extreme and sensitive, so that if associations are formed they rarely succeed. This second society will put forth less of productive power than the first.

— COURCELLE-SENEUIL, *Traité d'Ec. Pol.*, T. 1, p. 111.

Take an example, the trade of the pin-maker : a workman not educated to this business (which the division of labour has rendered a distinct trade), nor acquainted with the use of the machinery employed in it (to the invention of which the same division of labour has probably given occasion), could scarce, perhaps, with his utmost industry, make one pin

THE SCOPE OF THE SCIENCE

in a day, and certainly could not make twenty. But in the way in which this business is now carried on, not only the whole work is a peculiar trade, but it is divided into a number of branches, of which the greater part are likewise peculiar trades. One man draws out the wire, another straightens it; a third cuts it, a fourth points it, a fifth grinds it at the top for receiving the head; to make the head requires two or three distinct operations; to put it on is a peculiar business; to whiten the pin is another; it is even a trade by itself to put them into the paper. And the important business of making a pin is, in this manner, divided into about eighteen distinct operations, which in some manufactories are all performed by distinct hands, though in others the same man will sometimes perform two or three of them. I have seen a small manufactory of this kind, where ten men only were employed, and where some of them consequently performed two or three distinct operations. But though they were very poor, and therefore but indifferently accommodated with the necessary machinery, they could, when they exerted themselves, make among them about twelve pounds of pins in a day. There are in a pound upwards of four thousand pins of middling size. Those ten persons, therefore, could make among them upwards of forty-eight thousand pins in a day. Each person, therefore, making a tenth part of forty-eight thousand pins, might be considered as making four thousand eight hundred pins a day. But if they had all wrought separately and independently, and without any of them having been educated to this peculiar business, they certainly could not each of them have made twenty, perhaps not one pin in a day; that is certainly, not the two hundred and fortieth, perhaps not the four thousand eight hundredth part of what they are at present capable of performing, in consequence of a proper division and combination of different operations.

—ADAM SMITH, England, *Wealth of Nations*, Book 1, c. 1.

CHAPTER II

UTILITY AND WEALTH

Is food wealth?
Is the strength which comes from it wealth?
Is medicine wealth?
Is whiskey wealth?
Accurately speaking, can one's face be one's fortune?
Suppose that A devotes a year to clearing the land for a farm;
B to constructing a locomotive;
C to perfecting an invention, or an industrial process;
D to the study of a profession: —
Are intellectual acquisitions wealth?
Is health wealth? eyesight? a good voice? strong muscles? our inherited characters? our digestive apparatus? our bodies? our minds?

8. The French economist, Gide, neatly observes that the concern of the economist is with the wants of men — of the lawyer, with his rights — of the moralist, with his duties. Man is a creature of needs and desires. Primarily, and as a condition to his mere existence, he requires food, commonly, also, clothing and shelter. He has appetites for art, music, philosophy, cigars, and vice. He desires comforts and luxuries, — protection from the violence of nature, — from the wrongs of men, — and from the attacks of beasts and microbes. He wants his steak broiled and his clothes brushed. He likes to be preached to and sung to. He wants books and boats, and race-horses, laces, parks, theatres, and eyeglasses, chairs, balloons, railroads, panoramas, fortune-tellers, phrenologists, and humbugs. In a secondary way he wants the machines and inventions and tools and processes by which his primary wants are helped towards satisfaction. Look at the price-currents, the

The scope of desire and the nature of utility.

tariff schedules, the inventories of stocks in trade, or the advertising pages of the daily paper, and you get some suggestion of his manifold desires. He wants also love and pity and respect and place, and sometimes these also are bought and sold upon the market. All these things he wants because they minister to his desires — that is to say, because they are, in his thinking, useful to him. The one characteristic common to all objects of human desire is this quality of service to a human requirement. This attribute of serviceability we term utility. Put in another phrase, utility is desirability in relation to a person who desires. The thing or fact possessing this attribute of utility we call a good.

There is need to get this concept of utility clearly in mind. First, it must be remarked that in ultimate analysis utility is necessarily a matter of service to individuals. Things are not desired by men classwise, but by men as units. That which is greatly desired by one man may be not at all desired by another.

Again, the commendable character of the desire in question, or the good sense of its satisfaction, is not suggested in the economic use of the word "utility." Men put forth efforts and undergo privation for the possession of whiskey, cigars, and burglar's jimmies, as well as for food, or statuary, or harvest machinery.

9. It is unjustly charged, however, that in the view of the economist evil and right living stand together and in equality of respect, and that there is no distinction for economic purposes between virtues and necessities on the one hand, and luxuries and vices on the other hand. Once more, economics is a science as well as an art. The economist did not make the world. On one side his province is to advise and help. On the scientific side it is to describe and study. On neither is it to lie or to palter. While men are influenced by evil purposes or by ignorance to buy and sell foolishness and evil, so long the student must recognize these desires as economic facts and the commodities as of market standing. At any rate, whether

As art political economy regards the moral qualities of things.

we like it or not, the term "utility" in the terminology of the subject points merely to adaptability under conditions of desire or want to human desires.

10. A distinction must always be drawn between those things in the outside world which are useful to men, and those **Goods are both external and internal.** things which in ultimate analysis are a part of man himself. This distinction, sometimes working out in seemingly arbitrary results and occasionally causing considerable perplexity, is fundamental to the subject and must be firmly held in thought.

Useful facts must be divided into two classes. Bread, for example, is clearly enough an outside good — an external fact appropriate for human needs. When it is eaten, we say that it is consumed. It no longer exists as bread. Its service is rendered in maintenance of life or increase of strength. But how shall we conceive of this result, this strength? In the primary division of economic facts into man and environment, does strength fall into one classification and bread into another? The thing was bread. It is now life or strength. Is it now something possessed by man or is it part of the term Man? Is it subject or object, possessor or possessed, Man or environment?

Man is the beginning and the end of productive effort. The creation of utility is purposed by him for his consumption. **Are internal goods wealth?** He puts forth effort that he may enjoy its rewards. The economic cycle begins and ends in him. He works that he may live. He is the producer and not the thing produced. The more strength, the better producer — later, the larger product; but the strength is not product. So the mixtures prepared by the chemist, and the doctor's compounding of medicinal gums, fall within the class goods, while your good health to resist contagion, and my good sense to avoid it, are ranked as human attributes.

Let it be noted, however, that while the knowledge which avoids disease is to be conceived of as a human attribute and only in a secondary and half-figurative sense as a good — the outside fact from which this knowledge is obtained, the book or the advice of a physician, is a good. The mental power of the physician — his knowledge — is the source of his ability to do a useful thing — to speak a word or write a prescription which shall be of service to another human being. This knowledge is a part of the physician's equipment for the production of useful things. When this equipment shall come to service, the result will be a good. As equipment, however, it is not utility or good, but physician.

The full bearing of this distinction and the importance of it will become clearer in the following discussion of wealth.

Suggestive Questions

Define utility.
Why is not knowledge wealth?
Are all outside goods wealth?
Must there be some degree of scarcity?
How about services? What is the line of distinction?
If useful things must be in some degree of shortage to constitute wealth, is wealth a measure of well being?

WEALTH — Continued

11. The useful things external to man — goods — are in part those which come without effort or sacrifice, — which are freely at the disposal of all who desire them. Air and water, for example, are of infinite usefulness to men, but are commonly at hand in so large supply that they are obtained without effort or sacrifice. So, for the most part, of the advantages derived from climate, or from the laws, institutions and social organization which are a part of civilization. On the other hand, there are goods which are characterized by a greater or less degree of scarcity relative to the demand for them. When utility and scarcity concur, the phenomena of values and prices emerge.

But we are not yet prepared for a discussion of value, or even for a definition of it. Clearly enough the things of utility which are in surplus do not get bought and sold. Political

Economy has small concern with them — otherwise than to make them as numerous as possible. Our reasonings will be mostly occupied with the things which are attained through effort and struggle, and which upon the market are bought and sold at a price.

12. It is commonly said that all useful things of value are wealth. This statement requires considerable explanation if it is to stand as accurate. If all *things* of value are wealth, it remains true that there are many cases of value which do not fall within the meaning of the word "wealth" as used in Political Economy or in common speech. For example, when we have decided that the medical learning of the physician is not wealth, but is a human attribute, and that his activity is not wealth, but labour, what shall we say of the service which results from his activity? Wealth is paid in exchange for this utility. In what essential regard, then, does the result differ from wealth? It is not final that it is not fixed and embodied in matter. In a certain sense all utilities are dependent on matter, since any satisfaction must reach the consciousness by the intermediary of the senses, and the senses are affected only by material means or causes. But if the philosophical or unphilosophical distinction is to be allowed between the material and the immaterial, it must be admitted that the important characteristic of the picture or book is not the matter.

<small>Immaterial utilities — services.</small>

The fact which distinguishes services from wealth as popularly conceived is the difference in permanency. Consumption and production take place at the same instant. The services of the singer or actor are not wealth before they are rendered (though from the individual point of view the right to have them — the ticket — is wealth) nor after they are ended. Services cannot be hoarded or capitalized as such. This is an important distinction, and taken in connection with the departure from common speech involved in including services in the term "wealth," justifies the adoption of the established economic term "services," as indicating a particular sort of valuable utility.

13. We have seen that the class of things called valuable subdivides into wealth and services — the principle of subdivision being the question of whether the given utility is or is not incorporated in some material basis. We have now to observe how unimportant, and in fact how questionable, is this basis of distinction for other purposes than convenience of classification. *Do material existences furnish any measure of wealth?* To say that the wealth of the world is the sum of all material things that are valuable would seem to be wide enough. An account which should include all lands, houses, furniture, books, cattle, tools, machinery, goods in stock, money, merchandises in the possession of consumers, etc., would strike one as exhaustive. But to measure wealth in any degree in terms of material existence is misleading. There is no more matter in the world at present than a thousand years ago, but matter has been modified better to answer human needs. The house which was mere clay or stone, the cloth, the material for which was not grown but was in the earth or in the air, are now wealth to mankind. Work produces no new matter, no new forces. The applicability of matter and force to human uses does change. The iron in the earth, mined, melted, freed from impurities, hammered and flattened, forms a pocket knife. Nothing has been added to the matter of the world. Something has been added to the wealth.

14. No limit can be assigned to the possible increase of wealth, by reason of the development of the human race in knowledge, skill, and desire. We shall meet this fact again in our discussion of the law of increasing returns. "Of the one hundred and forty thousand species of vegetable life, we find only three hundred of sufficient value to cultivate; and of the thousands of species in the animal kingdom we make use of but about two hundred." (De Candole.) *The measure of wealth.*

There are two aspects of the truth which we are considering. Whatever adds to man's knowledge normally tends to add to the utility of the outside world to him. But also it is true that man himself develops new needs and desires as well as greater intensity of needs and desires. Thus objects which answered to no human desire now take on the character of wealth, and that which was before wealth is now greater wealth by its service to stronger desires.

15. Since wealth is found in the relation to man of the things outside man, there are in the relation two essential terms — the object to be enjoyed (used) and the capacity to enjoy (use). Thus wealth develops along the two lines: first, of changes which man impresses upon outside nature in making it more fit to his uses; second, of changes in the nature of man in strength, in knowledge, in desires, by which he becomes better able to make use of the outside world. For example, one who has a cigar, and can do nothing with it, lacks one of the essentials of wealth. So a book is not wealth to a savage. That a mineral may become wealth there must be a human use to which it may be put, an ability to mine it, and a knowledge to adapt it to use. The fallacy which underlies the terms "intrinsic value" and "intrinsic utility" is evident. Usefulness is a relation rather than a quality.

The lines of increase.

It thus becomes evident enough that the sum of material existences is no measure of wealth. It should again be noted that it is no part of the argument to show that knowledge, strength, taste, and desire are in themselves wealth. They are merely part of one term of the relation of which nature is the other term. They belong to the term Man.

16. We therefore turn to the reassuring fact that economic science is not greatly concerned with the metaphysical difficulties which surround the concept of matter. That a certain very respectable body of philosophers deny the existence of matter as conceived by the human mind, or regard matter as a manifestation of force, thereby implying that there exists no ultimate ground of distinction, does not fundamentally disturb a science which deals with utilities only, and uses the terms "material" and "immaterial" but as conveniences of classification. So far as

Is the notion of matter important in our science?

UTILITY AND WEALTH

the economist is concerned, it is sufficient that the *somewhat* in question satisfies certain needs and desires of men. It may do this by warming him — a certain effect on certain surface nerves — by pleasant excitations through eyes, nose, mouth, or ears — by an appeal to the emotions — to the love of art or of music or even of abstract truth.

17. We are to remember, then, that man's power over matter or force is that of use simply — of re-combination or re-distribution. To say that a man owns a piece of land is no more than to say that he has certain rights in and over it. If he has all rights, he is complete owner. If he has most of them, he is owner subject to easements, franchises, liens, etc. In such cases there are essentially coöwners. Wealth is to be computed not by the objects of ownership, but by the number and quality of uses which these objects permit and to which they are put under given social conditions.

Suggestive Questions

Are eyes wealth? eyeglasses?
What do you mean by intrinsic or extrinsic utility?
By intrinsic or extrinsic value?
Are charms and relics now greatly prized?
Have they changed their intrinsic quality?
Are colour and weight intrinsic qualities?
Did Niagara roar before there were ears?
Is heat a quality of an outside thing, or a mere effect on consciousness?
Is the difference in value between winter and summer ice an intrinsic or extrinsic matter?
Why not call singing wealth? acting? preaching?
A dog has been trained to guard sheep: —
Is there an increase in wealth? Is it a material or immaterial increase?
Is the ability to sing wealth?
What is matter? How do you know there is any?
What is an atom?
Define services. Why not call them wealth?

WEALTH FROM DIFFERENT POINTS OF VIEW

18. The student has probably remarked that the term "wealth" stands for no very definite or accurate concept. It

points simply to material things of commodity-nature, value-bearing, material facts, and has seemingly no relation to the degree or amount of value. It indicates merely the junction of utility with scarcity.

But we have now to analyze some modifications in the meaning of the term corresponding to various points of view in its application.

19. Most men if asked to estimate their wealth would experience no difficulty in the method. Each, after listing all his material property, would add his stocks, bonds, mortgages, rights, franchises, and claims of different sorts, and his money in hand. He would make as a list of offsets the debts he owed and the different sorts of liabilities to which he was subject. These matters of claim and demand would occupy a considerable place in his schedule. But evidently that which he adds to his wealth as due him must be subtracted from the wealth of somebody else, and *vice versa*. For every credit there is a debit. In estimating social wealth these claims must be cancelled. They are proper items in the individual reckoning, and are proper items in a national reckoning so far as they are against another nation.

Individual point of view. Credits and rights.

There are, then, increases or decreases in individual wealth which are irrelevant to the total social wealth. These are mostly if not entirely cases where men's relations to each other are immediately involved — as, for example, patents and copyrights, rights of goodwill in business, and in general all claims against one man in favour of another.

20. It deserves notice here that from the point of view of the individual, the line of separation between goods and wealth is hard to draw. Men commonly estimate their possessions with strict regard to exchange power and market values. Wealth, being at the best in large degree relative, those goods which are common to all members of society are readily omitted from the reckoning. But obviously the advantages of social life, the institutions, the religion, and the science of the civilization into which each of us is born, are infinitely important. Yet it falls out rarely

Uninventoried wealth.

UTILITY AND WEALTH 23

that we are more than obscurely conscious of this. These advantages come to us as matter of course for the most part — unobtrusively and inevitably. They are commonly unincumbered with conscious effort or sacrifice. And yet in fact social life imposes upon each of us its obligations and limitations. The liberty of each suffers that there may be liberty and safety for all. Men move from place to place or from country to country in search of better schools, better society, better levels of social intelligence or morality. The differences in the market values of city property are mostly explicable only as a buying and selling of social advantages. We occasionally make great sacrifices in order to obtain or retain these advantages. All men would ordinarily make such sacrifices, were enjoyment dependent thereon. That is to say, these opportunities of social life are valuable (admit of being valued) to each one of us. When the question is sharply raised we know it, as when our religious feelings are aroused we devoutly recognize it.

21. Within the concept of wealth from the social point of view must be placed the different forms of government property — buildings, records, railroads, postal and telegraph plants, streets, sewage and water systems, etc. But a difficulty arises parallel to the one just examined with reference to individual wealth. What shall we say of rivers, seas, and climate — in a word, of the race or national habitat? From the social point of view these advantages must be regarded as goods. Many a people would gladly buy a climate if it could, and makes for itself substitutes for humidity by expensive methods of irrigation. Nations war for possession of these natural advantages; entire communities, *e.g.* those of summer and winter resorts, derive their wealth from these advantages, and in some cases the exchange value of real property consists of practically nothing else. *The social point of view.*

22. The factors entering into the production of goods, other than the factor man himself, must be found in the nature of his environment — in the elements, in the varying conditions of temperature, *Wealth a question of correspondence.*

rainfall, sunshine, humidity, healthfulness, etc., in the soil, or more widely in the land, in its fertility and workability, its mineral resources, its accessibility to industry and commerce, in the varying sum of natural forces more or less within the control of man, such as winds, tides, electricity, gravitation, and steam. This enumeration is doubtless incomplete and inexact. Climate cannot be definitely distinguished from winds, electricity, and light; nor can natural forces be treated apart from questions of navigation and accessibility to commerce. Light which may be utilized as a natural force for power, or for the purposes of chemistry or art, is from another point of view an important factor in the fertility of the soil. But it is essential merely to hold in mind that wealth depends on the correspondence of two factors: first, man himself; second, the conditions surrounding him. He may in a large degree modify surrounding conditions. But it will still remain true that the arctic regions and tropical deserts do not offer favourable conditions for the exercise of his wealth-producing activities. He may adapt himself, in a manner, to an unhealthful climate; but also in a measure, an unhealthful climate must exercise an unfavourable influence on his powers. Though he may make for himself artificial lines of communication, yet rivers, lakes, and seas will preserve an economic importance for this purpose. He may subsist, making small use of the opportunities offered by natural forces, but it will remain true that in these rest the possibility of greatest economic efficiency and the widest field for economic progress.

23. We are now in position to discuss the vexed question of the origin of wealth. Is the position defensible that all wealth results directly or indirectly from labour? Certainly some wealth results from labour in the added utilities which are impressed upon matter. All services are evidently enough due solely to labour. In the coöperation of capital in production, labour is more remotely concerned. But the question is not the same with regard to the soil, the mines, the climate, the air for breathing, and the water for drinking. It is true that no mat-

Is wealth always a product of labour?

ter how fertile the land is, it is valueless until man goes to it. The mine may be never so rich—it gives out no wealth of itself —man must dig. Even if diamonds lie upon the surface of the ground, man must go to them and pick them up. If the fruit has ripened uncared for and unknown on the tree, man must gather it. But it is also true that the reward of labour in most of these cases is vastly disproportionate to the labour applied. It is true that the diamond would be worthless without man; but it is man's existence and not man's labour that is essential. Man is a necessary term in the wealth-relation, the other term of which is an exterior fact. But this is widely different from declaring that man or labour creates all wealth. He picks up the diamond because it is valuable. It is not valuable because he picks it up.

The following diagram will serve to indicate the point to which our analysis has proceeded:

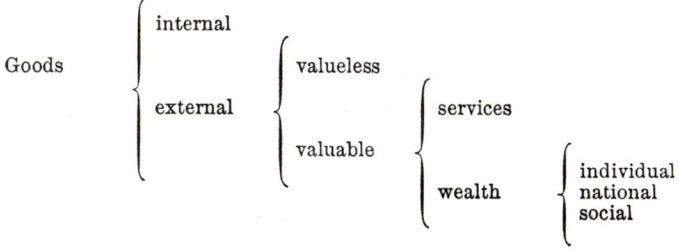

QUESTIONS

Is a field wealth?
Is a plough?
Is a waterfall?
Is a river?
Is the wind?
Is a railroad?
Is the sea?
Is society?
Is security?
Is the system of laws?
Within which subdivision should each of these be placed?

NOTES

Included in riches are, therefore, the territory occupied by nations, a road, a harbour, a canal, a church, a government building or a court-house; a triumphal arch, fortresses, cannons, arms of all sorts, munitions of war, as truly as are those objects which make up individual or family fortunes. . . . When land is appropriated, air, water, and light likewise constitute riches. The sovereign has the undoubted ability to permit or refuse entry to the national domain, exactly as the owner of an estate may permit or refuse enjoyment of the water, or air, or light upon his property. This right of enjoyment, therefore, is not open to all.

— Courcelle-Seneuil, *Traité d'Ec. Pol.* T. 1, p. 36.

Immoral books, poisonous beverages, and adulterated articles of food are wealth of an actual but irrational sort; so also are all things that minister to vice. These are real commodities, because somewhere in society are men whose impulses crave them. They are irrational, because the reason that is inherent in society as a whole, does not want them, and would cast them out if it could.

— J. B. Clark (America), *Phil. of Wealth*, p. 205.

Personal attainments, as subjective and immaterial, are excluded from the meaning of the term [wealth]: they are not a possession; that implies externality to the possessor. They are what he is, not what he has. Popular thought and speech broadly distinguish the able man from the wealthy man. A man has a potential fortune, not an actual one, in his abilities. The term indicates a state of being able, and implies a possibility, not an attained result. Labour creates wealth, and acquired abilities are potential labour. They are to be regarded as the potentiality of the human factor of production, and it introduces an element of confusion into the science to class them with the completed product. If these considerations were not sufficient to settle the economic status of a man's subjective qualities, it would at least suffice for that end to apply to them the test of the traditional definition itself, in which exchangeable value is made to be the essential attribute of wealth. . . . Nothing can be subjected to this process which is an inseparable part of one man's being. — Clark, *Phil. of Wealth*, p. 5.

Man is the author and the end — the subject of riches. We cannot confuse him with them without mixing in a kind of economic chaos cause and effect, subject and object — without involving the entire science in an impenetrable obscurity.

— Courcelle-Seneuil, *Traité d'Ec. Pol.* T. 1, p. 37.

Doctor Roscher has called attention to the intrinsic absurdity of calling a violin manufacturer a productive labourer and the artist who plays the violin an unproductive one, as is expressly done by Mr. Mill and his followers. [Wie auffalled aber, dass die Arbeit des Violinfabrikanten productiv heissen soll, die des Violin Spielers unproductiv, obschon das Product des ersten gar keinen Zweck hat, als den vom letzten gespielt zu werden. List adds in exclamation, Who raises pigs is said to labour productively ; who develops men unproductively !] The violin would thus be classed as wealth ; the music, the sole end of its manufacture, not wealth. The product, music, satisfies a direct want, — the violin only an indirect want. The latter is an instrument for producing that which satisfies direct desire. The direct want-satisfying product is, if anything, more obviously wealth than the indirect one. Relative durability and tangibility are non-essential attributes. The mechanic who makes the violin, imparts utility to wood ; the artist who plays it, imparts utility to air vibrations. One product is perceived by the senses of sight and touch, the other by the sense of hearing. — CLARK, *Phil. of Wealth*, p. 16.

The articulate sounds of the speaker are the ferry boat ; the ideas are the cargo, and the latter may exceed the former in value to an indefinite extent. In this case boat and cargo are a simultaneous product ; the boat is fitted in form to every different lading, and the two, as an industrial product, are inseparable. This illustration affords the most searching test of our definition of wealth. The thought, as existing in the mind of the speaker previous to its utterance in words, does not fall within the conception. It is subjective to the man, and like his mental faculty itself is inalienable. It only acquires the attribute of transferability when it attaches itself to the agent, — the vocal sound.
— CLARK, *Phil. of Wealth*, p. 18.

There would seem to be a certain absurdity in saying that people are poorer because they cure their diseases by medical advice instead of drugs, improve their minds by hearing lectures instead of reading books, guard their property by policemen instead of man-traps and spring-guns, or amuse themselves by hearing songs instead of looking at pictures. . . . Thus the mending of shoes is commonly treated as a service, because we pay for it separately ; but we consider that a cook at a restaurant " produces " a dish because our payment for his operations is lumped together with our payment for the material on which they were exercised.
— HENRY SIDGWICK (England),
Principles of Political Economy, p. 78.

Though we do not call permanent skill and culture any more than transient services by the name of wealth, still they resemble wealth in

the two important characteristics of being the results of labour and sources of satisfaction. The economist, no less than the statesman or philanthropist, must keep them in view in contemplating the growth of the resources of refinement and elevation of life, which the progress of civilization tends to furnish in continually increasing abundance.
— SIDGWICK, *Principles*, p. 89.

CHAPTER III

THE ECONOMIC FORMULA

Suppose yourself to have a pear and a peach — and some one tries to take them from you. You can protect but one, — the peach, — letting the other go. What has the peach cost you?

If one offers you a ride or an evening at the theatre, and you choose the ride, what have you paid for it?

If your work will produce for you two bushels of corn or one bushel of wheat, and you raise corn, what opportunity has been sacrificed?

If the work is the equivalent of its product, how much wheat has the corn cost you?

Why do men work?

When they stop, does this indicate that they want no more product?

If you were picking berries to eat, when and why would you stop picking?

Children enjoy playing, yet do not play indefinitely. Why?

If you were given $100 to spend, would you probably buy one thing or several?

Would your purchase of a second or third variety of goods show that you did not care at all for more of the first. Why not limit your purchases to one thing?

Do industrious men always work till the time comes to sleep? Why do they ever take amusement?

Every misery that we miss is a new blessing; therefore let us be thankful. — Complete Angler. Criticise this doctrine.

24. Our subject of investigation has been stated to be man in some of his aspects as a member of society. Each human being, however, leads some sort of economic life of his own. The study of society involves the study of man as a unit. The social forces are merely the summation of individual forces; social movements are aggregates of individual movements. For the purpose, then, of understanding social phenomena, it is necessary to seek the ultimate principle of individual action.

25. The fundamental assumption of Political Economy has been too often asserted to be that of the general prevalence among human beings of the motive of self-interest. Possibly enough, selfishness is the most general characteristic of the race, and possibly enough, there is no other so regular and reliable in its manifestations, and therefore so readily lending itself to the purposes of scientific prevision and orderly treatment. And yet when we think of the great and growing rôle of philanthropy in the world, we suspect of unstable foundations that science which takes no further account of man than of this one trait of selfishness. Obviously, that man who shall in his good time codify philanthropy into the laws and generalizations of science, will adopt a different human fact as his basis of procedure.

Is human selfishness the basis of the science?

There is a paradox here somewhere. Yet if Political Economy can do no better, it must get on as well as possible with what it has. If its assumptions are open to suspicion, its conclusions may well in some cases be found inaccurate or at best approximately true. But at all events the economist did not make man, and there is no occasion for calling the science ill names if it proceeds upon a somewhat dismal but general fact in human nature. Still, in a science intended to serve the purposes of every-day life, one wishes it were possible to proceed from man as he is, rather than from some abstract phase of him.

We are about to analyze the production, distribution, and consumption of wealth, and to face the truth that men produce in order that they may consume, and that demand is the motive force behind production. It is then in no small degree disconcerting, in view of the selfishness formula, to discover that if relatives, wives, and children are taken into account, two-thirds of all market commodities reach their consumers through gift, and that the motive of giving therefore furnishes two-thirds of the conscious purposes of economic effort.

It seems then that the formula of selfishness does not sufficiently exhaust the facts, and that some larger view of human nature must be found. We are in substance seeking a formula for human choices — a principle which shall be a working fact for economic reasonings, and which shall at the same time be true to human nature and applicable to the entire range of human activities.

26. The economic formula generally accepted is that proposed by Courcelle-Seneuil — the satisfaction of our wants with the least possible sum of labour. Jevons approves of this formula, but amplifies it: "To satisfy our wants to the utmost with the least effort — to procure the greatest amount of what is desirable at the expense of the least that is undesirable — in other words to maximize pleasure, is the problem of economics." *Is the pursuit of maximum satisfactions the ultimate fact?*

But while it is true that men occasionally work for the pleasure of working, they more commonly work to avoid the pain to themselves or to others of unsatisfied wants. Not the pleasure of eating or the pride of adornment, but the dread of hunger, exposure, or criticism is the main incentive to labour. To most men the question is one of comparison between the irksomeness of effort and the irksomeness of unsatisfied desires; and to all men the question comes to this case if labour be sufficiently prolonged. The desires of man outrun his performance. He ceases to labour, not because he covets no more of labour's rewards, but because the pain of continuance is greater than that of unsatisfied desire. Desires become less intense with partial satisfaction, and labour, even if pleasurable in the beginning, passes the line of pain if long continued.

27. For most purposes, then, it would seem preferable to state the problem of economics as the minimizing of pain rather than the maximizing of pleasure. Still, some provision must be made for the case of the man who works for the pleasure of working, and stops with the cessation of pleasure, or of the man who chooses as between two lines of agreeable work that kind of work which is for him the more agreeable. The economic formula must be wide *The minimum of sacrifice the ultimate fact.*

enough to cover these cases. There are possibly as many men who prefer work without reward, as there are men who prefer idleness to any of the rewards of work. Nor is this pleasurable labour to be classed, for theoretical purposes, with play. Though the activity be enjoyable, yet if its aim is the creation of utility, and performance takes place not simply for the pleasure of performance, but in some measure with a view to the resulting product, it must be classed as work.

But there is a formula which is wide enough to cover all of these cases, and which is yet serviceable. Economic activity, whether of the pleasurable or the painful sort, may be stated in terms of sacrifice. For the man who works because he finds work pleasant, it would be a sacrifice to refrain from work; he chooses that line of work which he prefers in view both of the pleasures of activity and the accompanying compensations in productiveness. He ceases to work at the point where continuance would be a sacrifice. The man to whom all effort is irksome chooses that line of activity which, in view both of the quality of the work and of its compensations, involves the smallest sacrifice. For him who prefers idleness to activity, activity would mean the larger sacrifice.

The economic problem can accordingly be stated as the minimizing of sacrifice. This formula includes in logical generalization, not only all of the phenomena commonly regarded as belonging to economic science, but also many classes of phenomena not ordinarily so regarded. The underlying law of economics is found to be identical with the primary law of physics, psychology, and sociology; namely, that force follows the line of least resistance.

28. This, then, is the ultimate principle which we are seeking as a generalization of human choices as affected by the forces of the industrial and commercial world. We find it to be a formula equally well adapted to the non-economic facts of life, and to be in substance a particular application of a law general in the physical and the moral world. Men follow their preferences. But preference is an outcome of a complex of internal and external factors. Man is himself a part of the

THE ECONOMIC FORMULA

problem. There are outer inducements, temptations, penalties; there are inner appetites, antagonisms of conscience and sympathy, — hopes, loves, hates, and fears, — all phases of moral, mental, and physical weakness and strength. Out of the combination of these complex and varying factors results a line of new direction — one of least resistance when all the varying factors are allowed for — humanly speaking, a choice.

We are fortunately free from the necessity of investigating the origin of choices or any of the psychological difficulties surrounding the question. It is sufficient for us that these choices take place as human nature presents itself. Men follow the line of least motive resistance.

SUGGESTIVE QUESTIONS

Suppose we say that men seek the maximum of satisfactions at the minimum of effort. Explain under this formula why the labourer works only eight hours a day ; or ten.

Under the minimum-of-pain formula explain why the farmer stops working ;

Why another man tramps ;

Why another man begs ;

Why another man hoards as a miser.

Why does one rich man work, and another take his ease ?

Can you explain these cases in terms of the minimum of pain ? Why not?

Explain in terms of sacrifice.

Do you see any analogy in the fact that in pressing the spring you find a point of equivalent resistance ?

Are there any subjects which you have studied which are worth knowing, but which you do not think were worth your learning ? How can this be ?

Why not produce silk in the United States ?

NOTES

Our instinctive indisposition to labour exists not to prevent our working, but to guide us in order that in each of our industrial actions we may attempt to attain the object of our desires with the expenditure of the least possible sum of labour. Thus, these two primitive impulses which

seem at first thought to be in opposition, one of which, desire, pushes us directly to labour, while the other, the love of repose, moves us toward idleness, work together in the same direction and move toward one end — that of satisfying our needs with the least possible sum of labour, or in other terms, toward increasing continually the effectiveness of our labour. This law of progress, long since observed and formulated by the physicists, is the axiomatic basis of all industrial science as well.
— Courcelle-Seneuil, *Traité d'Ec. Pol.*, T. 1, p. 34.

When labour produces more commodity, there is more reward, and therefore more inducement to labour. If a workman can earn ninepence an hour instead of sixpence, may he not be induced to extend his hours of labour by this increased result? This would doubtless be the case were it not that the very fact of getting half as much more than he did before, lowers the utility to him of further additions. By the produce of the same number of hours he can satisfy his desires more completely; and if the irksomeness of labour has reached at all a high point, he may gain more pleasure by relaxing that labour than by consuming more products.
— Stanley Jevons (England), *Theory of Political Economy*, 3d ed. p. 179.

A is interested to rob B; B, the weaker, has likewise his interest in allowing himself to be robbed in order that he may avoid something worse. But the state? — J. C. Sismondi (France), 1772–1843.

CHAPTER IV

VALUE

Would any system of political economy be possible for a man alone on a desert island?
Is there any sense in which Crusoe could be said to buy one thing with another or to exchange things?
Mention Crusoe's probable wants.
Which would be the most pressing?
What would he set himself to obtain first? secondly? thirdly?
What would determine him to change from first to second?
Why would Crusoe work?
Why do men in society work?
Do we live to eat or eat to live?
Do we live to work or work to live?
Why does water sell for less than wine? Iron than gold? Wool than silk?
Does the clerk in the candy shop eat much candy? Why?
Why bring wood or hay to town? Is this bringing an act of production? What does it produce?
Is the increase in value intrinsic?

29. It is a commonplace fact that if you are going to sell things at a very high price, you will not sell many of them. While apples are at ten cents each, most people purchase in limited quantities. If I am exceedingly hungry for apples I may buy one at this price. As the price falls, my desires express themselves in larger numerical volumes. While my wants have not in truth enlarged, there have new conditions arisen in which apple appetites of lower intensity make themselves manifest in actual purchases, as one may imagine to himself the gradual subsidence of a lake or sea, and the appearance one after another of reefs, bars, and islands.

Desires grow dull.

30. It has already been remarked that useful things may exist in such abundance as to bear no value. Water, for example, may be worth nothing — not that any particular amount of water has become less capable of satisfying human needs, but because the supply of water is greater than the total need. Some part of the total stock is thus absolutely without utility. This is simply another manner of stating the fact that human desires or needs are not infinite in any particular direction. It is also true that needs and desires become less intense with partial satisfaction. One will not ordinarily give as much for a second glass of water as for the first. The utility of each successive addition to the supply is commonly unequal per unit to the utility of the separate units of the previously smaller supply.

This same principle is daily illustrated in our current expenditures. One does not apply his entire income to the purchase of food or shelter. Food is the primary necessity, but clothing is more acutely required than is a second dinner. We supply our wants in the order of their intensities. When one has purchased himself a reasonably large wardrobe, the fact that he makes no further purchases in this line does not prove that he has no further desire for clothing, but that he has a stronger desire for something else. He follows the line of least sacrifice. So the purchase of apples at ten cents each would mean to you or me the lack of other things which we desire more intensely.

So again, if one is picking and eating wild berries, it is certain that somewhere he must tire. The first berries are well worth climbing ledges for. Finally there comes a berry equally as large and juicy, which is just worth the bother of picking. The next berry does not get picked at all. Remember for future purposes that the last berry picked and the first berry not picked are called marginal berries. They lie on either side the line of choice. The direction of least resistance changes at this point from picking to not picking.

31. In a certain fashion all the phenomena of exchanges are comprised in the above examples. A castaway upon a desert

island has no one to trade with, and yet can essentially trade one thing for another, and manifests in his own life a complete cycle of economic activities. So far as Crusoe's work was rationally planned, he was constantly turning his efforts to that undone thing the doing of which was of leading importance. At a certain point fishing was abandoned for game. More fish were refused in the interests of more game. The game cost fish, or the fish bought game, since the work which was potentially fish or game was applied to game and withdrawn from fish.

32. Marshall excellently illustrates the principle as follows:

"The primitive housewife, finding that she has a limited number of hanks of yarn from the year's shearing, considers all the domestic wants for clothing, and tries to distribute the yarn between them in such a way as to contribute as much as possible to the family well-being. She will think she has failed if, when it is done, she has reason to regret that she did not apply more to making, say, socks, and less to vests. That will mean that she has miscalculated the points at which to suspend the making of socks and vests respectively; that she has gone too far in the case of vests and not far enough in that of socks, and that therefore, at the points at which she actually did stop, the utility of yarn turned into socks was greater than that of yarn turned into vests. But if, on the other hand, she hit on the right points to stop at, then she made just so many socks and vests that she got an equal amount of good of the last bundle of yarn that she applied to socks and the last she applied to vests."

Emphasis has been placed upon what we may term individual or non-social economics, because from no other point of view can the laws of markets and prices be subjected to ultimate analysis. The unit of market action is individual action. Market outcomes are resultants from varied and conflicting individual movements. Social political economy rests upon individual economy. *Individual economy underlies social.*

33. If one were asked to compare in point of utility a river of pure water with a pound of gold, he would find little hesitation in rating the river above the gold. The economist would unquestionably pronounce the river to constitute the greater social wealth. *General notion of value.*

He would not decide the matter in the same way if the question were one of value. Most of the utility of rivers can be enjoyed by any one without price. The sum of these utilities for future distribution rests substantially undiminished with use. Obviously no one will pay, however great may be the benefits enjoyed, for that which is exhaustless in quantity and freely at the disposal of all who come. Again, whatever may be the relative utilities of water and wine, there is little doubt which of the two will bear the higher price. It is in this that the notion of value differs radically from that of utility. If men have enough of a thing to supply their needs and to spare, in so far they are fortunate, but the thing will have no value. No one will give anything for it because no one has to give anything for it in order to get it. It satisfies a need or desire — therefore has utility; but it commands no sacrifice. The notion of value contains, in addition to the meaning implied by the term utility, the idea of sacrifice. Value is not the measure of utility. *Value is the measure of the sacrifice involved in obtaining utility.* Market value is the measure of the sacrifice involved *through exchange* in obtaining utility.

34. Too great insistence cannot be placed upon this distinction. The useful things external to man are objects of desire — they furnish service, afford satisfaction, or protect from discomfort; if sacrifice is a condition to their enjoyment, they command sacrifice. The quality of utility and not the attribute of value is the measure of desirability. In view of this fact, the field of economic investigation needs to be re-surveyed. Economics, as a science, is mostly concerned with questions of value. As an art, however, economics is the application of economic principles to the well-being of society. Our concern is, therefore, not merely with wealth in the form of material valuable things, nor simply with any aggregate of values material or immaterial, but with goods. It is true that the difficult questions of political economy mostly range themselves about the concept of value.

As art economics mostly interested with utilities.

Antagonism between utility and value.

We shall come, indeed, to appreciate that, as a science, political economy is little more than the development of the definition of value into its corollaries and applications. In questions of distribution value-doctrines are all important. But this is only another statement of the fact that value emerges in human life only where obstacles and difficulties are found in the path of enjoyment, where satisfactions are saddled with deductions, where needs impel to burdensome effort. We are richer in our rain-falls than in our irrigation ditches. Value is an expression of the niggardliness of nature — of resistance to be overcome — of the disparity between man's desires and his opportunities — of the necessity which rests upon him for sacrifice. Economic progress expresses itself in successive reductions of the sacrifices necessary to the satisfaction of desire, in the approach of commodities to the margin where value disappears, — in short, in the cheapening of things. Human interests are not in parallel with value, but in antagonism. Commerce constantly affords verification of this truth. The destruction of the ship-load of spices has become a classical example. The progress of monopolies is a series of illustrations. A short crop commonly sells for a greater aggregate price than an abundant crop. Human weal, social welfare, is out of harmony with the current concept of wealth. That water should become so scarce as to command a high market price, would mean that society had not grown richer, but poorer. Value measures sacrifice, and not well-being.

THE DETERMINATION OF VALUE

If transportation is productive, what do you say of storekeeping ? of trading generally ?
Why should any one want to trade ?

35. The notion of market value is not, however, complete, until the nature of the sacrifice and the manner of its determination are examined. It is clear that the sacrifice will fix itself between

two limits, — at its lowest, at the utility of the commodity in question, to the owner, for his own purposes, if exchange does not take place; at its highest, at the intensity of the desire or need of the purchaser. This will be made clear by an illustration in the concrete. A wants a hat, B has a hat for trade. B will insist on something in exchange — something of utility to him in use or sale — and something that he cannot get for nothing. A must make a sacrifice in some form or other, or more accurately A must turn over to B something which would require of B sacrifice to get it. It may be that B will consent to receive services; but on whatever terms the exchange takes place, each must render to the other some good in exchange for some good. Nor will either consent to the exchange unless the utility turned over to him is greater than that of the thing in hand, and would involve a sacrifice in obtaining it from some other source. The fact to be emphasized for present purposes is that A could not get a hat on other terms than of dispossessing himself of other useful things or of rendering utilities of service.

Sacrifice for sacrifice.

36. Note, however, in passing, that the payment rendered by A is no measure of the utility to A of the thing purchased. Probably he would have paid more had a higher price been imposed. He finds his personal schedule of values to differ from the market schedule greatly to his own advantage.

Is value a measure of utility?

These utility-producing effects of exchange are sometimes overlooked or misconceived. It is evident that the transportation of a commodity from one place to another may add vastly to its usefulness — as, for example, wood from the forest, coal from the mine, water from the spring. It is equally true, also, that the legal transfer of the commodity adds to its usefulness in a similar manner. To recur to the cigar illustration: through the method of exchange, the man who has the cigars and does not care for cigars, is able to make the cigars useful to himself in proportion as they are useful to some other man; but until ex-

Is exchange productive?

change becomes a factor in the case, the cigars remaining with him who cannot utilize them, and the taste for cigars continuing with him who cannot satisfy it, the cigars form no part of the effective utilities at the disposal of men. This illustration of the benefit of exchange is still incomplete until the commodity transferred by the second man to the first is considered, where again by a change in ownership a utility is created or increased.

37. We are now prepared for a full definition of the term value. It is the measure of the sacrifice — generally in utility, possibly in effort, involved through exchange in obtaining utility. We may put it in other words as follows: The value of a thing is its power in exchange by virtue of its utility of commanding sacrifice. *Value defined.*

Stated shortly, then, value does not measure utility, but the sacrifice made for utility. Utility corresponds to motive, value to resistance.

38. This is complete enough in the way of definition, but it remains to inquire how the sacrifice gets measured. What in actual affairs determines how great a sacrifice A must make to obtain the hat? It is evident that it cannot be greater — in fact, it must be less — than A's measure of the utility to him of that which he parts with. *Mode of determination.* B will not part with the hat unless the measure of his sacrifice falls below the utility to him of that which he gets. If the two men are monopoly possessors of their respective commodities, the adjustment of terms must depend on many factors, such as skill, courage, independence, endurance, and the intensity of the respective needs or desires involved. But as a rule, exchanges are of commodities which are not monopoly commodities — where the terms of the transaction between A and B are approximately fixed by what some one other than B will do with A, if B will not agree, and what B can find some one other than A to do, if A will not agree.

What another man will do, that is, will consent to do, depends upon the adjustment which takes place between his individual desire and the total of other desires as bearing on the commodity in question. For the purposes of simplicity assume a single and perfectly organized market, in which only two kinds of commodities are being exchanged, — as for instance, hats and silver bullion, — and that there are ten offerers of hats, each with one hat for sale, no substantial difference in quality existing, and that each possessor is willing to receive silver in exchange. There are also ten holders of silver of a disposition to exchange for hats. Let it be assumed that —

A is willing to exchange a hat for 20 oz. of silver.
B " " " 18 "
C " " " 16 "
D " " " 14 "
E " " " 12 "
F " " " 10 "
G " " " 8 "
H " " " 6 "
I " " " 4 "
J " " " 2 "

Z is willing to exchange for 1 hat 16 oz. of silver.
Y " " " 15 "
X " " " 14 "
W " " " 13 "
V " " " 12 "
U " " " 10 "
T " " " 7 "
S " " " 6 "
R " " " 3 "
Q " " " 1 "

Evidently Q cannot make an exchange, since no one will part with hats for the amount of silver which Q is willing to give. Hats cannot exchange for silver at lower than two ounces of silver. On the other hand, A and B cannot find buyers, because no one is willing to sacrifice over sixteen ounces of silver to get a hat. But hats cannot go at sixteen ounces, because only one man will give that amount of silver for a hat, and there are seven other holders of hats willing if necessary to sell at less than sixteen ounces. But the hats will go higher than four ounces of silver, since there are two hat-owners who will exchange at this rate, and eight silver-owners who are willing to pay more than this if necessary. With hats at six there are three hat-men willing to trade and still eight silver-owners willing to trade. With hats at ten there are five hat-owners and six silver-owners disposed to trade. The price will then be at over ten ounces of silver for each hat, but it will not be as high as twelve ounces of silver, since at twelve there are six hat-owners and only five silver-owners willing to trade. The trades must then take place at somewhere from a little above ten to a little below twelve. It is conceivable enough that, in the higgling of the market, the sales should take place at very little over ten, though concerted and skilful action on the part of hat-owners might push prices up to nearly twelve.

It is unnecessary to remark that in actual affairs this margin for fluctuation and higgling is much narrower, unless when monopoly holders confront each other, or when buyer and seller arrange terms of exchange for articles, at least one of which is by reason of some peculiarity of fancy in one of the traders, or of quality in the article, incapable of accurate comparison with others of its class.

39. Evidently also in the above analysis, Z, who would, if necessary, have given sixteen ounces of silver to get a hat, but who on the market found it necessary to give but ten or twelve, has greatly profited by the institution of exchange. So of J., who would, if *Exchange is productive. Quasi-rents.* necessary, have exchanged a hat for two ounces of silver, but found the opportunity for exchanging for ten. This increase of social wealth, through the method of exchange, — that is to say, this addition to the total usefulness of commodities through the adjustment of consumption at the point of greatest comparative utility, — is beyond measurement. So in the cheapening of commodities by more effective methods of production, the gain to consumers represented by the difference between what they do sacrifice, and what they would if necessary sacrifice, while vast, is incapable of measurement, not only in totals, but commonly by each individual in his own case.

40. It is sufficiently obvious that for most of the buyers and sellers on the market, a change in market price would not result in their retirement from the market. By most of the buyers a higher price would be paid were the purchase conditioned upon a higher payment. So with most of the sellers, a lower price would be accepted were the sale possible only upon this condition.

In the adjustment of prices, however, in the great markets, there are producers and sellers who are on the point of ceasing to produce or of offering to sell, if price goes in any degree lower. There are purchasers, also, whose demand is of such a character that they will be excluded from the market if prices go in any degree higher. For all buyers and sellers other than these whom we term marginal, there is a surplus, a differential advantage measured from the point of actual market sacrifice. These differential quantities are denominated quasi-rents.

41. The law of margins is thus the key to an understanding of market adjustments, and value appears as the market outcome of differing individual estimates of utility.

Value measures merely marginal relative utility. For purchasers other than the marginal purchaser value furnishes no measure of utility. It is at most the measure of the marginal utility — marginal utility being defined as the utility to that purchaser who is willing to sacrifice least for a given commodity, or an additional supply of it, and who at this sacrifice obtains it. Nor even for the marginal purchaser is market value a measure of absolute utility, but only of relative utility. The poor man foregoes what the rich man purchases, not because the absolute utility to the poor man is less than to the rich man, but because the relative utility is less. A pound of meat may be many times more useful to the poor than to the rich man. But to the poor man, to have the meat means to lack for bread, while the choice for the rich man lies between bread and a cigar or some unthought minor comfort on a prospective European trip. So again, one may forego the bread to-day which he would have purchased a week or a year ago, though no less hungry to-day. The strength of the desire for other things is a necessary element in the decision. The marginal case is, then, a case of marginal *relative* utility; that is, of marginal sacrifice. A given case is marginal, simply because the utility gained and the utility sacrificed are approximately equal.

42. We say approximately equal. The equality cannot be absolute, since enough of inequality must remain to tip the scales of choice. There seems to be danger here of getting into infinitesimal quantities. But in every marginal adjustment there must be a marginal trade, a marginal buyer and a marginal seller, a marginal pair of sacrifices. Not that these two people exchange with each other — this is evidently improbable. Yet the market price which suits all exchanging parties must be one which suits these two. The hat-seller who is nearest the point of retirement — he who estimates hats most highly relatively to silver — must get silver enough to induce him to trade. Among the silver-sellers there is one also nearest to the verge of retirement. The market ratio of exchange is the point of adjustment between the two marginal dispositions — a rate which preserves a sufficient trace of quasi-rent to induce both doubters to trade.

Note, also, that there is as well a marginal excluded pair, — two men, each disposed to act as market factors, if prices swerve in their respective directions; but with the price as it is, each sniffs doubtfully at the bait and retires. These men lead the forces of demand and supply which are in reserve in the event that prices are modified.

43. That sales generally take place in terms of money against services or commodities, introduces no modification in theory. The utility to each man of his money is the utility of its most desirable application — of that thing into which he will turn his money by exchange. He who exchanges money for hats does so because this is for him its application of highest utility. The marginal purchaser is that purchaser to whom the other things which he might procure with his money most nearly approach the importance of a hat. The marginal seller is the seller for whom to part with his hat

most nearly approaches in importance that which the money obtained for the hat will buy.

44. In our analysis of demand and supply, in the succeeding chapter, we shall see that in the long run sellers' sacrifices are the market statement or market equivalent of producers' sacrifices. The marginal producer's sacrifice is to be stated as the sacrifice of that producer to whom other employments offer relatively the greatest attraction, that is to say, approach most nearly to an equality of advantages with the chosen line of production.

The following diagram will perhaps aid in clarifying the student's notions of the adjustment of demand and supply at market price; the relations between actual demand and sup-

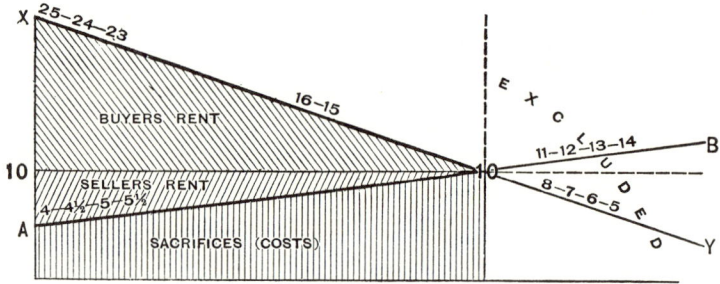

ply and potential demand and supply, the quantities described as costs or sacrifices of production, and producers' and consumers' (sellers' and buyers') rents.

Let XY represent the different degrees of intensity of demand, 25, 24, etc.

Let AB represent the scale of producers' sacrifices rising from 4, 5, etc., to 11, 12, etc.

Let 10 represent the point of market equation between demand and supply — that is to say, the price.

Those who will not sell as low as 10, and those who will not pay as high as 10, are retired, — are merely potential elements in the market.

Questions

Find the market price in the following problems: Boys desire base-balls according to the following schedule: 100, 95, 94, 87, 82, 78, 60, 55, 53, 49, 47, 45, 39, 36, 31, 26. With only six base-balls in the market, what will be the price? With 9? 12? 15?

Let the above schedule represent the falling intensity of one boy's disposition to buy base-balls: will this affect the results?

Sellers' minimum prices are as follows: 36, 35, 33, 31, 30½, 29½, 28 ; buyers' maximum payments as follows: 40, 38, 36, 34, 33, 32.

Sellers', 19, 18, 17, 14, 12, 7, 6, 5, 4, 3 ; buyers', 1, 2, 3, 4, 5, 6, 7, 8, 9.

NOTES

But had not also Crusoe an economic system? Are, in truth, the products which the peasant consumes in his household, the labour which he directs to his own consumption, less clearly economic facts than his marketed products or than the labour of his hired men? Schaeffle rightly observes that ordinary breathing is not an economic function merely because it is an unconscious natural necessity.

— Wilhelm Roscher (Germany), translated from *System der Volkswirthschaft*, Einleitung, c. 1, sec. 2, n. 6.

Thus, in a besieged city the total utility of food supplies has not risen, but solely the exchange value. According to Cordier, the wheat harvest in France amounted,

In 1817 to 48,000,000 hectolitres with a market value of 2046 mill. francs
" 1818 " 53,000,000   "   "   "   1442   "   "
" 1819 " 64,000,000   "   "   "   1170   "   "

—*Memoire sur l'agriculture de la Flandre Française.*

If the climate of England could suddenly be changed to that of Bogota, and the warmth which we extract imperfectly and expensively from fuel were supplied by the sun, fuel would cease to be useful except as one of the productive instruments employed by art ; we should want no more grates or chimney-pieces in our sitting-rooms ; what had previously been a considerable amount of property, in the fixtures of houses, in stock in trade and materials, would become valueless ; coals would sink in price ; the most expensive mines would be abandoned ; those which were retained would command smaller rents. — N. W. Senior (England).

Surely, a fertile soil, a mild climate, a fine network of navigable rivers and safe and deep roadsteads, are the earnest of wealth for a country, and yet they have no exchange value. It is even possible to establish an antithesis between these two terms; wealth corresponding to the idea of abundance, value answering to the idea of scarcity. Let us suppose, for example, that by a lucky miracle worked by human industry, all products were to be so multiplied as to become as abundant as spring water or the sand of the shore; should we not have to regard this marvellous multiplication as an increase of wealth, nay, as the climax of wealth? Yet, according to the above hypothesis all things precisely on account of their superabundance would have lost all value; they would have neither more nor less value than that very spring water or those grains of sand which we just compared with them.

— CHARLES GIDE (France), *Principles of Political Economy* (D. C. Heath, 1892), p. 41.

If the objects the most essential to the maintenance of life were the most costly, then would humanity have much difficulty in living and much claim to pity. But in truth it is the things which from the physiological point of view are superfluities, that are the most costly; and in this fact the mass of humanity find small cause for complaint.

— Translated from PAUL LEROY BEAULIEU, *Précis d'Economie Politique*, 2d ed., p. 202.

At first sight it may appear strange that so few persons, and those so little conspicuous, should decide the fate of the whole market; but, on closer examination, this will be found quite natural; if all are to exchange at one market price, the price must be such as to suit all exchanging parties; and since, naturally, the price which suits the least capable contracting party suits in a higher degree all the more capable, it follows quite naturally that the relations of the last pair whom the price must suit, or as the case may be, the first pair whom it cannot suit, afford the standard for the height of price.

— BOEHM-BAWERK (Austria), *Positive Theory of Capital*, 1st ed. (Macmillan), p. 213.

So far as is consistent with the inequality of wealth in every community, all commodities are distributed by exchange so as to produce the maximum of benefit. Every person whose wish for a certain thing exceeds his wish for other things, acquires what he wants provided he can make a sufficient sacrifice in other respects. No one is ever required to give what he more desires for what he less desires, so that perfect freedom of exchange must be to the advantage of all.

— STANLEY JEVONS, *Theory of Pol. Ec.*, p. 141.

There has been a long controversy as to whether "cost of production" or "utility" governs value. It might as reasonably be disputed whether it is the upper or the lower blade of a pair of scissors that cuts the piece of paper. — ALFRED MARSHALL (England), *Economics of Industry*, p. 221.

Leon Say (*De la Richesse Individuelle et de la Richesse Publique*, p. 29) measures the worth of goods after the grade of discomfort involved in their loss. This is in substance the notion of "effective utility," developed at length by J. B. Clark in his *Philosophy of Wealth*, Chap. V.

Dresses that are no longer worn, books that are no longer read, pictures that have ceased to be looked at, remedies that no longer cure, — how long the list would be of those riches which have lost their value ; and yet, if by chance the desire of the collector, perhaps the most intense of all desires, happens to settle on these dead riches, they will receive a new lease of life, and will immediately obtain perhaps a far higher value than they had in the course of their previous existence. But value varies not only at different times, but also from country to country, and even from individual to individual. We all know the proverb, *de gustibus non disputandum ;* let us add " and values " ; for they, too, depend on each man's tastes. — CHARLES GIDE (France), *Political Economy*, p. 45.

CHAPTER V

COST OF PRODUCTION

45. It has been stated that the value of a thing is fixed by the sacrifice — generally in utilities — which it commands in exchange in obtaining it. Cost of production should be stated in analogous terms. As to any particular article, *cost of production is the sacrifice of other possible values produceable by the application of the same productive energies.*

46. That values exist otherwise than as the result of labour, has already been remarked. There is evidently little relation between the value of a nugget of gold, stumbled upon in a careless walk, and the effort devoted thereto. The value of the nugget rests primarily upon the fact that gold is the object of intensely strong desires; secondarily, upon the fact that gold is to be had only in small quantities, and commonly upon terms of great effort. Supply being limited relatively to the demand, only those desires attended with high possibilities of sacrifice obtain satisfaction. Were it true, however, that a pound of gold was ordinarily to be had at the effort commonly applied to raising a bushel of potatoes, pound nuggets and bushels of potatoes would come to exchange at an approximate equality. Until this equality was reached, effort would be directed to obtaining one of the commodities to the entire or partial exclusion of the other. It is clearly not true that the value of each particular commodity corresponds to the quantity of labour which resulted in its forthcoming. Market value is the equilibrium point at which demand and supply are in equation. Values, then, tend to stand at a point compensating the production of the more expensive, rather than of the less expensive portions of the

Value exists apart from labour,

but tends roughly to correspond to it.

market supply; since if price falls, the marginal producer will cease production. If nuggets were obtainable on easy terms of effort, their market value would of necessity fall, until by reason of the fall the special advantages of nugget gathering were cancelled.

47. It is then not unreasonable to infer, that in general the value of any commodity, while not dependent upon the cost of production, does depend upon the cost of reproduction, which cost of reproduction is measured by the labour immediately or remotely expended therefor. *Does labour measure product or product value labor?* The reasonings of the previous pages, however, make for another view, namely, that instead of the labour expended being the measure of the value of the commodity, the value of the commodity is the measure of the labour rationally to be expended in its production. For most purposes these two views are not antagonistic in results; but they are so in theory. As long as two things are and must be approximately commensurate, it does not greatly matter which is made the measure of the other. Values of commodities commonly correspond approximately to the labour quantities in production; and it is equally true that the labour expended upon different commodities, commonly corresponds approximately to the value of the commodities when produced. This labour measure of value is safe enough, and absolutely correct, when there is a clear choosing between the indisposition to labour and the gratification of some particular desire. If a man desired only one sort of satisfactions, only one sacrifice would be required of him, — the sacrifice attendant upon effort. But when exertion is certain in one direction or another, and when therefore non-exertion is not the alternative in the choice, and when therefore the sacrifice involved in obtaining one thing is the deprivation of another thing obtainable by the same labour, the measure of the value of the first is in the sacrifice of the unobtained thing, and not in the sacrifice of mere effort.

48. If, for example, you have the opportunity of going to the theatre, or to a picnic, or for a walk, and prefer theatre

to picnic, and picnic to walk, your attachment to the theatre is better measured by your picnicking than by your walking disposition, — by the most you will sacrifice rather than by the least.

If for a bicycle you would give your bull pup or your Irish setter, or even your pony, your pony best indicates the degree in which you desire a bicycle.

If with your next week's wages you determine to buy either a new coat or a tennis set, and finally decide in favour of the tennis set, not your week's work, but the coat, measures what your tennis set has cost you.

It has been said that greater love hath no man than that he should lay down his life for his friend. If so, not the lesser services of kindness, but the very love of life, measures a man's highest devotion to his fellow.

If you would pay a dollar for a hat, you would with still greater readiness pay any smaller sum; thus a dollar, and not fifty cents, is the sacrifice yard-stick of hat values to you.

49. But the real difficulty with the labour measure of value lies still deeper. Man produces that he may consume; labour is a process of value creation. Man labours because this is the condition on which his enjoyment of certain goods depends. Labour, however, is not the cause of the utility; the utility is the cause of the labour. So utility is the cause of value, — the scarcity which entails effort being a mere condition. Product is the reward of effort. Labour has value merely in the sense that the value of the product may be conceived as reflected back upon the means by which it is obtained. It is, then, not logical to measure the value of the product by the value of the instrument of production. The labour measure of value, therefore, means nothing unless understood as suggesting the different productive possibilities in the application of labour. In the last analysis it is not the labour itself, but its product, which satisfies desire and therefore commands sacrifice.

In what sense has labour value?

50. The importance of this very obvious distinction will repeatedly become manifest in our succeeding discussions. It

is worth while, however, to point out in this place that wages are really never paid for labour. Nobody wants labour as such. It is commonly disagreeable to perform, or even to watch. Mere motion, simple activity, is as valueless as it is void of beauty. Only for product, and in proportion to product, can labour command a price. Ultimately, the employer purchases not labour, but the goods which labour affords.

If it should strike the student that all this is a saying of undisputed things in unnecessarily solemn fashion, it will suffice to remind him that the prejudice against prison labour originates mostly in forgetfulness that wages flow from product, and that increase in social product means increased average wages, or to call to his mind that whatever may be the merits in the tariff controversy, the question is generally argued as one of wages. It is asked how we are to compete with ill-paid labour. The discussion starts from the notion of wages as a cause instead of as an effect, and gets nowhere in consequence. Wages are a fact to be explained, instead of to explain with. Should this last fall short of clearness, it will receive further elaboration in the course of various discussions to follow.

51. The measure of value is then not in the labour devoted to the production of any good, or in the utility of that good, but in the sacrifice, commonly of other goods, involved in obtaining the good in question. The quality and quantity of labour applied are irrelevant, except in so far as the application of labour is a sacrifice of other possible goods.

52. The usual statement of cost of production, and of its relation to market prices, proceeds from the point of view of the individual, and is obscured for theoretical purposes by problems of wages, rent, and interest. It conforms, however, clearly enough, to the facts of individual experience. *Usual statement of cost of production.* The producer pays his different expenses of production, and if the market returns are inadequate, withdraws from production at least in a measure. If the returns are gratifying, production is increased. Increased production tends to follow rise in price, and decreased

production to follow fall in price. On the other hand, lower prices tend to follow increase of production, and higher prices decreased production, other things all the while being assumed equal. Differences between market price and cost of production constantly tend to be obliterated by resulting changes in the total supply. The market price will average high enough to induce an ordinarily sufficient supply for the market, and this average price will be approximately the cost of production of the necessarily most expensive portion of the market supply.

53. But while this analysis of market movements is faithful to the facts, it is not ultimate in theory; it is still to be asked why the producer ceases production when price falls.

Criticism. From his point of view, it is sufficient to say that further production is a matter of no profit or of absolute loss; but the ultimate answer is that productive energies can be employed in other directions to results commanding larger rewards from society. If these productive energies, applied in other directions, will produce larger market values, production ceases not because cost of production is too high absolutely, but too high relatively. Continued application of productive forces in the same direction would be a sacrifice of greater market values possible in other directions. The term "cost of production" does not express the final analysis of the facts; it only half suggests, or altogether fails to suggest, the decisive influence behind — namely, the demand. The difficulty is not that cost of production is too high, but that other things produceable at the same effort are more desired by society.

Clearly the price in any given market at any given time is determined without reference to cost of production, otherwise than as bearing on the prospect of future supply. In fact, nothing is claimed for cost of production further than that it indicates a normal or ideal price around which market price fluctuates, and from which in either direction it cannot long or widely depart. This normal price is, however, to be reached or approximated only through future expansions or contractions in supply. Professor Senior remarks that "any other cause limiting supply is just as efficient a cause of value in an article as the necessity of labour in its production." President Walker adds "that if supply is limited it does not matter whether there is any cost of production or not." And even if supply is not limited, and the term "cost of production" be understood to cover cost of reproduction, the irrelevancy holds, speculation aside, until reproduction takes place and affects the supply. If the cost of reproduction necessitates prices beyond the desires of consumers, it is again irrelevant. And we may safely go farther. If desirable at all, any commodity will be produced unless demand is stronger for some other. What the thing costs to produce it is irrelevant, except so far as its production displaces other products. Production does not adjust itself to cost of production, but to intensity and quantity of demand. To say that something is not produced because the cost of production is too high, is really to say that productive energies are more fertile of satisfactions when applied elsewhere. The so-called necessity for a protective tariff, for example, is stated to be a high cost of production in particular industries. A more accurate statement would be that at equal expenditure of productive energies other industries afford a greater amount of satisfactions. This is the important fact in international trade. An industry never ceases to exist because, rightly speaking, it is unable to compete with foreign industries, but because it is unable to compete for its labour supply with home industries. Simple depopulation is the only manner in which an industry can fail through foreign competition alone.

This manner of statement assimilates all questions of price to the general law of demand and supply, and does away with unnecessary distinctions of principle between the phenomena of competitive and those of monopoly prices, and between the phenomena of prices over long intervals of time and those of prices as fixed in any given market at any given time. It is true that in the long run, different forces modify in some degree the conditions of supply, but this is not an ultimate difference in theory. Prices do no doubt approximate to the cost of production as the term is generally used, but cost of production is a secondary or resulting fact, or rather, an aggregate of facts, being in itself an expression of demand working upon a large number of commodities simultaneously.

Cost of production must, then, as a formula for value, be interpreted to mean sacrifice of production, and to indicate merely that each industry must be equally remunerative with every other for the kind and quantity of labour applied, — or more accurately, that the normal price in each industry must remunerate each producer at least as well as would be possible for him in any other industry.

54. Even under the interpretation of sacrifice, the cost-of-production formula is open to the objection that it states as the ultimate cause of value that which in its nature is purely subordinate and secondary. Utility is the primary cause of value; sacrifice, merely a condition. Needs and desires, not sacrifices and costs, are the ultimate facts. Utility furnishes the motive for sacrifice, while value is the measure of the sacrifice. Demand controls supply, and supply adjusts itself to demand as expressed in market values. Producers in any line will continue to produce, so long as the remunerations obtained in the chosen line of activity exceed the resulting sacrifice of the remunerations possible in other lines. Differing degrees of advantage in different industries for different producers induce a constant change in the applications of productive energies.

Sacrifice of production formula not ultimate.

Demand the ultimate force.

But a change in activity is not the cause of existing values, though it may affect them. Men adapt their productive activities to price conditions as the market has determined them; not with any hope of fixing prices (except in cases of monopoly), and never with any idea of determining price by cost of production. The problem is always to adjust cost of production to price, — never price to cost of production. Changes in value modify supply, and changes in supply resulting from changes in value, in turn modify value; but demand is the motive force behind supply, and expresses itself as motive force in terms of value. In practical affairs producers as an aggregate and producers individually comport themselves in full harmony with this theoretical fact, and in complete recognition of it. To explain *production* in terms of the cost-of-production doctrine violates the facts or means nothing. To explain *values* under that formula, is to emphasize the secondary factor in the question to the exclusion of the primary factor. Value is a resultant from the forces of demand and supply, supply being itself a resultant from demand. Sacrifices of production are important only as modifying the supply term. Prices rise whenever demand tends to raise them, unless counteracting tendencies in the volume of supply are thereby set up.

55. The physical sciences excellently illustrate social forces in this respect. Water flowing from one receptacle to another sets its own limit to the process. Freezing brings an end to the solidifying process through a self-manufactured protection against the frost. A coal fire finally smothers itself with ashes. A spring, hard pushed, increases its resistance to a new point of equilibrium. Chemical reactions themselves bring about new equations. The larger part of social phenomena are of this self-limiting type, where forces set in action counteracting tendencies. Wars bring the peace of exhaustion. Satisfaction lowers desire to satiation. Continued labour makes ever shriller the cry for rest. The core of economic theory is the doctrine of margins, indicating a shifting point of adjustment between opposing forces initiated from one primary fact of demand.

Suggestive Questions

What was the value to Crusoe of a day's labour?

Would the value have been something else had his island been another island?

Do you think the value of a man's working powers depends upon what it has cost to rear him? Why?

Is there any sense in which you may say that apples in your cellar draw interest? Ice in the icehouse? Bread in a lunch basket? Money in your pocket?

Does money sometimes increase in utility to you without increase in amount?

Why do you not study Hebrew? Do you think it altogether useless? What do you expect to do for a living? Why not something else?

What is the reason that all farmers in your neighbourhood do not raise cabbages exclusively?

NOTES

There is no connection between cost of production and price in the cases of food in a beleaguered city, of quinine, the supply of which has run short in a fever-stricken island, of a picture of Raphael, of a book that nobody cares to read, of an armour-clad ship of obsolete pattern, of fish when the market is glutted, of fish when the market is nearly empty, of a dress material that has gone out of fashion, or of a house in a deserted mining village. — MARSHALL, *Ec. of Ind.*, p. 245 n.

The fact is that labour once spent has no influence on the future value of any article; it is lost and gone forever. In commerce by-gones are forever by-gones; and we are always starting clear at each moment, judging the value of things with a view to future utility.

— JEVONS, *Theory of Pol. Ec.*, p. 164.

Mill and some other economists have followed the practice of ordinary life in using the term "cost of production" in two senses; sometimes to signify the difficulty of producing a thing, and sometimes to express the outlay of money that has to be incurred in order to induce people to overcome this difficulty and produce it. But by passing from one use of the term to the other without giving explicit warning, they have led to many misunderstandings and much barren controversy.

— MARSHALL, *Ec. of Ind.*, p. **214 n.**

That Tokay is not valuable because there are **Tokay vineyards**, but that the Tokay vineyards are valuable because **Tokay** has a high value, no one will be inclined to deny, any **more than** that the value of a quicksilver mine depends on the **value of** quicksilver, the wheat field on the value of wheat, the **brick kiln** on that of brick, and not the other way about. It is only this many-sided character of most goods — their capacity of being employed in many different uses — that gives the appearance of the contrary, and a little consideration shows this to be an appearance, and nothing more. As the moon reflects the sun's rays on to the earth, so the many-sided costs reflect the value which they receive from their

marginal product on to their other products. The principle of value is never in them, but outside them in the marginal utility of the products.
— BOEHM-BAWERK, *Pos. The. of Cap.*, p. 189.

I hold labour to be essentially variable, so that its value must be determined by the value of the produce, not the value of the produce by that of labour. — JEVONS, *Theory of Pol. Ec.*, p. 165.

I must absolutely deny that wages can in any sense be taken to represent the labour element in cost of production. Wages, as Mr. Mill observed in the passage already quoted, may be regarded as cost to the capitalist who advances them; though perhaps it would be more correct to say that, so far as they go, they measure his cost, which really consists in the deprivation of immediate enjoyment implied in the fact of the advance. But to the labourer wages are reward, not cost; nor can it be said that they stand in any constant relation to that which really constitutes cost to him. If they did, wages in all occupations, in all countries, and in all times, would be in proportion to the severity of the toil which they recompensed. . . . The point for which I am contending will possibly appear to some persons to involve a purely theoretical issue. A theoretical issue no doubt is at stake, but I believe a better example could not easily be found of the intimate connection between theory and practice, and of the way in which an unsound theory can invert for people the true relation of phenomena and mislead in the practical business of life, than is furnished by this doctrine. The truth of this statement will only fully appear in later chapters of this work; but even here I may give an example or two. What, for instance, is now the grand argument with the people of the United States for the maintenance of protection? Why, the high cost of production in that country. And what is the evidence of the high cost of production? Simply the high rates of wages which prevail. How, they ask, can we with our high-priced labour compete with the pauper labour of Europe? I must frankly own that accepting the point of view of the current theory of cost, I can find no satisfactory reply to this question, and I am quite sure that Mr. Wells, who implicitly adopts this point of view, has wholly failed to furnish one.
—JOHN CAIRNES (England), *Leading Principles of Pol. Ec.*, p. 53.

That which is called cost of production of an object or a service is the price at which this object or service can be obtained in a permanent way in approximately the quantity which is commonly demanded. . . . In truth, things take place in the following order: (1) the market value determined by causes we have studied fixes the remuneration of the work which has served in production; (2) this remuneration, according as it is

sufficient or more or less than sufficient, brings about continuation, or increase or decrease, in future supplies; (3) this production results in an equal increased or decreased offer of product in a fashion to render the offer of each commodity of no great variability, and to force ceaselessly toward a level the remuneration of different services.
— COURCELLE-SENEUIL, *Traité d'Ec. Pol.*, T. 1, p. 283.

Between contemporaries the value of different commodities is measured simply by gold or silver, and when it is said, for example, that a particular product is commonly worth a kilogramme of gold, this indicates simply that it is necessary to put forth, in order to obtain the product, a sum of productive energy equal to that which the acquisition of a kilogramme of gold requires. — COURCELLE-SENEUIL, *Traité d'Ec. Pol.*, T. 1, p. 322.

According to the reports of English manufacturers, an English workman produces on the average almost twice as much as a Frenchman; the latter in turn more than an Irishman. An English wage-earner who had worked in a French factory spoke before the Parliamentary Committee his opinion of the French as follows: "It cannot be called work they do; it is only looking at it and wishing it done." Thus, for example, a good English spinner with an eight-hundred spindle machine could produce daily sixty-six pounds of yarn; a Frenchman only forty-eight pounds. . . . The report of an Agricultural Interest Commission places the North American workman above the English in good conduct, fidelity, and interest. A Berlin wood-cutter accomplishes as much in ten days as an East Prussian in twenty-seven days (Hoffman). English planters on the Hellespont prefer to pay Greek labourers ten pounds sterling yearly, besides their keep, rather than Turkish, three pounds. So, the Malay field labourer gets two and one-half dollars per month, the Malabar four, the Chinese six.
— WILHELM ROSCHER, *System der Volkswirthschaft*, Book 1, c. 1, sec. 40 n.

Physicists and chemists have recognized two classes of changes: first, those which tend to go on indefinitely until all the matter present has suffered the alteration in question; second, those which give rise to products which are unfavourable to the original force at work; — such changes are self-limited, and may cease therefore long before all the material has been used. . . . In reality the self-limiting are vastly the more numerous.
— JOHN W. LANGLEY in *Pop. Science Monthly*, Feb., 1895.

The term cost of production is used in at least four different meanings in economic discussion.

1. It may mean the fatigue or irksomeness of labour. Those engaged in extractive industries are most conscious of its meaning. Thus a

farmer, doing much of his work with his own hands, instead of paying for it with wages, will often count the cost of this or that farm operation, or this or that crop, in terms of his own weariness. Prof. J. E. Cairnes, in his "Leading Principles of Political Economy Newly Expounded" (New York: Harper & Brothers), stated that in economic theory cost of production must always mean the fatigue of muscle and brain. Wages, interest, etc., he said, are not the cost of production. Labour and enterprise drift to those places and into those occupations in which they get the greatest rewards in proportion to cost; *i.e.* the greatest wages and profits in proportion to exertion of body and mind.

2. Cost may mean the destruction of one objective or material utility in the production of other utilities. Agriculture uses up seed, grain, manures, and implements, destroying the utilities embodied in them, to produce further harvests; manufactures and transportation destroy coal to produce steam power. We have to use "cost" in this sense whenever we inquire whether a nation is increasing its material means of satisfaction by the means in which it consumes its resources.

3. Cost may mean the sacrifice of an alternative utility, opportunity, or value. The blacksmith might be able to make $1.50 a day as an agricultural laborer, when any other man in the neighbourhood could make but $1.25; but, being able as a smith to make $2 a day, he stays at the forge. He will estimate the cost of production of his work at the value of his best alternative employment — the $1.50 a day. It is in this sense we constantly use the word "cost" in discussion of international trade. Thus a nation that could produce iron at $11 a ton may import it at $13, simply because the labour and capital that would produce a ton of iron at $11 may be productive of enough wheat or cotton to buy a ton and a half or two tons at $13.

4. Finally, cost may mean the sum of all the prices paid for the materials and labour and sacrifices involved in production. This is what the business man ordinarily means by cost.

Cost in this latter sense is not always a cause of value or price; that is, the price of a product is not necessarily determined by its cost of production in terms of the prices of labour and materials. On the contrary the price of the final product may determine how much the producer will offer for materials and labour. It is impossible here to trace out all the relations of cause and effect, but one general principle will hold good. More than one final product is commonly made from the same raw material, and the prices of those products, even after allowing for all the other differences in expenses, may be unequal. Nevertheless, the various producers will buy their raw material at subsequently the same price, and that price cannot exceed the market value of the least valuable product made from the material. It is, therefore, the least valuable product that determines the cost of production for all other products made from the same raw material, or by substantially the same kind of labour. This cost of production, acting on the supply of the other products, tends to bring down their market prices to an equality with the least valuable product; that is, it becomes, in their cases, a cause of value.

— Prof. F. H. GIDDINGS, *6th Ann. Rep. Com. of Labour*, p. 9 n.

COST OF PRODUCTION — *Continued.*

What different motives might one have for laying aside money?

Do people commonly get interest on money deposited in national banks?

Did you ever pay for having your travelling-bag guarded?

Is it conceivable that money should draw negative interest? money-lenders pay charges for keeping?

Would any saving still take place?

56. This difference in manner of statement becomes important as we attempt an analysis of the factors which make up cost of production. Approaching the wages question from the point of view of comparative demand, it is easy to understand why the labourer is employed in one industry rather than in another, or why wages differ in different industries or for different men. That the labourer is employed in one industry rather than in another, simply means that the adjustment of demand has resulted in a rate of wages sufficient, in comparison with the wages of other industries, to attract and hold the services of this particular labourer. The labourer will remain in this industry until the same labour applied elsewhere will obtain for him, directly or through exchange, a greater sum of satisfactions,— more accurately, will involve for him a smaller sum of sacrifices.

Wages from point of view of labourer.

57. Considering the question from the point of view of the employer, the reasonings are parallel. So long as profits are adequate, employers in any particular industry will compete with each other and with employers in other industries for more labourers. Wages must stand in any industry at a rate

COST OF PRODUCTION

which, under conditions of competition with employers in other industries, will attract employés. The demand of the employer for labour is the mere working out of the demand of society for some particular commodity. As long as the social demand is sufficient to permit the payment to producers of as great means of satisfaction as they could obtain in some other industry, so long will employer and labourer consent to continue the relation. From point of view of employer.

58. It remains to inquire whether any important principle or dangerous error is involved in the term "cost of production of labour." This term occupies something like the same relation to the wages question that "cost of production of commodities" occupies to the price question (price means value expressed in terms of money). Is there a cost of production for labour? The adjustment of demand and supply is the ultimate fact in either case. Cost of production in either case is irrelevant, excepting as bearing on the volume of the future supply. Any Malthusian or other population law is, as concerns wages, at most an indication of tendencies and a prophecy of ultimate results. (Read in the Encyclopœdia, article on Malthus.) But in a most important respect cost of production of labour offers no parallel to the cost of production of commodities. As to commodities, cost of production is a summary of the working out in industry of the social demand for some commodities as compared with others. Demand must be understood in the sense of the human desire for goods. No parallel demand exists for an increase of population, nor is there any commodity satisfying a desire, with which labour may be compared in the working out of comparative demand, other than the desire for rest, — the indisposition to labour. For the purpose, then, of general reasonings, there is no force in the phrase "demand for labour" otherwise than as an expression of the different lines of activity in which different human desires are seeking their satisfactions. The nature of the demand for labour.

Inertia, friction, displacements, and confusion aside, the total demand for labour is as constant and immeasureable as are human desires. It thus seems best, as regards the total of in dustries, to avoid any consideration of the demand and supply of labour, and to regard wage payments as, for immediate purposes, merely a question of subdivision among the labourers of that part of the total product to be ascribed to labour. For industries or individuals the wages question is one of distribution of the industrial product. The portion of the product falling to the share of any labourer or group of labourers is approximately the measure that his or their production ministers to the social demand.

59. So far as relates to the determination of rates of interest, the current cost-of-production formula is more than superficial — it is misleading. Accurately employed, the term can mean nothing more than compensation for abstinence, without which saving would not take place, and without which capital would not be created. But savings are not in general made with a view to interest, but with a view to future needs. The French people save more closely than the American, while rates of interest with them are lower than with us. Savings would take place in large amounts if no interest were paid, or even if charges for safe keeping were usual. Presumably less saving would take place if interest were lower. In some measure, probably in a large measure, a higher rate of interest results in a larger supply of loanable funds to borrowers. But some saving would take place if no interest were paid; and this is a demonstration that the payment of interest is not a necessary condition to the existence of loanable funds. That the rate of interest ranges far above what is necessary as an incentive to save, and differs so widely in different countries, shows that it is the marginal advantage derived by borrowers from loans, and not the compensation of the abstinence involved in the saving, which fixes the rate of interest.

The cost-of-production doctrine as related to interest.

The law of demand and supply is here in full force, and supply is only in small degree affected by so-called cost of production; that is, the rate of interest is only in slight measure

COST OF PRODUCTION

made up of necessary compensation for abstinence. Interest is continually lowering, and yet both capital and loan funds are continually increasing. Saving does not stop because interest is lower to-day than five years ago, nor does the lower rate of interest of to-day mean that saving has become a matter of greater ease or of lower abstinence. It means simply that for one reason or another, abstinence included, there are now more wealth for use and funds for loan to be had for interest. If all people were to-day as willing to save, even without recompense, as they are now willing to save with recompense, the interest rate would not in any degree alter.

60. It is conceivable enough that the advantages derived from loan funds should so far fall as to furnish an insufficient inducement to producers to forego consumption, except to the degree that provident forethought for the future should be effective. *Demand rather than supply must explain interest.* In this event, the volume of loan funds would be approximately limited by the saving for prudential purposes, and interest would be limited by the marginal desire of borrowers. It is also conceivable enough — indeed the condition is probably the existing one — that the advantages from the use of capital should be in many parts of the world more than sufficient to postpone the consumption of commodities, even without the provident motive of insurance against future needs. But in this case, also, interest would be fixed in the adjustment of demand and supply at the marginal desirability of loan funds.

Suggestive Questions

Does the marginal producer's or seller's sacrifice fix price? or is it the marginal purchaser's sacrifice? or is it the equation of demand and supply? Which is the primary force?

Why does the nearest excluded buyer not buy? Nearest excluded seller not sell?

Why do some producers stop producing when price falls?

What do they do then?

Why do others continue to produce?

Do producers expect to determine price by their sacrifices?

Would it be well for most of them if they could? Or do they adapt production to price ? Do they lead or follow ? How do these answers apply to monopoly producers ?

Are wages determined by demand and supply, or by productiveness of labour, or by both ? How may you reconcile affirmative answers ?

Do you think that our higher standard of comfort makes our wages higher than European wages ?

Is there any relation between high standard of living and high efficiency ?

What does make our wages higher ?

Has the fertility of our soil anything to do with it ?

What limits the employer's disposition (ability) to pay wages ?

Can the farmer increase the crop by being hungry ? If so in what sense ?

Can he increase his ability to pay wages from the fact that his hired man has a large family ?

Can the hired man use this fact to increase his wages ?

Do wants = wages, or wages = wants ? Which is the nearer the truth ?

Are women's wages lower than men's because they can afford to work for less ?

Why does not the employer have to pay them more ? Why may he not pay them still less ?

Do employers make more by hiring women than men ?

Where do manufacturers get their materials ? What do they cost the producer ?

Is it possible to lose on the product of one's own labour ? How ?

What do you mean by cost of that which you produce with your own labour ?

What do you mean by cost to you of your own labour ? By cost to you of X's labour ?

Whose sacrifice of production is commensurate with market price ?

Criticise the term "Cost of production."

Mention all the different reasons which might impel you to borrow, and to pay interest.

Suppose you were working a farm, what would impel you to borrow ?

Where and when would you stop borrowing ?

Does borrowing ever take place for other than productive purposes ?

Is it accurate to say that interest is paid solely because of the productivity of capital ?

NOTES

Although, then, we have traced its instrumentality in production to nature and labour, is capital itself not productive at all ? Certainly it is, in more than one sense of that too ambiguous word. It is first "productive" because it finds its destination in the production of goods; it is further productive because it is an effectual tool in completing the roundabout and profitable method of production once they are entered on; finally, it is productive indirectly because it makes the adoption of new and profitable methods possible. One thing, however, it is not; it is not independently productive in the sense on which the most important part of the controversy turns. As the old economist Lotz expressed it briefly and succinctly: "Of any independent labour in capital there is simply no question." — BOEHM-BAWERK, *Pos. Theory of Cap.*, p. 99.

If the insecurity of compensation is so great that people who have wealth will not lend it, the disposition to hoard will be intensified, and the reason is that the motive for saving is the provision against emergencies, and that this feeling is stronger and more enduring than for the sake of profit on loans. It is a mistake with many economists to say that saving is due to the desire of profit. If people could get no profit or but a small profit or interest, they would still save; perhaps save all the more, for it is found necessary with prudent people to save for the sake of security; and we may be sure that people saved and hoarded with the greatest energy before they could find the people whom they could trust as borrowers; and similarly a very low rate of interest stimulates saving.
— THOROLD ROGERS (England), *The Economic Interpretation of Hist.*, p. 235.

For, after all, family affection is the main motive of saving. That men labour and save chiefly for the sake of their families, and not for themselves, is shown by the fact that they seldom spend, after they have retired from work, more than the income that comes in from their savings, preferring to leave their stored-up wealth intact for their families; while in this country alone twenty millions a year are saved in the form of insurance policies, and are available only after the death of those who save them. — MARSHALL, *Ec. of Ind.*, p. 153.

This power of anticipation must have a large influence in economics; for upon it is based all accumulation of stocks, of commodity, to be consumed at a future time. That class or race of men who have the most foresight will work most for the future. The untutored savage, like the child, is wholly occupied with the pleasures and the troubles of the moment; the morrow is dimly felt; the limit of his horizon is but a few days off; the wants of a future year or of a lifetime are wholly unforeseen. But in a state of civilization a vague though powerful feeling of the future is the main incentive to industry and saving.
— JEVONS, *Theory of Pol. Ec.*, p. 35.

CHAPTER VI

PROFITS DEFINED

Would you call interest received on notes profit? A dividend on bank-stock? Rent of a house?
Salary received and spent?
Salary received and put by?
Wages received and spent?
Wages received and put by?

61. Leaving out of consideration the bounties of nature, all goods may be said to result from the application of human energies to the human environment. Natural forces may or may not be concerned in the, process. Any activity so modifying or distributing matter or force as to contribute immediately or remotely to the creation of utility, is productive activity; and if this activity be human and purposed to the creation of utility, it is labour. Natural forces are best conceived as taking in the process, the part of aids or multipliers of human energy. Natural forces are not, however, essential to the production either of utility or of profit. Wood may be whittled or stone be carved to an increased usefulness without the aid of any natural force. Goods in the form of services are commonly independent of natural forces. It is true, however, that some of the goods necessary to the existence of man, namely, food products, are conditioned for their supply on the reproductive powers of nature. And while it is not true that wages or profits result in every case and necessarily from the aid of natural forces, it is true, as we shall see, that the rate and total of both are intimately associated with the employment of natural forces.

62. In the ordinary business sense, if one plants a field he must get back more in return than he sowed, else there is no

PROFITS DEFINED

profit. If one hires labourers, buys materials, pays interest and rent, and produces a machine which will not sell for enough to replace the expense, there is no profit. But if one apply himself, or the productive energies in his control, to results in products less in value than the value he might otherwise have produced, the case is not so clear.

In fact, the word "profit" is used in ordinary affairs with perplexing indefiniteness. One man means by profit that surplus which remains to him after charging against the gross gain interest and rent and a fair compensation for his own services. For example, a storekeeper owning his own store building worth $5000, and carrying a stock of goods worth $10,000, makes a gross gain per year on his sales of $4000. This $4000 is merely the difference between the cost price and the selling price of the goods he has sold. It is not unusual to find this entire $4000 included in the term "profit." A second merchant would insist upon deducting interest on' capital invested in land and stock, say $900, and would regard the residue of $3100 as profit. Another would deduct also the value of his own time and effort, say $1500, and would allow but $1600 to stand for profit. Yet another would look at his inventory of wealth at the end of the year as compared with the beginning, and would regard as profit whatever increase had been made, treating his living expenses as part of his expenses of business, and regarding his land and stock in trade as coöperators with him in the general process of earning him a livelihood and gaining him a surplus.

Term is indefinite in ordinary use.

To the merchant, the question is mostly one of bookkeeping, the facts, and not the names for them, standing to him as important matters. For us, however, it is necessary to fix upon some definite and specific meaning for the words which we must use. Some clearness of thinking also comes about with clearness of definition. Were one to ask a real estate speculator what profit he had made upon a lot costing him $1000, which he had held for one year and sold at $1500, he would answer either $500, or $500 minus interest, and if asked what he had done with the profit, he would have no hesitation in replying that he had used it in his living expenses. Nor would it ever occur to him in fixing his profit to deduct the wages of his own superintendence. His business is to make profits and to live off them. So with the trader in grain or live-stock. And in no one of all these cases would it ordinarily occur to charge up anything for risk of loss.

Crusoe, if asked, at the close of his harvest season, what the season's work had profited him, or what wages he had made, would probably interpret the question as an inquiry into the effectiveness of his season's labour, after deducting his outlays of seed and the wear and tear of his primitive appliances. If he could have done better on another piece of land, or with a different crop, he would not find it unnatural to say that another course would have been more profitable. In this sense, evidently all labour is profitable as compared with idleness. Different lines of production are only relatively, never absolutely, unprofitable as long as anything remains above expenditure.

The sense in which the term is used in this Crusoe illustration, extended and developed to apply to the complex relations of the business world, is the economic sense. Profit is one form of remuneration for labour — for human effort.

63. The existing industrial system is a competitive system organized upon lines of division of labour and exchange.

Profit may be absolute or relative. Social life adds important factors to the Crusoe problem. Division of labour becomes possible only on terms of possible exchange of products. We will suppose, for illustration, that a man needs or desires ten different sorts of commodities, which he may, if he will, produce for himself. If he finds that by producing some few or one of these commodities in large quantities, and obtaining the others of the ten by exchanging for them some portion of his product, he can thereby obtain in the aggregate a greater sum of satisfactions than by the other method of direct production, he will make use of the opportunities afforded by exchange. In this he simply follows the prospect of the greater profit, and if the outcome justifies his expectation, his labour is relatively profitable. Even if the outcome is disappointing, his labour may be absolutely profitable.

The further development in the exchange system by which the producer employs not only his own activities, but the activities of others, — immediately in the form of services, or remotely in the form of commodities, — involves no essential modification in the nature of profit.

64. Profit is merely one form of the remuneration of labour, and is essentially in strict parallel with wages. Had usage so decreed, the two terms might well have been merged in one. But as the terms are established in use, profit points to remuneration without the intervention of an employer, — where the labourer is himself the projector (imprenditor, undertaker, unternehmer, entrepreneur) of the enterprise. Wages indicate the intervention of an employer. Profit may be conceived as a form of wages from society as employer. Rightly considered, all individual workmen, other than wage-earners, are imprenditors. That enterprise promises to be *relatively* profitable which affords prospect of a better return to the imprenditor than with equal sacrifice he may reasonably expect in another line of activity. And if no line of activity promises profit as compared with wage-earning, or with production for direct personal consumption, the imprenditor can without sacrifice betake himself to one of these courses. *Distinguished from wages.*

It is important to note at this point that this phrase " relatively profitable" points to an element in wages and profits, which from another point of view we have considered under the aspect of producers' and sellers' rent.

65. Inasmuch as, in the present form of social organization, that life which excludes exchange and any form of industrial interdependence with one's fellows, is practically out of the question, we may safely consider that some one of the different forms of wage-earning furnishes for each man that marginal type of activity by which for him the comparative profit of any other activity is to be estimated, and to which, meeting

elsewhere with unsatisfactory remuneration, he may betake himself without sacrifice.

From this point of view the intimate association of wages, profits, and interest becomes manifest. If wages are anywhere **Relation of profit to wages, rent, and interest.** found to be high, profits may also be expected to be high,—in any event, as high as wages,—since otherwise employers and self-directed labourers would tend to become wage-earners. Also where labour is productive of large results in goods, capital, which is an indirect application of labour to like ends, may normally be expected to be highly productive of goods, and therefore to command a high rate of interest.

66. It will be noticed that the element of compensation for risk, which enters largely into the business man's notion of **Relation to risk.** profit, is rigorously to be excluded from the economic definition of the term. It is true that remuneration for risk and true profit are seldom capable of accurate discrimination in practical affairs, but in theory it is clear that so far as the return of any venture is compensation for risk, it is not compensation for labour of management, and that unless the return is more than compensation for risk there is no room for profit. And with equal care must be excluded from the notion of profit that portion of the return which is in fact interest upon capital. Interest bears the same relation to capital as does profit to labour.

It will be helpful to summarize at this point the factors in production, and the names which are applied to their respective forms of compensation,—remembering that capital stands for what man has done to adapt his environment to his purposes, the useful changes which he has impressed upon the outside world.

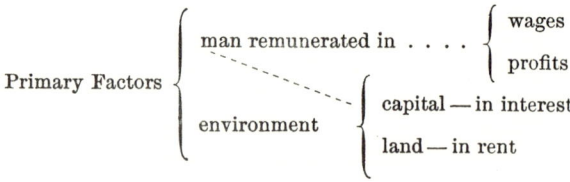

SUGGESTIVE QUESTIONS

Does nature produce anything? Is Henry George correct in saying that it produces everything of profit?

Is man a producer?

What do you call his productive activity?

Is labour the only productive fact?

In what different forms is productive labour remunerated?

What aids does man have in production?

Does he consume immediately all that he produces? Why not?

Is any part of this residue an aid in production?

What do you call that part? What do you call its compensation?

Is a lawyer a producer? A minister? A cook? A factory hand? The employer of the factory hand? A school teacher?

What do you call their respective remunerations?

A farmer has a farm worth $1000, machinery and stock worth $1000, hires a man at $300 per year, works himself, gets $1000 worth of crop. Apportion this into wages, interest, rent, and profits.

A carpenter takes the contract for the carpenter work on a building at $1000, works six months himself and pays his men $800. It costs him $300 to live during the six months. He might have worked by the day, receiving $400 in wages. What is his profit?

Is it possible to have absolute profit and relative loss?

NOTES

We come to the conclusion that the wages of the employer and of the workman are generically identical and only specifically different. The question between the two parties engaged in joint product is, what is the share which each party shall receive, the cost of materials being deducted in the residual distribution?—ROGERS, *Ec. Int. of Hist.*, p. 21.

Now it will be plain that, in the language of logicians, the two first elements of profit are objective, *i.e.* they are external to the agent, and determined by conditions which the agent cannot control. The third, his own labour, is subjective, and it is plain that on this his real profits depend. Our analysis, therefore, shows that the capitalist employer is a labourer, and that his remuneration depends entirely on the efficiency of his labour. Whether or no he gets too much in the distribution of the gross value is another question, but the more necessary workmen make him by being as much as possible unlike him, the greater will be his share. — ROGERS, *Ec. Int. of Hist.*, p. 19.

As Adam Smith says, "The real wages of labour may be said to consist in the quantity of the necessaries and conveniences of life that are given for it; its nominal wages in the quantity of money. . . . The labourer is rich or poor, is well or ill rewarded, in proportion to the real, not to the nominal wages of his labour." But the words "that are given for it" must not be taken to apply only to the necessaries and conveniences that are directly provided by the purchaser of the labour or its products; for account must be taken also of the advantages which are attached to the occupation, and require no special outlay on his part.
— MARSHALL, *Ec. of Ind*, p. 271.

CHAPTER VII

RENT OF LAND

If you were renting land for farming would you pay more for some land than for other? Why?

How much do you think you could handle advantageously without hiring men?

Why not try to get along with half as much? One-fourth as much? Twice as much? Four times?

If you had 320 acres, do you think two men in diversified farming could get twice as much from the land as one? Four times as much as two? Eight as four? Sixteen as eight? Where would this stop, if ever?

Would it matter for this purpose whether the crop were strawberries or wheat?

Would the advantages of increase in numbers ever stop with strawberries?

Can two men harvest more hay or wheat than one? Two times as much? Three times as much?

Would you prefer good land at high rent or poor land at low rent? Why?

67. It is a matter of every-day observation, that from one piece of land one man makes large profits, that from another piece of equal quality a second man obtains a greatly less return, while a third man may fail to recover his actual outlay. If these men are renters, the first makes large profits over and above his rent, while the third is getting mortgaged.

The returns of agriculture result from the effectiveness of human energies coöperating in production with the energies of nature. Capital is to be conceived as an indirect application of human energies. This is not to deny that in some measure nature affords perfected and valuable goods, commodities which are to be regarded as gratuitous to man, as an unearned value, rather

What produces the crop?

than as products of his labour. It is to be remembered, however, that these values are fixed in the market by the marginal sacrifice process, — where labour of necessity has part, — and that the unearned value appears, therefore, as an accidental increase in wages or profits, or as attached to land under the form of rental or selling prices. Natural forces and advantages furnish instruments or opportunities for the exercise of human activities, and are best conceived in the aspect of aids and multipliers of human energies. The results are not to be ascribed to man alone, or to land and nature alone, but to human energies applied to the land. Rent, therefore, is broadly to be defined as payment for the use of land. The amount of the payment will tend to be proportional to the value of the opportunity.

68. The Ricardian theory of rent, from which, for the most part, we shall not widely diverge, is not difficult of statement.

Ricardian theory stated. It rests fundamentally upon what is known as the law of diminishing returns. Were the capacity of any one field unlimited, and were successive increases of product possible without at some point reaching a condition where increased outlays of productive energies were recompensed less bountifully in products than were previous outlays, rent, so far as it is a question of agricultural products, would mostly disappear, being limited to the differential advantages of some one field over any other offered field for the purposes of this entire production. Transportation charges are not allowed for in this illustration. The tendency towards diminishing returns is not an economic theory, but is one of the most commonplace facts of agriculture. The very existence of rental and sale values of land sufficiently attests it. "Were it not for this tendency, every farmer would save nearly the whole of his rent by giving up all but a small piece of his land, and bestowing all of his labour and capital upon that." (Marshall.)

Law of diminishing returns.

The reader should note that land, in economic phrase, includes rivers and seas and mineral deposits. It is not clear that the law of diminishing returns applies to all extractive industries equally. It is questionable whether it applies to the sea at all. The returns of mining are in a measure to be conceived as a consumption of the resources of the earth, rather than as a mere using.

The origin of rent as a historical inquiry, the fluctuations which rents in the aggregate and rents in particular have exhibited and still exhibit, and the probable tendency of rents in the future, are questions which cannot be separated in treatment from this agricultural law of diminishing returns. "Whatever may be the future developments in the art of agriculture, a continued increase in the application of capital and labour to land, must ultimately result in the diminution of the extra produce which can be obtained by a given extra amount of capital and labour." (Marshall.)

With increasing population and expanding demand for agricultural products, it therefore comes about that cultivation tends to extend itself to less and less desirable land. As soon as market prices make the cultivation of 24-bushel land practicable, the opportunity to cultivate 25-bushel land becomes equally practicable at a rental payment of one bushel per acre. Competition compels payment of this rental. When cultivation extends to 23-bushel land, the 24-land pays one rental and the 25-land two. Mark that prices all the while stand at a level which remunerates the production on the poorest grade of land, and that the rent payment is the market price of the differential advantage measured from this point.

69. Thus the Ricardian reasoning concludes that increasing population tends towards rise in rents, and that this rise measures the tendency toward increasing difficulty in obtaining the requisite quantity of agricultural products; but that since market price gravitates **Does rent add to price?** always toward that point which compensates the producer at the margin where no rent is paid, rent cannot be said to add anything to market price or to be paid at the expense of the purchaser or consumer. Rent is the outcome of a competitive

distribution between landlord and tenant of that which the consumer could not avoid paying in any case.

70. The foregoing statement contains the essentials of the Ricardian theory, so worded as to avoid unnecessary controversies. But it is important to note that the Ricardian reasoning necessarily assumes as in cultivation a large body of land at or near the no-rent line, and the existence of other lands uncultivated and just beneath the line of cultivation, so that with every rise in market remunerations, lands pass from potential to actual competition, and with every fall, cross from actual to potential competition. A ready flexibility is thus given to the marginal line which would be impossible if all land were utilized, or if gradations from better to worse, instead of being gradual and regular, were irregular and marked.

It is further worthy of note that the statement, as above worded, carefully avoids the imputation that market price is fixed or regulated by the marginal cost of production. Market price and marginal cost (sacrifice) are evidently commensurate quantities, but this fact does not indicate which is cause and which effect, if indeed cause and effect are accurately to be distributed.

71. There are several factors in the determination of rent, each of which deserves close examination. First, there is the demand for agricultural products, — the disposition on the part of human beings to refrain from producing other goods in order to produce agricultural goods, or to produce these other goods for the purpose of obtaining agricultural products in exchange.

The different factors in the rent problem.

Second, there are possessors of opportunities for the production of these goods offering these opportunities competitively for rent or for sale. These offered opportunities are broadly termed "land." It must also be held in mind that there is a large body of uncultivated land, capable by change in market conditions of being brought into the lists of competitive production.

Third, there are possessors of productive energies, — labour or capital — competitively seeking opportunities to supply the market demand for agricultural products.

72. The economic demand, that is, the desire for satisfactions and the disposition to sacrifice in order to obtain them, is particularly strong and persistent in the case where room for subsistence and nourishment for subsistence are concerned. The utilities of mere space are of small importance in respect to agricultural lands, but of great importance in respect to urban lands; fertility and food-producing power are not of great importance as regards urban lands, but are of chief importance as regards agricultural lands.

<small>(1) Demand for product.</small>

But it is an entire misconception of the problem of rent to omit from consideration certain other utilities of lands offered by landlords and purchased by tenants, — utilities of healthfulness and beauty and social advantage, which do not manifest themselves in increase of the number of bushels or tons of agricultural product, or in the market price for which these bushels or tons are sold. These utilities are as necessarily, and perhaps as prominently, a factor in the rent of agricultural land as they are in the sale price. They are likewise prominent factors in the rent of urban lands, oftentimes as important as are the quality and cost of improvements, or as are the opportunities afforded for convenience or profit in business.

<small>Different sorts of product.</small>

It is, for example, within the experience of every one that the selling-price of a farm is often affected very considerably by the beauty or healthfulness of its location, by the general character of the neighbouring families, or by the proximity of schools or churches. It is commonly found that farms situated near towns or villages bear a high market value altogether disproportionate to the diminished expenses of transportation or to the greater convenience of market facilities. Considerations of this sort become of overshadowing importance in the investigation of rents and values of city property. The location, with respect to sightliness, or neighbours and social privileges, or nearness to the business centre, is the main element in the case. Rents and values climb to enormous figures on business streets, the value of the land often greatly outweighing the expense of very costly improvements. Evidently, then, the explanation of rent by differences in the wheat-producing power of land can be taken as illustrative merely.

73. With more than an ample supply of land, not all land will be cultivated, and not all the residue utilized even for pasturage and forestry. Somewhere there will be land the use of which will command no payment; somewhere there will be land just worth using if no payment is required. This land, wherever and whatever it may be, is to be regarded as the land of marginal utility, from which the differential advantages and rent-bearing capacities of all other land may be measured. Under present conditions, however, this marginal land is not cultivated land. It is land used for hunting and fishing, or pasturage or forestry. In order, therefore, to avoid misconceptions, the term "marginal utility of land" is preferable to "margin of cultivation." Land which is at the margin of *cultivation* is almost of necessity rent-bearing land, since, under present conditions, land which would be worth while to cultivate at all, even without rent, would have an appreciable value for purposes of pasturage, forestry, etc. Were there, however, no non-rent-paying lands, — were the supply all utilized, — the above reasonings would not be greatly modified in the absence of effective combination among land-owners. The rent of the least desirable land, plus the value of the advantages of better land, would give the rental value of the better land.

(2) **Supply of land. The margins.**

It does not rest then with changes of customs or laws or institutions to abolish rent. So long as different parcels of land offer differing degrees of advantage for human purposes, and the supply of the best land is limited, rent will continue to exist. It is indeed possible enough that the handling of land should by law or custom be confined to owners, that renting cease, or that the State become landlord, or that the State by taxation appropriate the rental value in whole or in part.

But these methods would none of them destroy the differential advantages attaching to land.

It is to be observed, however, that our investigations have been mostly limited to the forces determining rent at any given time, and that we have for the most part postponed any examination of the historical question with its associated problems of justice, and of the economic outlook with its associated population problems. Nor have we departed widely from the Ricardian doctrine. We have somewhat enlarged the Ricardian conception of products to include the utilities not properly termed agricultural attaching to the use of land. We have substituted as the vanishing point of rent the margin of usefulness in place of the margin of cultivation. Lastly, and more importantly, we have omitted to investigate what portion of land or rental values has resulted directly or indirectly from human agencies, — or what portion is due to the original qualities and peculiarities of the land, — or what subtraction or destruction of these original qualities men may have worked. The Ricardian statement defines rent as "that portion of the produce of the earth which is paid to the landlord for the use of the original and indestructible powers of the soil." It is clear enough that some of the original powers of the soil are as capable of destruction as they are of improvement. But for the purposes of our present inquiry, it is unimportant to determine, even were it possible, the degree in which the present condition of the land is due to the beneficial action of birds, or men, or corals, or insects, or to what extent deterioration is due to men, or animals, or insects.

Supply of land merely a present fact.

The factors which enter into the determination of the value of land, and the value of its temporary use, are very complex. Present usefulness depends in part on the quality of past treatment. In this respect, however, there is nothing peculiar in principle about land. The question of land and rental values remains, like all questions of value, a matter on the one hand of advantages obtainable, and on the other of sacrifices submitted to in the adjustment of demand and supply. It is to be expected that as stores of capital, arts of cultivation, methods of transportation, and habits of consumption are modified, land values will undergo great variations in the aggregate, as well as relatively to each other. This, however, is not peculiar to land, and will not serve as a denial of the laws of rental and land values. Wampum, sacred relics, talismans have, with the lapse of years, almost lost their value. Every attic is filled with articles which have outlasted the human desires served by them at an earlier time, or which have been superseded by appliances more effective to the same or similar ends. This perpetual flux in prices characterizes in varying degree all exchangeable objects. The mill owner finds his machinery out of date, though not outworn; his buildings possibly useless for their original purpose by reason of changes in lines of transportation, in the sources of supply, in the centres of consumption, or in habits of consumption. The mill, if operated, may pay returns only upon the floating capital applied, the fixed capital being correctly considered as lost. It may be that the rental value of an improved farm is no more than its value for purposes of household occupancy, or it may be that the rental value is not greater than the value for purposes of cultivation, the opportunity for household occupancy being neglected and valueless. The entire usefulness of agricultural land may be due to drainage operations, or may be considerably diminished by such operations. No parcel of land exists, the utilities of which can be asserted to be permanent and indestructible. That which was once regarded as the best land, and which was the best, in view of the arts and appliances and conditions of that time, may have been at an earlier date, and may again become, not worth the using. " A mere increase in the demand for produce may invert the order in which two adjacent pieces of land rank as regards fertility. The one which gives the smaller produce when both are uncultivated, or when the cultivation of both is equally slight, may rise above the other, and justly rank as the more fertile when both are cultivated with equal thoroughness. In other words, many of those lands which are the least fertile when cultivation is merely extensive, become among the most fertile when cultivation is intensive. . . . We therefore cannot call one piece of land more fertile than another until we know something about the skill and enterprise of its cultivators, and the amount of capital and labour at their disposal; and until we know whether the demand for produce is such as to make intensive cultivation profitable with the resources at their disposal. If it is, those lands will be the most fertile which give highest average returns to a large expenditure of labour and capital; but if not, those will be the most fertile which give the best returns to the first few doses. The term 'fertility' has no meaning except with reference to the special circumstances of a particular time and place." (Marshall.)

74. Possessors of productive energies are of unequal skill, unequal strength, unequal capacity, and inclined to different estimates of the importance to themselves of the subsidiary utilities above set forth. Each who (3) **Cultivators.** betakes himself to agriculture does so because agriculture offers to him, as he thinks, in the goods obtainable through exchange, plus the goods of nourishment directly obtained, plus advantages of health and comfort and convenience and beauty, plus immunities from inconveniences of various kinds, the maximum of advantages in proportion to the labour and capital applied. Each might have betaken himself to cloth-making or machine-making, or to any other one of the countless occupations of human energy. Those who become renters or purchasers of land for agricultural purposes, become so because, under all the conditions of personal aptitudes, personal tastes, amount of capital in hand, market prices of products, the esteem in which the employment is held, etc., they think the best to be had for themselves out of agriculture.

75. These men enter the real-estate market competitively, as buyers of the temporary or permanent use of land; that is, as renters or as purchasers. They confront land- (4) **Land-owners.** owners who offer all sorts and qualities of land, with all sorts and degrees of improvements, affording all degrees and all kinds of advantage. There is, then, nothing

peculiar in the fact that different lands sell or rent at different prices. There is nothing peculiar in principle in the sale of the temporary use of land as distinguished from the permanent use. Lands which, in view of the market prices of products, of fertility, location, healthfulness, and beauty, offer no inducements for purposes other than pasturage or forestry, will bear no rent for other than their value for these purposes. If, under all the circumstances, fertility and the market prices of products being the most important, the land is desirable for cultivation, it will bear a rent at least equal to the rental value for pasture, forestry, hunting, or fishing. Other lands will bear higher rents in proportion to their differential advantages.

76. It is evident, however, that in the competitive buying or hiring of lands, the advantages obtainable from the possession of particular lands will tend to be cancelled, and will ordinarily be mostly cancelled, by the higher rents or prices paid therefor, but that the advantages obtained from the possession of the land by reason of the exceptional qualities in skill, capacity, or taste of the occupier, will not tend to be cancelled by rent, excepting in so far as the skill, etc., become general. That is to say, the remunerations of the cultivators differ as widely as differ the cultivators.

Renters' quasi-rents.

77. All remuneration for personal activity, without the intervention of an employer, will be recalled as covered by the term "profits." The profits, then, of cultivators differ as widely as differ the cultivators. Whoever obtains the use of land is held to pay therefor its rent or value as determined by market adjustments — by the amount which another will pay if he will not. Each piece of land attains its rental value by virtue of its differential of advantage over the marginal land. But because of the great diversity of advantages offered by different lands, the rate at which this differential shall be appraised is in considerable degree a distinct question for each piece. Similar lands are in some degree in competition with each other, — as

Some monopoly features.

are different horses, for example, — but in considerable degree, also, the owner of each piece of land stands as a monopoly possessor offering his commodity to competitive bids. Whatever the tenant obtains from the land as net return after deducting rent, interest, and the outlays of cultivation, is to be ascribed to him in his rôle of productive agent. So, if there is something in the position or quality of the land peculiarly adapted to his condition or abilities, whatever he is able to get from the land more than would another cultivator, is to be attributed to himself as producer rather than to the land as opportunity.

78. We have found, then, that an analysis of the forces determining rent at any particular time reduces itself to an application of the notion of value to questions concerning the occupancy of land. The law of rent is the law of value to the extent that both rest upon demand and supply, that both are the working out of that compromise between the indisposition to work and the desire for the results of work which manifests itself in the tendency to follow the line of least resistance, *i.e.* of least sacrifice. The differences in the hire of land rest upon differences of advantage in use. <small>Rent doctrines in some degree familiar.</small>

But we have seen, also, that while the law of demand and supply is equally applicable to all commodities, there are important differences in commodities in point of the possible variations in the volume of demand and in the volume of supply, and in point of the terms and conditions of increase in either demand or supply. <small>In what degree peculiar.</small>
We have seen that if the arts of agricultural production — the term being understood to include transportation — remain unchanged, an increased supply of product is possible only in conformity with the law of diminishing returns; that is, only upon terms of increased proportional expenditure of productive energy. We shall be called to observe, in a subsequent chapter, that with many other commodities, a tendency towards increasing returns is equally manifest by reason of the increased efficiency of the productive energies applied.

79. The very existence of rents is conditioned upon this commonplace agricultural fact that increased labour and capital applied to land bring a less than proportional return. This fact we have called the law of diminishing returns. In large measure, the past and the future of rent movements are to be deduced from this law. The increases in population which have already taken place have enlarged the demand for the products of land, and, by compelling the cultivation of less desirable lands, have necessarily brought about an increase in rent payments corresponding to a larger differential of advantage as measured from a lower margin of utility. Future increases of population must likewise be attended by increased rent, unless their influence is overbalanced by other tendencies.

Relation of population, machinery, and methods to rent.

There are such other tendencies; in truth, the law of diminishing returns falls far short of a full theoretical equipment for the analysis of rent movements. This law points merely to one very important fact in the supply aspect of the problem. But diminishing returns are the condition upon which rents depend rather than their ultimate cause. As we have already seen, and shall repeatedly see, no economic explanation in terms of supply is exhaustive or satisfactory. The volume of the demand for agricultural products must be examined before the tendencies characteristic of supply can safely be estimated. How rapidly, for example, rents may advance with an enlarging market for products, must depend upon the measure in which demand will be retired by rising prices. How rapidly rents may be made to fall by the opening up of new lands, is incapable of estimate till something is known of the degree in which falling prices may be expected to attract a larger consumption. All rent tendencies must be studied not alone from the point of view of the facts peculiar to supply, but as well from the point of view of the peculiar nature of the demand.

Commodities vary greatly in what is known as the elasticity of demand. With falling prices, the demand for books, for example, greatly expands, while higher prices would be met by greatly decreased consumption. Where demand is very elastic, small changes in price work large changes in consumption. It follows, then, that small changes in supply must work small changes in price, while large changes in supply work only limited changes in price.

But where the demand is inelastic, the reverse of all this is true. Small increments in supply are marketable only at considerable decrease in price, while large increases in supply work enormous price reductions. Much that is peculiar to rent movements is to be explained by the fact that the demand of society for the products of the earth, and particularly for agricultural products, is extremely inelastic. Consumption of food products cannot be very largely increased, nor is it possible without acute suffering greatly to reduce consumption. It is true, that in considerable measure one product may be substituted for another by reason of minor changes in price, but the total volume of consumption adjusts itself to the total volume of supply only through relatively great price fluctuations. Were the fact otherwise, advances in rents following upon increased population would have been much less considerable, and a fall in rents resulting from the opening up of new supplies of land would be relatively unimportant.[1]

Bearing in mind that increasing supplies of agricultural products are unmarketable unless at rapidly falling prices, it becomes evident that all causes tending to increase the per acre productiveness of land will mostly manifest themselves in

---

[1] Attempt has been made under the formula known as Gregory King's law to express mathematically these relations of price to supply. Necessarily under modern conditions of commerce the whole world must be included in the reckoning. Statistics for this purpose are not obtainable, and the conclusions must, therefore, be taken as, at best, only loose estimates. With defective harvests, prices are said to rise as follows:

A defect of 1 tenth raises prices	3 tenths
2 tenths	8 "
3 "	16 "
4 "	28 "
5 "	45 "

Taken as applied to any one cereal product, this is probably an overstatement. As applied to the total of agricultural products, it probably errs greatly in the other direction.

the abandonment of marginal lands and the decrease of rental totals. Thus all progress in agricultural skill, — like better methods of crop rotation, or improvements in the applications of chemistry to the production of fertilizers, — by which the per acre output of land is increased, will tend toward the disuse of the poorer qualities of land. Likewise all improvements in transportation facilities by which new and more fertile lands are brought into use and the abandonment of poorer lands made possible, must reduce the rent differential.

And even with the new lands only equally fertile with the old, the reductions in the cost of transportation would reduce the differential of advantage enjoyed by the lands nearer the market. Not less land would be used, but the difference in advantages would be lowered. In the diagram the transportation charges of 2, 4, 6, 8, etc., give rentals of 14, 12, 10, etc. Reducing the cost of transportation by one-half lowers the differentials to 7, 6, 5, 4, etc. It is true that this cheaper transportation would cause some of the more distant lands to be brought into cultivation. But only a small increase in products could be marketed without so great a fall in price as seriously to affect rents generally.

LAND.

14	2	30	1	7
12	4	30	2	6
10	6	30	3	5
8	8	30	4	4
6	10	30	5	3
4	12	30	6	2
2	14	30	7	1
	16	30	8	
		30		

Assuming, however, that the land opened up is of distinctly inferior quality, one might look for a rise in rents. But the question is whether this wider differential of fertility can be sufficient to more than offset the diminished differential of transportation.

Suppose that the land is 30, 28, 26, 24, etc., in productiveness, and that the transportation charges are 2, 4, 6, 8, 10, etc., as in the previous illustration. Each grade of land from the margin, increases in rent by 2 for differential of fertility, and by 2 more for differential of freight.

If now the freight differential falls to 1 for each grade, the rent payments will fall from $20 + 16 + 12 + 8 + 4$ to $15 +$

$12 + 9 + 6 + 3$. Even could cultivation extend two grades lower without a material fall in prices, this would carry the rent payments only to $21 + 18 + 15 + 12 + 9 + 6 + 3$. In fact, however, prices would greatly fall upon the assumption of this extension. These lands could no longer be treated as 30-, 28-, etc. (bushel) times one (dollar) lands. The 2, 4, 6, 8, etc., as differential in bushels, would still remain, but these bushels would have greatly shrunk as measured in terms of market value.

	LAND.	
$10 + 10 = 20$	30	$10 + 5 = 15$
$8 + 8 = 16$	28	$8 + 4 = 12$
$6 + 6 = 12$	26	$6 + 3 = 9$
$4 + 4 = 8$	24	$4 + 2 = 6$
$2 + 2 = 4$	22	$2 + 1 = 3$
	20	
	18	
	16	
	14	

It is worth remarking, also, that this tendency of improved transportation facilities to lower rents can be asserted only where marginal lands are rendered accessible. In the absence of new lands, as for example upon a densely inhabited island, or in a country mostly cut off from outside influences, as is China, lower outlays for transportation must inure entirely to the benefit of the landowners. It is not even true that improvements in the art of agriculture necessarily lower rent, if these improvements are such as to apply solely or mostly to the better lands. If for example there were in cultivation

        3 units of 30-bushel land
        4 " " 29- " "
        5 " " 28- " "
        6 " " 27- " "

and some method were devised of doubling the output of classes 1 and 2, it would still remain necessary to cultivate some of the 27-bushel land, while the 30 and 29 lands would have become 60 and 58 lands with their rent differential measured from the old margin of 27-.

80. In no case, then, is it safe to assume that the mere fact

of the extension of cultivation to inferior lands means of necessity an increase in rents. For anything like an accurate forecast of rent tendencies in any case, there is required a Gregory King's law of altogether unattainable accuracy. Were the demand for agricultural products as elastic as is the demand for books, or sewing-machines, or bicycles, improved arts of transportation would probably raise rents. If, for example, rent differentials were due one-half to lower expenses of transportation, and these expenses were reduced by one-half, it would become practicable to cultivate much larger areas of land, if the demand for products were such that the prices should not sharply fall. In this case, rents would increase in the total.

30	30	29	29	28	28	27	27	27	27
26	26	26	26	26	25	25	25	25	25
24	24	24	24	24	23	23	23	23	23
22	22	22	22	22	21	21	21	21	21
20	20	20	20	20	19	19	19	19	19

If, for example, all the land better than the 22 is under cultivation, transportation differentials accounting for one-half the rent payments, and if these charges fall by 50%, rents may advance, if it is assumed that the demand is sufficiently elastic to sustain prices so that all lands of the 19 quality or better may remain in cultivation. Upon the original conditions the 23 lands were marginal.

```
5 units of 24-bushel land paid 5-bushel rent + 5-freight rent
5   "     " 25-    "    "     " 10-   "     "  " 10-    "    "
5   "     " 26-    "    "     " 15-   "     "  " 15-    "    "
4   "     " 27-    "    "     " 16-   "     "  " 16-    "    "
2   "     " 28-    "    "     " 10-   "     "  " 10-    "    "
2   "     " 29-    "    "     " 12-   "     "  " 12-    "    "
2   "     " 30-    "    "     " 14-   "     "  " 14-    "    "
                                  82-   "     "  " 82-    "    "
```

Under the new conditions,

5	units of	20-bushel land pay	5-bushel rent +		2½-freight rent	
5	"	" 21-	"	"	" 10-	"	"	"	5-	"	"
5	"	" 22-	"	"	" 15-	"	"	"	7½-	"	"
5	"	" 23-	"	"	" 20-	"	"	"	10-	"	"
5	"	" 24-	"	"	" 25-	"	"	"	12½-	"	"
5	"	" 25-	"	"	" 30-	"	"	"	15-	"	"
5	"	" 26-	"	"	" 35-	"	"	"	17½-	"	"
4	"	" 27-	"	"	" 32-	"	"	"	16-	"	"
2	"	" 28-	"	"	" 18-	"	"	"	9-	"	"
2	"	" 29-	"	"	" 20-	"	"	"	10-	"	"
2	"	" 30-	"	"	" 22-	"	"	"	11-	"	"
					232-	"	"	"	116-	"	"

The supply of products has risen from $60 + 58 + 56 + 108 + 130 + 125 + 120 + 115 = 772$, to $772 + 110 + 105 + 100 + 95 = 1175$. Under the old conditions, 82 bushels could be claimed by the landlord as rent; under the new conditions, 232 bushels. If these 232 can be sold for more than were the 82, rents have risen irrespective of 34 increase in freight differentials. Ultimately, then, we fall back upon the character of the demand as the critical point in our rent investigation. The law of diminishing returns explains the existence of rent only after demand is assumed. The degree of rise or fall in rent can be guessed at only in view of the demand.

Some questions we can hardly even guess at. It is commonly assumed that improvements in farm machinery work in line with improved fertilizers and improved methods to reduce rents. This is correct for such machinery as increases the per acre output. But for the most part, these labour-saving devices are not land-saving devices. They increase the amount of land employed in producing a given amount of product; thereby they lower the margin of fertility, exactly reversing the effect of fertilizers. If rents fall, it must be from the fact that cultivation is carried so far upon inferior soils as, through a considerable expansion of supply, to lower prices, and to do this to such an extent that the influence of an increased differential in product is overcome by the necessity of marketing the products at lower prices.

This case is parallel to that where improved transportation facilities carry cultivation to poorer lands, excepting that with the machinery there is a distinct and important first-effect toward the use of more rather than of less land, irrespective of any increase in total output. The influence of machine methods upon rent is more nearly parallel to that of lower rates of interest. The product sells more cheaply by reason of lower production-sacrifices at the new margin, but the new margin is a lower margin. The lower market prices correspond solely to lower outlays in the direction of labour or capital. If rent is not increased as measured from this lower margin, it is because such a fall in prices has occurred as to more than offset the wider differential in fertility. The problem is to determine the point of adjustment of two opposing forces, the strength of neither of which have we the ability to estimate.

Mere space values of land must, however, be expected to advance with an increase in population, without reference to any improvements in agricultural arts. Better facilities for suburban transportation, on the other hand, must tend to the reduction of urban rents, and of the aggregate of land values, and possibly to the reduction of the tendency towards booms, with the resulting unsteady growth of population centres.

Urban rents.

81. Substantially, nothing has thus far been said of the so-called unearned increment. It is, however, evident that a considerable portion of the advantages offered by land for human purposes, exist by reason of the natural and original qualities of the land; that another considerable portion of these advantages arise from the possibility of applying to the land the great store of scientific and practical knowledge which the race has acquired, as well as from the enjoyment of the means of transportation, the social privileges, and the conveniences and comforts which society has created; and that another considerable portion of these advantages would entirely fail to exist but for the opportunity offered by society of exchanging agricultural for other goods. It is clear, then, that in many cases and in large

Henry George.

degree, the value of land is not the creation of the owner. As far as he is concerned, there exists an unearned increment. It is true, also, that in some degree there exists a value in land which, as regards the race at large, is unearned, — in the existence of which the race has had no part other than of mere presence. There is also equally clearly a value in some land — in much land — which is to be ascribed to the efforts of the possessor and preceding possessors. And it is clear, also, that unearned decrements follow certain social improvements, discoveries, and changes in habits of consumption. Agricultural lands in Europe and in the eastern states of America have fallen considerably in rental and sale value during the last thirty years.

Suggestive Questions

Suppose the State owned the land, should we pay any rent?

Do we now in any way pay what amounts to a land rent to the State?

If you were a renter, and the landlord forgave you your rent, would you have to, or would you, sell your products at lower prices?

Suppose all land rents were forgiven; how would this affect prices?

What does a perpetual lease without rent amount to?

What effect would the general forgiving of rents have on the margin of utility? On demand for products? On supply of products?

What effect on prices from a tax on all land, marginal or otherwise? What effect on consumption of products?

Effect of a percentage tax on rents?

Would the landlord be able to shoulder it off upon the tenant? Tenant upon consumer?

If a large body of fertile land — a new continent, for example — were discovered, what effect on rents in Europe?

Rents and land values, rural, have largely fallen in Europe. Why?

What would be the tendency of rents on the new continent?

Which of the tendencies would predominate in importance? Why?

What effect on supply of products?

On margin of utility of land?

On social dividend? On average comfort?

If the land of the world were all owned by one man or company, could rents be raised profitably for the owner?

Is there any reason why landowners cannot combine?

Would some land be thrown out of use? Why?

Who would lose the rent on this?

If a large amount of land were taken from agriculture for parks, etc., what effect would this have on the aggregate of rents? On prices of products?

Is it the increase of rent or the decrease of supply which causes prices to advance?

For rents to affect prices, the supply must in some way be modified so as to bear upon buyers near the margin. How would a general advance in rents do this?

What will the tenant do if prices fall?

Will all tenants do this?

Which ones?

What bearings have producer's rents upon this question?

If you were a farmer with a large farm, would you hire men to work for you? Why? How many?

When and where would you stop?

Could you fix prices of products? Wages of employés? Rents?

What is your rôle as far as price is concerned?

What bearing has productivity of marginal land on agricultural wages?

What bearing have wages in other employments on agricultural wages?

An increased demand for agricultural produce exercises what effect on the margin of utility of land? On rents? On prices? On agricultural wages? On wages generally?

Is the wages question the solution of the fraction *social dividend* over *social divisor?*

Interpret the following:

$$\text{wages} = \frac{\text{social dividend} - \text{rent} - \text{interest}}{\text{wage-earners}}.$$

What would you do with taxes here?

What makes a town lot valuable?

Who made it valuable?

Who gets the advantage?

What do you mean by the unearned increment?

In what sense are the interests of landowners opposed to the interests of all other classes of society?

Read in the Encyclopedia articles on Malthus and Malthusianism.

Prove that rent does not commonly add to price.

In justice ought the tenant to pay rent upon the improvements which he himself has made upon the land?

How may he be compelled under free competition (rack rent) to do this?

What effect on the condition of farmers?

What effects upon the habits of husbandry?

What relation do you perceive to the history of Ireland?

What effect on rents from improved machinery?

What effect on rents from improved methods and science?

What effect on rents from improved transportation?
What effect on social dividend from improved machinery?
What effect on social dividend from improved methods and science?
What effect on social dividend from improved transportation?

NOTES

The condition of agriculture in a new country is often to some extent similar to that of mining; so far as tillage is applied to naturally fertile lands, whose fertility is gradually exhausted by the comparatively unlaborious methods of cultivation, which are also the most economical methods so long as the land is plentiful and cheap. But this state of things passes away as the country gets filled; and at any rate, after a certain density of population has been reached, the most economical are such as continually maintain the productiveness of the land cultivated.
— SIDGWICK, *Principles*, p. 380.

On the other hand, services which land renders to man in giving him space and light and air in which to live and work, do conform strictly to the law of diminishing return. It is advantageous to apply a constantly increasing capital to land that has any special advantages of situation, natural or acquired. Buildings tower up towards the sky; natural light and ventilation are supplemented by artificial means, and the steam lift reduces the disadvantages of the highest floors; and for this expenditure there is a return of extra convenience, but it is a diminishing return. However great the ground rent may be, a limit is at last reached, after which it is better to pay more ground rent for a larger area than to go on piling up story on story any further; just as the farmer finds that at last a stage is reached at which more intensive cultivation will not pay its expenses, and it is better to pay more rent for extra land than to face the diminution in the return which he would get by applying more capital and labour to his own land. — MARSHALL, *Ec. of Ind.*, p. 122.

RENT — *Continued*

82. The relations of the rent of land and of the margins of utility and cultivation to the prices of agricultural products deserve examination. The statement of Ricardo is in most respects correct. "Corn is not high because rent is paid, but rent is paid because corn is high. . . . No reduction would take place in the price of corn although landlords should

forego the whole of their rent. If the high price of corn were the effect and not the cause of rent, prices would be proportionally influenced as lands were high or low, and rent would be a component part of the price. But that corn which is produced by the greatest quantity of labour is the regulator of the price of corn; and rent does not and cannot enter in the least degree as a component part of the price." That is to say, that corn, the cost of production of which is more than remunerated by the market price, is the only corn which affords rent, rent, therefore, being paid at the expense of the producer's profits, and not by means of an increased price to the consumer.

83. The only exception to be taken to this statement is to the proposition that the corn which is produced by the greatest quantity of labour is the regulator of the price of corn. As has been shown in previous pages, the more accurate statement would be that the price of corn is the regulator of the quantity of productive energy devoted to producing corn. But these two statements do not materially differ for our immediate purpose; they may perhaps profitably be combined as follows: If a cultivator finds that upon a certain piece of land he can, with the application of a certain quantity of productive energy, and with the payment as rent of what the land would be worth for pasturage, forestry, etc., produce at average market prices a product sufficient to decide him to continue in this line of production, and no more, he cannot and will not continue to pay for the land more than the above-mentioned non-agricultural rent. He can and will, ordinarily, consent to pay a higher rent for other and better land, to the extent that the other and better land gives to the productive energies applied larger returns in marketable and non-marketable advantages; and if this man is that producer to whom other productive employments offer comparatively the greatest inducements, those prices for products which will induce him to continue in working this minimum-rent land will be the average market prices. Ultimately speaking, these prices are not prices representing the highest cost of production of the necessarily most expensive portion of the

Does margin of cultivation fix price?

supply; they are the prices which will remunerate the highest sacrifice necessarily involved in furnishing the supply, — sacrifice being, of course, understood to contemplate the remunerations possible in other employments.

84. From the point of view, however, which we have adopted, treating rent as the compensation for the use of land and its improvements, — excluding from rent all payments for the right to impair or exhaust the land or improvements, such payments being assimilated to the case of a partial purchase, — something must be said of the relation of rent payments to prices, so far as such payments are remuneration for the use of improvements. Clearly if improvements cannot be removed, no reason exists relative to rent for regarding them as other than land. To impair or to destroy them influences rent as would any other injury done to the land. Payment for the use of them adds nothing to price, price being remuneratory to the producer at greatest continuing sacrifice, and it being irrelevant to his sacrifice whether he hires poor land at low rent or better land at correspondingly higher rent. *Relation of improvements to price.*

With regard to contemplated improvements, it is clear that they will not be made unless it is believed that the outlay will be compensated by an increased product to the cultivating owner, or by an increased rent to the landlord; and it is clear that this compensation must, all things considered, seem as advantageous to the maker of the improvements as that obtainable from any other use of the capital applied. So if capital already applied is capable in some degree of removal, it will be removed unless it can with equal advantage be continued in its present use. In these two cases, capital applied to land receives, or is expected to afford, returns after the analogy of interest rather than of rent. But confusion is possible in determining whether these returns do or do not enter into price. Put in other words, the question is, whether prices are high because of this interest element in rent, or whether the interest element is paid because prices are high. Evidently this is a wider question than the rent question as ordinarily conceived. Not only the relations of interest and rent to prices, but as well the relations of wages and profits, are concerned. It is difficult to see how wages or interest can be held to enter into price, if rent does not enter. Yet as Ricardo has clearly demonstrated, rent does not enter, inasmuch as the cancellation of rent would neither increase the agricultural product nor decrease the demand for it.

85. If we assume, for purposes of theory, an entire absence of non-rent-paying land, and the payment of a considerable rent on even the poorest land, the question whether rent enters into price becomes altogether unanswerable other than by way of objecting to the question. In truth, it involves an entire inversion of logical theory. It can with equal correctness be answered by yes or no. So far as by its sale or rental value any land is proved to aid in production, the use of it must be remunerated in the selling price of the product; in this sense rent enters into price. Likewise profits must at least remunerate the continuing sacrifice of the marginal producer; they may much more than remunerate any other producer. The extent of society's disposition to sacrifice other utilities in order to obtain agricultural utilities determines the quantity and kind of productive energy which may be remuneratively applied to agriculture instead of to something else, as well as the amount of rent which will be competitively paid to any landlord.

If there were no no-rent land.

86. The fact is that, from the social point of view, the sacrifice or cost-of-production notion is in danger of stopping at superficial conclusions. So far as it can rightly indicate anything, it indicates the price at which the producer can as advantageously to himself produce the utility in question as to produce something else. But wages are the *reward* of the labourer; interest the *reward* of the capitalist; rent the *reward* of the land-owner. Wages are not the cost to the labourer of that which he produces, they are the result of his efforts; they are rarely even the measure of his sacrifice in refraining from the production

What does cost or sacrifice of production ultimately mean?

Wages—interest and rents are results.

of something else, since he may be altogether incapable of other work, or indisposed thereto, without of necessity reducing his remuneration. Musicians and artists perhaps illustrate this fact.

The argument will be made clearer by recurring for a moment to the discussion of value (Section 38). We have seen that the value of any good is the measure of the sacrifice submitted to in exchange by purchasers, and that this sacrifice fixes itself generally at considerably above what would be necessary to divert from other employments a large proportion of the productive energies engaged in this particular line, and ordinarily at considerably below the sacrifice which would be submitted to by some or all of the consumers, were such sacrifice necessary in order to obtain the good in question. On the other hand, no producer will continue in this line of production, if he can, preferably for himself, as he thinks, do something else; what he gets more than he could get elsewhere will be due to his ability or his good fortune.

Values, then, do not correspond to producers' sacrifices, except in so far as they tend to remunerate that one highest sacrifice necessarily involved in supplying the demand. Normal value is the exact remuneration for this marginal producer only. The commodity exactly compensates the sacrifice of that purchaser only who was least disposed to sacrifice other products therefor; that is to say, of that purchaser who among actual purchasers placed the highest estimate on the other goods of which he deprived himself. Value results primarily from the disposition of purchasers, if necessary, to undergo sacrifice. Producers competing with each other get therefrom such advantages as they may; in competitively seeking these advantages, they force down market values to such a point that, normally, some few producers — in theory one producer — derive no advantage therefrom, as compared with the advantages possible in other lines of production. But as to no other than these producers at the margin, can the term cost or sacrifice of production correctly indicate anything.

87. If now we attempt an analysis of the relation to prices of non-marginal lands under cultivation by their owners, we shall meet with some striking corroborations of the conclusions already drawn.

Assume a case of land of high rental value under cultivation by its owner. That the land should be retired from cultivation is out of the question. By some person or other, in some crop or other, this land is certain to be utilized. Doubtless there is land somewhere in the world which would go out of cultivation, if prices for the product to which it is applied and to which it is best adapted should fall. But our cultivator has no concern with this fact, or with rental values in any way. No matter whether his land would rent for little or much, it is worth working, and his concern is merely to choose the best-paying crop for cultivation. Cost of production is for him exactly what it is for the cultivator of marginal land, — the sacrifice of other values possibly obtainable by the application of the same productive energies, — with this difference, however, that with the non-marginal land it is a question of one agricultural product as against another, — with the marginal land, a question of agriculture as against some other occupation. Each cultivator produces in response to the social demand, and produces what best pays him in view of current or prospective prices, enlarging his output as far as it can be done without an outlay too great for the market prices, and without displacing more remunerative products.

Prices in relation to non-marginal lands.

Well, what of it? This of it, — agriculture is not a mere question of wheat-raising. Beans, corn, pumpkins, and radishes must be included in the reckoning. The marginal sacrifice in wheat or bean production may as well be at one grade of land as at another. There is much land so well adapted to other things as to be too good for beans. It is true that any product raised upon marginal land must be raised at the marginal sacrifice, since if the price falls, or a rent be imposed, production must cease and the land lie idle. But many agricultural products are not produced upon

What of it?

the poorest of the cultivated land; and, as has already been pointed out, lands at the margin of utility are rarely, if ever, cultivated. A fall in the price of wheat or maize would change more land to other agricultural uses than it would exclude from any sort of agricultural uses.

88. A few facts emerge from this discussion with helpful clearness. Neither rent, nor the margin of cultivation, nor the margin of utility has much to do as a determining cause with market value. The marginal sacrifice principle, as bearing on values, does not of necessity point to land at or near the margin of rent disappearance. The margin of utility of land is the key to rent determinations, but analy- *Value is a resultant — rents and margins a result from value. Demand is primary.* sis of demand for products and of supply of land must explain the determination of this marginal utility. The causes which lie back of high prices, lie back of high rents. Prices serve as an intermediate step in explaining rent. Neither rent nor margin of utility of land, nor margin of sacrifice in production, can explain the phenomena of values as a question of ultimate causes, but only as a process of adjustment.

If, as the outcome of all these analyses, the rent question should begin to seem one of interminable confusion, it only needs be pointed out that all attempts to explain value solely or mostly by examination of the supply term of the value equation, necessarily lead to this result. Approaching these questions from the point of view of demand, the difficulties vanish. Demand controls supply, and supply adjusts itself to demand as expressed in market values. Men adapt their productive energies to price conditions as the market has determined them, not with any hope of fixing prices (except in cases of monopoly), and never with any idea of determining price by cost of production. The problem is always to adjust cost of production to price, never price to cost of production. Changes in value modify supply, and changes of supply, resulting from changes in value, in turn modify value; but demand is the motive force behind supply, and expresses itself as motive force in terms of value. To explain production in terms of the cost-of-production doctrine violates the facts or means nothing. To explain values under that formula is to emphasize the secondary to the exclusion of the primary factor. Value is a resultant from the forces of demand and supply, supply being itself a resultant from demand. Prices rise whenever demand tends to raise them, unless counteracting tendencies in the volume of supply are thereby set up.

89. It follows that from other than the individual point of view, none of the forms of compensation attributed to productive forces are to be regarded as primarily causal elements in market values, — but rather as distributive shares received by different coöperating factors out of the apportionment of the value product. Wages and interest, as well as rent, are compensation and not cost — result and not cause.

It is true that were the wages lower in any industry, the product could and would be sold at a lower price, since the supply would be increased until lower prices of product would offset lower outlays in production. But this analysis is superficial, and carried only thus far makes for erroneous conclusions. It is easy to say what would happen if wages were lower; but wages can be lower and remain lower only upon the condition that wages fall along the whole line of industry. Wages are results. What forces determine the level of wages in any given industry? Why are they as they are? Why not half as high or doubly high? Evidently if they were higher, prices of products would have to be higher. Why may not this be? If wages were ultimately a cause, almost anything might be, and the striking trades-unionist, the eight-hour agitator, and the protectionist would have foreclosed the argument. But the production of each commodity means the displacement of some other. Wages in all industries fix the wages in each, since the market values of the products in each industry operate as a standing offer of employment at corresponding wages. Thus it follows that market values in all industries fix the wages in each. Wages in each industry must be sufficient to induce on the part of some labourers a refusal of the remunerations possible in other industries.

90. This reasoning applies to interest equally with wages. The ultimate force is demand, and wages and interest are forms of compensation received in ministering to it. Likewise with rent. The extent of society's disposition to sacrifice other goods in order to obtain agricultural goods, determines the quality and kind of productive energies which may be remuneratively applied to agriculture instead of to something else, and as well, also, the amount of rent which will be competitively paid to any landlord. If this demand is such as to render all land utilized for products rent-paying land, it is idle to ask whether this rent-payment is a part of price. The market demand consenting to pay, if necessary, a given price, cannot be satisfied without cultivating all this land. The poorest of the opportunities afforded obtain through the competition of cultivators a considerable rental and sale value. If there is an abundant supply of land, it is price which determines the point at which the marginal line is fixed. It is the same force acting in precisely a similar fashion which fixes the rent-payment where all land is rent-paying land. So long as there is marginal land to be had for the taking, rent clearly enough does not add to price. Nor, in the second case, does rent increase the price, since by the very fact that the land is limited, the high price is unavoidable on any assumption, and the rent is therefore a mere question between owner and cultivator in the distribution of a produced value, and is entirely without interest to consumers. Unquestionably, were there an unlimited supply of land, this rent would not be paid, and prices would be lower; but mark, not lower because the rent is not paid, but lower because conditions exist which, in making a lower price possible, make this rent impossible. And mark, also, that the poor land, when it crosses the marginal line into utilization, crosses as a result of market values, and only in a secondary and derivative way, by affecting supply, becomes a factor in the determination of value. Demand has carried prices up, and the rise in prices has set in operation forces of supply tending in some measure to counteract the rise or to set a limit to it.

Distributive shares are results.

We conclude, then, that rent, like wages, profits, and interest, is primarily a share in the distribution of the social product, — an outworking of the competition of producers for the most favourable opportunities for production, — and that cost of production for agricultural, as well as for non-agricultural products, points merely to the compensation upon which is conditioned the displacement of other values.

91. This seeming diversion from the subject of rent proper will have justified itself if it shall serve to bring out more clearly the necessity in economic reasoning of regarding man as the subject and central point in economic science; his environment as his opportunity; his industrial product as his remuneration; his economic activity as his attempt to produce and distribute this product along the lines of least resistance (sacrifice). Normal price is to be conceived as the line of least resistance, not only for the sellers and buyers directly engaged, but also for the producers in other employments searching for those lines of activity affording the highest remunerations. Market prices are found to fluctuate in either direction about these normal or ideal prices, and cannot, in the competitive adjustment of sacrifice, long or widely depart therefrom. In short, the normal price is that price at which no producer can, to his own thinking, better employ himself in some other line of production. Prices generally would stand at their normal, if no producer or consumer could to his own thinking advantageously change his manner of economic action. But, like the ocean, market values have no rest. Prices ripple and wave above or below their ideal level, as desires and appetites, opportunities and abilities, slowly or rapidly change in force; yet they are none the less tied to the level fixed by social demand, and confess the controlling power of this level as truly as do crest and trough their subjection to the ideal level of the sea.

The point of view.

Normal price.

It remains to observe that an increase in population would not, necessarily, even with stationary arts of agriculture, compel an increased proportional application of productive energies

RENT OF LAND

to the land, provided the average consumption of agricultural products should diminish for any cause, or the direction of consumption should change to products of the soil more readily produced; as, for example, if corn should take the place of wheat for general use as food.

Questions

Assume an island with lands ranging in productive quality from 28 to 20 as by diagram. Consider that with each 100 of population, a new tract has to be cultivated, and that the diagram covers all the land to which the society has access. What will be the sum total of rent with a total population of 900? 1300? 1800? 2300? 2500? 2900?

20	20	20	20	20	20
21	21	21	21	21	21
22	22	22	22	23	23
23	24	24	24	25	25
25	26	26	26	26	26
27	27	27	28	28	28

What effect, other things being equal, does population have on total rent?

Improved machinery?
Improved fertilizers?
Better scientific knowledge of agriculture?
Improved transportation methods?
Answer these questions under two assumptions.
First, that land is in large supply; second, that all is in cultivation.
Is price fixed by margin of cultivation, or margin by price? Which is primary?
Trace analogy to a spring under pressure.
What have producer's sacrifices to do with it?
Which producers?
Explain how rent is not a part of price.
Are wages and interest a part of price? Why?
Why does a farmer abandon his land or change his crop?

CHAPTER VIII

TENDENCIES OF POPULATION

92. In economic discussion, there is a close connection, logical or illogical, between the doctrine of cost of production, as ordinarily stated, and the tendencies of population. If labour, instead of the product of labour, be held to be a thing of value, — a commodity, — and if the normal market value of a commodity be held to depend upon its cost of production, it is a ready conclusion that the cost of labour — wages — cannot permanently stand above the cost of rearing and maintaining the labourers. This conclusion is, perhaps, not a necessary one; in fact, not all the writers who adopt the prevailing "cost-of-production" notion apply it with equal emphasis and confidence to the wages question.

Does cost of production apply to labour?

The probable effect from large increases of population in the future can mostly be deduced from the law of diminishing returns. Rents would rise as cultivation was pushed to poorer soils — while wages would tend toward fall from two causes: first, this larger share of the landlord in the division; second, the lower product per capita to be divided. But the fear that idleness, lack of employment for any part of the race, would follow from over-population is groundless. As long as needs and desires remained unsatisfied there would remain open to all producers a market for commodities upon advantageous terms of exchange. Not as sellers, but as producers in an increasingly unfavourable environment, would humanity suffer.

For the purpose then of making these principles of practical application to the economic outlook, we are interested to examine into the tendencies of population as actually manifested. This investigation is perhaps not strictly a matter of economic theory, but belongs rather within the province of biology or sociology.

The theoretical aspects of the population question are not entirely covered by the law of diminishing returns. We have also to deal with the law of increasing returns. Great progress in the methods of the extractive industries seems probable. It would be hazardous to assert that during any given period, even with a very rapid increase in population, the industrial advance may not be sufficient to overcome the tendencies indicated under the law of diminishing returns. But, to our present knowledge, it seems probable that at some point this tendency to diminishing returns must assert itself in the balance; that population cannot endlessly multiply without at some point meeting with resistance in lessened supplies of food products and of the raw materials of industry. It is conceivable enough that the arts and processes of manufacture may advance; that a constantly greater proportion of the productive energies of society may be applicable to the extractive industries; that by this method the elastic limit of want may for a long time be extended. But, if population is to be assumed to increase continually, the harsh pressure of this limit seems ultimately certain. That time, if it comes, will illustrate the iron law of wages; when the remunerations of labour will be just sufficient to maintain the supply of labourers; when inevitable death will counteract all excess of births; when, in Malthus' vigorous metaphor, the covers laid at Nature's banquet will be found insufficient for the invited guests.

Is over-population imminent?

93. But, assuming that the remunerations of labour may at some time become so meagre as to inaugurate a veritable struggle for existence and to negative further expansion of population, it by no means follows that the remunerations of all participants in the struggle will stand at the margin of subsistence; it merely follows that there will be effectively a margin of subsistence, and that population will be held in check by the death of those members not able to attain to this margin, — and that differen-

How the marginal doctrine applies.

tial advantages measured therefrom will accrue to all members other than the marginal labourer. While weaklings die, the strong may prosper. In truth, the ominous quality of this alleged population law has been greatly exaggerated. It points not to an average rate of wages for all labourers, but to a death-line minimum for many. Nor is this assumed condition so far wide of the present condition as may be imagined. Even now, yearly, many human beings die of want, in its varied relations with idleness, vice, and disease. But the Malthusian forecast points to a time when nothing but a diminishing birth-rate can avoid for many a threatened extinction. At present such inevitableness as exists is of inner rather than of outer conditions.

94. It must be remembered that whatever Malthus' disciples have since done, Malthus himself did not assert that overpopulation is the unavoidable fate of the race, but rather that it is a danger against which only a conscious and continuous resistance can offer a remedy, and toward which he believed that the Poor-Law system of England exercised a strong influence.

The evidence in support of the Malthusian foreboding is very considerable. During the past two hundred years, at least, population has increased over the civilized world with startling rapidity. This will be seen from the following table: —

What is the evidence?

COUNTRIES.	POPULATION IN THE YEARS.		
	1789	1882	1889
	Million	Million	Million
France	26	37	38
England	12	36	38
Germany	24	45	48
Russia	25	90	100
United States	3	52	62
Totals	90	260	286

So far as our knowledge goes we are justified in believing that the tendency to increase has been general throughout history. Observation of lower forms of life discloses this tendency toward increase to the outside limit permitted by the means of subsistence. An unquestionable increase in marriages and births accompanies periods of prosperous business; to at least a large proportion of human beings, the number of children raised is limited only by the number that can be cared for; and in newly and thickly settled countries, where the necessaries of life are comparatively abundant, the tendency to increase is especially marked.

95. The present tendencies of European populations will be examined in detail.

It is computed that in the average of European peoples, the child-bearing age of women covers about twenty-two years, and that in each one thousand of population there are approximately 167 child-bearing women; and that a birth-rate of twenty children per year among each thousand of population would be ordinarily sufficient to maintain a population at a stationary figure. As the annual percentage of births increases, the percentage of mortality increases also — other things being equal — because of the especially high rate of mortality among young children.

Tendencies in Europe.

The following table gives, for the years from 1878 to 1887, the average birth- and death-rates of European peoples, and their respective periods of doubling at these rates: —

Countries.	Birth-rate per Thousand.	Death-rate per Thousand.	Doubling Period.
France	24.4	22.2	445.5 years
Switzerland	29.7	22.5	135 "
Sweden	30.1	17.9	82 "
Norway	30.9	15.9	67 "
Great Britain and Ireland .	31.5	19.2	81 "
Belgium	31.7	21.9	102 "
Germany (1881–1887) . .	38.46	26.82	85.9 "
Austria	39.06	30.57	80.7 "
Saxony	43.08	30.4	75 "
Hungary	45.4	34.9	85 "
Italy	38.2	29.2	111 "

The following tables will show, for several of these countries, the tendencies of births and deaths for a period preceding 1886: —

Countries.	Year.	Rate of Births per Thousand.	Rate of Deaths per Thousand.
Belgium	1865	31.4	24.5
	1875	32.5	22.7
	1885	31.7	21.8
Sweden	1865	26.2	19.2
	1875	31.0	30.3
	1886	30.5	17.4
Italy	1872–76	37.13	32.06
	1877–81	36.32	28.87
	1882–86	37.31	27.31
Great Britain and Ireland	1865	30.7	20.7
	1875	31.2	21.6
	1885	31.0	18.8
Germany	1841–50	37.8	28.2
	1851–60	36.8	27.8
	1861–70	38.7	28.4
	1871–80	40.7	28.7
	1881–85	38.5	27.2
Saxony	1865	42.9	31.9
	1875	45.7	32.0
	1885	43.6	30.3
Norway	1865	31.7	16.5
	1875	30.6	18.7
	1885	30.8	16.

It will be seen that of this list all the countries named, excepting Norway, show an increased birth-rate, and all, without exception, a decreased death-rate, and that Norway is the only one of these countries which does not indicate a general tendency toward a more rapid increase in population. These facts are perhaps to be attributed to rapid commercial and industrial development, to increased facility for obtaining food supplies through importation, and to a general advance in the knowledge and practice of hygiene.

96. On the other hand, analysis of population tendencies in England, France, and the United States during the last one hundred years, reduces somewhat the overwhelming force of the above figures. In fact, the past one hundred years disclose a marked tendency in France toward a stationary condition of population; even, perhaps, toward a decrease. In the absence of immigration and of the relatively large birth-rate among immigrants and their immediate descendants, it is clear that French population would be, at present, diminishing. French emigration is so small as to be a neglectable factor:—

Year.	Rate of Births per Thousand.	Rate of Deaths per Thousand.	Increase.
France —			
1801–10 . . .	32.3	...	...
1811–20 . . .	31.6	25.9	5.7
1821–30 . . .	30.8	25.0	5.8
1831–40 . . .	29.0	24.8	5.2
1841–50 . . .	27.4	23.3	4.1
1851–60 . . .	26.3	23.9	2.4
1861–70 . . .	26.3	23.6	2.7
1871–80 . . .	25.4	23.7	1.7 (war)
1881	24.88	22.0	2.88
1882	24.88	22.2	2.68
1883	24.81	22.2	2.61
1884	24.75	22.6	2.15
1885	24.34	22.1	2.24
1886	23.71	22.3	1.41
1887	23.47	22.0	1.47

The following are the figures for Great Britain:—

Years.	ENGLAND. Per Cent of Increase.	SCOTLAND. Per Cent of Increase.	WALES. Per Cent of Increase.
1821-31	16.	13.0	12.2
1831-41	14.6	11.8	13.2
1841-51	12.8	10.2	10.3
1851-61	12.0	6.0	10.5
1861-71	13.4	9.7	9.5
1871-81	14.5	11.2	11.8
1881-91	11.7	8.0	11.6

In England and America, the most noticeable decrease in the birth-rate has manifested itself in the last ten or twenty years. This decrease is especially marked among the well-to-do classes, and seems especially characteristic of the cities. The immigrant populations of the United States are by far the most prolific of children. The following table contains data for the United States during the last one hundred years. It is generally admitted that the census of 1870 is untrustworthy. (The asterisk denotes an estimate.)

Date of Census.	Population.	Total Decennial Increase.	Immigration during Decade.	Natural Increase during Decade.	Per Cent of Total Increase.	Per Cent of Increase due to Immigration.	Per Cent of Natural Increase.
1890	*62,032,672	11,876,889	5,245,530	6,631,359	23.68	10.45	13.23
1880	50,155,783	11,597,412	2,812,191	8,785,221	30.07	7.29	22.78
1870	38,558,371	7,115,050	2,433,524	4,833,908	22.63	7.74	14.89
1860	31,443,321	8,251,445	2,579,590	5,611,889	35.58	11.12	24.46
1850	23,191,876	6,122,423	1,753,251	4,469,148	35.87	10.27	25.60
1840	17,069,453	4,203,433	599,125	3,604,308	32.67	4.65	28.02
1830	12,866,020	3,232,198	143,439	3,088,759	33.55	1.49	32.06
1820	9,633,822	2,393,941	*118,385	2,303,941	33.07	*1.64	31.43
1810	7,239,881	1,931,398	*70,000	1,851,398	36.38	*1.32	35.06
1800	5,308,483	1,379,269	*70,000	1,299,269	35.10	*1.78	33.32
1790	3,929,214	...	...	...	...	...	...

Parallel facts are obtainable from France in greater detail; the most wealthy departments show relatively the lowest birth-rates; the most wealthy quarters of Paris relatively lower birth-rates than the less wealthy and poor quarters. The number of births in France entire in the years 1841–45 was 976,000 per annum; in 1888 the total was 882,639.

97. It is not easy to deduce a law from these facts. We observe, however, that the three countries in which a pronounced tendency toward a decreased birth-rate has developed, are precisely the three countries in which are the greatest development in wealth and industry and the highest well-being; that the tendency manifests itself most strongly among the classes of greatest financial prosperity; and that improvidence and recklessness in child-bearing are especially characteristic of that class of people most inclined to improvidence and recklessness in everything else. But over against these reasonings stand a multitude of figures making toward a seemingly contrary conclusion. If any reconciliation is possible, it will hardly leave the field free to Malthusianism or to its opponents. It is at any rate not incredible that the first effect of easier conditions of existence is to stimulate population, and that the final effect, for peoples of the European grade of civilization, is in the other direction. But that which may stand for a law for one nation, or for one stage of civilization, may be entirely inadequate for other nations or conditions. The question is intimately connected with the standard of living (or comfort), and its possible variations among different peoples and in different circumstances. It does not necessarily follow that because the labourer obtains larger remunerations, he will therefore raise more children; he may apply his larger income to better nourishing himself and the family already dependent upon him; his larger wages may be a source of increased ability to earn yet larger wages; he may devote his increased wages to vicious indulgences, or he may hold to his previous scale and manner of expense, taking to himself greater leisure, or providing more adequately for the future of himself or his family. It

Is there a population law?

seems probable that easier conditions of life, to the very vicious or very improvident, will result in increased vice and improvidence, sexual and other.

98. To a hard-working and ill-fed population of the European type, a considerable proportion of any increase in remunerations will probably go to increased nourishment, increased intelligence, and increased reproductiveness. Increased remunerations to the point of luxury (an indefinite term) may result in increase of leisure or increase in positive satisfactions, and may be followed finally by a higher standard of living, or by an increase in population, or by both, or even by a decrease. I quote from Lord Brassey's *Work and Wages*, Chap. III.: "At the commencement of the construction of the North Devon Railway, the wages of the labourers were 2s. a day. During the progress of the work their wages were raised to 2s. 6d. and 3s. a day. Nevertheless, it was found that the work was executed more cheaply when the men were earning the higher rate of wages than when they were paid at the lower rate. Again, in London, in carrying out a part of the Metropolitan Drainage Works in Oxford Street, the wages of the bricklayers were gradually raised from 6s. to 10s. a day; yet it was found that the brickwork was constructed at a cheaper rate per cubic yard, after the wages of the workmen had been raised to 10s., than when they were paid at the rate of 6s. a day.

"On the railways of India it has been found that the great increase of pay which has taken place has neither augmented the rapidity of execution, nor added to the comfort of the labourer. The Hindoo workman knows no other want than his daily portion of rice; and the torrid climate renders water-tight habitations and ample clothing alike unnecessary. The labourer therefore desists from work as soon as he has provided for the necessities of the day. Higher pay adds nothing to his comforts — it serves but to diminish his ordinary industry."

99. The laws of population, when once discovered, will be of enormous importance to almost all practical applications

of Political Economy. There is hardly any economic question that is not, from some point of view, a population question. We have seen the closeness of the relation to rent and wages. There is an equally impor- **Practical bearings.** tant connection with the different methods of charity administration; and it is possible that socialism may finally stand or fall with the outcome of investigations along this line. In these investigations the services of Malthus and his disciples have been of great importance, however questionable for theoretical purposes may have been their conclusions. So much cannot be said for the practical applications of their teachings. If it be true that in any country there is danger of over-population, it is reasonably certain that the classes of society with whom the danger mostly lies will neither hear nor heed Malthus' teaching; that the only people with whom the teaching will at all avail are the very people who least ought to heed it, and who are already too prone to make large practical applications thereof. Not only this, but the question is more than a national question, — it is a race question. The western races bear to the rest of the world a similar relation to that borne by the better classes of society to the poorer classes; if the western races do not people the world, the other races will. (See Sections 252–258.)

SUGGESTIVE QUESTIONS

What bearing has the population question on rent?
On wages?
On charity administration?
On public expenditures for general education and culture?
Explain the law of the survival of the fittest as it applies to the lower orders of life.
Why does it not apply in equal degree to humanity in the complex conditions of human society?
Do we let it apply?
Easier conditions of life among lower orders result in a larger maturing of offspring: does there result from easier conditions any change in birth-rate?
How with humanity as to maturing of offspring?

How as to birth-rate?

Do the poorer classes show higher or lower birth-rate than the rich or well-to-do?

Have lower orders of life any standard of comfort similar to that among men?

Do their standards change? Do ours?

If society refuses to care for poverty, disease, and vice, will there be any effect upon the birth-rate? Will it rise or fall?.

Will there be an appreciable effect upon the percentage which mature? What will be the effect upon the quality of those who mature?

As a general question, is it better to abandon the disease and vice in the hope that it will perish without offspring, or to attempt to cure in the conviction that multiplication will take place anyway?

What have population tendencies to do with socialism?

What is the probable future of Russia as an international power? Of China? Of France? Of the English race?

What bearing do you perceive upon the question of immigration? Of public schools?

What did Henry Ward Beecher mean when he called the public school the national stomach?

Suppose a given ancestral pair to bring up two children, these children in turn each two children, and that there are no intermarriages among these descendants. In ten generations how many people can count this original pair as among their ancestors?

Had there never been any intermarriages among your ancestors, how many strains of ancestry would meet in you, reckoning back thirty generations?

Without allowing for intermarriages or immigration, how many generations must we reckon back to find a common ancestry for all of us, supposing an ancestral stock of 50,000,000?

Suppose a village containing 100 families, — entirely unrelated by blood, the rate of production two to each family, — and no marriages made with outsiders. In how many generations will marriage become impossible for all, unless relatives intermarry?

Assuming a nation of 70,000,000 people, — no immigration or outside marriages, the rate of production as before, — in how many generations will intermarriage between descendants of the same stock become unavoidable?

How long will it be in the widening circles of intermarriage before your descendants will be as much interested as mine, — intermarriage among relatives aside, — in the question of how I have lived?

In view of our genealogical histories, which are the harder to explain, the similarities or the differences in people of the same nation?

Do we probably greatly differ other than to the extent that education and environment have in one, two, or three generations developed latent powers?

What has this to do with charity administration?

NOTES

Many years ago I stated it as my opinion, and gave my reasons, that the population of England and Wales, from the beginning of recorded economical history to the end of the sixteenth century, was never in excess of two and a half millions, and was often less. At the end of the seventeenth century it was from five to five and a half millions.
— ROGERS, *Ec. Int. of Hist.*, p. 157.

Population instead of increasing decreases slowly in Normandy, and this since about thirty years. Never, however, has industry there been so flourishing, never agriculture so productive; never the fields so rich, or the inhabitants in enjoyment of as high a degree of comfort; never, likewise, have the wages of workmen employed in farm labour attained so high a point; they have increased by two-fifths. . . . Whence comes, then, this decrease in population? It is not the effect of immigration, for the Normans are so well off at home as not to go abroad in search of the means of subsistence which at home they find abundantly. It is the effect of a lower fertility from marriages in the rural districts, and solely in the rural districts. . . . The same thing is true in some other parts of France, and as well in some other of the countries of Europe. Increasing wealth brings about, — I will not say purposed continence, — but the fear of having too many children, and families become smaller and smaller in number. This is what is taking place in Switzerland, for example, in several of the Cantons where the rural people enjoy real and well-assured well-being.
— JOSEPH GARNIER (France), translated from *Du Principe de Population*, 2d ed., p. 347.

Whatever be the fashion or desire which is first developed in the mind of any community, it makes a demand upon the existing body of goods, or upon the current production of wealth, which at once antagonizes the strong and urgent disposition to the consumption of wealth in the support of an increasing population. The newly awakened passion or desire cannot be gratified out of the existing fund of wealth, unless the procreative force receive a check. Whether this shall be done or not is a question,

upon the answer to which depends the whole economic future of the community. . . . Since the procreative force increases rather than diminishes in case of poverty and squalor, there is no natural resting-place for population, if once it passes below the plane of ample subsistence, until it reaches the point where it meets the positive checks of famine and disease, and, it may be added, of war.
— WALKER, *Advanced Course*, sec. 397.

It is impossible that a positive check so goading and remorseless as famine should prevail without bringing in her train all the others ; pestilence is her uniform companion, and murder and war are her followers.
— N. W. SENIOR (England).

The population under ten years of age in 1880 (in America) was 26.7 per cent. In 1890, 24.3 per cent. Now what does this mean ? It means that if the population of 1880 had been maintained in 1890, the population of the country would have been greater by sixteen or seventeen hundred thousand, and the aggregate population over 64,000,000. This would have been equal to the most liberal estimates of our population, and the fact that the actual enumerated population did not equal the estimate can be explained entirely by the falling off in the birth-rate during the previous ten years.. . . . Again, the falling off in the birth-rate finds corroboration in the returns, showing the falling off in the size of families from 5.9 in 1870 to 4.9 in 1890. . . . Elkanah Watson in 1815 estimated the population of the United States for each decade until 1900. In 1820 he was only about 8000 out of the way ; in 1830 about 32,000 ; in 1840 about the same neighbourhood ; in 1850 something like 630,000 ; and in 1860 over 310,000. Then he took a mighty fall, and was millions too much in 1870 and 1880, closing nearly 15,000,000 too high in 1890, while his estimate for 1900 of 100,235,985 will probably exceed the actual amount by 25,000,000.
— ROBERT PORTER, Supt. of Census, 1890, Article in Chicago *Inter-Ocean*, Sept. 11, 1894.

CHAPTER · IX

CAPITAL

100. The ambiguities in the term "capital" are nearly parallel to those examined under the head of wealth. They arise from insufficient attention to the distinction between the things internal to man and those external, or from confusions due to changes in point of view.

If one man works a year in making a machine, and another a year in learning his trade, it seems clear that each is bending his energies towards the future with a purely commercial motive, and it is not at first thought easy to grasp the necessity of different classifications for the two cases. The term "intellectual capital" has been invented to distinguish mental acquisitions from acquisitions of what may properly be termed wealth. Probably no great harm results from the use of this term; and yet if there are intellectual capitals, there ought also, logically, to be capitals of morals, health, and beauty. Again, capital is logically a classification inside wealth. These intellectual acquirements are not wealth, but preparation for the creation of wealth. It cuts across established classifications to make them wealth; and finally, and as it seems conclusively, it destroys all line of distinction between possessions and possessor — capital and capitalist. The question is, however, mostly one of definition. Admittedly, the analogies are strong in some respects between intellectual acquirements and capital.

Are there intellectual capitals?

Restricting the meaning of the term "capital" to external utilities, there yet remains a deal of perplexity, resulting mostly from insufficient recognition of the fact that capital means different

Individual and social point of view.

things accordingly as it is considered from the individual or the social point of view.

Adam Smith defined capital as that part of a person's stock from which he expects to derive an income. This answers fairly well to the meaning of the word as used by business men. This concept includes, for example, lands, food on hand for labourers, deposit accounts with banks, patents, and goodwill in business.

The other concept is almost entirely unfamiliar to the business man, but is most important for purposes of economic theory. It proceeds from the point of view of society instead of the individual. It conceives capital as (a) an article of wealth, (b) the product of human labour, (c) used as a means of further production of wealth (utility).

From the individual point of view, all that is capital which is intended to minister to the increase of individual wealth. From the social point of view, all that is capital which, having been derived from labour, coöperates with labour in increasing social wealth.

Social capital, then, includes tools, machines, factories, raw materials, coin, etc., and, in general, all social wealth which is not consumption wealth. Private capital includes all these, and, in addition, all "consumption goods which the owners do not require for themselves but employ by exchange (sale, hire, loan) in the acquisition of other goods" (Boehm-Bawerk); *e.g.* real estate, legal claims, means of subsistence to be supplied to labourers.

101. Even this line of distinction is hard to apply in particular cases. The intention with which wealth is held determines whether it is capital or not. Thus, with changing purposes and varying uses, any particular form of property may pass out from the lists of capital or back again. The physician's horses serve now as capital, and again, when he drives for pleasure, as mere consumers' goods. The actress's gowns are in one case mere raiment; in another, stage costume; in a third, business advertising. A considerable part of the living expenses of the

Some ambiguities.

foreign ambassador are mere incidents of his official position.

Again, the utility of any commodity is partly dependent on questions of place and time. Soda from the plains, coal from the mines, wood from the forest, gain in utility by mere transportation. Ice preserved from winter to summer acquires all its utility from mere lapse of time. No one would question that when cider is stored to await the change to vinegar, the cider is capital, and the change to vinegar the production of utility. It is difficult to regard the ice in any other light. As has already been pointed out, the merchant is a producer in the sense that from the physical, as well as the legal point of view, he is engaged in the transportation of goods. Warehouse and cold-storage men produce both time and place utilities. Goods in a merchant's stock in trade fall, then, within the category of capital rather than within that of consumers' goods. They are not mere wealth until they have passed the last process of manipulation and are truly ready for consumption. This last is more than a question of nomenclature; it is ultimately the social justification for the existence of middle-men.

CAPITAL AND ITS CREATION

(Sections 102 to 108, inclusive, may be omitted in class work.)

102. Under the present industrial organization, some common commodity of exchange and measure of value is essential to the transaction of business. And it is evident that the commodity or commodities selected and used for this purpose must be held to serve a function as important to the creation of utilities as that of any other of the tools of industry. Currency is one of the most effective of labour-saving contrivances. The bullion utilized for this purpose is not only wealth, but it is wealth at a high degree of productiveness.

103. But what, for purposes of classification, shall be said

of fiat legal tenders, of bank-notes, checks, bankers' credits, and generally of the whole body of credit and fiat substitutes for coinage currency. From the point of view of the individual, they are undoubtedly proper items in an inventory of riches. From the point of view of society as a whole, and regarded as matter of debt and credit, they would seem to be clearly subject to the cancellation process previously outlined. Yet, while uncancelled, they serve the purpose, however imperfectly, of a medium of exchange, and dispense with the use for that purpose of large amounts of wealth. If coinage currency is a labour-saving device, credit currency is a bullion-saving device. Considered as a created or saved utility, credit currency may with some force be claimed to be a form of social wealth. But the objection is a forcible one, that knowledge and experience are also effective for the saving of labour and wealth, and are yet not wealth — whatever other or better thing they may be held to be; and that if a method in affairs were devised for dispensing altogether with currency of any sort, no room would remain for asserting that an increase of wealth had taken place.

<small>Is paper money either wealth or capital?</small>

It appears to be true that, for purposes of classification, no better ground exists for regarding circulating credit as social wealth than for so classing the institution of exchange, the form of government, or the grand total of virtue, experience, and intelligence, which are the heritage of the race.

But if circulating credit cannot be held to be wealth, something remains to be said of the material paper, the ticket, so to speak, which circulates as currency. If the credit right is not wealth, or its circulating characteristic wealth, it seems at least true that a new and remarkable utility has been discovered in paper utilized for currency purposes; and in this sense it may be correct to claim that paper currency is social wealth.

104. Whether one shall regard the foregoing conclusion as reasonable or fanciful is not of particular interest to a correct understanding of currency questions. But to measure correctly the great function performed by credit currency in the affairs

of the commercial world is important. In the business of Great Britain and London, which is, in a considerable measure, the business of the world, the proportion of metallic currency to bankers' deposits is something like one to seven (Palgrave's *Notes on Banking*). Notwithstanding the fact that not only the business of one of the most wealthy, and industrially most energetic of nations is transacted in England, but that a considerable proportion of the world's business also is transacted there, the legal tender currency of Great Britain is noticeably less in amount, per unit of population, than among any other of the great industrial peoples. And the explanation of the fact is found not in an exceptionally great expansion of the credit system generally, but in a comparatively great extension and centralization of the deposit banking system. Doubtless, so far as promissory notes, bills of exchange, stocks, bonds, and book accounts are the subject of transfer from owner to owner in *payment of indebtedness*, they serve *pro tanto* to supply the need for currency. But it is the bank check and clearing-house in England which supply the greater part of the credit currency for exchange purposes.

I quote from Sidgwick's *Principles*: "It is undeniable that, in England now, wealth is chiefly transferred by the intervention of a medium of exchange complex in com- **Both paper and** position; consisting partly of gold coin, partly **credit serve as** of bank-notes, but to a greater extent of bank- **currency.** ers' obligations to pay coin on demand, not represented by notes; and it is chiefly this medium that is actually lent and borrowed in commercial and industrial loan transactions. And it is no less undeniable that the immaterial part of this instrument has functions precisely similar to those of the material portion; that it is as effective in purchasing goods; that borrowers pay the same interest or discount for the use of it; and that it, no less than metallic or paper money, is, in ordinary times, currently accepted in final settlement of all debts,— except, of course, the debts of bankers. The essential and fundamental function of money is to be used in exchange and in other transfers of wealth, where the object is to transfer not some particular commodity, but command over commodities generally; it is as a medium of wealth-transfer that money is qualified for performing its other important function of measuring values. If, then, we take this function as essential; if we understand by money that which passes freely from owner to owner, throughout the community, in final discharge of debts and full payment for commodities, then, in all ordinary conditions of modern commercial societies, bankers' debts payable on demand, however acknowledged and transferred, are as rightly called money as they are commonly so designated; and in all consideration of the quantity of money available for commercial or other purposes, this fact ought to be recognized.

"This leads me to notice an objection that is likely to be brought against the view above expounded. It may be said that what I have called Money is merely a part of what other economists have called Credit; and that it is more convenient to keep this term as indicating its real quality. And I should quite admit that for some purposes it is important to insist on the fact that bankers' debts are after all debts, no less than those of private individuals. But in a general consideration of the manner in which functions of money are performed, it seems to me more important to point out that there is as much difference between one kind of credit and another, in respect of its currency, as there is between gold and 'goods.' If a private individual (A.), obtains any valuable article from another (B.), by promising to pay for it hereafter, and *does* pay for it, the credit he receives obviously does not operate as a substitute for money at all in the long run [unless the items of an open account offset each other], though it tends, *pro tanto*, to raise prices temporarily. Only if B. uses A.'s debt to him as a means of purchasing another commodity from C., does this credit begin to be a substitute for money. If C. uses it similarly in a similar transaction with D., its efficiency as a substitute is doubled. But it is not until such a debt has come to be taken without any idea of using it otherwise than as a means of payment that it has completely acquired the characteristics of money. That this

Credit one form of currency.

is in ordinary times the case with bankers' obligations taken in the aggregate is undeniable; though (as I have said) the fact is obscured by the continual liquidation in gold of a small portion of such obligations." (*Principles*, Book II., c. 4.)

105. The foregoing discussion of currency, otherwise outside our immediate purpose, has been introduced as essential to a correct understanding of the relations between savings, loan capital (loan funds), industrial capital, and the process of capitalization. Speaking generally, and excepting from consideration the bounties of nature and the increase in values which flows directly from progressive development of human tastes, needs, and desires, it may be said that all wealth results from human activity, and is a surplus of production over consumption. Of the entire volume of wealth existing at any time, one portion is destined to consumption — to the direct satisfaction of human needs and desires; another portion is destined to use in the reproduction of wealth. It is to the second portion that the term "capital" is applied. That is to say, capital is wealth, other than nature and natural forces, used as an aid to human energy in the reproduction of wealth. It is to be noted that this definition conceives capital from the social instead of the individual point of view. So far as concerns questions of production and reproduction of wealth, nature and natural forces are to be regarded as forms of capital. For this purpose the only important distinction is between "consumers' wealth" and "producers' wealth." The question of origin is immaterial.

106. It is, however, particularly to the manner in which savings become capital that attention is directed. Were the industrial organization of the socialistic type, the process of saving would be a matter, for theoretical purposes, of extreme simplicity; a certain percentage of the social product would be withdrawn from the reach of consumers, or a certain percentage of the social energies would be directed to the creation of aids to future production, — the labourers so directed subsisting meanwhile upon the current product of industry or upon stored-up products. The date and manner of the sav-

ing would be for social purposes clearly open to analysis. In the first case, the saving would take place at the time at which, but for the withdrawal, consumption would occur. In the second case, the saving would date from the time when the aids for future production — the capital — were created; that is to say, the time at which the products consumed were rendered into equivalent capital.

In the existing industrial system, however, there is no such thing as a parallel withdrawal of commodities from consumption. **Savings result in loan funds — not directly or necessarily in capital.** The saving which one member of society makes in his daily or yearly consumption is not at all certain to be a social saving. In the average case he has secured a certain income, and has refrained, in some measure, from making purchases in the market. The aggregate social consumption is not less because of this abstinence; the other purchasers have simply profited by this diminution of demand. When the labourer concludes — as an equivalent of past abstinence — to consume in excess of his current production, other purchasers will suffer by the resulting extension of demand. In short, individual abstinence, in the present industrial organization, is a condition precedent to social saving, and therefore to possible capitalization of wealth; but it is not social saving, nor is it capitalization. The labourer in the above case has saved himself a right to direct in purpose and manner a future application of wealth or activity. It is upon his decision that capitalization will depend. It is of course true that the labourer may have followed a manner of creating capital as simple as the socialistic method. He may have reduced his production for purposes of immediate use, perhaps lessening his current consumption, perhaps subsisting on products of past labour, and have applied his energies directly to the production of capital; as does oftentimes the farmer, for example, in digging a ditch or building a stone wall. That is to say, capitalization is possible without an appeal to the loan market. Nor is it an easy matter to estimate the relative importance of this simpler type of capitalization. At all events, it calls for no especial labour of analysis, and is for the most part unrelated to the phenomena indicated under the terms "capital" and "interest."

107. But, in the typical case of an appeal to the loan market for so-called capital, there is usually neither capital nor social wealth in existence, which in itself, or in equivalent existences, owes its origin to the savings now represented in the form of loanable funds. There exist against society in the form of hoarded money, or against banks in the form of bank-notes, deposits, and savings-accounts, or against individuals in the form of different species of claims, rights of direction over the application of labour and commodities. Every credit represents such a right. The loan market consists of these rights and of nothing else. It is not because of her store in hand of iron or wood or provisions that England is able to supply the so-called capital for endless railroad building; and the construction of railroads in America or Africa by means of English capital does not ordinarily mean the transportation from England of any considerable amount of commodities for this purpose. Nor, ordinarily, have the supply of loanable funds and the creation of capital any necessary relation to the prevailing condition of plenty or scarcity in the industrial society. It is true that there is a theoretical outside limit to the amount of capitalization which can take place during any particular period. Only so much productive energy can be diverted to future production as can be spared from the necessities of immediate consumption. But the demands of immediate consumption are very flexible. Practically, no limit exists of any sort except the food limit; and the supply of food being mostly periodic, and, if scanty, incapable for a period of some months of being largely affected by an immediate application of labour, and not ordinarily increased above the average by the application of an exceptional amount of labour to the production of a new crop, it results for practical purposes that the amount of labour applicable to remote ends is not greatly lessened by insufficient harvests. It may, indeed, be increased by the sharp competition of wage-earners to obtain as large a share as pos-

Why is England so rich in so-called capital?

sible of the short food supply. It is true that this view leaves out of consideration the average of years; for, in this average, a sufficient number of labourers will devote themselves to the production of a supply of necessaries sufficient to meet the average demand. Normally, the application of energy for future purposes must be secured from labourers not requisite to this production of necessaries for immediate consumption. But how much of this labour, possibly applicable to remote ends, will be so applied, will depend not on the possessors of capital in the form of shops, and tools, and lands, nor upon the possessors of products ready for consumption, but upon the possessors of these *choses* (claims) in action against society or against individual members thereof, — these rights of direction of labour, of which bank and savings deposits form a large proportion and are typical examples. Nor, usually, does any possessor of material property or wealth become effectively a capitalizer until he has parted with his material wealth and become a holder of some proportion of these rights. Capitalization in practice ordinarily takes place through transfer, in the form of loans, of these rights of direction to projectors of enterprises. A borrowing of products instead of rights may result in capitalization, without involving any preceding saving, — in that case, however, necessitating a concurrent decreased production of commodities for immediate consumption. It is true that the borrowing may have resulted in the consumption of really surplus products, but more commonly the borrowing is of these saved rights of direction. When payment of a loan is made, it is commonly made not in commodities, but in the right to commodities or labour, and this right is often used, not in obtaining these commodities for purposes of mere consumption, but in a new direction of labour or wealth to the creation of more capital.

Credit relations are the reservoir of loan funds. We conclude, then, that whether capitalization does or does not take place is practically independent of the total supply of consumer's wealth, whether in excess or scarcity. The question is substantially one of whether the persons having the right to consume are disposed to exercise that right in one direction or in another.

108. A thorough grasp of this truth is necessary to a full understanding of the subject of interest. The usual definition of interest as the hire of capital, or as compensation paid for the use of capital, opens the way to possible misconceptions as to the real nature of capital. It may be true that borrowing commonly takes place in order to obtain capital, but that which is borrowed is commonly a mere right to wealth. It is not essential that the right borrowed be used in the acquirement or production of wealth. The proceeds of the borrowing may be expended in luxurious living expenses, in education, or in vice.

If the term "loan funds," or some equivalent, were used to indicate the subject-matter of borrowing, a deal of confusion would be avoided, and less hazy conceptions would find place with regard to the "centres of capital" and the "increase of capital" and the "countries rich in capital."

Capital is wealth used as an aid in the reproduction of wealth. Loan funds are something entirely different, — the mere right to obtain possession of capital or wealth, or to direct the application of productive energies. The abundance of loan funds is measured more by degree of complexity in credit relations than by the quantity of wealth or capital in actual existence.

NOTES

Every one is aware that England has much more immediately disposable and ready cash than any other country. But very few persons are aware how much greater the ready balance — the floating loan fund, which can be lent to any one for any purpose — is in England than it is anywhere else in the world. A very few figures will show how large the London loan fund is, and how much greater it is than any other. The known deposits — the deposits of banks which publish their accounts — are, in

London (31st December, 1872)	£120,000,000
Paris (27th February, 1873)	13,000,000
New York (February, 1873)	40,000,000
German Empire (31st January, 1873)	8,000,000

And the unknown deposits — deposits in banks which do not publish their accounts — are in London much greater than those in any other of these cities. The bankers' deposits of London are many times greater than those of any other country.

— WALTER BAGEHOT (England), *Lombard Street*, c. 1, p. 4.

The latest (1895) estimate of bank deposits in Great Britain places them at £700,000,000.

INTEREST

Mention the different reasons for which one might desire to borrow money.

If for use on a farm, what would determine the rate which one could pay?

Could a starving man afford to borrow at 100 per cent per annum?

Is a given amount of wealth always of the same total of utility to you?

Does a loaf of bread vary in its utility?

Is money always of constant utility per unit?

Does the borrower get an advantage from borrowing? How?

The lender from lending? How?

109. Money is seldom an object of desire for itself. As in the sale of commodities for money, the ultimate remuneration to the seller is not in the money received, but in the commodities into which he later exchanges the money; so in the borrowing of money or other forms of loan funds, the thing desired by the borrower is commonly not the money or the borrowed right, but the wealth or capital into which the borrowed fact may be exchanged. To say, then, that interest is compensation made for the use of wealth, is obviously not an unreasonable statement, though we shall shortly find reason to question its entire accuracy and exhaustiveness.

The quickest way to produce wealth is not always the most effective way. If one were dependent for his living upon the results of the chase, he would do well to nourish himself somewhat scantily, if necessary, for a time, in order to devote himself not to hunting, but to preparing to hunt in a more effective manner, — to making for himself traps and bows or guns.

The roundabout way is ultimately the more productive of results. So instead of wading for fish, it is profitable to set aside a share of effort for the production of poles and lines. The traps or the poles illustrate the aid to production afforded by the use of capital.

If one were without a fish-pole, and should wish to borrow the pole of another, it would manifestly be fair that the lender of the pole should receive some part of the product in fish. On these terms the owner could possibly afford to part with the pole for a time. Even at a high rate of payment, the borrower, also, could afford to borrow. If poles could not be loaned at a rental, no one could be expected to have more of them than would be sufficient to answer his own requirements.

In what sense is capital productive?

A farmer finds that with the expenditure of $1000 in drainage improvements, he can increase by $200 the annual productiveness of his meadow. If necessary, then, he can afford to pay nearly 20% for borrowed money with which to effect this improvement. If the market rate of interest is 6%, he can profitably borrow more than this $1000. Suppose that the gain in productiveness from added increments of capital is as follows:

2d, $1000	. . .	$150	5th,	. . . .	$70
3d,	. . .	120	6th,	. . . .	60
4th,	. . .	90	7th,	. . . .	50

With the rate of interest still at 6%, he can afford to borrow at least $4000 additional. To borrow yet a full 1000 more would profit him only as much as the necessary interest payment. He will therefore borrow, say, 750 at an increase in productiveness of, say, 50. The account then stands as follows:

1000 at	60 interest and		200 advantage.	
1000 "	60	" "	150	"
1000 "	60	" "	120	"
1000 "	60	" "	90	"
1000 "	60	" "	70	"
750 "	45	" "	50	"
5750 "	345	" "	680	"

Note that his demand for capital at an established rate finds its limit at the point where usefulness falls to a level with interest payment. Were some more effective method of ditching discovered, it might be advantageous to increase his borrowings.

Note, also, that the limit of his demand is not at all affected by the amount which his preceding borrowings have already profited him. Each addition of capital stands on its own merits.

The manufacturer likewise may find it of great profit to increase the volume of his business, or to improve his processes of production. He also stops at the point of disappearing advantage in view of the rates of interest which he is compelled to pay.

110. If one has to-day a great appetite and no dinner, and will later have at his disposal two dinners but no increase of appetite, borrowing will be to his enormous advantage, and, if necessary, he may pay enormous interest rates without exhausting this advantage. Neither money nor wealth is of stable utility to men, but shifts in utility relatively to needs. So the young man rationally borrows the money with which to complete his education, counting upon paying from a later relative abundance. So the business man, in straits for means to save his credit from injury or his property from forced sale, pays with advantage for the right to await a better market, or for time to muster his resources.

<small>Other rational demands for loan funds.</small>

The cases mentioned are typical of the rational demand for loan funds to be expended as capital or otherwise. There is also an improvident demand, — the spendthrift's near-sightedness which mortgages a needy future in favour of a luxurious and wasteful present.

111. The doctrine, therefore, that interest is merely compensation for the use of capital in virtue of its productivity, is not entirely tenable.

First, as has been intimated, borrowing is not always an intermediate process in the hiring or buying of useful things.

Money is sometimes an object of desire in itself; the demand for it exists at any given time, not merely for the purpose of effecting the current exchanges of products, but as well for obtaining discharges of obligations left over from earlier transactions. The volumes of unliquidated transactions remaining at different times vary widely, for reasons which we need not here discuss; and the disposition to make or require immediate currency settlements, is a matter of constant variation; hence it often occurs that a rate of interest considerably higher — or lower — than would be paid for the use of utilities obtainable through currency, is paid for currency itself.

The constant fluctuation of interest rates at money centres is largely a result of this demand for currency for what we may term non-intermediate uses.

112. *Interest is* then to be defined as *a difference in value of present over future goods.* This difference results in part from the general tendency to underestimate the needs of the future, and to prejudice the future to the advantage of the present; in part from the fact that with the aid derivable from wealth, a larger product is possible than could be produced without such aid. That is to say, the demand for present goods on terms of a larger payment in the future is *The demand.* due in part to the helpfulness of wealth in productive processes, in part to a desire for wealth for uses which are nonproductive. This demand for unproductive uses depends in part upon the necessity for the liquidation of existing indebtedness, in part upon the disposition of improvident men to discount the future, in part, also, upon the fact that in some cases a larger service is afforded by present consumption of a given sum of values than is expected to be sacrificed by the later payment of a greater sum.

113. Over against this demand volume is the supply volume. Many men have reason to expect greater needs in the future than those to which they are now subject. *The supply.* These men would save irrespective of the fact that saved values may be made to increase by interest. Other men save because, comparing present needs with future needs,

and comparing the amount of wealth in hand with the amount which by the aid of interest additions may in the future come to hand, they find the course of abstinence preferable. Still others save from miser-like exaggeration of future needs, or from miser-like satisfaction in the mere possession of wealth. But whatever motives lie behind demand and supply volumes, the final fact is that they exist, and that the interest rate results as a point of adjustment between them. This resulting rate expresses the relative market values of present and future goods. Capitalists have present goods for trade against promised future goods; borrowers promise future goods against present goods. The terms of sale are determined by the equation point between demand and supply.

114. To conceive of a loan as a sale of present for future goods, and of interest as the market premium of present over future goods, is a great gain over the production formula, both in clearness and in exhaustiveness of statement, and is due to the Austrian economist Boehm-Bawerk. It includes whatever truth is contained in the doctrine that interest is compensation for the use of wealth. But interest paid upon a loan made for consumption purposes cannot be explained under the use formula, unless by referring interest to some use which some one might have made, but did not make. This explanation, however, must be regarded as insufficient, since, were all consumption loans changed to production loans, the rate of interest would tend towards fall by reason of a larger supply and a resulting lower marginal productivity of capital.

Productivity and use formulas criticised.

No one factor in demand should be mistaken for the entire market demand. Nor should we commit the error of mistaking one factor in supply for the entire supply, as have those theorists who regard interest as mere reward for abstinence. We are not concerned to inquire whether the marginal borrower borrows for purposes of production or for purposes of consumption, or to inquire what use for the wealth offered for loan the marginal would-be borrower may have had in thought. Nor from the point of view of supply, are we concerned to know whether the marginal lender is at choice between loaning and consuming, or between loaning and some manner of productive application of his capital in connection with his own supervision and effort.

The terms of sale of present against future goods — that is to say, the rate of interest — are determined in a competitive market through the adjustment of demand and supply.

115. It is to be noticed that in this adjustment allowance must be made — first, for imperfect competition; secondly, for differences in volume and intensity of demand at different places and times; thirdly, for differences peculiar in point of supply and demand to some particular forms of wealth or capital. *Imperfect competition.*

(1) It often happens that by reason of ignorance of the market, or non-acquaintance with lenders, or by reason of lack of reputation and standing in the market, or by reason of oppression or injustice on the part of the lender, a rate of interest is demanded and paid which is, in a measure, not competitive in character and cannot be fully ascribed to difference in risk. For example, a merchant doing business with a banker, and in need of money, may be compelled by the banker to pay almost any rate of interest. The banker alone is likely to be familiar with the business situation of his customer, and if the banker will not loan, no one else will.

(2) The opportunities for profitable applications of capital, and the rates of return to be derived from increased applications, as well as the total supply of loan funds offered in the market, differ at different times and in different places; and although the resulting differences in rates of interest, so far as higher rates are not ascribable to risk, tend to be overcome by more rapid local increases in loan funds and by displacements and inflows from other localities, yet these differences in interest rates are of considerable permanence.

(3) Not all forms of income-paying wealth are held and owned with equal regard to what are ordinarily considered as income-bearing capacities. In a general way it is doubtless true that upon different sorts of income-bearing wealth, mar-

ket values are usually adjusted in proportion to the incomes derivable therefrom, and that the tendency to such an adjustment is constant. But this is only approximately true unless the notion of income is expanded, as it ought to be, beyond its usual signification. The possessor of a picture may receive some portion of its income-bearing revenues in definitely marketable advantages, but receives probably a larger proportion in direct personal satisfactions. Land-rents bring to many landlords low rates of interest on market values, the difference not being fully explicable by difference in risk. The deficiency is compensated by social or other advantages attaching to the position of landlord.[1]

But after making the necessary allowances for various forces affecting both the demand and the supply of loanable wealth, including powers of direction over wealth or energy, — differences between the present and future values of wealth are determined in conformity with the forces determining the value of other commodities through the competitive adjustment of demand and supply.

116. Different men, differing in aptitudes for the profitable employment of wealth as capital, some of them having, in fact, no purpose to employ wealth as capital at all, but only for personal consumption, — some of them borrowing currency for purposes of debt-discharging, enter the loan market, demanding loans differing both in amounts and duration. On the other hand are possessors of capital and currency and rights of direction over labour and wealth, possessors who have different abilities and dispositions personally to utilize their own possessions and who are disposed to loan, if necessary, at different rates of interest, and are desirous of making investments

Demand.

Supply.

---

[1] Boehm-Bawerk regards all of these income utilities as aspects of consumption — denies that a house, for example, is productive in any sense, and traces the market value of the use of property of this sort to the power of the same wealth invested otherwise of commanding remuneration. I cannot agree. A difference between the present and future value of a house might exist even did the house not deteriorate, and even were there no other productive use possible for the capital invested.

for different periods of time. It is, therefore, intelligible that loans for a given period should, in the adjustment of demand and supply, command in some cases a higher, and in other cases a lower, per annum or per diem rate than other loans for a different period. And we find that the rates for long-time, short-time, and call loans do in fact greatly fluctuate upon the market relatively to each other.

117. At the rate as determined upon the market many lenders receive a high rate of interest relatively to the income which they could or would themselves make from their possessions. Many borrowers obtain their loans at a very low rate of interest com- **Quasi-rents a part of profits.** pared to the advantages they expect to derive, and will derive, from the use of the loans arranged. This surplus of advantage is no part appropriable by third persons in the form of interest, wages, or rent, but forms a part of the remuneration of the labour of management. This surplus may be helpfully conceived as a kind of rent accruing always to ability of management, and appearing as one element in profits.

Thus it appears that the rate of interest offered and paid does not tend to fix itself at the average of advantages believed to be derivable from the loans made, but at the minimum advantage expected to be derived from **The marginal doctrine.** any of the loans made or from any part of any. That is to say, there is in the loan market a clearly defined marginal utility for any class of loans, which marginal utility is the normal rate of that class. The demand for capital — that is, for wealth for purposes of reproduction — forms the most considerable part of this borrowing demand. It is thus evident that the discovery of a new field for capital, or of new opportunities for the more productive employment of capital, will, by increasing the demand, tend, other things being equal, to raise the rate of interest. Increases of capital, without enlarging opportunities for productive uses, must make toward fall in interest rates. There is nothing, however, peculiar in theory to interest in this respect.

RISK

118. Something must be said of the relations of risk to interest. Indeed, the question of risk has many important connections with many aspects of economic theory. It was remarked in Section 66, that so far as gain is mere compensation for risk, it cannot be included accurately within the term profit, which strictly used points only to compensation for the personal element in economic activity. Evidently the line between adequate compensation for risk and the compensations for enterprise and far-sightedness is hard to draw. In fact, there are gains which come to men as altogether unearned — by mere luck or chance — which are hard to include in any economic category, and which have been by German economists specially distinguished under the term conjuncture profits. For example, one buys a tract of land upon which coal or iron is afterwards discovered, or a town lot which enhances in value through the location of public buildings or by the construction of a railroad; or one stumbles upon a nugget of gold, a valuable invention, or a new industrial process. It is difficult to regard these as cases of compensation. In these cases of fortunate discoveries in science, the difficulty does not strike one as so considerable. On the other hand, when one receives a fortune by gift or inheritance, we regard it as a mere question of distribution of wealth and trace the title back to that of the giver.

The line between production and distribution.

Bearing in mind all the while that the line is hard to draw between merit and luck, — effort and gratuity, — we may yet place all these cases in one. of the two categories, production or distribution. The fortunate individual is either the producer, the bringer forth of wealth, or he is the receiver of wealth already in existence. In the latter case, he is the lucky recipient, under a seemingly lawless system of distribution, of a social product or of a gratuity of nature. Possibly it would be well that society should assert its claim to many of these gratuities, as has been attempted at some time in some systems of jurisprudence, as, for example, under the ancient law of treasure-trove, and of jetsam and flotsam, or in later years under the state ownership of all mineral deposits. But in the present state of society, the list of "conjuncture" profits is a considerable one, and can hardly in any society entirely fail of place. In moral, as well as in theoretical aspects, we shall find the subject of speculation to brush constantly against this difficulty.

119. How risks shall be treated as related to interest, depends something on the notion of interest which one adopts. Viewed as the reward of abstinence, interest clearly cannot include the risk share in the amount received. Viewed in any sort as compensation to the owner for depriving himself of the use of his capital, risk cannot enter. Viewed again as the difference between the present market value and the future market value of wealth, interest cannot cover risk. To include risk, interest must be defined as the difference between a present value and a probable future value. Adopt, however, not the standpoint of the lender of market values, but the standpoint of the borrower, and risk takes on another aspect. Omitting from consideration all cases of dishonest borrowing, — where the borrower does not intend to pay, — and omitting, also, all cases where the borrower is consciously speculating on the possibility of his becoming unable to pay, interest becomes a payment for the use of capital, or more accurately a payment for the difference in value to the borrower of present over future goods. As applied to the marginal borrower, interest is the full equivalent for this difference. The fact which we are interested to observe is that the risk payment is received by the lender in one character, and is paid by the borrower in another. It is a quantity which separates them, — a kind of neutral ground. It profits the lender nothing; it burdens the borrower; it presses as an incubus on the loan relation. In fact, it burdens the lender by working out a reduction of the net or pure interest received by him; this truth, however, must be taken on trust for the time being. For theoretical purposes, risk may be regarded

Risk and interest.

as in analogy to a tax imposed upon the relationship of debtor and creditor. Discussion as to the incidence of this tax — its distribution between borrower and lender — must be postponed until we are prepared for a discussion of the general topic of taxation.

SUGGESTIVE QUESTIONS

In what case does a physician treat his horses as capital? In what case as mere consumption goods?

Would an increased supply of money affect the crop from any piece of land? The butter made from any cow? The ratio between the yearly output — dividend — and the market value of any property?

Assuming that doubling the currency would double the price of cows, sheep, and farms, would it do the same thing for calves, lambs, and harvests?

What effect, then, on interest rates?

In what sense is interest a ratio?

What forces determine this ratio? Which is ultimate?

NOTES

The price of a loan is not altogether founded, as one might imagine, upon the profit, which the borrower hopes he will be able to make with the capital, the use of which he buys. This price is fixed, like the price of all commodities, by the debate between buyer and seller — by the equation of offer with demand. Men borrow with all sorts of views and for all sorts of motives. This one borrows to enter upon an enterprise which shall make his fortune; that to buy a tract of land; another to pay a gambling debt; still another to cover a loss of revenue due to accident; yet another in order to live until he may earn something by his labour. But all of these motives which influence the borrower are altogether indifferent to the lender. This latter is concerned but with two things, the interest which he shall receive and the safety of his capital. He takes no more thought of the use to which the borrower will put it than does a merchant of the use which a buyer will make of the food supplies which he buys. — TURGOT (France), 1727–1781. Translated from *Œuvres de Turgot* (Guillaumin), T. 1, p. 47.

We have already noticed that the demand for new capital to be productively invested, depends, at any particular time, not upon the actual productiveness of such capital, but upon the general estimate of what it will produce. There seems, indeed, no ground for supposing that this estimate tends, on the average in the long run, to diverge decidedly from the facts in either direction. But experience shows that the general view of the possibilities of profitable employment of capital is liable to marked ebbs and flows. — SIDGWICK, *Principles*, p. 368.

Capital is an immediate product of nature and labour, nothing more. Its own origin, its existence, its subsequent action, are nothing but stages in the continuous work of the true elements, nature and labour. They, and they alone, do everything from beginning to end in bringing consumption goods into existence. The only distinction is that sometimes they do it all at once, sometimes by several stages. In the latter case the completion of each stage is marked outwardly by the appearance of a fore-product, or immediate product, and capital has emerged. . . . Capital is an aggregate of products destined, not for immediate consumption or use, but to serve as a means of acquisition. . . . So, just as everybody would include among instruments of production and capital the horse and cart which assist the peasant in carrying in his grain and wood, must we reckon as capital the objects and apparatus of that more extensive "leading in" of the national harvest — the conveyed products — the streets, rails, ships, and the commercial tool, money. . . . The greater the stock of capital, the larger is the share taken by the productive powers of the past in providing means of consumption for the present, and the less are the new productive powers of the present drawn on for the present.
— BOEHM-BAWERK, *Positive Theory of Capital*, c. 3, passim.

What, then, are the capitalists as regards the community? In a word, they are merchants who have present goods to sell. They are fortunate possessors of a stock of goods which they do not require for the personal needs of the moment. They exchange this stock, therefore, into future goods of some form or other, and allow these to ripen in their hands again into present goods possessing full value.
— BOEHM-BAWERK, *Positive Theory of Capital*, p. 358.

There are three factors, each of which, independently of the other, is adequate to account for a difference in value between present and future goods in favour of the former. These three factors are: The difference in the circumstances of provision between the present and future; the underestimate, due to perspective, of future advantages and future goods; and finally, the greater fruitfulness of lengthy methods of production.

The needy and the careless value present goods more highly because they urgently require them in the present or think only about the present; the well-off and the saving value them because they can accomplish more with them in the future. And thus, in the long run, every one, whatever

his economic position and whatever his economic temperament, has some ground for valuing present goods more highly than future.
— BOEHM-BAWERK, *Pos. The. of Cap.*, p. 277.

"Experience has shown that peasant cultivators are liable to become loaded with debt to money-lenders who, either through the absence of effective competition, — partly in consequence of a certain discredit that often attaches to their business, — or perhaps, sometimes, through unavowed combination, are enabled to exact very onerous interest."
— SIDGWICK, *Principles*, p. 539.

CHAPTER X

WAGES, PROFITS, AND DISTRIBUTION

What is the effect of machinery on the average productiveness of labour?
What effect on average consumption of products?
Is machinery humanity's assistant or its competitor?
Is machinery the labourer's assistant or his competitor?
Would wages be higher if we had one arm instead of two?
Would wages be higher if our environment were poor?
Would wages be higher if our strength were less?
Would wages be higher if our intellects were weak?
Would wages be higher if our scientific knowledge were small?
Would wages be higher if our control over natural forces were small?
Would wages be higher if we had to use gas for heat in place of sunlight?
If products can be produced at small effort, will labour be well or ill rewarded in commodities?

WE are now prepared for a more extended examination of wages and profits than was possible in Sections 61–64. The identity in principle of wages with profits was there shown.

120. In Section 61 was examined the proposition that but for the reproductive power of the land and the aid afforded by the powers of nature, labour products could never surpass in value the value of the labour applied. From the point of view which we have adopted this statement is unintelligible. Labour has no value in itself. Its results have value, and it is only in this secondary sense that value can be predicated of labour. Indeed, this is equally true of all utilities which fall within production rather than consumption goods.

Does value of product depend on value of labour?

It is unquestionable that utilities may be created by labour without the aid of natural forces or of any of the reproductive powers of nature (Section 61). It is nevertheless true that the reproductive energies of nature furnish the sole opportunity to procure food, and that most industrial processes derive great aid from natural forces such as electricity, chemical action, gravitation, heat, and the expansive power of steam. It is in these, for the most part, that the machine-using industries exhibit a productive superiority over the hand industries. But all the processes by which natural energies are made of service in production require the coöperation of human effort. These natural forces stand, then, as aids or multipliers of human energy.

121. With varying abilities, moral, intellectual, and physical, and with varying intensities of desire for the satisfactions possible through effort, men set themselves to the production of utility, applying thereto their energies directly in the form of labour as well as indirectly in the form of capital, and applying also thereto such natural forces and opportunities as they may have been able to appropriate. So far as measured by competitive market adjustments these appropriated forces and opportunities, under the form of land, patent rights, and capital, are marginally determined to aid in the creation of values, they bring to their possessors the remunerations analysed under the forms of rent and interest. So far as human energies directly applied are determined to aid, they bring to their possessors the remunerations indicated under the term "profit" or "wages."

The personal equation.

Each labourer — the term "labourer" being intended to indicate any sort of economic actor — determines for himself, as best he may, the line of activity which will involve for him the minimum of sacrifice. He does not decide the question after the manner of some hypothetical or abstract economic man, who seeks solely that line of activity in which he can obtain the maximum of wealth. Men in actual affairs do not in all cases follow the line of their highest producing capacities. They follow in a considerable measure lines of taste or even of lack of energy or of weakness. It is not at all uncommon that a man prefers to preach or to paint at one income, rather than to do something else at twice that income. Many men prefer to study without salary, other men to do nothing at all on the same terms. The wage received by an artisan may be materially less than that which he is conscious of being able to earn in some less congenial work. The profits of whiskey selling are in some countries far above a fair remuneration for the intelligence and energy required in the business.

The motives, however, which induce men to follow certain lines of activity instead of certain others, have no influence on the wages or profits received therein, except in so far as these motives influence the supply of labourers in any particular line of production, *thereby affecting the market supply of that line of products.* Whatever may be the influences involved, whether of congeniality of the work, or of the profits obtainable, or of heredity or habit or capacity, the ultimate fact is that at a certain price at which the market will consume a certain quantity of commodities, there are for various reasons, among which price in most cases figures as the most important, sufficient products to supply the demand. Should an intensified demand raise the price, the number of persons willing to forego other lines of activity or idleness and to enter this employment would doubtless be increased. The supply of commodities in this line might also be affected by changes in the capacities and preferences of workers, or by modifications in the public esteem in which the employment was held. *What influence has labour supply on wages?*

It must all the while be held in mind that these changes in capacities and preferences are matters of slow accomplishment. Capacity and incapacity tend to perpetuate themselves through heredity and education. Lack of means in the parent may result in the inability of the child to become more than an unskilled labourer. From a theoretical point of view, this seems to cover all that is important in the doctrine of non-competitive groups. *Non-competing groups.*

122. An investigation of wages and profits is, therefore,

146   OUTLINES OF ECONOMIC THEORY

from one point of view an investigation of the causes modifying the demand for particular goods, and of the causes modifying the supplies of labour energy applied to the production of these goods. Thus wages in any particular employment may be permanently low if by force of public opinion or law, or by lack of aptitude for other employments, certain large classes of workers are restricted to few employments.

Wages a question of demand and supply of products.

This, taken in connection with relatively inferior productive energies, is the explanation of the strikingly low average wages of women. If countless women go into shirt-making, they must get, per shirt, wages corresponding to the low price at which shirts must be sold in order to market the whole product. Prices fall to the measure of the marginal shirt, and wages for all shirt-makers come to be fixed at this same margin. Nothing can be done in the case but to decrease the number of shirt-makers, or to find a way by which people shall be willing to buy the same number of shirts at a higher price per shirt. This last is not only impossible, but would, if possible, bring about the production of still more shirts.

Why are women's wages low?

That the wages of one employment are high is due, primarily, to the fact that society consents to consume at a high price the goods produced; but that these wages continue high is due, secondarily, to the fact that the quantity of labour energy applied to that employment is for some reason or other limited. The goods produced, and therefore the labour thereto applied, command a scarcity value. This scarcity may result from the rarity, relative to the demand, of inherited or acquired capacity, or from the indisposition of labourers, for some reason, to enter this line of employment.

123. If all men were labourers, each working for himself, the problem of wages would not be over-complex; the entire social product would constitute the social dividend, — market values would determine the gross receipts of each producer, competition between producers would fix the compensa-

What is starting-point in wages problem — the independent labourer?

tions paid for land and capital. These payments deducted from the gross receipts would leave net wages or profits. Land and capital would be estimated in point of their remunerations by their final increment of desirability.

This is not difficult to see in regard to capital; the rate of interest must be low enough so that all loan funds seeking investment shall find takers; the rate is the lowest rate of desirability among actual borrowers. Different units of capital do not differ in desirability; that is to say, loan funds do not differ in quality: it does not matter whose brand you borrow.

The analysis is a little more difficult with land; here the commodities offered are not of exact similarity. The case is in some degree like that where one monopoly possessor offers a commodity to the competitive bids of different seekers. Nevertheless, other lands fix narrow limits within which this one-sided competition can act. At any great increase of rent or price, other lands become relatively more desirable. Thus rents so adjust themselves that each piece of land commands a rent corresponding to the service it renders over and above the land obtainable without rent payment; that is to say, a rent proportional to the advantages which the possession of the land commands.

124. Or, were it possible to regard land and capital, or the owners thereof, as a class employing labourers, the analysis would be relatively easy. Machines require men to run them, and land requires a force to work it. Market values would become adjusted by processes already analyzed, and in view of these market values the competition of employers to obtain workmen would force the wages up to the point of the marginal productivity of labour. To illustrate: So long as the land-owner could increase his crop of wheat by five bushels through the employment of an additional labourer, he would pay, if necessary, approximately this amount of wheat or its money equivalent in order to obtain the labourer. If land were of such quality and abundance, and other industries of such degrees of productive-

Is it the wealth-owner?

ness, and capital at so high a rate of interest, that all labourers willing to work in agriculture could be there employed without the last addition of labour failing to produce as much as five bushels of product, wages would stand in agricultural employments at approximately this figure. The surplus over and above wages would go to the land-owner or to the capitalist. Suppose, for example, that the land-owner finds that by working his farm alone he can obtain per day 10 of product.

If he hires one man he gets net increase of .	9	of product.
One additional, an additional increase of . .	8	"
One additional, an additional increase of . .	7	"
One additional, an additional increase of . .	6	"
One additional, an additional increase of . .	5.1	"
Increase from five labourers	35.1	"

We have assumed that these labourers are of equal efficiency, each, so to speak, a labour unit. If differences are to be allowed for, we should merely need to change the figures to 9.1, 7.9, 6.9, etc. Wages stand at a little over 5 per labour unit, the five labourers receiving in the aggregate 25 +. The difference between this aggregate wage and the aggregate increase in production must go to the land-owner in his capacity either of owner or of supervisor of labour and capital.

But it is not in fact correct to regard the owners of land and capital as a class employing labourers. Land-owners borrow capital and capital-owners hire land. So, in the above example, if the land-owner finds that by buying or hiring a reaper he may discharge a man and thereby lessen his outlay without diminishing his product, capitalistic processes will be substituted for labour processes. That is to say, capital and labour are in a certain sense competitors.

125. Shall we find it more practicable to start from the point of view of the capitalist as the employer of land and labour? But we have found that the compensation of the capitalist, as such, is determined by the marginal productivity of capital applied to processes of production. That is to say, interest is explained

Is it the imprenditor?

WAGES, PROFITS, AND DISTRIBUTION

by means of land and labour, and cannot therefore itself serve as the basis of explanation.

These attempts at analysis appear to move in a circle — wages a residue after paying rent and interest — rent a residue after paying wages and interest — interest a residue after paying rent and wages. Which is first — which is the centre? or have we a case like that of the planets, a moving equilibrium where each is held in place by all, and all by each, and no one is primarily more cause than effect or more effect than cause?

126. However, we may start to unravel the tangle by recalling that capital does not in fact employ men — nor does land. These are all relations of men with each other. Men employ the capital of capitalists. Landlords employ men and the capital of capitalists. Capitalists employ capital from capitalists and land from landlords. Men employ each other. *It is man.*

The problems of distribution are cases of men against men, and not of men against inanimate things. Where land-owners and capital-owners employ their own capital, they are also free to loan for hire or to hire more and other land and capital. In their character as men they are not lost or merged in the character of land-owners or capitalists. All utilities serve for the benefit of men. Production finds its outlet in consumption. The machine which does the work of men differs for economic purposes from the labourer in this, that the labourer works for himself, while the machine works for something not itself: its product goes to men and not to machines. Capital and land are means for human ends. Economically speaking, they exist not for themselves and are not to be personified or made objective goals for any purpose. Capital does not serve for productive purposes excepting as subsidiary to man and directed by him. So of land. Neither is productively independent. The economic point of view conceives of man as an actor, and of all other things as raw material at his hands.

In the double sense, then, that demand is human demand, and supply the outcome of human effort, we look to solve our difficulty by regarding man as the economic actor, and distribution in all its aspects as a question of reward for his activity. Capital and land are compensated by the measure of what they can profit man for the purposes of production. That which remains, after this service of land and capital has been marginally fixed and payment rendered to the owners, goes to the producing man as the net reward of his efforts.

Wages and profits are residue.

127. This analysis is complicated, however, by the addition of another practically, if not theoretically, most important fact. There are what are called the employers — men whose business it is to stand between labourers and the market — middlemen in production. The producers are not all independent actors. Some employ others. The distinguishing fact about these undertakers or imprenditors is exactly this, that they manage their fellows, and do it not for the profit of their fellows, but for their own profit. The imprenditor is not necessarily a capitalist — though he may be that also — or a land-owner — though he may be that also: he may as well, however, borrow or rent, and often does.[1] As imprenditor, he is mere operator. Wolves hunt their prey in packs; men likewise often hunt value in herds. But there is this difference: the industrial hunt is not in motive coöperative, whatever it may work out to in results. The imprenditor pays the landlord and capitalist what he must, purchases from labourers their utility-product as cheaply as he can, sells the result in the market at the best terms possible, and having assumed all the risks, appropriates all the gains. It is true that all the different productive elements may be centred in one man; he may labour at the bench or in the field; he may be at the same

The imprenditor.

---

[1] Corporations illustrate the union of the functions of capitalist with those of imprenditor. Through directors elected by the stockholders and through officials chosen by the directors, the management of the corporation traces back to the stockholders. It is like a great partnership acting through a committee of direction. The dividend received by the stockholder is a compound of interest on capital, true profit, and remuneration for risk.

WAGES, PROFITS, AND DISTRIBUTION 151

time land-owner and capitalist; but he is imprenditor simply in his capacity of employer of his fellow-men — in his character of industrial captaincy.

The employer (imprenditor) class exist because, by reason of the possession in peculiar degree of capital owned or hired, or by reason of superior ability in management, or by reason of economies in production possible only in industries conducted on a large scale, they are able to procure from labour larger utilities, and to provide for it a larger recompense, risks being considered, than labourers could obtain from society without the intervention of the employer. It is always open to employés, if the imprenditor system seems to work them ill, to return to the system of decentralized industry where each labourer may be his own employer.

The demand of the employer is an intermediate form of the demand of consumers for the goods produced. The employer may be regarded as the agent or representative of the social demand, engaged in the purchase of the results produced by labor, and compelled by competition, if effective, to recompense labourers approximately in proportion to the services rendered. No distinction in principle exists, for present purposes, between the goods commonly termed services, and those goods fixed and embodied in matter commonly termed commodities. Likewise, the occupations of merchants and carriers in the production of utilities of legal condition or of place, offer for present purposes no occasion for special treatment.

Imprenditor is a middleman.

Relatively to society, employers stand as a class of wage-earners whose remuneration, other things being equal, is competitively determined by the supply of them. This supply is modified by influences parallel to those recited with reference to labourers. As with other forms of wages or profits, so with imprenditors' profits, peculiar advantages in ability or capital will bring correspondingly large returns, the amount of the profit being mostly determined by the degree in which the imprenditor is able to reduce his expenses of production below those of the marginal producer. A tendency toward fall in the profits peculiar to ability, analogous to the tendency toward fall in rents, exists in the degree that the differential advantages of ability become by increase in intelligence and education less marked.

128. But the ability of one employer to make large profits, relatively to another, is not entirely a matter of superior ability in production, nor to any great degree a matter of superior advantages in the possession of capital, since under present conditions aggregations of capital are readily made through borrowing or through stock companies. To some extent these differential profits result from superior ability and readiness in tricks of adulteration, in the lying of advertising, and in oppression of employés. The entire body of consumers suffer from the first two of these causes; employés, individually, from the third cause. An examination of the question of remedies lies outside of our immediate purpose. We are in the presence, however, of one of the most acute phases of the labour problem. Were all labourers capable of changing their places of habitation and their manner of occupation, were the question uncomplicated by their ignorance, improvidence, and lack of energy, and were some degree of oppressive combination impossible among employers, there would always remain as causes of non-employment the normal and abnormal changes and fluctuations in the conditions and methods of industry and the inertia and friction of rearrangement. Through the famished competition of the unemployed, in itself an index of imperfect competition, the employer may always find himself largely set free from effective competitive laws, and to a considerable degree at liberty to profit at the expense of his employés by methods of injustice and oppression.

Evil aspects of imprenditors' competition.

Nor is the matter greatly helped by the fact that, even of the wages of this oppression, employers are mostly dispossessed by the competition of other employers in the same lines. There is a strong tendency in business towards the survival of the morally most unfit, and toward the permanent establishment of a low competitive plane of business morality.

To illustrate: If all merchants adulterate their coffee, no one of them gets any benefit out of it, and some good beans get wasted. Yet, if the process is profitable for any, all are pressed toward doing it if any do it. Whenever skilful adulteration succeeds, those who practise it tend to gain the market. Lying, shoddy, and oppression are, in the degree that they are successful, forced upon competitors. And yet, since all follow, the benefits or evils do not for the most part remain with the competitors, but rest with the employés or are passed along to the consuming public.

The wage-earner's assurance of receiving as wages an amount approximately equal to the value of his product, marginally determined, rests solely upon the effectiveness of competition among employers. His wage is, however, guaranteed from falling very low by the possibility which always remains to him of producing directly for the market. The practical difficulty is commonly that when the necessity arises, he is rarely possessed of even that small capital requisite to find himself quarters, tools, and materials. Labour unions will one day find their best field of usefulness in this direction.

Suggestive Questions

If labourers in manufacturing get higher wages without higher efficiency, what will be the effect on the price of their products?

Can they get such higher wages without a lower total product to be sold?

Who will be injured?

If labour unions increase the efficiency of labourers, who will get the benefits?

Will the direct effect be to raise or lower their own wages per piece? How about decreased efficiency?

What harm is done by putting paper soles into shoes? Who suffer?

Would workmen be benefited if labour organizations acting together should stop " scamping " ?

Is it well for society that apprentices be restricted from entering a skilled industry?

In what ways do the unemployed injure the employed?

Do you see any way for labour organizations to manage this problem of the unemployed?

Under influence of labour unions does remuneration correspond accurately to services rendered?

What effect does this hiring labourers by the hundred have in good times on (a) employer's profits? (b) the wages of efficient men? (c) of inefficient men?

How does the system work in bad times?

If X. gets half as many yards of cloth from his machine as does A. from his, will X. get fully one-half the wages paid to A.?

Why?

What effect does prison competition have on (a) social dividend? (b) wages of free labour? (c) average consumption of wealth? (d) taxes?

What effect from women's labour on (a) social dividend? (b) wages of men? (c) average consumption of wealth? (d) morals? (e) health? (f) intelligence?

What would be the effect in the same directions of the eight-hour day?

What do you mean by fair wages?

What influences bear upon salaries different from those on wages?

Is competition equally effective?

How about honesty, fidelity, efficiency?

Is a school-teacher a producer?

Is the minister a producer?

Is a doctor?

Is a lawyer?

Does competition work in these cases in accurate fashion?

Is it possible, commonly, to get a cheaper teacher, doctor, or minister?

What holds up the remuneration?

Is there any meaning in "fair wages" with reference to salaries?

Do you suppose high government officials save much from their salaries? Why?

Is a doctor's outlay for horses productive, or is it consumption?

How about the receptions which the President gives?

Is there any analogy here to the drummer's expense account?

Do officials take their pay, to some extent, in honour?

In what respects does this work well?

In what respects ill?

Is there objection from the point of view of justice?

Would a far-sighted farmer feed his oxen liberally?

A slave-owner his slaves?

Why not, then, an employer his employés?

In what sense do low wages tend toward lower wages?

Would a rise in the American standard of living — in average wages — lead to a further increase in wages?

What effect should you expect on morals?

NOTES

Labour adds to the wealth of its employer. The addition is necessary and continuous; from the moment when the mill begins to run to the moment when it stops, labour, assisted by capital in different forms, is increasing the possessions of the man or the company that employs it. Let the wheel of the engine make a dozen revolutions: there is an inch more of cloth upon every loom. The employer recognizes this addition to his assets, and would not fail to take account of it if he were making an accurate inventory. All through the day and the week the sum of his wealth is growing; and when he pays his men on Saturday night, he takes the amount of their wages . . . from the value that has come into existence during the working days.

Let a man pump water into a full tank, and get what he wants for use from the overflow; does the water for consumption come from the tank or from the pump? In a sense from both; and if important interests were dependent on the answer given, there would be here an opportunity for a fierce logomachy like that which has actually arisen over the origin of wages. The particular drops which are used come immediately from the tank; but the amount in it is undiminished, and the draught virtually comes from the supply furnished by the pump. Moreover, the size of the tank has no influence on the amount of the overflow; that is gauged by the volume of the inflowing stream. In like manner wages are taken immediately from a reservoir of capital; but the amount in the reservoir is undiminished, since the quantity which was drawn from it has already been added to it by the stream of products resulting from industry. It is the volume of products which sets limits to the amount of wages.

The hydraulic figure will perhaps bear straining to the extent of representing one other fact in the relation of capital to wages. If the water which overflows from the tank be regarded as better in quality than that which is pumped into it; if, for example, it loses its sediment by standing, the service rendered by the reservoir corresponds to a certain useful office performed by capital. — CLARK, *Phil. of Wealth*, p. 127.

Have you ever had occasion to witness the fury of the honest burgess, Jacques Bonhomme, when his scapegrace son has broken a pane of glass? If you have, you cannot fail to have observed that all the bystanders, were there thirty of them, lay their heads together to offer the unfortunate proprietor this never-failing consolation, that there is good in every misfortune, and that such accidents give a fillip to trade. Everybody must live. If no windows were broken, what would become of the glaziers? Now this form of condolence contains a theory which it is proper to lay hold of in this very simple case, because it is exactly the same theory which unfortunately governs the greater part of our economic institutions.

Assuming that it becomes necessary to expend six francs in repairing a damage, if you mean to say that the accident brings in six francs to the glazier, and to that extent encourages his trade, I grant it fairly and frankly, and admit that you reason justly.

The glazier arrives, does his work, rubs his hands, and blesses the scapegrace son. *This is what we see.*

But if, by way of deduction, you come to conclude, as is too often done, that it is a good thing to break windows — that it makes money circulate — and that encouragement to trade in general is the result, I am obliged to cry halt. Your theory stops at what we see, and takes no account of what we don't see.

We don't see that since our burgess has been obliged to spend his six francs on one thing, he can no longer spend them on another.

We don't see that if he had not this pane to replace, he would have replaced, for example, his shoes, which are down at the heels, or have placed a new book on his shelf. In short, he would have employed his six francs in a way in which he cannot now employ them. Let us see, then, how the account stands with trade in general. The pane being broken, the glazier's trade is benefited to the extent of six francs. *That is what we see.*

If the pane had not been broken, the shoemaker's or some other trade would have been encouraged to the extent of six francs. *That is what we don't see.* And if we take into account what we don't see, which is a negative fact, as well as what we do see, which is a positive fact, we shall discover that trade in general, or the aggregate of national industry, has no interest one way or other whether windows are broken or not.

Let us see, again, how the account stands with Jacques Bonhomme. On the last hypothesis, that of a pane being broken, he spends six francs and gets neither more nor less than he had before, namely, the use and enjoyment of a pane of glass. On the other hypothesis, namely, that the accident had not happened, he would have expended six francs on shoes, and would have had the enjoyment both of the shoes and of the pane of glass.

Now, as the good burgess, Jacques Bonhomme constitutes a fraction of society at large, we are forced to conclude that society, taken in the aggregate, and after all accounts of labour and enjoyment have been squared, has lost the value of the pane which has been broken.

— FREDERIC BASTIAT, (France), 1801–1850. Translation by Francis Walker. See *Œuvres Choisis* (Guillaumin) *Bastiat*, p. 107.

If we suppose free competition excluding combination — the remuneration of labourers paid by employers, so that the results of their labour become a portion of the employer's capital, is not determined in a manner essentially different from the remuneration of labourers who work on their own account and are directly paid by consumers: except that in the latter case the worker is commonly paid later, and therefore his remuneration must, *ceteris paribus*, be increased by interest proportioned to the interval that he has to wait for payment [and, we may add, to the risks which he has borne]. — SIDGWICK, *Principles*, p. 307.

Manual skill that is so specialized as to be wholly incapable of being transferred from one occupation to another, is becoming steadily less and less important. Putting aside for the present the faculties of artistic conception and artistic creation, we may say that what makes one occupation higher than another, what makes the workers of one town or country more efficient than those of another, is chiefly a superiority in general sagacity and energy which is not specialized to any one trade.

— MARSHALL, *Ec. of Ind.*, p. 141.

There is thus no reason why a sudden fall in the demand for any particular kind of skilled labour [for its products] should not reduce its remuneration to the level of that of altogether unskilled labour; or even below the average of this latter so far as the skilled labourer's previous habits of work have unfitted him for unskilled labour. Nor, indeed, is there any economic reason why an extensive change in processes or local displacement of any particular industry might not reduce the remuneration of any kind of labour in a particular district even below the point sufficient to furnish the labourers with the necessary means of life; as they might be too numerous to be absorbed by such migration as their resources enabled them to effect. — SIDGWICK, *Principles*, p. 320.

In a society in which wealth is distributed as unequally as it is in our own, it is likely — quite apart from any influence of combination or governmental interference — that certain kinds of skilled labour will normally be purchased at an extra price considerably above that required to replace, with interest at the ordinary rate, the expense of acquiring the skill, through the scarcity of persons able and willing to spend the requisite amount of money in training their children and supporting them while being trained. . . . Mill has pointed out that there are important differences in normal wages which are due to relative scarcities of various kinds: chiefly to scarcities arising from the unequal distribution of wealth, which limits the power of performing certain kinds of services to the minority of persons whose parents have been able to afford the expense of prolonged training and sustenance for their children. The freest competition has not in itself any tendency to remove these scarcities, unless the present inequalities in the distribution of wealth are first removed. — SIDGWICK, *Principles*, 322.

The worse fed are the children of one generation, the less they will earn when they grow up, and the less will be their power of providing adequately for the material wants of their children, and so on. And again, the less fully their own capacities are developed, the less will they realize the importance of developing the best faculties of their children, and the less will be their power of doing so.
— MARSHALL, *Ec. of Ind.*, p. 278.

It should be observed that when we speak of rare skill, the term is always used relatively to the demand for the products or services of the skilled worker. It is quite possible that a given kind of skill may be confined to an extremely small minority of the members of any community, and yet may be so abundant relatively to the demand, that no one possessing it is able to earn extra remuneration for his labour. This is the case *e.g.* with the faculty of writing second-rate poems. . . . The competitive remuneration of any kind of labour does not tend to include compensation for the extra aversion felt to it by some of the labourers, except so far as such compensation is required to obtain the whole amount of the labour in question, that society is willing to buy even at the raised price. — SIDGWICK, *Principles*, p. 327 n.

There often came about with a falling demand an increasing supply, and, on the other hand, with improving conditions, a lessening of the labour supply which offered itself at the factories. Thus, for example, I found that the poor hand-weaver brought his children the earlier to their trade the more the trade was depressed, while better conditions enabled him to allow them to learn a better trade. The lad who, from his tenderest years, has been occupied at silk weaving, as man rarely becomes an agricultural labourer, when agriculture prospers and silk weaving languishes. His members, having become adapted to his inherited calling, make him awkward for almost every other. Thus, he by no means diminishes his production with falling demand; on the contrary, he lengthens his hours of labour, since, at the lower price, he can only in this manner supply his extreme necessities. — LUJO BRENTANO (Germany). Translated from *Die Klassische National Œkonomie*, p. 10.

The disagreeableness of work seems to have very little effect in raising wages, if it is of such a kind that it can be done by those whose industrial abilities are of low order. For the progress of sanitary science has kept alive many people who are unfit for any but the lowest grade of work. They compete eagerly for the comparatively small quantity of work for which they are fitted, and, in their urgent need, they think almost exclusively of the wages they can earn; they cannot afford to pay much attention to incidental discomforts, and, indeed, the influence of their surroundings has prepared many of them to regard the dirtiness of an

occupation as an evil of but minor importance. And from this arises the strange and paradoxical result that the dirtiness of some occupations is a cause of the lowness of the wages earned in them.
— MARSHALL, *Ec. of Ind.*, p. 275.

In most occupations, even that part of the work which affords the worker more pleasure than pain, must, as a rule, be paid for at the same rate as the rest; the price of the whole, therefore, is determined by that part of the labour which is most unwillingly given, and which the worker is on the verge of refusing to give; or, as we may say, by the Marginal Disutility of labour. . . . As with every increase in the amount of a commodity offered for sale, its marginal utility falls, and as with every fall in the marginal utility there is a fall in the price that can be got for the whole of the commodity, and not for the last part only, so it is with regard to the supply of labour. If there is an increase in the amount required of a certain kind of work, and some of it has to be done with greater difficulty so as to cause a greater disutility (sacrifice), then a higher price must be paid for this; and the price of all the rest of the work will rise at the same time. This surplus price which has to be paid to all the rest of the labour in some respects resembles rent.
— MARSHALL, *Ec. of Ind.*, p. 103.

TENDENCIES OF DISTRIBUTION

Already in considerable part, though in fragmentary manner, questions of tendency in distribution have been covered. To some of the more difficult of the special problems, special attention will later be given under the titles of Speculation, Combination, and Monopoly.

129. The problems of distribution refer to the subdividing of the social dividend between labourers, employés, land-owners, and capitalists. Put in different phrase, we are concerned with the forces and tendencies affecting the apportionment of the shares indicated under the heads of wages, — including salaries, — profits, rent, and interest.

It may appear a truism to say that the first concern of society in the problem of distribution is to have the largest possible product to divide. In later discussions we may find reason to question how far human weal is bound up with the maximum consumption of wealth; but the question of distribution is

What is relation between social dividend and the distributive shares?

evidently one for the various participants of how to obtain the largest outcome from the distribution. Back of distribution, then, is production.

For each of the factors in production there are but two possible methods of increasing its distributive share: (1) By increase in the total social output, or (2) by increase in one share at the expense of some one or all of the other shares.

Primarily, in the attempt to attain the highest possible social dividend, the interests of all are parallel. In the distributive process, it is equally clear that the interests are adverse. When, for example, two lads go fishing or hunting on shares, harmony is probable until the time comes for dividing the spoils; then peace is less certain. So partners in business are each as loyal to the partnership interests as either would be were the enterprise all his own. Against the business world they stand united. In the division of the profit and in the settlement of the partnership accounts they are not one but two.

Unfortunately, production and distribution cannot be as neatly separated as is indicated by the above statement. All the producing factors are interested that the largest output be reached, but each is at the same time interested to get the largest share of this output. There arises another instance of that antagonism between utility and value which was remarked in Section 34. It constantly falls out that while the interest of each is that the others should produce at the maximum, it is also the interest of each that its own product be materially limited. A small product often has a greater market value than a large. It is better to receive 50% of 75 than 30% of 100.

Thus we must beware of the sweeping proposition that the interests of all classes or of all countries are parallel, — or that the interests of capital (capitalists) and labour (labourers), or of employers and employés are one. They are never so in distribution, and not always strictly so in production. This fact is strikingly illustrated in trusts, monopolies, and combinations.

But excepting in cases of the sort just mentioned, the apportionment of the shares called wages, profits, rent, and interest is brought about by ordinary competitive adjustments.

130. We have analyzed in detail the origin, determination, and tendency of these four factors considered separately. We have observed the general tendency toward an increase in the social dividend through the development of man. Upon the assumption of an increasing population we have observed the tendency toward an increasing proportional importance of rent, subject to such modifications as may be effected by progress in the arts of agriculture and transportation. We have remarked the tendency toward increasing supplies of capital; but on account of the impossibility of forecasting future opportunities for the profitable use of capital, we have found the tendencies of demand for capital relative to supply to involve some degree of conjecture. There is a question, also, as to the direction and degree in which changes in the hazards of loaning may vary the market interest in excess of net or pure interest. It is, however, evident that if no changes take place in the rate of interest, an increasing supply of capital will involve an increased aggregate of interest on capital; and even with diminishing rates, the increase in amount of capital may be such as to render possible an enlarging aggregate of returns. But it is not clear whether this aggregate would or would not tend to increase proportionally with the entire social product. Assuming, as is probable, though questionable, that opportunities cannot be found in the future for investment of continued increments of capital, except on terms of a tendency toward fall in rates of interest by reason of a lower marginal productiveness, there would appear to be a probable tendency toward a constantly increasing social advantage on the use of capital. This social advantage — a quasi rent — must be distributed to the benefit of consumers generally, to employés, to wage-earners, or to landowners; but assuming a stationary population, or such improvements in the arts of agriculture and transportation as to

The distributive shares considered separately.

The share of the capitalist.

negative an increase of rent, these advantages must inure to the wages of labour, or to the wages of management, or to the benefit of consumers as a whole.

These tendencies may be more clearly indicated by the use of a diagram. Assuming an increase in the volume of capital, and falling rates of interest resulting from this increase, a smaller proportional share of the increasing advantages from capital will go to capitalists and a larger share to society.

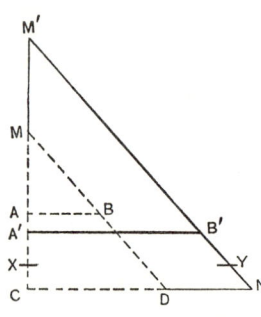

Let the smaller triangle represent the present aggregate productiveness of capital, and the figure $ABCD$ the share going to the capitalist by way of interest; AMB the advantages accruing to other members of society. Out of the increased advantages of capital as represented by the larger triangle, capital at a low rate of interest is represented as receiving an increased absolute return, $A'B'CN'$, but a smaller proportion of the aggregate advantage. Society receives an increase both absolute and relative from ABM to $A'B'M'$. Interest might so fall, as, for example, to XY, that the share of capital should decrease absolutely.

131. It is evident that, with a rising average of intelligence, the advantages from increased capital and improved productive processes will tend in less and less degree to be intercepted by imprenditors under the form of profits, excepting possibly so far as the risks of business and the resulting compensations therefor may increase; since a fall in profits must take place as the requisite ability for management becomes more general. This fall in profits results from a rise in the margin of ability and the consequent lessening of differential advantages, that is to say, from a larger and closer competition of employers with each other. Doubtless some tendency toward a rise in the marginal productivity of capital would accompany the increased productive efficiency

The tendency of profits.

of capital in the handling of more efficient imprenditors; but this tendency would be largely counteracted by further increases in the supply of capital.

For the most part, then, the benefits of lower interest and of improvements in production will be passed along to wage-earners as a class, or to society as a whole; in other words, the inquiry remains to us whether these benefits will be distributed among producers as a class or among consumers as a class.

Perhaps upon closer analysis this inquiry will not be found over-full of meaning, since to the degree that land and capital aid in production their possessors may for this purpose be said to produce. Essentially, our problem is to determine whether the above-mentioned benefits are shared solely among wage-earners, or among all classes of producers, including therein land-owners and capitalists. A correct understanding of the subject of profits is necessary to this solution; the detailed working of a reduction in prices must be examined.

In the competition of different imprenditors with each other, market price measures the sacrifices of the marginal imprenditor. Differential profits can from no point of view be regarded as forming an addition to price. The marginal imprenditor is driven from business by the ability of his competitors to achieve economies in production to which he cannot attain: prices go too low for him. At the same time that prices are falling, the profits of imprenditors are becoming, by reason of a raised marginal efficiency, less. It thus appears that the imprenditor's savings in interest payments and his savings through economies in productive processes are passed along to other classes solely by way of reductions in price. It is, then, all classes of consumers who share the advantages of lowering interest and lowering profits.

These views are so nearly parallel with those of President Walker that it will be profitable to examine the divergence. President Walker reasons that in the distribution of the social dividend, whatever does not go to the landlord in the form of rent, or to the capitalist in the form of interest, or to the imprenditor in the form of profits, must go to the wage-earner. If I understand him correctly, he considers the wage-earner as the residuary beneficiary of industry, gaining by whatever is deducted from rent, interest, or profits. Reasoning in substance as we have reasoned that profits must fall with increased supply of imprenditors' ability, he concludes that the wage-earners must monopolize the advantages from this fall.

But it is not so clear that the entire reduction from imprenditors' profits goes to the increase of wages. President Walker's argument seems to rest upon the proposition that the competition of imprenditors must, in lowering the marginal profit and driving from business some of the competitors, increase directly the nominal wages paid. But it is to be remembered that these competitions of imprenditors are competitions within the limits of separate industries; that commonly the first effect of economies in production is to throw out of employment some portion of the employés; that improvement moves now slowly and now rapidly in each particular industry. Thus, taking into view the extent of the labour supply relative to the improvement at any one time in any particular industry, it does not seem probable that appreciably higher wages could result directly from such improvement, even were the case one where an increased total of labourers was immediately called for.

Thus, the lowering of prices due to employers' competitions is distributed between all market purchasers of products in proportion to their purchases. The fall in interest makes to the advantage of landlords, capitalists, employers, and employés, in their character of consumers. The capitalist's 2% interest may purchase for him more of the good things of life than did his 4%, and this irrespective of the fact that, with an increase of capital, he will reckon his per cent upon a larger base.

But while the capitalist's share in the product of industry may increase absolutely, it cannot fail, with falling rates of interest, to decrease relatively to the other distributive shares. This is also true of the imprenditor's share, for reasons already sufficiently set forth.

It is, in fact, imprenditors and wage-earners who are the residuary legatees of industry. As it is the exercise of human energy which is the first fact, the actor fact, in production, and as land and capital are mere tools and auxiliaries in the process, so human effort obtains the compensations of production after the possessors of land and capital have received their hire. Wage-earners may profit — probably will profit — at the expense relatively of the possessors of capital. They may profit, also, — though they probably will not — relatively or absolutely at the expense of the landlord. Wages, also, are likely to trench relatively upon profits; but that profits should decrease absolutely is not probable, although it is doubtless possible. That imprenditors' ability should become more abundant, would tend to enlarge the social dividend; but that it should tend to lessen the differential between the best and poorest imprenditors is not a necessary result, unless in the tendency of modern industry toward consolidation the number of imprenditors should lessen. Fewer imprenditors, relative to wage-earners, would tend toward a lower aggregate of profits *relatively*. Fewer imprenditors absolutely would mean a reduced aggregate of profit, unless this should be offset by the general tendency toward advance in the remunerations of human activity.

<small>Men generally — not wage-earners alone — the residuary legatees.</small>

<small>Relative tendencies of wages and profits.</small>

QUESTIONS

Who are ultimately benefited by lower rates of interest following upon larger supplies of capital?

By lower rents?

By lower profits?

Do lower profits come about mostly through payment of higher wages or through fall in prices?

How does the marginal law apply to employers?

Do wages and profits tend to preserve any general relation to each other? (See Section 65.)

Does the labourer get wages in proportion at all to the profits of his employer?

Ought he?

The wage-paying ability of what imprenditor is commensurate with market wages?
Is this fair to the wage-earner?
Can it be changed by trades-unionism?
Or in any other way?

NOTES

Stanley Jevons has compared the process of production in which the three factors of production are joined together to the kitchen of the three witches in *Macbeth*, who throw into their cauldron and stir up therein the most heterogeneous substances for the purpose of brewing their "hell-broth." In such a blend as this how are we to set about finding what each man's share should be? What analysis shall we use, what law shall we follow, so as to arrive at this determination?
— GIDE, *Political Economy*, p. 424.

We shall never fully understand either distribution, exchange, or simple production, considered as results of individual economic effort, until we get firm hold of the truth that these are not three separate processes, but only three developments of one process, in which distribution cannot be separated from exchange and simple production, or exchange from that production of utility by labour which it presupposes. The traditional partition of economic science into departments of production, exchange, distribution, and so forth, not only does not correspond to the objective fact; it misrepresents the objective fact.
— FRANKLIN H. GIDDINGS (America), *Sociology and Political Economy*, *Publications Am. Ec. Ass.*, Vol. III. No. 1.

People fail to see that the fact of there being so many men in the world who have so small a share of wealth does not spring merely from the unfair distribution of this wealth; the chief reason is that there is not enough of it. The gravity of the problem does not arise so much from the unequal distribution of goods — for that might be fairly easily overcome — as from their insufficiency.

The enunciation of the fact leads to this: Whatever mode of distribution may be proposed, it should always be subordinate to the mode of production; however conformable the plan might otherwise be to the ideal of distributive justice, it should be sternly rejected if it might lead to a diminution of production. Otherwise the attempt at cure would aggravate the disease. The *sine qua non* is "not to discourage productive activity." On this reef we shall find that all the socialist systems founder. — GIDE, *Political Economy*, p. 408.

Is, then, the demand for capital likely to balance this increase in supply ? On the whole, it seems to me most probable that this will not be the case, for the non-industrial demand for the savings of individuals — chiefly for warlike purposes — which so markedly characterizes the century that has just elapsed, can hardly be regarded as likely to be a normal incident of the preponderantly industrial period of civilized history which seems to lie before us; and though hitherto, no doubt, industrial improvement has been accompanied by an increase on the whole in the industrial demand for capital, I do not see — as I have before said — why this should always be the case. Some recent inventions have tended importantly to diminish the demand for capital: *e.g.* the use of the telegraph by traders has tended to reduce the amount of goods that it was necessary to keep in stock, for the most economical performance of the functions of trade: and it seems quite within the limits of probability that the inventions of the future may have this effect to a greater extent. On the whole, therefore, I should be disposed to conjecture that this demand for capital will not increase so as to balance the increasing supply, and that therefore the rate of interest will slowly decline. I should expect the decline to be slow, owing to the check that the fall will give to accumulation; but I see no reason for placing a definite limit to it. I do not see why it should not go on till the interest on capital not employed by its owner does not amount to more than a fair insurance against risk, so that the desire of obtaining interest ceases to be an important motive for accumulation: — though there is no reason to think that this limit will be reached until after a very long interval.

— SIDGWICK, *Principles*, p. 383.

CHAPTER XI

MINOR MARKET MOVEMENTS

132. We are not yet prepared to consider questions of currency and the fluctuations in prices related thereto. So far in our investigations, possible disturbances from currency sources have been assumed as safely to be disregarded. This course must still for a time be pursued. At present, we need go no further into currency questions than to assume price to be the measure in money of value.

Already in developing the theory of value and the notion of normal value, there has been rendered unnecessary in considerable part any special treatment of market values and market prices. There is, however, one case of permanent tendency in price to which only casual attention has been drawn; this is the tendency usually expressed as the law of increasing returns.

In a sparsely settled country enterprise will commonly be found to busy itself for the most part with the extractive industries, since these are the industries which, for the time, offer the highest remuneration and require the smallest outlay of capital. But these are the industries to which the law of diminishing returns applies. As population increases, this law tends to become increasingly manifest, and the advantages of extractive industries correspondingly less. On the other hand, as population and capital increase, the relative disadvantages of manufacturing and kindred industries decrease. Manufacturing industries soon obtain foothold; nor is this entirely due to the tendency toward diminishing returns in extractive industries; it is in part due, also, to the tendency toward increasing returns manifested in other industries. It is easier to make ten hats after one pattern than to make ten different patterns of hats. This

The law of increasing returns.

is true even with the methods of hand industry, — and more noticeably true in more highly developed conditions. The larger the market, the greater the possible economies in production; the more extended the division of labour, the more marked the advantages to be derived from machinery, and the more important the economies possible in the use of capital. Every improvement in transportation, which enables a larger number of customers to be served from one centre of supply, renders possible larger economies of production at this centre. An increase in population acts in a parallel manner. So manifest is this tendency toward diminished proportional expense in manufacturing industries, that it is rarely overcome by the tendency toward advancing expense characteristic of raw materials, excepting in cases where the manufacturing processes have comparatively a small part in the value of the finished product.

It is not clear that, as usually stated, the tendency toward increasing returns deserves to be termed a law. The economies possible from larger markets and increased division of labour give no indication of being inexhaustible. But the tendency toward increased productiveness, through the development of man in tastes and desires, as well as in the science and technique of industry, is seemingly persistent. On this side, only, the law of increasing returns is open to no question.

Is there such a law?

Suggestive Questions

Why have cities grown so rapidly within the last fifty years ?

What kinds of business centre in cities ?

Do improvements in agriculture tend rather to the increase of the rural or of the urban population ?

Is the great growth of cities peculiar to the United States ?

Are there proportionally more or fewer people employed in agriculture now than fifty years ago ? Why ?

Is this growth of cities likely to continue ?

What effect will improvements in transportation have ? Improvements in machinery ?

What effect from improved suburban transportation on the density of cities ?

On health ? Vice ? Population ?
What effect may the electric motor as power have on the large factory system ?
In what degree ?
Why do city debts increase so rapidly ? In what degree is this justifiable ?
What has your city to show for its indebtedness ?
Ought cities to own their gas, water, and electric light plants ?
Is the price at which the services are rendered a fair test ? Why not ?
Does the city plant pay taxes ? interest ? rent ? full cost of management ?
Does it have to advertise ? fight competitors ?
Does it make profits ? Is it expected to pay dividends ?
Discuss the relative merits of the following methods of treating these questions : By city operation ; by city ownership, and leasing under competitive bids ; by progressive taxation on profits ; by some combination of these methods.
Which manner would probably tend least to corrupt city politics ?
Is the modern city a purely governmental body or in large degree a business corporation ?

NOTES

It is easier for a dense than for a sparse population to have good roads, good streets, beautiful avenues, large theatres and good actors, a water service, cheap lighting, and as well literary and scientific libraries, thorough and general education, and a public opinion which restrains by the general sentiment of social interest the excesses of individual interest.
— COURCELLE-SENEUIL, *Traité de l'Ec. Pol.*, p. 176.

A working man who is well versed in political economy once told me that the reading of Ricardo had convinced him that there is no hope for the labouring class under the existing system of industry. Competition, as he was compelled to think, must sooner or later reduce workmen to the starvation limit and keep them there. In times of exceptional distress, it must drive them below that limit, and only restore them to it through the lessening of their number by actual death. His hopes for the future of his class were founded on a change in the industrial system, which should substitute coöperation for competition. This man is representative ; his premises are those of Ricardo, and his school and his conclusions are those to which many readers are forced. This fact explains the popularity of orthodox economic literature among declared socialists. It prepares the soil for revolutionary seed. A demonstration of the hopelessness of the old economic system is, to a man who retains his natural optimism, equivalent to a proof that a new system is coming. . . . If the law of diminishing returns in agriculture were admitted, it would be necessary to accept the conclusion that crude nutriment will become costlier as population increases. It would then be of importance to note that there is a class not noticed in the traditional theory in the case of which the reverse of the above law is true. Commodities consisting mainly of form utilities are unquestionably becoming cheaper; and among these are all products which minister to intellectual, æsthetic, and spiritual wants. If the conditions of the future were to involve plainer living, they would at least be more favourable to high thinking; and we might welcome a tendency which would make it necessary for men to forego some of the sensuous enjoyments of life, if it, at the same time, enriched them in intelligence, refinement, and moral character. If the man of the future is to be wiser and better than the man of to-day, we need not be troubled with the question whether he will or will not be happier. We do not admit, however, that the spiritual gain is to be purchased by physical sacrifice. The world is, in fact, becoming more tolerable to man as an animal, and it is becoming indefinitely more favourable to him as a rational being. — CLARK, *Phil. of Wealth*, p. 149.

A sudden increase in the demand for anything will raise its market price; but whether the permanent effect of an increase of normal demand for it will be to raise or lower its price depends on whether it obeys the law of diminishing or increasing return. . . . In other words, we say broadly that while the part which nature plays in production conforms to the law of diminishing return, the part which man plays conforms to the law of increasing return, which may be stated thus: An increase of capital and labour leads generally to an improved organization; and therefore, in those industries which are not engaged in raising raw produce it generally gives a return increased more than in proportion; and further, this improved organization tends to diminish or even override any increased resistance which nature may offer to raising increased amounts of raw produce. — MARSHALL, *Ec. of Ind.*, p. 246.

RETAIL PRICES

133. There are minor and temporary fluctuations of market price about normal price which require attention. Among the most noticeable are the indefiniteness and variety of price characteristic of the retail trade. Buyers and sellers in the wholesale markets deal

<small>Ignorance and carelessness of retail purchasers.</small>

in large quantities, have large interests at stake, and are by training and information well able to follow their respective lines of interest; competition is close and approximately perfect. But in the retail trade purchasers are, to a large extent, ignorant of prices and qualities, and to a large degree not interested to learn. The immediate subject of bargain is seldom of great importance to the purchaser as compared with the annoyance of further seeking; and in the confusion of makers and brands he knows himself to be at best largely dependent on the good faith of the seller. Considerations of acquaintance, habit, credit, and fashion enter.

Fashion. Social distinction, for example, may depend in some measure on buying goods at X's shop at exorbitant prices. Stated shortly, competition is imperfect in retail trade; exalted retail prices, bearing unfavourably upon consumers, and a multiplicity of dealers far beyond the social need, are common results.

A second cause of departure of market price from normal price is to be found in the impossibility, in many cases, of a quick adjustment of supply to demand, on **Inertia of capital and labour.** other terms than a considerable change in price. Agricultural products furnish the best examples. The supply is produced periodically. Shortage can be remedied, in some measure, by the substitution of other commodities, and by importation from other markets; but a new supply is possible only after the expiration of considerable time.

Some cases of variation from normal price and some cases of long-continued departure therefrom are to be explained, as we have seen, by the inertia of labour — the indisposition of labourers, or their inability through lack of information or otherwise, to move about from place to place. There is also an inertia of capital. The time necessary for placing capital, the difficulties incident to moving it, the frequent impossibility of employing fixed capital for other than the purposes originally in view, and the certain loss incurred in stopping business, all explain the tendency of any deviation from the market price to continue over a considerable period of time. This tendency is, of course, in considerable measure limited by modifications of supply due to the influence of outside markets.

SPECULATION

134. The question of risk lies at the very heart of the subject of speculation. In many cases risk is best conceived as part of the cost of doing business, or as a tax imposed upon trade and commerce. This has already been pointed out as related to interest; it is equally true with reference to all the processes of producing and marketing goods. *Risk in some cases part of outlay in production.* Farmers must, in the long average, obtain a price upon their products sufficient to compensate them for the crops which they do not harvest. The non-harvested crops make part of the expense of the harvested. So the bad debts of the wholesaler or of the retailer are a part of the expense of getting goods into the hands of the paying customer. The analogy to the case of transportation charges is close.

But what of the risk to which the wholesaler is subject when he buys his supplies, that prices will fall, or what of his hope that prices may rise? How about a gain in this sort if he makes it? Is it profit? Or, how about the loss when loss befalls? Is the gain more than compensation for risk? *In other cases difficult to classify.* Is the loss the business equivalent of the gain which was equally in prospect when the purchase was made? Has the insurer lost merely because his property did not burn? or had his property burned could the insurance company rightly have called it a loss? Answers to these questions fit awkwardly into the nomenclature of political economy. Possibly the term "profits" should be enlarged to include returns on risk. If so, profit becomes something wider than a theoretical equivalent for wages, — a form of compensation for the human element in production. Or, possibly, it would be well to construct a new term, "risk-profit," to cover this class of cases.

At any rate, one who buys goods or land buys at a price which different estimates of future developments have helped to fix. Whoever wins, wins because his judgment, or his guess, or his luck, was superior; loss comes by reverse title. In either case the gain or loss has no relation to any productive purpose on the part of the speculator.

The benefits of speculation. 135. We say that in purpose there is nothing productive in speculation. Is it productive in effect, and, if so, in what cases and in what degree?

Utilities, as we know, are never absolute, — but are relative to human needs, and rest in their very nature upon questions of place and time. Ice, in summer, has gained a time utility; so of apples or potatoes in winter. The surplus from to-day's banquet may possibly shield you from starvation to-morrow. Here is room for productiveness in some sorts of speculation.

I find no clearer or more accurate discussion than that of Cairnes, of which the following is, for the most part, either quotation or abridgment: "It can be shown that there is in every market a price at which it is desirable that the commodity, whatever it is, should sell at that time and place, — desirable ultimately in the interests of consumers, but in a certain sense desirable, also, in the interests of dealers, — taking buyers and sellers together, — and which the combined operations of both, so far as they are well informed respecting the conditions of supply and demand, tend to establish." (*Leading Principles*, pp. 107–110.)

An undue fall will, on account of increased consumption, be compensated by a corresponding rise, to the loss of the dealers who sold while the lower price prevailed; and an undue rise, by checked consumption and a corresponding fall, to the loss of all dealers who purchased at the higher rate. "It is to the interest of both buyer and seller to know the point beyond which in one direction the buyer, and in the other the seller, cannot pass without loss; and this is precisely the point which stands identified with the consumer's interest." For, in order that the entire supply shall furnish the maximum of utility, there must be avoided, not only temporarily large consumption and a low average of utility, but also that condition of scarcity which results in a high average utility and greatly diminished consumption. One apple per day for thirty days will afford greater service than thirty all in one day. It follows that "such oscillations are at variance with the interest of consumers," and the price, therefore, which renders them unnecessary, which is just sufficient and no more than sufficient to carry the existing supply over, "with such a surplus as circumstances may render advisable to meet the supply forthcoming," we may conveniently term the " proper price," a price which adjusts in the most advantageous way the existing supply to the existing demand, pending the coming forward of fresh supplies from the sources of production.

A speculative restriction of consumption is also desirable against the possibility of shortage in the new supply.

The services to society of speculation and of the speculative features in ordinary business are thus evident: " A service which has been well compared by Archbishop Whately to that rendered by the captain of a ship, who, taking account of the stock of provisions at his disposal and the length of his intended voyage, adjusts to these conditions the rations of his crew." These speculative adjustments, by which an immediate surplus can be withdrawn from the market with a view to future consumption, or a future supply rendered immediately available to consumers, are made by men who set themselves for personal gain to the study of market conditions, and whose forecasts, as expressed in market prices, while doubtless liable to considerable error, are of immeasurable value to society as a whole. Famines are thereby greatly mitigated in intensity, and future plenty made to lend itself to present comfort. The lack of effective machinery of this kind is theoretically one of the weak points of socialism. (But see Section 239.)

136. But Cairnes' view of speculation seems to assume for all cases the necessary coincidence of speculators' interests

with social interests. Mill, in fact, says "that the interests of the speculators as a body coincide with the interests of the public; they can only fail to serve the public interests in proportion as they miss their own." While this is true of speculation against an approaching food shortage, it certainly is not true in all cases or with reference to all kinds of speculation. It is not true, for example, of land, upon the price of which speculation can have no desirable influence. In this case, as well as in case of some other commodities, erroneous or extensive speculative operations are often productive of widespread and severe business disturbances. In many cases the speculator foresees permanent changes in values, and profits by them. Profits of this kind are made at the expense of the public; no corresponding social advantage exists in economizing supplies, nor any considerable advantage in rendering the advance less abrupt. Nor is there any social advantage in the fluctuations of prices caused by false reports or by "bearing" or "bulling" the market through the influence upon an ignorant public of the example of the speculators themselves, by which later the speculators step forward to profit.

The evils.

Land.

Nor, as regards those commodities like food products, where, if half the supply is destroyed, the aggregate selling price may be doubled, is there room for doubt that speculation may result most injuriously to the public, by precisely reversing the beneficial action of speculation, as previously outlined. So far as the effects of the successful corner extend beyond the gains and losses of speculative operators and touch the interests of consumers, it is by raising the price for immediate consumption, whereby the total of current consumption is diminished and a later increased consumption is made to follow at a low average of utility.

Corners.

But whatever may be relatively the good and evil in speculation, and to whatever degree speculators may in particular cases profit from each other, it is evident that in the end the consuming public pays in larger part the profits of speculators as of

The ultimate incidence of speculators' profits.

middlemen generally; since, however unfavourably speculation may in some cases affect producers, it is evident that the producers must in the average obtain remunerations equal to those obtainable by them in other branches of industry.

There is, however, here also a theoretical question similar to that suggested by the relations of risk to interest. Speculators' profits are an intermediate quantity between producers' and consumers', a kind of charge upon trade. The distribution of this charge will be considered under the head of taxation.

NOTES

The highest kind of business talent is shown in forecasting rightly all these various changes, and continually adapting supply to demand; but the forecast tends to become more difficult as the range of coöperation through exchange extends. Producers are more and more led to manufacture for markets too numerous to watch carefully, too remote to understand adequately, and exposed to modifying influences of continually increasing complexity; and hence fluctuations in the adaptation of supply to demand, and the consequent fluctuations in the income of producers, tend to become greater and to contain a larger element of mere luck.
— SIDGWICK, *Principles*, p. 366.

Such operations are of doubtful legitimacy, even according to the ordinary standard of commercial morality: since the speculators do not merely expect to profit by the mistakes of others, but by the mistakes which they have themselves intentionally caused.
— SIDGWICK, *Principles*, p. 338.

CHAPTER XII

INTERNATIONAL TRADE

Make a list in writing of the different arguments in favour of protection which you have heard or can suggest.
Do you see that any one of these conflicts with another ?
Make a like list on the free-trade side.
Do any conflicts strike you on this side ?
Do machines add to wages or subtract ?
What controls wages ?
Is it generally well or ill to lower cost of transportation ? For a people to possess fertile land ? For mineral deposits to lie near the surface ?
What effect in these cases on wages ?
Define cost of production.
Separate the conditions of wealth production into two classes: (1) human, and (2) non-human.

137. It was pointed out in Section 63 that division of labour is possible only upon condition of the possible exchange of products. Each producer must provide for a considerable number of different needs. The system of exchange renders it possible that he apply the productive energies in his control to some one line of goods, and obtain the other goods desired by him through the exchange of a portion of his product for these other goods. He foregoes (sacrifices) some of the goods possible through direct production, in order to obtain a greater total of satisfactions through exchange; nor is he deterred from this course by the fact that his productive abilities, in some or all of these other lines, equal or exceed the productive abilities of the producers actually engaged therein, if his abilities are relatively more marked in some particular line. He follows the prospect of greatest remuneration (least sacrifice).

Advantages of division of labour.

Likewise it often happens that the inhabitants of some particular locality devote themselves, because of their peculiar aptitudes, or because of advantages peculiar to their environment, to the production of some one line or some few lines of goods, and obtain their supply of other goods through exchange. One community is found to be engaged for the most part in mining; another in agriculture; a third in manufactures; and a fourth in commerce. The deciding cause, in any of these cases, may be a special adaptation either of the people or of the place to the chosen industry, or a special lack of adaptation to any other industry. In short, exchange between different communities comes about for reasons parallel to those which induce exchange between individuals in any community. The need of special treatment of trade between different communities or different countries rests upon the relatively large importance, in these cases, of transportation outlays, and upon the lack of mobility of labour and capital across long distances or across geographical frontiers, marking changes in language, customs, laws, and institutions. That England sends cloth to France, and France wine to England, does not of necessity indicate that France cannot produce cloth at as small an application of productive energies as can England, or that England cannot produce wine at as small an application of productive energies as can France; it simply proves that wine, produced in France and exchanged in England for cloth, will obtain for the French producer more cloth than seems possible to him by the application of the same kind of productive energies directly to the production of cloth; and, similarly, that English producers believe they can get more wine by making cloth and exchanging for wine than by producing wine. It is theoretically possible that the French producer possesses, in comparison with the English producer, advantages in both lines, and yet, because of advantages greater in one industry than in the other, finds it profitable to follow only one of these industries, to the entire or partial exclusion of the other.

Not absolute but relative advantages govern division of labour.

138. The orthodox economists are accustomed to make of

some phases of international trade an exception to the application of the cost-of-production idea; but in our view, international trade is a mere illustration of the doctrine of value, and results from the choice by each producer, in whatever country, of the line of least sacrifice for him. In international trade, no less than in domestic trade, normal values are those values indicating the line of least resistance for all persons producing and consuming in any given market, or in trading relations therewith. The normal market price in each market must remunerate the highest continued sacrifice involved in supplying that market. Costs of transportation are a part of this sacrifice; these costs must therefore be remunerated in the market price, and unless the difference between the price in the supply market and in the consuming market is believed to be more than sufficient to cover the charges for transportation, shipment will not take place. This statement does not, however, of necessity imply that this difference must exist entirely in the prices of any one commodity, as, for example, of the wine in the above illustration. The difference may be, and ordinarily is, found in part in the prices of that commodity which serves as return cargo; for example, if corn is five cents per hundred higher in London than in New York, and iron ten cents higher in New York than in London, corn may be shipped to London and iron to New York, even though, if the return cargo in either case were omitted from consideration, it would be impossible to charter a ship from New York to London at as low a charge as five cents per hundred. It is necessary only that the markets be so circumstanced that a profit be possible, both outward and homeward trips being considered. It is immaterial whether the exchange be conducted by one operator or by more than one. In the competitive adjustment of demand and supply, transportation services will be obtainable at a charge enabling both the corn and iron exchanges to be carried on remuneratively. It is evident that the consumer of iron will, in the case assumed, reimburse the larger part of the transportation outlays of the entire transaction. The final incidence of these

An example of line of least sacrifice.

outlays will vary with variations in the market prices of the products involved. No definite distribution of transportation charges is *a priori* possible in any case of exchanges, international or other. Market conditions may be such that trade can take place in but one line of commodities; in this case, for so long as it endures, consumers of these commodities will commonly bear the greater part of all transportation charges, including the cost of payment, whether through bankers' exchanges or by shipment of coin. The incidence of these charges is parallel to that of taxes. (See Sections 155–161.)

139. It is evident that benefits are expected to accrue in some measure to both of the parties to international trade, but the relative degrees of benefit cannot be measured by the apportionment of transportation charges. As Ricardo acutely observed, "Every transaction in commerce is an independent transaction." If foreign purchasers find the export trade sufficiently profitable, the volume of trade will expand until, by increased marginal sacrifices in production or by falling prices (lowering marginal consumer's sacrifice), further expansion is checked; but the aggregate profit to producers above the margin is a necessarily indefinite quantity, and the advantages to consumers measured by the difference between what they do pay for the foreign product, and what they would, if necessary, pay, are equally indeterminate. *Quasi-rents in international trade.*

Exchanges between people of different localities, as well as exchanges between people of the same community, take place by reason of differences in the comparative sacrifices involved in the production of different commodities. If, for example, it is found in Australia that the advantages in wheat production are relatively greater than in the production of cloth, wheat will be produced to the exclusion of cloth, till the marginal sacrifices in wheat production reach an equality with the sacrifices involved in cloth manufacturing. It is quite possible that the superiority in absolute productive power should be with Australia in respect to cloth as well as to wheat, but cloth must continue to be imported as long as relatively greater remunerations are possible in wheat raising. The following quotation from Cairnes refers to the condition of affairs in Australia during the few years following the discovery of gold: "Australia became the importer of everything that from its nature admitted of being imported; and, what is especially to be noted, among the things thus imported were many which she could have produced herself at far less labour and abstinence than they were produced at in the countries from which they were brought. For example, timber was imported from the Baltic, although there were forests in Australia capable of yielding timber quite good enough at least for mining purposes, for which timber was mostly required. Butter was largely imported from Ireland, and I believe also from England and Holland, though the advantages possessed by Australia for dairy farming in her unrivalled pastures and abundant cattle were exceptionally great. Similarly, with unlimited areas of fine agricultural land, she imported nearly all her food; and with the materials of leather cheaper than in any other part of the world, she imported all her shoes. What was the explanation of these facts? In all cases one and the same: it was to be found in the principle of comparative cost. Australia had considerable advantages over other countries in respect to timber, butter, food, and shoes; but she had a greater advantage still in respect to gold; and so it became her interest to obtain the former things by means of the latter. I have always regarded the commercial results of the Australian and Californian discoveries (for things in California followed a very similar course) as one of the most striking experimental verifications which a purely abstract doctrine has ever received."

140. As has been observed, international or any other division of labour may be determined either by special adaptation of people or locality to some particular line or lines of production, or by lack of adaptation to any other. So far as special advantages attach for particular industries to particular localities, an interchange

The inertia of labour and capital.

of commodities may be expected to take place. Personal advantages and disadvantages are of parallel importance to the extent that they are permanent; but to the extent that larger remunerations are possible to labour and capital through changes in location, the differential advantages accruing to labourers and capitalists on account of changes in location must tend to be cancelled by rearrangements. These rearrangements are, however, matters of long duration. Migrations of labour and capital are of every-day occurrence, and of increasing importance; yet there remains a large degree of immobility, depending in part upon ignorance, stupidity, or pure inertia, in part upon differences of laws, customs, languages, etc., in part on the risks and inconveniences of change.

There is, however, an economic aspect of the question which economists have largely disregarded. Not all the goods for which men make sacrifices are marketable commodities. A portion of the immobility of capital, as well as a considerable portion of the immobility of labour, arises from the fact that many men prize above high wages or high interest the established associations and social and family ties in which their lives have been cast. A change, though offering a prospect of higher market remunerations, involves in many cases a greater sacrifice in the total. Nevertheless, the remarkable degree in which migration is taking place, both between different countries and between different portions of the same country, indicates the tendency of industrial advantages toward a level, so far as these advantages depend upon differences of environment. Only to the extent, however, that the mobility of labour and capital is effective, can foreign competition tend to injure some domestic industries otherwise than to the extent that it benefits others. So long as the people and the capital cling to established locations, the manner of industrial employment will not be modified, excepting to the extent that some competing domestic industries become relatively more remunerative than others. We may then recur to the proposition already stated in Section 53, that domestic and not foreign competition is the cause of failure of particular industries, except in so far as the superior inducements offered abroad result in an outflow of labour and capital. Only to the extent that this outflow is more injurious to one industry than to another, can foreign competition tend directly to the prejudice of any one industry. The bearing of these propositions upon tariff and immigration questions is evident, so far as such systems are intended to be permanent. For the purposes of a temporary revenue policy or of a temporary stimulative policy, much may be said from a practical point of view in favour of tariffs "protective" in their effects.

Suggestive Questions

Why does X work on hats? Y on shoes? Z on law?

Why does England produce coal and woollen cloth instead of bananas? or instead of silk?

Would silk cost too much in England? Why?

Why does America tend rather to wheat and beef than to silk or sugar?

Why must we have tariff in order to produce sugar?

Is it because wages are high?

Why are wages high?

Is it because wages are low "there"? Why are they low "there"?

Are wages high because people consume much, or *vice versa?*

Would it be well for us if our mines were deeper or our lands less fertile? Would there be more work?

Do men lack work because there are no more desires to be satisfied?

If we could get woollen cloth from abroad at three-fourths the price here, would it be well to buy it? At one-third? At one-tenth? At nothing at all?

Is some one worsted in every trade?

Suppose foreigners should become able to undersell the British iron producers, what could the British iron producers do then?

Why would they not work at wages low enough to meet the foreign competition?

Complete your list of arguments on each side, cancelling such arguments as you see to be fallacious.

Suppose 100 units of energy to produce, in America 200 wheat or 100 sugar — in France 100 wheat or 100 sugar. What measured in wheat is cost of sugar in France? in America? Will America best buy or produce its sugar?

NOTES

Take a man belonging to the more modest classes in society, a village cabinet-maker, for example, and take note of all the services which he renders to society and those which he receives; we shall quickly be struck by the great and apparent disproportion. This man passes his day at planing lumber and at making tables and bureaus; he bemoans his condition, and yet what does he, in fact, receive from society in exchange for his labour?

Every day, on awaking from sleep, he dresses. He, himself, has made no one of all his articles of clothing. But in order that his garments, simple as they are, should be at his disposition, an enormous quantity of labour, of industry, of transportation, of ingenious inventions, must have been accomplished. Americans must have produced cotton; Indians, indigo; the French, wool and linen; the Brazilians, leather; and all these materials must have been freighted to different cities, spun, woven, coloured, etc.

And then he breakfasts. That he may have the bread of which he daily eats, lands must have been cleared, fenced, tilled, fertilized, sown; the harvests must have been preserved with care from force and theft; a certain degree of security must have been guarded in the midst of a numerous society; the wheat must have been garnered, ground, and kneaded; iron, steel, wood, and stone must have been made by human labour into instruments of industry; certain men must have thereto applied the energies of animal life, others, the force of falling waters, etc. All these are things each one of which, in itself, presupposes an incalculable quantity of labour energy thereto applied, not alone in space, but in time.

No day passes when this man does not make use of some small quantity of sugar or of oil, and does not enjoy the help of various tools for his work. He will send his son to school to receive instruction, which, though limited, must have required researches and preceding investigations, and knowledge astounding in extent.

He steps from his door to find the streets paved and lighted. His property rights are attacked. He will find attorneys to defend his rights; judges to maintain them; officers of justice to put them into execution; all of these are things which presuppose a fund of acquired knowledge.

He enters the church. In itself it is a wondrous monument to human intelligence, and the book which he carries with him is yet a more wonderful monument. There his moral nature is developed, his intelligence strengthened, his purposes reinforced. That this should happen, another man must have been able to apply himself in the libraries and the seminaries . . . and to live without the necessity of applying himself directly to the satisfaction of his bodily needs.

Should our artisan desire to travel, he finds that, in order to save his time and spare him trouble, other men have graded and levelled the soil, filled valleys and made mountains low, bridged rivers and constructed carriages running over pavements of stone or rails of iron, and have tamed to the work the strength of horses or of steam. . . . And that which makes this phenomenon all the more strange is that every member of society finds himself in the same condition.

— BASTIAT. Translated from *Harmonies Economiques—Organisation Naturelle. Œuvres Choisis, Bastiat* (Guillaumin), p. 211.

Suppose the French nation to be alone in the world, or to be surrounded by impassable deserts. Some portions of its territory are very productive of grain, other moister districts adapted only to pasture, others made up of barren hillsides valuable only for vintage ; still others, more mountainous, productive of nothing but timber. If each one of these districts is shut up by itself, what must happen? It is evident that, in the grain district, a considerable population may maintain itself, there being an opportunity to fully satisfy the primary human need, — that of food. However, this need is not the only one ; clothing and shelter are essential. These inhabitants will then be compelled to apply to forestry and pasture and unproductive vineyards a large part of these good lands, a very small part of which would have sufficed through exchange to obtain the things which were lacking, while the remainder would have maintained a considerable added population. Thus this people will never become as numerous as if they had taken advantage of commerce ; and, at the same time, they must lack for many things. The same thing is still more true of those people who inhabit the hillsides adapted only to vine culture. These people, even if they possess some industries, will produce wine only for domestic uses, having no place in which to sell it. They will waste their energies in ungrateful labour in attempting to produce upon their barren hillsides poor crops of grain, not knowing where to purchase it, and will want everything else. The population, even though agriculturists, will be small in number and poor. In the country of lowlands and swamp, too moist for grain, too cold for rice, the case will be still worse. . . . In the forest country, no means of living is found but the chase of wild animals whose skins are without value. Such must be the condition of France if all communication between its different portions were cut off, — one half savage, the other half poor. — Translated from DESTUTT DE TRACY, *l'Esprit des Lois*, Liv. XX., XXI.

Franklin supposes a country X having three manufactures, for example cloth and silk and iron, drawing their supplies from three other countries, A, B, and C, and making the attempt to benefit the producers of cloth by increasing sales and raising prices. For this purpose fabrics coming from country A are prohibited. A retaliates by shutting out the silks from X. It follows that the silk producers complain of decreased trade. Thereupon X excludes the silks from country B; B in response excludes the iron from the forges of X. Thereupon the proprietors of the forges complain of diminished trade. Thereupon X prohibits iron coming from C; C in response excludes the cloth from X. What results in the total? Each of these countries experiences a diminution in the aggregate of wealth and well-being which it can command.

SOME CONCESSIONS

I

141. It has been repeatedly emphasized as fundamental to all economic reasoning that needs and desires are the motive forces behind productive effort, that supply comes about in response to demand, and that demand is as inexhaustible as are human needs and desires. For the human race as a whole, production limits consumption. Wages, interest, rents, and profits are quantities necessarily limited by product, and as limited by product are mere questions of distribution inside it. Thus the doctrine of the early economists that no one distributive share, as, for example, wages, can increase, unless at the expense of another or others, is not an accurate statement. The position is tenable only upon the assumption that other conditions remain the same. If the social production is increased, it is possible enough, indeed perhaps probable, that rent, wages, profits, and interest advance concurrently.

The argument for free trade rests ultimately upon the foregoing principle. The desirability of international division of labour, as dictated by advantages of race or habitat, seems clear enough, when once the truth is grasped that the question is one merely of maximum of product. And the argument is even stronger than at first appears. We tend to confuse the question of product, which is one of utility purely, with questions of value. The well-being of the world is not measured in the values at its disposal for consumption, but in the utilities. Abundance means fall in value or absence of value. The commodity which by abundance in supply more than neutralizes the energy of demand, ceases to be commodity by that fact, falling out of the list of exchangeable products. Human interests, therefore, are not parallel with the maximum creation of value, but only with the maximum creation of utility. Economic progress expresses itself in successive reductions of the sacrifices necessary to the satisfaction of desires, — in the approach of commodities to the margin where value disappears, — in short, in the cheapening of things (Section 34). If what we now get on terms of effort we were able to get without effort, all these things would be valueless, but society would be richer with all its energies free for new conquests of product. That water should become so scarce as to command a market price, would mean that society was not richer but poorer.

Thus it is clear that value measures do not correctly represent the economy of human energies worked by international division of labour. Product, and not price, is the ultimate fact, utility, and not value.

142. But while this is unquestionably true for the human race as a whole, it as clearly falls short of the truth in exceptional cases of nations or individuals. (See Section 150.) While increasing values do not of necessity tend toward increasing social product, they do unquestionably in the interests of their producers tend toward an increasing share of this product. In questions of distribution, utilities sink in importance, and values take precedence. Thus it may become for the interest of any individual in a community, or for any nation in a community of nations, artificially to redistribute the applications of productive energy for the purpose of reducing in certain lines what would otherwise be the commodity output.

The monopoly principle in international trade.

Nor do cases of this sort present any inconsistencies with the general theory of value, or call for any extensions of theory. On the contrary, these cases serve to bring out with helpful clearness the antagonism between utility and value, which is fundamental to the very existence of value. Value is the measure of the sacrifice involved in obtaining utility. Value emerges in human life only where enjoyment is conditioned on some form of sacrifice; where there is both debit and credit in the account; where a balance is to be struck; where the gain of the consumer is not gross but net. That there may be for humanity utility without value is but another aspect of the fact that things of utility may exist in superfluity, and this again but restates the truth that human needs and desires are not infinite in any particular direction. The increase in the utility afforded by successive increments of supply is not proportionate to the increase in supply. It thus often comes about that an increasing aggregate of utility is accompanied by a decreasing aggregate of value. When any line of commodities affords its maximum of possible utility, there is no place for value. "Value is an expression of the niggardliness of nature; of resistance to be overcome; of the disparity between man's desires and his opportunities; of the necessity which rests upon him for sacrifice." (Section 34.) But while values tend to rise with greater scarcity, the maximum aggregate of value is not found at the very extreme of scarcity, but at some middle point, where the tendency toward increasing value from scarcity is overcome by decreasing demand consequent upon higher prices. This is readily illustrated from market movements; a short crop of wheat commonly sells for a greater price aggregate than an abundant crop.[1]

---

[1] There is one law of prices which you must know and understand before you can make the least progress in interpreting the simplest problem. It is known to some economists, I do not say all, for it is most unaccountably neglected or obscured in most treatises on the subject, as Gregory King's law. We take it a defect in the harvest may raise the price of corn in the following proportions : —

Defect:	Above the common rate:
1 tenth raises the price	3 tenths
2 " " "	8 "
3 " " "	16 "
4 " " "	28 "
5 " " "	45 "

The price of any article in demand, but at present in defect, rises in price

One billion bushels of wheat at forty cents per bushel command a lower price aggregate than eight hundred million bushels at sixty cents per bushel. It does not, however, follow that this increase may continue indefinitely with every decrease in the quantity of wheat for sale. The point of maximum price aggregate is dependent upon the volume of the demand for the commodity as affected by modifications in price. Food products furnish the best illustrations, and perhaps the only important ones, of increasing value aggregates following upon decreasing supplies.

143. It then becomes evident that, while the general welfare may thereby suffer, far-sighted individual or national policy may dictate that course of reduction of product which manifests itself in daily affairs in what are commonly termed "monopoly methods." The inducements to this course are indeed stronger than are indicated by the foregoing analysis. Assuming that the billion bushels of wheat sell for four hundred million dollars, and that this covers approximately the cost of production, the restriction to eight hundred million bushels, while increasing the selling price but from four hundred million dollars to four hundred and eighty million, would increase the producers' profits not only by the eighty millions increase in price, but by the saving in outlay accompanying the decrease in output. This course would be attractive enough even on terms of maintaining the displaced labourers and capital in idleness. But these productive energies are not lost; they profit the monopolistic company or nation in applications to other productive employments.

---

by a different ratio from that indicated by the ascertained amount of the deficiency; and *e converso*, the price of any article in demand, but at present in excess, falls in price by a different ratio from that indicated by the ascertained amount of the over-supply. The operation of the above law is always most dominant in articles of prime necessity, in which no notable economy can be made without suffering on the part of the people when supply is short, and no notable increase of consumption can be expected when the quantity is in excess of supply. If the article is relatively perishable, the phenomena increase in intensity on either side.
— THOROLD ROGERS, *Ec. Int. of Hist.*, p. 250.

Doubtless, the practical bearing of these principles upon the tariff policy of nations is not great. It falls out rarely that any people possesses an industry fulfilling in considerable degree these monopoly conditions. But where conditions of this sort exist, if they ever do exist, a protective tariff may be a practicable, almost an ideal, method of effecting a profitable readjustment of industrial energies. And doubtless these conditions do occasionally exist. The nitrate and guano industries in South America are probably examples; possibly, also, our cotton and copper interests may be placed within this class. With world-wide opportunities for agriculture and world-wide agricultural products, it is clear enough that our agricultural industries do not, for the most part, meet these requirements. It is, however, important that the case be based upon correct theory.

How does this apply to America?

But it is worthy of note in passing that while we may regard a protective tariff system as an almost ideal policy in the case assumed, it yet falls something short. Export duties would operate with equal effectiveness in foreign trade and commonly present fewer difficulties in practical administration. Not only this, but it is very possible that, under a protective tariff, profits of foreign trade in monopoly products should be more than counterbalanced by higher prices and wasted energies at home. No case of this sort could arise if the entire product of the industry in question were exported, or if the productive energies set out of employment could be applied in other branches of industry with not greatly diminished effectiveness. If, however, we assume 1000 units of productive energy, — say, for convenience, men, — to be employed in copper production with a daily output of 1000, of which 300 goes for export, and if we assume that the imposition of a tariff upon other products works a twenty-five per cent reduction in output of copper and a thirty per cent advance in price, and that the foreign and domestic consumption are affected proportionately, the question stands as follows: Domestic consumers will suffer in opportunities for consumption a loss of $700 \times .25 = 175$. Over against

Export duty a better method.

this, it is to be computed that the foreign export now commands a selling price of 225 × 1.30 = 292.5 in place of 300, and that 250 units of production have been set free for application to other branches of industry. If these 250 displaced units are capable of producing in their new employment more than 175 + 7.5 = 182.5 units of value, the tariff has made for profit, — otherwise for loss.

The fallacy which underlies all attempts at creation of home markets is indicated by this analysis, but space forbids elaboration.

II

144. The theoretical relations of import duties to the incidence of taxation require examination in this connection.

It is commonly asserted that tariff burdens are necessarily borne in the outcome by consumers. Since the tax adds itself to the cost of production, it is therefore asserted to add itself in its entirety to the selling price.

Does the foreigner pay the tax?

That this is commonly true in a rough fashion may be admitted; but that it is almost never completely true must also be admitted.

A rapid survey of the phenomena of rent will afford us helpful analogies. The rent-bearing capacity of any tract of land is measured by its differential of advantage over the lands called marginal; these marginal lands bear no rent; they are lands barely worth cultivating at the ruling level of prices if no rent is paid; a fall in price would therefore work the abandonment of these lands and the direction into other employments of the capital and labour thereto applied. Better lands, however, will continue in cultivation as long as some part of the differential termed rent still remains uncancelled. What lands shall remain in cultivation or what be abandoned is determined by the market prices obtainable for their products.

These reasonings apply with equal force to all other lines of production. Market values fix in every industry both the volume of demand and the volume of supply. As with agricultural products, so with all others: a rise in price does not imply that the entire demand volume is retired, nor does a fall in price close all the avenues of supply. Normal price is that price which is sufficient to maintain the normal volume of product. Put more accurately, normal price is the price which barely remunerates that portion of the normal production carried on under the most unfavourable conditions, — a price which scantily compensates the marginal producer, and which, if lowered, will direct his productive energies to other employments. For all producers other than those termed marginal there is a differential of advantage measured by the difference between what is received and that lower price which might be accepted without determining the producer to a different line of production. Likewise, for all purchasers other than marginal purchasers, there is a differential termed consumers' or purchasers' rent, — the difference between what is paid and that higher price which would be paid were the higher price imposed. Thus the distribution of any tax is determined by the point at which a new marginal alignment is made necessary, a new point of equation between demand and supply.

To illustrate: let it be assumed that there are upon the market for sale 26 units of any given commodity, the cost of production of these ranging by unit stages from 75 to 100, and that there are upon the market 26 purchasers disposed to buy each one unit of commodity, and to pay therefor, if necessary, prices ranging respectively from 100 to 125. Evidently, the price which will place demand and supply in equation is 100. Now, suppose a tax of 10 to be imposed. Assuming that the consumers must bear the entire burden, 10 of them will be excluded from the market and 26 of commodity will confront 16 of demand. If, on the contrary, the sellers were to bear the entire tax, the result would be 26 of demand to 16 of supply. The point of equilibrium is then at 105, five producers and five consumers being excluded from the market. Under the conditions assumed, the tax has divided itself equally between producers and consumers, and is paid in diminution of the quantities termed producers' and consumers' rents.

For ordinary cases this illustration greatly exaggerates the facts. The rent quantities are commonly of less considerable magnitude. Especially is it true that in industries other than agriculture producers' differentials are measured by narrow margins. But the principle holds and is theoretically important as bearing upon the distribution of taxes on imports. Some part of the tax is always paid at the expense of the producer. If a wide choice of markets is open to him, he pays but an inappreciable portion. If the industry is agricultural, where land rents largely enter, he is more readily and more considerably affected. Likewise, during the time that capital and labour are readjusting themselves to new conditions and redistributing themselves in new employments, a large tribute may be collected; and if his industry is one fulfilling monopoly conditions where the production outlays fall considerably within the market price, he may be made to bear permanently the entire weight of the tariff burden. (See Chapter XIV, Taxation.)

III

145. The argument for protection, based upon the desirability of stimulus to industries in their experimental stages, is not a novel one, and has long been admitted by free-traders to be theoretically valid. The difficulties incident to providing machinery and plant for a new industry, to establishing sources of supply for raw materials, to operating the plant with labour at first unskilled, to organizing market connections and attracting consumers' demand, are so great that, though the industry may ultimately demonstrate its practicability and profit-earning capacity, it may also never requite the pioneers for their exceptional outlay. These original projectors have no monopoly of the possible success, but only of the probable failure. In its most important bearings the experiment is of social rather than of individual interest, and during the period of experiment society may fairly be called upon to stand be-

Tariff as temporary stimulus.

hind, in some measure at least, as guarantor. On any other terms it is very possible that capable projectors will not undertake the experiment.

But on grounds of experience the advocates of free trade seem fairly to have turned the argument. To admit that the State may profitably interfere is far from admitting that the interference is commonly profitable. American and European history unite in convicting the State of exceeding stupidity in selecting the experiments in which it shall coöperate, — in indicating that the unsuccessful experiment commonly fails of abandonment when abandonment is due, and that the successful experiment commonly receives greater protection in nearly the proportion that it ought to receive less, — in short, that the system inaugurated to overcome the inertia and loss incident to planting a new industry, inevitably develops by the dark ways of politics into a persistent attempt to maintain in existence an energy-wasting failure, or into grotesque solicitude for industries grown vigorously independent. But the theory stands.

IV

146. It has been made a basis of attack upon the American tariff system, that the industries maintained by it are industries of exceptionally low wage-level, and that they are clustered in cities notorious as centers of lawlessness, poverty, and ignorance. The system with us does manifestly tend toward the increase of urban populations with whatever of political and social evil is associated therewith. This result, however, does not inhere of necessity in a protective system, but is due to our peculiar conditions. The direct effect of protection in England would be greatly to stimulate agricultural industries, and to relieve, in corresponding degree, the congested population centres. Nor is it true in America that the employés of the iron, cotton, and woollen interests are poor, unintelligent, and lawless, because of their employment in these industries, so much

Effects on distribution of population and wealth.

as that these industries require cheap labour, and this class of labourers supply it.

But admitting the evils which, from the point of view of health and morals, attach to the extension of the great manufacturing industries, there are important considerations in favour of these tendencies, as bearing upon the domestic distribution of the social dividend. Production may be helpfully viewed as a purchase, from nature, of utility at the price of effort. Upon the assumption of perfect competition, all productive energies are compensated by their full product. Employers and workmen constitute the human element in the aggregate of productive energies. Any cause which makes toward increased wages must be taken to make toward increased profits, since wages and profits are but different aspects of remuneration for human effort. Changes in relative compensations must direct employers into the ranks of labourers, or *vice versa*. Capital also is an indirect application of human energies to the purposes of production; whatever causes tend to increase the productiveness of labour, will, therefore, other things remaining equal, tend to the increased productivity of capital; in short, wages, interest, and profits tend to move in parallels. It is, therefore, not credible that tariff regulations should affect any one of these distributive shares permanently to the prejudice of another. Protection will not raise profits without at the same time working to the advantage of wage-earners; nor can interest be moved toward rise or fall without a sympathetic tendency becoming manifest in wages and profits.

We must, however, face the fact that rents commonly tend toward advance from the very causes which make toward fall in interest, wages, and profits. This is a corollary from the agricultural law of diminishing returns.

Peculiar effects on rents.

Increasing difficulty in procuring agricultural products means a diminishing social dividend, — a diminishing wage quotient. It at the same time means the cultivation of poorer land in response to the larger demand, and, therefore, for landlords, an increasing differential of advantage as measured from a lower margin of utility. If, then, we may conclude, as seemingly we may, that for a country circumstanced as is our own, protection, as judged by the test of maximum value product, is a distinct loss, it may yet remain true that this loss is more than offset by the advantages of a better distribution.

It is important to place the terms of our problem clearly before us; for this purpose the illustration used by Sidgwick in his *Principles* (Book 3, c. v) will serve us as the basis for our necessary analysis. Sidgwick assumes a case of a country occupied in both agricultural and manufacturing industries, and so thickly populated that additional agricultural production is impossible except at a rapidly increasing expense. Let it be supposed that this country, having been strictly protected in aid of its agricultural interests, now adopts free trade. What, then, are the manufacturing labourers thrown out of work by this change to do? Suppose the entire community of workers to be represented by 100, sixty of whom are employed in agriculture, forty in manufacturing, and that the value product (as it would fix itself under conditions of free international exchange) of the sixty is seventy units, of the forty, thirty units. With the advent of free trade, these forty manufacturing producers must find employment in agriculture, which, under the conditions assumed, affords a rapidly decreasing return. But, unless the fall in agricultural wages resulting from the inflow of some part of these forty labourers is so great as to permit the existence of the manufacturing industries on a free-trade schedule of wages, all the labourers must be employed in agriculture. Assume now that the forty increase in agricultural labourers results in but twenty increase in product, — Sidgwick would draw the following comparison: Under the protective system, the sixty agricultural labourers produce seventy units of value, while the forty labourers engaged in manufacturing produce but thirty units. This difference in actual production, as measured upon an international free-trade basis of values, has by assumption been overcome for distribution purposes by tariff adjustments. The aggregate production of the 100 labourers stands at 100 units of value with wages at the quotient of this value divided by the number of labourers. But under unrestricted world competition the manufacturing industries could not exist if wages stood at above $\frac{30}{40}$. Now, then, if the trade barriers are removed, the 100 labourers together occupied in agriculture produce an output of ninety. But free trade and a wage of $\frac{90}{100}$ will not permit the existence of manufacturing industries. Sidgwick therefore argues, that in some cases protection may conduce to a larger aggregate both of goods and of values than is possible under unrestricted trade. It may rightly be objected that conditions of this sort rarely, if ever, exist. Sidgwick, indeed, remarks with characteristic fairness: "The fear of such a result as that just described has undeniably been important among the motives that have operated on the side of protection; I think that the claim has usually been without much practical justification; but I think that it ought to be met, not by a fallacious general demonstration that the result cannot happen, but by a careful exposition of the reasons why it is not likely to happen in any particular case, to an extent that ought to influence a statesman's action." (Book 3, c. v.)

But on closer examination we shall find occasion to question the correctness of these reasonings. Our conclusions may make none the less strongly in favour of protection, but they cannot be the same conclusions. Insufficient attention to the relations between wages and rent has betrayed Sidgwick into a fallacy. The average wages of agricultural labourers are not measured by the quotient obtained in dividing the entire agricultural product by the number of labourers. Increasing rents are the correlative of decreasing returns in agriculture. Wages must be determined by the rate of productivity of the last increment of labour applied. Thus in the case assumed by Sidgwick, rents would increase with a rapidity corresponding to the rapidity of the decrease in agricultural returns; it is, therefore, misleading to compute at ninety divided by 100 the wage outcome of free trade in the above example. Wages in agriculture must fall to the level of the last increment in productiveness of the new supply of labour. This is clear enough when one reflects that on any other terms land-owners will refuse to hire more labour, or, accepting the last offer of labour, will discharge some labourers previously employed. The labourers, then, in the foregoing problem, will not, as directed by wages, forsake the manufacturing for the agricultural employments, except to the extent that the labour product in the new employment is greater than in the old. Whatever, then, should be the result upon the level of wages, it is clear that the social dividend would be increased by the removal of trade restrictions.

It is from the point of view of the distribution of the social dividend that the change to free trade would present undesirable features. Wages may fall despite an increased social product if only rents sufficiently advance. It is possible, for example, that the forty labourers displaced by free trade should find employment in agriculture, the social dividend then rising from seventy to something over one hundred, and yet that the increase in product due to the last increment of labour should permit a wage of but $\frac{75}{100}$.

We conclude, then, that the tendency of free trade, in a community whose productive advantages are mostly agricultural, must be toward an increase in rural rents and in rural land values, which might well overbalance the rise, under protection, of urban rents resulting from larger city populations. Where large supplies of unutilized or half-utilized land are in reserve, that is to say, where the law of decreasing returns is operative to an inappreciable degree, these theoretical reasonings have no important practical bearings; and even in the event that conditions of the sort to make the question one of practical importance should exist, the rational remedy for the case, as indicated by correct theory, would be found not in artificial readjustments of production and exchange, making inevitable a diminished social output, but in a system of progressive land taxation in which the increase in social product should profit society

Land taxation a better remedy.

in general rather than land-owners and landlords. Still, it is best first to master the theory.

ASPECTS AND ARGUMENTS IN TARIFF QUESTION

Infant Industry. — Correct in theory but inconsistent with permanent system argument; so abused in practice as to be bad; tends to fix itself permanently.

Diversified Industries. — Our industries sufficiently diversified anyway. In some cases a good argument from educational point of view. For us real question is one of economic profit.

Commercial Independence. — Peace and civilization furthered by interdependence. Division of labour as good for nations as for individuals.

Tax on Foreigners. — Temporary success. Consumers finally pay most of the tax — commonly not quite all. See Chapter on Taxation for full treatment.

To hurt Foreigners. — Trade helps both sides or there would be no trade.

To employ Labour. — Till there are no more unsatisfied needs there will be employment under either system. (Under which system are temporary derangements most likely?)

To offset Differences in Wages. — Need of protection proves low relative productiveness. General level raised only by increased social product. Wages cannot be increased by tariff at expense of interest or profits.

Ultimate Question, then, is
  Does Protection increase Social Product?
   Is the new industry more highly value-creating than the displaced industry? If so, why can it not without help pay the ruling wages? Higher cost of production means merely larger displacement of other products.
  Protection demoralizes Politics.

But under Monopoly Conditions protection may pay. Of one hundred apples better destroy fifty where fifty can be sold at three cents apiece than sell one hundred at one cent apiece.

Protection may, under unusual conditions, rest as a heavy tax on foreigners.

May work beneficially to modify distribution, but taxation would be a less wasteful method.

CHAPTER XIII

COMBINATION AND MONOPOLY

Why do manufacturers combine ?
Is this, in any sense, a result of competition ?
Could railroads do business more cheaply if there were fewer of them ? Would they lower their charges ? Would they make as many improvements ?

How many gas companies are there in your town or city ? Street railway companies ? Water companies ?

Why not more of each ? Would it be well to have more ? Would such a condition be permanent ?

Why does a short crop of wheat sell for more than an abundant crop ?

Can a factory employing 100 men undersell one employing 50 ? How about 400 as against 200 ? 1600 against 800 ? 2400 against 1200 ? 6400 against 3200 ? 26,000 against 13,000 ? Would these advantages ever be exhausted ?

147. Statements of economic laws assume for the most part the existence of competition. Their applications are definite and satisfactory nearly in proportion as this assumption conforms to the facts. It thus comes about that any incompleteness or failure of competition is a source of confusion in economic reasoning; the necessary allowances are found awkward to make. It has perhaps resulted that these breaches of economic analogy and simplicity have come to stand with economists in some measure of scientific and moral disfavour.

Any scheme of social organization which should exclude all phases of competition would seem to involve the loss of important advantages. Broadly defined, economic competition is a struggle for maximum economic rewards (minimum sacrifice). On the part of producers, it is an attempt to undersell each other, — to find a

Advantages of competition.

profitable way of offering more for less; on the part of buyers, it is an attempt to obtain most for least; speaking generally, it is a method by which each member of society gets most from society by rendering largest services. In outworking, it is a defective but automatic method of apportioning rewards to services, and in a secondary way, in some sort of rough approximation, a method of apportioning compensation to sacrifice. The apportionment is accurate only at the margins. In the absence of the ingenuity which competition has stimulated, the economic progress achieved by the race would hardly have been possible. Each producer, in his attempt to economize productive energies, has helped society to its present measure of economic comfort. Competition, always gravitating toward normal values, serves as a permanent indicator of the point of seemingly most profitable adjustment for all individual interests. (See Section 91.)

These advantages from competition are incontestable. No non-competitive scheme has yet offered an adequate substitute. Both for purposes of maximum production and of practicable distribution, competition seems to be essential.

This may all be granted, but it falls far short of justifying the doctrine of the economic harmonies. (See Sections 221, 222.) We may well believe the interests of society to be greatly subserved by the elastic energy and ingenious initiative which belong to individual interest, and which obtain their fullest manifestation in the competitive system; but we are not therefore compelled to admit that social interests are in every case subserved by the fullest play of individual interests. The interest of each is not always parallel to the interest of all. Even if the interest of each were always rightly understood by him, it would not always conform to the public interest; and if the individual not only goes wide of the social interest but of his own as well, there is not the less but the greater divergence between social and individual interests.

Evils of competition.

It does not strike the individual, for example, that he is greatly interested not to pollute the springs and streams below him. He is interested that a rule should exist against pollutions generally, and that other people should obey it, but not that he himself obey it. So, open and closed seasons for fishing and hunting are necessary for the aggregate good; but the better the laws are observed by others, the greater the advantage of each from violation. The very existence of monopolies rests upon the fact that while a large social product is for the aggregate good, a restriction of product in the special line of each producer is often of enormous advantage to him. So, again, it is for the comfort of the lucky possessor of four seats in the passenger coach that he lounge upon them all, while fellow-travellers stand; something like a government is necessary here in the presence of the conductor. Likewise it is well for the government, through a policeman, to stand at the street crossings and adjust the conflicting interests of foot-travellers and traffic; otherwise you and I could never get across the street. Almost all crimes against property illustrate the antagonism between the individual and the general good. One of the aims of socialism is to escape this clash of interests; perhaps, however, this is just where it will fail. How shall any one find strenuous effort to be for his own interest? If he produce twice as much, his share will be increased by one sixty-millionth, — no great matter. As a practical question, each will be interested simply that every one else work nimbly, while he himself takes things easily. It is hard, even in the small horizon of a school-room, for the individual to see that he must in his own interest guard the privileges and comforts of all.

While it is true that in competition there are strong tendencies toward economies in production, it is equally true that in some cases competition brings about great wastes. While it often results in improvement in the quality of the product or in reduction of prices, in other cases it results in the wasteful multiplication of retailers, in the dear cheapnesses of adulteration and "scamping," in the false pretences of advertising, in unjust, because imperfect, competitive divisions between employers and employed, in bad sanitation and bad hygiene for men and women, and in the moral, mental, and physical disasters of child labour.

If the individual's understanding of his own interest conformed at all times to the social interest, the need of laws would mostly cease. The doctrine of the economic harmonies runs close to anarchism. On the other hand, no purely socialistic scheme is justifiable, unless upon the assumption that there is no distinguishable and retainable balance of benefits in any of the tendencies of competition.

148. But some of the tendencies of competition seem destructive of its primary characteristics; for, from one point of view, **Competition sometimes destroys itself.** combination and monopoly are mere aspects of competition. It is a commonplace that the extension of the giant industry at the expense of the small is a competitive product; so of the tendency toward corporate organizations, — toward trusts, pools, monopolies, and the other forms of organized industrial combination. But these secondary aspects of competition differ in the degree in which they retain the primary competitive characteristics. In proportion as they fail of this, they become awkward of treatment to the economist and perplexing to the moralist and legislator.

There is nothing of especial seriousness in the mere organization of industry on a large scale, though considerable is to be said of its benefits — and dangers. But sufficient room remains for the competitive feature, in the rivalries of numerous producers; while, at the same time, organization seems possible to a sufficient extent to obtain all or nearly all of the possible economies in production. With some other of the different lines of industry (for example, with transportation industries and with industries in which expense consists largely of transportation outlays, as in the coal, oil, water, gas, and electric light industries), the maximum economies in production seem possible only on terms of exclusion of competition.

149. Now, it is evident that these resulting **What is the harm?** economies are not the sources of any considerable evil or perplexity; the awkwardness of the thing lies in the fact that, competition being excluded, it is

practically certain that society will get none of the advantages of these economies, but that, on the contrary, the low price possible to the monopoly will discourage all outside competition, and the monopoly be thereby enabled not only to reap the entire benefit of its possible economies, but to collect from society something over and above the price which would prevail under the full and wasteful action of competition. And not only is competition avoided by the superior advantages of the large combination, but it is also discouraged and destroyed by the method of cut-throat competition, — the trial of financial endurance in doing business at a loss. A discussion of possible remedies will come later. (Section 242.)

150. The theory of monopoly profits is a development from the theory of value. The normal competitive price is the price remuneratory to the highest continuing sacrifice in production. This price may be considerably lower than that possibly obtainable from some or all consumers, were such higher price imposed. With some commodities, a change in price does not greatly affect the disposition to consume. In these cases a considerable advance in price is possible, with no considerable reduction in sales, but with severe encroachment on that indefinite quantity indicated under the term "consumer's rent." It is the consumer's rent which the monopolist manipulates to appropriate. The extent of his operations will be limited at the outside by the point at which his increase in profit, by reason of increased price, approaches an equality with his decrease in profit on account of diminished sales. This adjustment is a separate problem for each industry; and the danger of attracting competition may fix a lower limit in price than the theoretical limit above indicated.

The theory of monopoly.

This monopoly principle finds frequent illustration. Fruit occasionally becomes so plentiful in the market as to sell for almost nothing. Half as much would sell for more. The price must go so low that all of the supply can find buyers. If the sellers could combine, it would be to their advantage to withdraw a half of the supply, and, if need were, let it rot. Again, one could hardly give away a hundred bananas to ten ordinary people for their own eating, yet could probably sell one-half or one-fourth as many at a very appreciable price. Not many decades ago an English company, having a monopoly of the spice trade, sunk a whole shipload of spices off the coast of England. These cases further illustrate that antagonism between utility and value already several times remarked.

151. The proposition that where combination is possible competition is impossible, would be approximately correct if changed to read that to the extent that combination is possible competition is impossible.

What are the limits?

But we are unable to determine the extent to which methods of combination may be applied. There are certain industries which seem rightly termed natural monopolies. Most or all of these depend to a peculiar degree on the use of natural opportunities or natural forces, or are intimately associated with the industries of transportation. To the degree that the sources of supply or the number of producers is limited, combination becomes more feasible and more dangerous. It is forcibly claimed that a large proportion of all such monopolies are legislation-made or legislation-permitted. To what degree, if at all, this is true will not be here discussed.

Those industries which manifest the tendency to increasing returns, offer inducements to combination to the extent only, that added economies are possible through constantly enlarging organization; further than this, combination cannot go, unless by force of cut-throat methods. The advantages of large organization in the *economies of production* appear to cease before the point of effective monopoly is reached.

152. Some attention must be given to combinations among purchasers. These are commonly more subject to competition and are less durable than producers' combinations; but, in theory, the analogies are close between the two.

Combinations among purchasers.

We have seen that, in the long average, price cannot fall below the marginal producer's sacrifice; it may remain above, though if perfect competition exists, this marginal sacrifice is to be regarded as indicating the normal price. If necessary, a large number of producers could afford to produce and sell at lower than the market price. It is evident, therefore, that by an actual agreement or tacit understanding among the purchasers in any given market, the price paid can be to a large extent controlled, to the positive loss of the marginal producer, and to a diminution of profits for all the producers above the margin. The buyers' combination is an attack on producers' rent, parallel to the attack, through sellers' combinations, upon consumers' rent. It is true that this buyers' combination must result in a restriction of the supply to the extent that the lower price discourages producers at or near the margin of sacrifice; but as to producers above the margin, the opportunity will still remain to the combination buyers — so long as the competition of new buyers does not intervene — of appropriating a considerable share of the producers' profits without any corresponding decrease in price to the consumer. Indeed, to the extent that the total supply in the consumers' market is diminished by the combination tactics of middlemen, market prices will tend toward advance, and a corresponding additional profit accrue to the operators; and if, as sometimes happens, these operators are at the same time in practical control of the selling market, the diminished expense of combination buying may be made the source of additional profit in combination selling.

It is asserted that the purchase of cereal products in rural markets illustrates the working of buyers' combinations, and that the meat-packing industries of the United States illustrate the cumulative effects of the double combination.

Suggestive Questions

In what degree can the large concern outdo the smaller in economies of production?

Is this equally true of the great farm or the great store?

Ought society to get the benefit of these economies?

What are the natural limits to the growth of giant industries?

May these limits be enlarged by trusts and combinations between different plants?

How much has cut-throat competition to do with this?

In what sense do you regard the law of increasing returns as a permanent fact in industry?

How does transportation open the way to the giant industry?

What benefits can you mention from competition?

How are honest manufacturers driven to doubtful methods?

Do you think it proper for the government to enforce regulations in regard to sanitation? child labour? adulteration? length of work day?

Under our form of government would this fall to the separate states or to the general government?

What bearing have protective tariffs on the ease of combination?

What is the harm in combination?

Could anything be done by taxation to obtain for society the benefit of cheaper processes, or to protect society from artificially high prices?

How about the justice of the thing?

Is it a moral wrong to attempt to wreck another's business by selling goods under cost? What should you say of an action for damages in this case?

Do you know of any instance of cut-throat competition? Who suffer? Who gain?

In case of street railways, city water works, gas works, electric light works, does the public suffer most from competition or from combination?

What do you think of city operation of these industries? City ownership and leasing? City taxation?

What effect do these industries have on city politics? What effect would come under city ownership?

What effect would national railways have on politics?

Is national ownership practicable while there is private ownership in land? What is the connection?

Do the same considerations apply to the telegraph or postal service?

To what extent do you regard railway discriminations as responsible for monopolies?

TRADES-UNIONS

In what senses are labourers' interests parallel with employers' interests?

In what sense adverse?

Is the labourers' contest a contest against capital? Is it an attempt to lower rates of interest?

Can anything be done by labour unions to lower rents?

Does the contest mostly concern wages as against interest, or wages as against profits?

In what degree are profits obtained by unfair treatment of individual workmen — by unwholesome or unsanitary conditions for work?
By labour of children and women?
By adulteration and lying?
From which of these do labourers suffer?
What can labour unions do in regard to each of these evils?

153. No attempt will be made here to discuss in full the practical advantages and disadvantages of labourers' combinations. Some ground exists for believing that such combinations tend, in many cases, to reduce the losses of friction between employers and employed, and to increase the productive efficiency of the average labourer. So far, at least, as this claim is well founded, labourers through unions can effect a permanent rise in compensations. *Trades-unions.* *Benefits from labor unions.*

Further effects of labourers' combinations, so far as they are successful, must be in the line of reductions of interest upon capital, or of the wages of management, or must be an addition to the prices paid by consumers. In the long run, labourers *in any particular industry* can limit the returns on capital and the profits of management only to the extent that they reduce investment in the particular line of industry in which the diminution takes place, which reduction must react unfavourably upon the labourers to more than a counterbalancing degree. But there is no sufficient reason for asserting that, if trades-unionism be general in industry, it may not in some degree reduce the proportion of interest to the whole industrial product, without any appreciable effect on the total productiveness of industry; but any balance of effects in this direction would probably be inconsiderable. *May interest be decreased?*

And it does not seem probable that the remunerations for the risks of business, or the profits of its speculative features, can be appreciably affected by labourers' combinations to the ultimate average advantage of the labourers. *How about pay for risk?*

Labourers can, then, as a whole, in no considerable degree

profit by combination (otherwise than as combination increases efficiency), except to the extent that employers and agriculturists are injured; nor can any particular class of labourers profit, except to the extent that other classes of labourers and employers and farmers are some or all of them injured.

Effects on purchasers.

So far as employers' profits are made up of the proceeds of oppression or of unjust treatment of labourers, combinations may be expected to prevent in some degree the employment of these methods, and to tend to a diminution of the profits therefrom; but, as we have already seen, competition alone cancels these profits for the benefit of the general consuming public, leaving to the employer a substantial profit therefrom to the extent only that his abilities are especially large in this direction. So far also as employers' profits are derived from the sale of a poor product at the price of a good one, labourers in combination can do something for themselves and much for society by refusing to be made parties to this waste and fraud. Here is a feature of trades-unionism that deserves development.

The wages of injustice.

Scamping.

154. Several conditions are essential to any considerable success in labourers' combinations. The combining labourers must exercise substantial control of the labour supply in any particular trade; it is also essential that the labour combination set some effective limit to its number, else wages must tend downward towards the outside level, to the extent that the supply expands. Again, the combination must control such a monopoly of the requisite skill that substitutes cannot be supplied from other trades or from the ranks of the unemployed, to an extent to defeat the organized action; and finally, the goods produced by the combined labourers must be of such sort that an advance in price will not materially reduce consumption or stimulate the use of substitutes. In point of fact, there are few industries of great importance in which there exists a working monopoly of skill; and where such monopoly does

Conditions of success.

exist, the consuming public protects itself, in some measure, by substituted consumption, or refuses to continue consumption at appreciably advanced prices.

Where the monopoly of skill does not exist, the difficulties in the way of effective combination are extreme. It is true that there is a kind of sympathy between trades, which in a considerable measure protects a labour combination from competition by workmen of other trades; but the competition of the unemployed is always uncompromising. It is from this arsenal that the employer derives his means of defence, as well as in other cases his weapons of oppression.

And it is to this problem of the unemployed that labour organizations must address themselves; for that matter, it is around this same problem, also, that are waged most of the uncomfortable economic and sociological controversies of the present time. The topics of socialism, anarchism, crime, prostitution, contagion of disease, charity administration, will suggest the bearings of the problem.

Suggestive Questions

If unskilled labourers all work, what determines their wages?

What effect from a combination which should raise the wages? Could as much product be sold? Could as many men be employed? What would the out-of-works do?

Is combination among unskilled labourers likely to be effective in raising wages? In protecting members from oppression by employers?

Inquire among employers, and see whether they find the labour unions a convenience in adjusting disputes. In avoiding disputes.

Is combination among employers possible for regulating wages? Probable?

Did the Chicago railroads practise it in 1894?

Would travellers and shippers ultimately get a benefit from these lower wages?

Do strikes commonly succeed? If not, does this prove the failure of strikes to benefit the workmen?

Does the armed peace of Europe tend to prevent war?

What do you think of government ownership of railroads from the wages aspect of the case?

Can skilled labour through combination get higher wages?

Must there be methods of excluding competition?

Is this desirable?

If as many men work for as long a time, can wages be changed?

If the number of workers or the length of the day be lessened, who suffer?

NOTES

In proportion, however, as the habits of the labourers, or the limitations of their intelligence or of their resources, operate as a bar to change of place or employment, the limit of the employers' possible gains through combination is obviously extended; since, supposing such change excluded, this limit would only be fixed, so far as the present supply of labour alone is concerned, by the amount of necessaries required to keep the labourers in fair working condition. — SIDGWICK, *Principles*, p. 341.

There is a second way in which employers' [or employés'] combinations react detrimentally upon wages. A curtailment of the production of a particular commodity means a lessened demand for labour within the group which produces it. A struggle between the groups to outdo each other in limiting production would mean, to the labourers, an effort on the part of each group to thrust labouring men into other groups. As the attempt becomes general, the result is a thrusting of labourers either into the reserve force of the unemployed, or into the one department in which combinations are impossible, namely, agriculture. The power of agricultural industry to absorb the working force excluded from other fields is becoming limited, and the army of the unemployed must receive an increasing proportion of them. — CLARK, *Phil. of Wealth*, p. 146.

CHAPTER XIV

TAXATION

The right of taxation has been called the essential fact of sovereignty; why?

What was the main difficulty with the Articles of Confederation?

What is the usual cause for revolution? How was it in American history?

Where does the food come from which the judge and the sheriff eat? The wool that they wear? Who pay for these ultimately?

In what sense are all taxes taxes on consumption?

What is a tax — not in terms of money but in terms of labour or product?

Why ought a good citizen to be willing to pay taxes? Does he get his money's worth? More? Is it a good investment?

Do you think even a poor government better than none? Mention the different ways in which the expenses of government return to us in services.

Discuss as to each of these suggested ways whether the rich man is more benefited than the poor man.

Ought the rich to pay more taxes than the poor? Why?

Should taxes be proportioned to wealth? Suppose A's wealth to be in a picture gallery; B's in unoccupied town lots; C's in a livery stable; D's in mortgages; E's in factories; F's in tenement houses; should taxation apply to all proportionately?

Ought taxes to be proportioned to income?

Should it matter that one has ten children to educate while another has none, or that one spends his income in charity and another in luxury or vice?

Should taxes rest especially on luxuries and vices?

Should taxes bear on that portion of one's income which goes into living expenses rather than on that which goes into savings and factories, or *vice versa?*

Do you regard the basis of taxation as in abilities or in benefits?

Who ultimately pays the taxes on a stock of goods? On imports? On factories? On machines? On mortgages? On wages? Incomes? Land rents?

Which is the better method, direct or indirect taxation? Mention different considerations.

Should churches pay taxes? Schools?

What moral right has society to compel the unwilling to contribute?

By what sort of taxes does the city get its revenue? The state? The nation?

Do you approve of inheritance taxes?

Should litigants pay all the expenses of court proceedings?

155. An exhaustive treatment of the problems of taxation belongs to the applications of economic science rather than to the science itself. The strictly theoretical bearings of the doctrines examined in the preceding pages are, however, of considerable importance to the theoretical aspects of taxation. But before entering upon an examination of these bearings, we are first concerned to notice that all questions of taxation are complicated in practice by constant considerations of justice on the one hand, and of expediency on the other. Government is interested to obtain its necessary revenues with the least possible injustice, and, as well, with the least possible friction. A rude sort of equity is doubtless attainable in the imposition of taxes consistently with the collection of necessary revenues, but neither close adherence to any principle of taxation nor strict consistency with any sort of ethical test is to be looked for in actual administration.

General considerations.

We shall, for immediate purposes, devote but small space to the definite moral rules proposed as guides in the imposition of taxes. The rule that taxation should be proportioned to wealth is defective unless modifications be made with reference to the sources of wealth or to the manner of employment. Money at interest, lands at rent, the ownership of a home and of a factory plant are not all safely to be reckoned for purposes of taxation in the same category. So, taxation proportioned to total income is defective, unless examination is made of the uses to which incomes are put. Expenditures for luxurious living, for the care of children, for the creation of capital, and for public education, are not safely included in the same classification.

For similar reasons, taxes proportioned to the quantity of consumption are objectionable as imposing relatively greater hardships upon the poor than upon the rich. Taxes upon surplus consumption are equally objectionable, as omitting from consideration that relation between benefits and burdens which should in some degree influence the collection of revenue. Again, taxation which apportions burdens to benefits, works great inequalities of sacrifice. An approximately perfect system would probably differ from present systems not in the application of any of the proposed rules to the exclusion of others, but in a more rational estimate of the relative importance of these rules.

For immediate purposes, however, we are concerned to examine only the ultimate incidence and secondary economic effects of taxation, leaving for later discussion the practical applications to be derived from our conclusions.

156. In Section 64 it was stated that some form of wage occupation furnishes for each economic actor that marginal type of activity from which for him the comparative profit of any other occupation may be measured, and to which, meeting elsewhere with no profit, he may betake himself. But the alternative, if one occupation is found unsatisfactory, *Tax shifts only through changed relation between demand and supply.*
is not of necessity wage-earning; there are many other lines of activity, any one of which may offer prospect of returns greater than the compensations possible in wage-earning; and there are important differences, also, in the wages obtainable in different lines of wage-earning. What we are concerned to note is that each economic actor follows the line of seemingly least sacrifice, and that whether the margin of difference between the chosen employment and some other employment be large or small, no change in direction of activity will be worked by taxation, unless the amount of the tax be sufficient to more

than cancel this margin of difference. It is commonly stated, and in most respects correctly, that a tax on land rents does **Taxes on rents and quasi-rents do not shift.** not distribute itself in higher prices of products. It is equally true — to the extent that taxation on wages or profits is taxation on that relative advantage of one line of employment over another which we have termed a quasi-rent — that such taxes do not tend to distribute themselves. It is, then, incorrect to assert that a tax on commodities increases the selling price of the commodities by the amount of the tax. Such taxes increase prices only to the extent that they increase the marginal sacrifices of production; they do not ordinarily work this increase to the amount of the entire tax.

Suppose, for illustration, that 50 hats are offered upon the market, the producers' sacrifices ranging by penny stages from 100 down to 51, inclusive, and that there are 50 seekers of hats upon the market, disposed, if necessary, to submit to sacrifices ranging by penny stages from 100 to 150, inclusive. Under these circumstances, prices will stand at one dollar for each hat. The imposition of a tax of 20 per hat will not raise the price from the old marginal sacrifice of 100 to 120, but from a new margin of 90 to 110. This results from the fact that, with almost all commodities, some part of the demand is retired by increase in price. There follows, also, a diminished supply through the retirement of those producers at or near the old margin of sacrifice. Prices adjust themselves to a compensation for the sacrifice at the new margin in which the tax necessarily finds place.

In other words, taxes on commodities, whether collected from the producers or from the consumers, are commonly paid in part from producers' and in part from consumers' rents. Where any tax will ultimately rest, and in what proportions, is a separate question for each commodity, and must rest on the conditions peculiar to the demand for it and the supply of it. Ordinarily the tax will be divided in its incidence between producers and consumers, resting, however, mostly upon consumers. Under monopoly conditions, or conditions approaching closely thereto, it is possible for the tax to rest mostly or entirely upon producers. (See Section 144.)

These cases illustrate the most important principle in the theory of taxation; namely, that a tax on rent of any sort cannot be shifted unless the tax is more than the rent, or unless by touching the margin where rent vanishes, a new marginal alignment at higher marginal sacrifice becomes necessary. Thus a tax on profits will remain where it is placed, to the extent that it is a tax on monopoly or on any sort of differential advantage of one line of production over any other, and will be shifted to the extent only that these relative advantages are overbalanced by the imposition of the tax. If taxation were so levied as to bear equally upon the relative advantages of different lines of activity, so that no rearrangement in the demand and supply of commodities and therefore no change in value should result, no shifting of the tax burden could take place. What is true of profits is true of wages. Unless the imposition of a tax upon wage-earners should result in the decrease of the products produced by wage-earners, either by inducing a change of labourers to other lines of activity, or by stimulating emigration, or by causing a diminution of birth-rate, or by pushing some portion of them across the death-line margin of subsistence, the tax would remain as placed.

157. It is not entirely clear that a tax on interest would have either the immediate or the final effect of diminishing savings. Certainly this diminution would not take place unless the net returns on loans were reduced; and even in such case, the necessity of larger accumulations for provident purposes might be of sufficient influence to overbalance any tendency toward lessened accumulations on account of lower rewards. *Taxes on interest.*

But it is clear that taxes upon interest cannot affect the interest rate otherwise than through a change in the quantity of loans offered and taken. To the extent that the tax is shifted to borrowers, and cannot be passed along from the borrower to third persons, there will result a diminution of the borrowing demand to correspond to the raised marginal sacrifice. To the extent that the tax remains upon the lender, there will be some tendency toward outflow of capital to other markets, and some disposition on the part of capitalists to utilize directly their own possessions. The new interest rate will mark the new point of adjustment between higher lenders' sacrifices and higher borrowers' sacrifices, — the point of intersection of two new lines of margin.

But it must not be assumed that because borrowers of capital have been compelled to share with lenders some part of the tax burden, the portion shifted to borrowers may not in turn be passed along by them in some part to other members of society. So far as the borrowers are the ultimate consumers of the borrowed wealth and its resulting utilities, we shall see that these borrowers will be unable to shift the tax; so far, however, as the borrowed capital is employed in placing commodities upon the market, a tax on interest is parallel to a tax on commodities, and will distribute itself in a similar manner.

To the extent that taxes are passed along to ultimate consumers, the tax will rest with these consumers, unless the commodity is one consumed in peculiarly large degree by particular classes of producers. In such case, the tax on the commodity will act as a tax on these particular branches of production, and will tend to work a rearrangement in the applications of productive energy. Such cases, however, are not common, nor are effects of this sort ordinarily of marked importance.

158. Income may, in any particular case, be made up solely from profits and wages, or from rents, or from interest, or it may be the aggregate of two or more of these elements. If, however, an income tax is so adjusted as not to modify the relative advantages of different forms of industry or of different lines of productive activity, no changes in values will follow the imposition of such a tax. Its burdens will not be shifted; it will in effect bear as a direct tax upon the total consumption of each receiver of income. This is usually the case with income taxes.

Income taxes.

159. We have now to note that every tax at its point of final incidence is of necessity a tax upon consumption. Taxes

on incomes and taxes on profits differ in this regard from taxes on specific commodities in this only, that taxes on profits and income tend to restrict consumption generally and cannot be avoided, while taxes on specific commodities do not in material degree tend to reduce the consumption of other commodities, and may in large degree be avoided. It is from this point of view that taxation of luxuries and vices especially recommends itself.

All taxes are consumption taxes. Luxuries and vices.

Taxes upon land rents are correctly said to rest where placed. But this proposition must not be understood to include taxes upon the value of improvements or upon the rents derived therefrom. Nor does it include taxes upon those consumable or destructible qualities of the soil which, under the new burden of the tax, are not profitably to be replaced when once consumed. A slowly working change in the applications of productive energies is certain to follow in a small degree the imposition of a land tax, if the tax touches land at the margin of production or touches improvements upon land. To this small degree the case is in strict parallel with that of taxes on commodities in general.

Improvements on land.

160. Finally, it must be observed that no tax is safe from further shifting until it has reached the point of consumption; that no tax is safe to rest in its entirety where placed, if by modifying the applications of productive energy it tends toward the disturbance of values; that general taxes on profits, rents, incomes, monopolies, or wages do not in general bring about this disturbance, and therefore do not in material degree interfere with those normal divisions and applications of productive energy which result in the greatest aggregate creation of utility. Such taxes are taxes on the general consumption of the contributor, and leave him free to arrange his consumption to the greatest personal utility. Taxes on specific commodities are in the comparison non-economic, excepting to the extent that the State may be expected to judge more wisely than the contributor as to what consumption is best for the contrib-

utor. And by this test, also, taxes on luxuries and vices are to be commended.

The tendencies indicated under the laws of increasing and diminishing returns, have some important bearings upon taxation. The law of diminishing returns may be restated as a tendency towards falling prices as production decreases. Thus, a tax upon products falling within this law will, if it reduce the entire consumption, increase the market price by less than the amount of the tax.

Increasing and decreasing returns as related to taxation.

On the other hand, the tax upon the production of those commodities which manifest a tendency towards increasing returns will increase the market price by more than the amount of the tax; that is to say, the marginal sacrifices of production irrespective of the tax will be increased.

161. The granting of bounties is a distribution of collected taxes. The process is not taxation, but its reverse. Nevertheless, the effects of such distribution are to be analyzed upon reasonings similar to those applicable to taxation.

The necessary result of any bounty is to modify the relative advantages of different lines of activity, and to this extent to compel a readjustment of values. We have seen that the burden of taxation is not entirely shifted to consumers; we shall also find that consumers are not able to monopolize the benefits of bounties, but must share them, in some measure, with producers. The hat illustration will again serve. If production and consumption have adjusted themselves at a price of 100, a bounty of 20 would admit 20 new producers to the market, on condition that with this increase of supply prices could be sustained at 100; but 20 more consumers must be found; these can only be found at a price of 80. But at 90 ten more can be found, and at 90 ten more producers can apply themselves to the production of hats. The bounty of 20 will thus have lowered the price by 10, and will have distributed its benefits equally between producers and consumers.

Bounties.

It is to be held in mind that, through this redistribution of productive energies, there has resulted a lessened production of other commodities, and thereby a diminished aggregate production of utility.

Suggestive Questions

Compare the tax bill with that of the grocer.
Ought the right to vote to depend in any way upon property or to be influenced by it ?
How does taxation differ from robbery ?
Why do anarchists object to taxation ?
What was Rousseau's theory of the social contract ?
Ought public funds to be used for Fourth of July celebrations ?
What is a poll tax ?
Are taxes better direct or indirect ?
Is it wise to assist private educational institutions with public funds?
Suppose A has $100,000 all invested in real estate mortgages, upon how much is he taxed ?
Can he shift this, in part, upon some one else ?
Suppose he himself owes $10,000 to the bank ; will this be deducted from the amount upon which he is taxed ?   Ought it ?
Suppose you own a farm worth $5000 and owe A $4000 toward the purchase price ; how much are you worth ?   On how much do you pay taxes, — $1000, $5000, $8000, or $9000 ?
Are all who are taxed citizens ?   Ought all to be ?
Are criminal courts of service to those who never have litigation ? How about civil courts ?
What harm in taxing the grain which makes the flour ?   Why better tax the flour ?
Is tariff taxation sufficiently near to the point of consumption ?   Is it economical of collection ?
Does it place unusual premiums on dishonesty ?
Does it bear in desirable proportions upon rich and poor ?
On what classes does taxation on whiskey or tobacco fall ?
Is this better than an income tax ?
On what classes does the income tax mostly fall ?
What should you say of the expediency of limiting taxation to two forms, — an income tax for the rich, a luxury and vice tax for both rich and poor ?
Would you add to this a land tax, or, more properly, a rent tax ?
Is an income tax best levied by measure of income received or of income expended ?
The French assess their income tax by measure of a few leading

indicia of the expenses of living, — rental value of house, amount of furniture, number of servants, etc. ; what do you say of this ?

Is it true that "tariff is a tax" ?

Is it true that the foreigner pays the import duty ?

Do producers or consumers pay charges of transportation ?

Do producers or consumers pay the profits of speculators ?

Do lenders or borrowers pay for the risk element in the loan ? Do consumers ultimately pay any part of this ?

Does a tax on land by the acre fall on landlords ? Tenants ? Consumers ?

Who would pay a percentage tax on rents ?

On whom does a tax on residence property fall ?

Where does a tax on a factory finally fall ? On mortgages ? On railroads ? On dividends ? On railroad stocks ?

What do you think of a succession tax (tax on inheritances) ?

Should taxation on incomes be progressive ?

Should taxation on public franchises be progressive ?

If a large amount of land were set aside for parks, etc., what effect would this have on the aggregate of rents ?

On prices of products ?

On profits of cultivators ?

Which would be the most considerable effect ?

Would producers' or consumers' rents suffer the most ?

NOTES

Some thinkers hold seriously that the burden of taxation ought to be as much as possible felt by those who bear it, in order that they may have the strongest possible motives for minimizing it; and perhaps in a very orderly and law-abiding and lightly-taxed community this might be desirable ; but in most actual societies the dangers arising from " ignorant impatience " of taxation are so much graver than any which "ignorant patience" would cause, that it should rather be a maxim of statesmanship to avoid if possible any species of tax that is particularly disliked by the persons on whom it falls, even if the dislike seems groundless and fanciful. — SIDGWICK, *Principles*, p. 565.

Neither excise or customs make a substantial revenue, unless they attack the consumption of the poor. — ROGERS, *Ec. Int. of Hist.*, p. 464.

A tax imposed on things that are partly esteemed as signs of wealth, and therefore of social status, *pro tanto* increases their utility in pro-

portion as it increases their exchange value ; so that the consumers do not lose what the government gains. And obviously taxes that reduce the consumption of commodities likely to be abused, such as alcoholic stimulants, tend to benefit consumers thus prevented from injuring themselves, and indirectly to increase production by diminishing the loss of efficiency caused by such production consumption.
— SIDGWICK, *Principles*, p. 580.

CHAPTER XV

CURRENCY

STANDARD OF DEFERRED PAYMENTS

162. It has already been made sufficiently clear that the borrowing of money is, in effect, the borrowing of the things which money will buy. Yet, as a matter of practice, all are familiar with the fact that when money is loaned the agreement commonly runs to pay back money. So, when property is sold on time, the terms are for payment later in money. One does not know what a house will be worth next year or the year after. At the time you sell your hay, for example, you know what it will exchange for of other things. If you are to be repaid at the end of a year, you want not an equal amount of hay, but an equivalent amount of purchasing power. Payment in hay would work out at under or over payment, accordingly as hay should become scarce or abundant, of high or low marginal utility. Yet, evidently, also, money fluctuates in purchasing power; that is to say, prices sometimes exhibit a general rise or fall. Money is, therefore, not a perfect standard of deferred payments, though it may seem to afford the closest practicable approximation thereto.

Credit relations commonly fixed in terms of money.

Before proceeding to a general discussion of currency questions, we are interested to inquire whether an ideal standard of deferred payments is either practically or theoretically possible; and, if so, to determine what commodity or method would afford this standard.

Suppose the question to arise with reference to the payment of a loan made forty years ago; would the theoretically proper payment be found in a number of days' work equal in quality and number to the days' work obtainable through the loaned money at the time the loan was made; or in a quantity of satisfactions equal to the satisfactions obtainable through the loan at the time of its making; or in a sacrifice of satisfactions by the payer equal to the sacrifice undergone by the lender at the time of the lending? If we have adopted sacrifice as the basis of value, are we not committed to the proposition that payment should be made in equal labour? *Long term relations examined.*

Estimating roughly, gold will buy now twice the merchandises which an equal amount of gold would buy forty years ago; it will buy only half the days' labour. To demand payment in sufficient gold to purchase labour equal in quantity and quality would be to demand double the original amount of gold. The gold having per dollar double the merchandise purchasing power, this manner of payment would amount to payment in quadrupled satisfactions.

But it is not so clear whether, in strict theory, payment should be by measure of equal goods or of equal sacrifices. Nor is this a mere play of words, though the distinction may seem an obscure one. In another form, the question is whether value or utility only shall be made the basis of payment. *Should payment be by utilities or by sacrifices?* We will assume, for example, that the $100 borrowed was sufficient to procure the satisfaction during a month of all the needs and desires commonly satisfied at the given time by the average man. It is conceivable enough that by reason of human development, or of discoveries and inventions, all the needs at that time satisfied by the average man should after forty years be satisfied almost as freely as if by the entire bounty of nature. That is to say, the means of satisfaction of the desires commonly satisfied at the earlier date may now bear almost no value. Payment in value, that is, payment measured in sacrifices, would mean payment in a vastly increased sum of satisfactions. Payment in an equal sum of satisfactions would mean payment in vastly decreased sacrifices of effort.

It appears to be true that the measure of payment should be found rather in the line of equality of utilities than of equality of efforts. But by the test of utilities, the problem is insoluble other than by loose approximations, since over long periods of time utilities offer no basis of comparison. Even were comparison possible, where food has remained, as in Europe, practically stationary in price, rents have risen and clothing fallen, and small luxuries and transportation have greatly fallen, — yet, in view of the fact that a host of commodities of luxury and convenience have come to exist which were not to be had at any price forty years ago, the essential unfitness of the problem for accurate solutions becomes manifest.

163. Yet, proceeding on the principle that an equality in satisfactions constitutes the ideal measure of payment, attempts have been made to outline a scheme for commodity payment which shall avoid the fluctuations in the purchasing power of money. Admitting the theoretical difficulties above examined, the case has yet seemed manageable for general purposes. Evidently no one commodity will do for a measure. It has therefore been suggested that a general average of prices should be taken at the time of borrowing and at the time of payment, and a sum of money equivalent to the borrowed sum in power over the general schedule of commodities be returned to the lender. This plan, however, has been rightly subjected to criticism, as giving in the reckoning equal importance to pepper with potatoes, and to mustard with meat. Only commodities in general use should be considered, and these should be given prominence as nearly as practicable in the proportions in which they are generally used. The outcome has been the scheme for deferred payments, called the multiple standard, — a method not intended to avoid the use of money as a means of payment, but to compute for purposes of justice the amount which, returned, would constitute a fair payment. It may be doubted whether the method will ever come into general use, or would prove entirely practicable if attempted; but the principle on which it proceeds has been accepted by most economists as

A commodity measure.

indicating an approximately ideal standard of deferred payments.

164. Some further modification seems, however, to be required; the commodity schedules must take account of human services rendered directly, that is, not incorporated in market commodities. The servant girl, the doctor, and the minister are important facts in our current expenditures. *Allowance made for services.* While it is true that gold commands a greatly increased sum of the commodity products of labour, it commands a smaller sum of labour itself. Human attentions, in the form of professional, artistic, or domestic services, have risen in value, as measured in money. Inasmuch, then, as every schedule of expenses is made up, in important degree, of outlays for singing, doctoring, teaching, and preaching, any multiple standard of deferred payments must take account of these items. We eat the broiling of our steak as truly as our steak.

165. Enough has been said to indicate the extreme perplexity of the question and the unsatisfactory nature of any possible solution. But there is a further element of difficulty, an element of great importance practically as well as theoretically. Our standard of living has changed. With increasing effectiveness of labour, human needs have expanded. That which was once relative comfort has become privation, — privation absolutely in view of higher standards of desire, — privation relatively in view of higher levels of comfort or luxury in society. *How as to changed standard of life?* The causes which have served to make greater consumption possible, have themselves made greater consumption necessary. Payment in an equal amount of control over the objects of human desire is not an adequate return for the earlier sacrifices. If even exchange of work would be over-payment, even exchange of utility would be under-payment. If on the one hand expanding desires and expanding powers of satisfaction are to be regarded as a human gain, on the other hand the possession of the desires without the power of satisfaction must be counted for a misfortune.

228   OUTLINES OF ECONOMIC THEORY

A just standard of payment would require that such return be made to the lender as should do equal service with that which he parted with, and as should command from the borrower a deduction from his satisfactions equal in importance to the addition obtained through the loan. That the creditor receive a volume of commodities — services included — merely equal to the volume loaned, would be enough, were the creditor substantially the same creditor in needs and requirements, — if, for example, the advance in labour effectiveness had taken place in a night, immediately after the loan was made and its proceeds consumed. The borrower in such case would find it possible by the application of a half day's energy to repay the loan which had required of the creditor a full day's labour. Yet the lender is in as desirable a case as if the advance in labour effectiveness had not taken place. Although the debtor has freed himself of fifty per cent of labour through sheer delay, he may rightly argue that this is no injustice to the creditor. All humanity, creditors included, share in the good fortune of higher labour efficiency. Mankind is fortunate in the fact that the application of a day's labour produces greater services. They are none the less greater services. The debtor rightly objects to rendering to the creditor greater benefits than were received. The obligation of equivalent benefits is admitted, — it is irrelevant that the labour requirement is lower. The creditor's industrial effectiveness has advanced as has the debtor's. The creditor may replace his original investment by one-half his original labour. Were the debtor now insolvent, the loss could be replaced on these terms. Ultimately speaking, things are not useful because they cost effort, but the effort is put forth because the things are useful. It was usefulness and not effort which the debtor borrowed; it was the product of effort and not effort which the creditor loaned. It is, then, in terms of usefulness that payment should be made. Labour is the producer of utility and not the measure of it.

Payment by utilities not sufficient.

166. But it must be remembered that by this very measure

of usefulness, payment must be made in something more than an equivalent command over commodities. The increased effectiveness of labour has brought about a higher level of consumption, — a raised standard of comfort and of life. This is a gain to such members of society as are able to attain to this new level; it is the reverse to those who fall short of it. A new need plus the ability to satisfy the need is an advance in well-being; without the ability, the need is a misfortune. The line, then, of compensation — of equality in sacrifice — must be found somewhere above equality in purchasing power, somewhere below equality in command over human effort. Something must be added to payment on account of the greater necessities of the lender; something, also, on account of greater requirements for the maintenance of social position and relative well-being. The point of fair adjustment is to be found where the direct gain from larger satisfactions is offset by the disadvantage of increased requirements and decreased command over social distinction.

Discussion of this question cannot profitably be carried farther at this point. Something will be said later, under the topic of Fashion, which may aid in estimating for theoretical purposes the relative importance of the two factors in this adjustment. Enough has already been said to indicate the difficulties, theoretical and practical, which lie behind the question of a standard of value intended to serve over wide intervals of space or time; enough, also, to discourage any disposition toward dogmatism in the premises. This discussion becomes of especial importance in what is known as the silver question.

Suggestive Questions

Have prices risen or fallen during the past twenty years? How about wheat? Dry goods? Meat? Machinery? Rates of transportation?

How about wages paid domestics?

Has the general average of consumption risen?

Do you think the increase of wealth in the world is a matter of congratulation in (*a*) health; (*b*) morals; (*c*) intelligence; (*d*) content?

How much of this increase in the value of life in (*a*) health; (*b*) morals; (*c*) happiness; (*d*) content, has come from increase in knowledge rather than from increased command over wealth?

MONEY GENERALLY

Why is value of gold more stable than that of coal or iron?
In what sense is the value of gold fixed by sacrifices of production? Is this a quick or a slow process?
In what sense can money be consumed?
What do you intend to do with the next money you get?
If a ten-dollar bill were given you on the condition that you should always keep it, would it be worth your while?
If a hundred-dollar bill were given you would this increase the total wealth of the world?
Would it increase your wealth?
Suppose each man's cash were increased by one hundred dollars, would this increase the wealth of the world?
If the money in the possession of each member of society were doubled, would this increase the wealth of any individual?
Do you suppose that after this doubling, each dollar would buy as much as before?
If there were no money, how would you go to work to buy a book? Would the bookseller be willing to take hay in payment?
Why would not iron make good money? Brass? Wheat? Cattle? Hay? Diamonds? Tobacco?
So far as we now see, in what important respects do gold and silver differ in characteristics from the above-named substances?
Is paper money useful otherwise than as money?
Mention some uses for gold and silver other than as money.
Mention some of the advantages of division of labour.

167. That the love of money is the root of all evil expresses in forcible, but inaccurate fashion, a general truth in life.

The root of all evil.
Cupidity in some of its forms is the root of endless evil. But people want not money, — they want the things which money will buy. Only people with diseased brains care for money as a thing in itself. When we speak of the love of money, we use a sort of shorthand expression for the love of the things in life which are

bought and sold. Money is the general form in which desires express themselves and temptations present themselves. The love of money for itself is a perversion of desire from the thing symbolized to the symbol. But human needs and desires are the source of all well-doing equally with all ill. If we wanted nothing, we should do nothing. The evil is in the improper direction and insufficient restraint of desires.

168. The function of money is analogous to that of tools; we do not desire these for themselves, but for the things they enable us to do; we do not desire labour for itself, but for the things which it produces; so money is helpful because it enables us easily and conveniently to make exchanges of goods. Barter would be an inconvenient and impracticable way of carrying on exchanges. The advantages of currency are best illustrated by assuming the absence of it. Suppose that A desires to exchange hats for boots; B has boots, but refuses to trade with A, because B himself wants not hats but flour. If it turns out that C, who has coats, wants neither boots nor hats but potatoes, the three men can do nothing with each other. A must hunt about until he finds some one who has boots and wants hats; B, some one who has flour and wants boots; C, some one who has potatoes and wants coats. And even if A finds a man having boots and wanting hats, it may be impossible to trade because of a difference in value between the desired quantity of boots and the desired quantity of hats. B and C may meet with similar difficulties. Jevons gives the following illustrations: "Some years since, Mademoiselle Zélie, a singer of the Théâtre Lyrique at Paris, made a professional tour round the world, and gave a concert in the Society Islands. In exchange for an air from *Norma* and a few other songs, she was to receive a third part of the receipts. When counted, her share was found to consist of three pigs, 23 turkeys, 44 chickens, 5000 cocoanuts, besides considerable quantities of bananas, lemons, and oranges. At the Halle in Paris, as the prima donna remarked, this amount of livestock and vegetables might have brought 4000 francs, which would

What use does money serve?

have been good remuneration for five songs. In the Society Islands, however, pieces of money were very scarce, and, as Mademoiselle could not consume any considerable portion of the receipts herself, it became necessary, in the meantime, to feed the pigs and poultry with the fruit. . . . When Mr. Wallace was travelling in the Malay Archipelago, he seems to have suffered rather from the scarcity than the superabundance of provisions. In his most interesting account of his travels, he tells us that in some of the islands where there was no proper currency, he could not procure supplies for dinner without a special bargain, and much chaffering upon each occasion. If a vendor of fish or other coveted eatables did not meet with the sort of exchange desired, he would pass on, and Mr. Wallace and his party had to go without their dinner. It therefore became very desirable to keep on hand a supply of articles, such as knives, pieces of cloth, arrack, or sago cakes to multiply the chance that one or other article would suit the itinerant merchant." (*Money and Exchange*, p. 1.)

If trading were impossible, each of us would have to produce everything which he consumed. We should be Jacks at all trades, masters of none. Under the opportunities of exchange, individuals and nations follow the lines of their greatest ability and advantage, and exchange their surplus in product for the surplus of others. Thus the aggregate social product is increased, and thereby the individual share — the quotient — is enlarged. Currency facilitates this specialization of labour, commonly termed division of labour, by facilitating exchanges. Whenever we trade, it is because the thing which we get we value more highly than the thing which we part with. Money, or more accurately currency, is a means of transportation as truly as are railroads and steamships.

169. It is important to understand what qualities are essential in any material used for money. Primarily the money commodity must be adapted to the needs of ordinary cash exchanges; great purchasing power must be contained in small bulk; all specimens must be of equal quality; division and combination must be

<small>The necessary qualities.</small>

possible without loss of value; the value must not be so great as to render the medium over minute for small transactions. Hay would be too bulky and too variable in quality; diamonds too valuable, too variable, and incapable of subdivision and recombination without great loss. The pin and needle business would not flourish with diamonds for money. Any material which should answer these requirements would serve acceptably as a medium of exchange, were it not for the fact that exchanges are sometimes a long while in completing themselves. When you sell your hats you may not want immediately to purchase their equivalent; possibly you do not yet know what you will purchase, or, if you know, you are not yet in want of the thing. Thus the money which you get must be something which will not fall in purchasing power by reason of chemical changes or by reason of fluctuations in supply. Your money is a note of demand payable by society in market products. Wheat and hay would deteriorate in quality, and are at one time in flood and at another in famine.

170. Again, while not so clearly, yet ultimately as truly, all cases of mortgages, notes and bonds, bank deposits, and credits in general are protracted instances of exchange. The wholesaler sells his groceries at three months' time. Instead of receiving his pay immediately in commodities or in money with which to buy commodities, the payment side of the trade is postponed for a term of months. It is important, then, that the medium of exchange shall be of stable character in purchasing power. When you loan, you really sell the right to things; when you are repaid, you get things in return. Thus a loan is, in essence, a long-time barter. When you have sold your hats, you allow X to take the money for which they sell. It is the same as if you had sold X the hats or the goods which he buys with the money. When he pays you, he really returns to you your remuneration for the hats. If the payment is a fair one, the money in which he pays you must not have gained or lost in its control over the means of satisfying

Credit is protracted exchange.

human needs. Thus, money has to serve not only as a medium of quick exchanges, but as a standard of deferred payments — a means of effecting exchanges requiring long periods of time for their completion.

Gold and silver approximate most nearly of all commodities to these requirements. Neither is greatly subject to rust, decay, or chemical action. Both are absolutely uniform in quality wherever found, and are subject, without loss of value, to division and combination. Both comprise large value in small bulk. Not only this, but the annual product of each is so small in proportion to the entire supply, that rapid fluctuations in value from supply causes are impossible. An amount of water which, poured into a wash-tub, will make things lively, will not greatly affect the shore line of a lake. Small tempests work great commotions in teapots.

Currency has, then, three distinct functions: that (1) of facilitating ordinary exchanges; (2) of serving as a measure of value in current business; (3) of affording a standard of deferred payments or reservoir of savings.

171. It may be admitted that no sort of currency, as we know it, serves as a perfect appliance for any one of these purposes. In the last chapter were examined the difficulties which seem to inhere in any currency in its deferred-payment function. Ordinary exchanges and measurings of value seem to be approximately well served by most forms of currency, in so far as these two functions do not shade off into the deferred-payment function. Even with a noticeably fluctuating medium, the day-to-day business of society could be satisfactorily performed, if it were not for the fact that the very necessity of following the day-to-day method would of itself introduce into business serious inconveniences. It has already been pointed out that the man who sells a hat for silver is not in all cases inclined to an immediate use of the intermediate commodity received; and if this intermediate commodity be one of fluctuating value, the speculative features involved in its retention may exercise an effectively deterrent influence upon the question of sale. If the sale of

Fluctuation important mostly in credit relations.

CURRENCY 235

the hat is a credit sale, the features of speculation and uncertainty become still more considerable.

It is thus evident that for cash transactions, as well as for transactions involving deferred payments, it is important that a currency shall be, as far as possible, free from liability to fluctuation.

172. We have seen that the utility of currency lies, for the most part, in its service in facilitating exchanges; in fact, its function as a standard of deferred payments is merely one aspect of its service as an exchange medium. Its service as a measure of value — a common denominator for trade — is incidental to its use as an exchange medium. There is, then, as truly a demand for money as for any other commodity. The demand for a medium of exchange is approximately measured by the volume of exchanges to be made. We say approximately, since barter is always possible, though ordinarily not of considerable volume. *Measure function subordinate to exchange function.*

Clearly enough there would be no necessity for money and no demand for it, if each of us were to produce everything that he consumed. It is equally obvious that division of labour becomes possible only on terms of possible exchange of product. It now becomes important to note that, population and per capita production remaining the same, the volume of exchanges increases as division of labour is more extended; that the aggregate of exchanges is approximately limited by the degree in which division of labour is extended; and that, therefore, the advantages of exchange are exhausted, when no further economies in production are promised by an increased division of labour. *Demand limited by division of labour.*

173. But population and per capita productiveness do not remain stationary; the population of the earth is rapidly increasing; the development, also, of the sciences and arts, and of machinery and transportation, not only stimulates the division of labour, the specialization of industry, but increases the per capita produc- *Demand is increasing.*

tion of commodities. The ends of the earth now trade with each other.

It ought, then, to be clear that the need for currency is not proportionate to population alone, or to wealth, or even to per capita productiveness alone. It is the volume of exchanging to be performed which furnishes the measure of the demand for currency. This is largely a matter of degree of civilization and manner of industrial organization. In a general way, the per capita requirement for currency is enlarging. No amount can be said to be required per capita simply, but only per capita in view of the average productive efficiency and the established industrial methods. A sufficient per capita for one country may be entirely inadequate for another.

174. The argument of the preceding chapter suggests that the sufficiency of the money supply may, however, be approximately determined by a careful examination of the tendency of prices. The value of the currency unit, the dollar or franc or pound, is determined by the relation between the demand for currency and the supply of currency. To this extent, there is nothing difficult or peculiar in currency principles. If the demand increases without correspondingly increasing supply, money rises, that is, prices fall. So, increases in supply tend toward higher prices, that is, toward depreciation in the purchasing power of the money unit. If the relation between demand and supply changes, the value of the unit changes to correspond. A permanently insufficient currency is therefore an impossibility; prices must fall until at the new unit value the supply is sufficient. So, if the currency is redundant, prices rise until the redundancy is cancelled. Currency is like a gas which always fills its receptacle. A currency out of equilibrium is always in process of becoming sufficient. But this process of becoming is rarely a comfortable one, and is always attended with injustice, and commonly with disaster, as will be more clearly seen in our examination of commercial crises. These fluctuations in prices are to be avoided if possible; it is by this test, then, that the normal supply of money is best determined. A supply

Prices test the sufficiency of supply.

sufficient in kind and quantity to maintain a price equilibrium, services considered, would be the ideal condition for all ordinary cases.

Suggestive Questions

Explain analogy between exchange and transportation.
Outline inconveniences of doing business without a medium of exchange.
Show that a sale for money is only half of an exchange of goods.
Show that a loan and repayment of money really equal an exchange of commodities.
What forces are working to increase the demand for a circulating medium?
As far as you can see, is gold alone, or are gold and silver together, increasing in volume with a rapidity corresponding to the demand?
If not, what strikes you as a necessary result?
What will happen if currency is in excess? Is insufficient?
Who are injured when prices rise?
Who when prices fall?

CHAPTER XVI

VALUE OF CURRENCY — HOW FIXED

What effect would falling prices have on the production of gold?
Would this result probably be sufficient fully to overcome the tendency toward fall in prices?
What effect would an increased output of gold at the mines tend to have?
Suppose the output of this year to be double that of last year, would this double prices?
Have you any gold about your person?
Is it in the form of money? In what forms?
Suppose the total supply of gold were doubled, would this double the amount used as money? Why not?
What effect would more plentiful gold have on its use for non-currency purposes?
Would this effect be sufficient entirely to prevent a rise in prices?

175. Assuming, however, that the social importance of the currency system in its function of economizing human energies, not only by removing obstructions to the division of labour, but as well by simplifying every transaction of exchange, is well understood, and assuming the peculiar adaptation of silver and gold for these purposes to be evident, it yet remains to question how the value of this measure medium itself gets established, and gets modified after establishment.

It is not difficult to see how a rise in the exchange value of the exchange medium is limited, if only there exist sources of **Value when new supply is possible.** new supply. The rise takes place to the extent only that the marginal sacrifice in production becomes greater. If the amount of gold for which a hat will exchange is less than the amount of gold which could be produced by the work which produced the hat, gold will be produced until an equilibrium is reached. The statement therefore holds, that the value of the circulating medium is fixed by the marginal cost (sacrifice) of production, if the medium is one the sources of supply of which are not closed.

But it does not yet appear how such a rise takes place in the value of the circulating medium as to induce further production at higher marginal sacrifices; nor does it yet appear what limit, if any, may be set to this rise if further production is not possible.

No especial difficulty presents itself with commodity currency so long as the currency value does not depart appreciably from what the value of the commodity would be, were it not employed for exchange purposes. Its market value, resulting from the adjustment of the demand for it, by virtue of its utility in consumption, to the supply of it, fixes approximately the value when employed for intermediate purposes. It is easy to see that with an increasing demand for purposes of consumption, any commodity, the product of an extractive industry, may be expected to rise in price through a rise in the marginal sacrifice in production. But it is not so clear why the demand for any commodity for intermediate purposes should tend to raise the value beyond the normal value for ultimate non-intermediate purposes. How does commodity as currency come to be worth more than commodity as commodity? How worth more for buying things than it is worth for use?

<small>What causes rise in value of money?</small>

176. An examination of the sources of demand for gold becomes necessary. Gold serves human desires not only in one, but in many ways,— for ornament, and for industrial, scientific, medicinal, and mechanical purposes. There are few, if any, commodities which afford but one mode of service. Almost every object of value is a bundle of utilities, generally, though not necessarily, bound together by a material basis. If the supply of gold were sufficiently restricted, gold might rise to a value corresponding to the highest utility of any part of it for any purpose. So, if for any reason a large

part of the supply of gold were subtracted from the ultimate use market, gold would undergo a marked rise in value, still not departing from its value as registered by its marginal utility for ultimate uses. But how does it come about that the use of currency is of such urgency or advantage to any particular individual as to effect, at an increased value, this withdrawal of gold from ordinary uses?

This difficulty will be better illustrated by supposing the sources of production of gold to be cut off, and by inquiring what would be the possible limit, if any, to a rise in value, and whether any ground exists for believing that a rise in value would, of necessity, be limited to the highest utility of gold for non-intermediate purposes (ultimate uses). Repeated experiences with paper currencies would seem to indicate that utility for purposes of consumption and utility for purposes of currency exhibit no necessary interrelation, and that, were the supply of gold for currency sufficiently limited, the exchange value of gold as used for currency might rise indefinitely beyond any possible margin of utility for ultimate uses. What, then, is the limit, if there is any limit?

Suppose the supply to be cut off.

177. The classic solution of this question is in substance as follows: Currency is of great social utility; it is a tool in exchange as useful for its purpose as are any other of the tools of industry for their purposes. The amount of exchanging to be performed furnishes at once the measure of the demand for currency and the measure of its utility. No more is needed than enough; prices must so adjust themselves that the volume of business to be transacted can be cared for with the existing volume of currency. The point of equilibrium between the demand for currency and the supply of it is the exchange value of currency.

Usual statement.

178. This is correct enough, but there seems something yet to be said: social utility and social demand must be translated into individual interests and personal demands, before market adjustments become intelligible. Social utilities and social demands are not known in the

Supplemented.

VALUE OF CURRENCY 241

markets, — "Every transaction in commerce is an independent transaction."

All economic activity is directed to ultimate consumption. Division of labour takes place, because, for each individual, the greatest total of satisfactions seems obtainable by this method. A produces shoes, because, by this course, he can get more cloth than by producing cloth. Each exchange by him of shoes for some other commodity affords for him, in some degree, that advantage commonly designated under the term "producer's rent." Something analogous to producer's rent is expected to accrue to each of the parties in any case of barter. Each has bought something and each sold something. Each has obtained something of greater utility to himself than that which he has parted with, and something which, if produced by himself, would have required from him greater sacrifice.

When a trade does not take place, it is because, for one or both of the parties, the utility of that which is offered is believed to be less than the utility of that which is in hand. If A, for what he possesses, refuses all offers of trade, it is because, to his notion, that which he has surpasses in utility anything offered for it.

179. The strenuous demand for currency, therefore, finds its explanation — its motive — in the rent elements hidden in every transaction of trade. The currency received will buy for the seller that which is of greater utility to him than the property sold. *Quasi-rents are the force.* When the volume of currency is insufficient for the needs of business, unless on terms of lower prices, these producers' and consumers' rents are the force which pushes money values up, — that is, prices down. There is no limit to the possible rise in the value of money excepting at the point of equilibrium, wherever found, between the volume of exchanges seeking fulfilment and the volume of currency. The rapidity of fluctuation, whether in rise or fall, is mostly unimportant, unless it becomes so marked as to cancel in considerable degree these rent quantities.

180. The process of market adjustment by which these

fluctuations take place is as follows: Assume a certain number of currency units with an established purchasing power for each unit. A, whose only possessions for sale consist of shoes, can acquire currency only to the extent that he sells shoes. If he obtain in any way more of these currency units than he is disposed to retain for purposes of later use, he becomes an offerer of currency on the market. His offer is the indication of his desire for commodities in place of currency. If, at the same time, the volume of currency in the hands of other men generally is also greater, in view of the purchasing power of the unit, than is their need or disposition to hold, the offers of commodities will be insufficient to absorb, at the current purchasing power of the unit, the currency offered. A, or some man in a similar case, will be able to obtain commodities only on terms of making concessions. The purchasing power of the unit will then tend toward fall, until an equilibrium is established between offered currency and offered commodities. If, on the other hand, the offerings of commodities are such, compared with the currency seeking investment in commodities, that concessions by commodity possessors are necessary in order to effect exchanges, the purchasing power of the currency unit will tend toward rise. If sources of currency supply are open, this rise will tend to induce an increased production of the currency commodity. If there are no available sources of supply, the rise will continue till, partly by the increase in the exchange value of the unit and partly by decrease in the number of the units withheld for future purposes from the market, — each separate unit having acquired a higher purchasing power, — the volume of currency becomes sufficient for the volume of exchanges.

The mode of adjustment.

We should, then, expect it to be true that times of unusual financial stringency and falling prices are for the industries of precious metal production times of unusual prosperity. That the facts lend support to theory may be seen from the statistics of gold production beginning with 1888 and covering the panic years up to 1895.

1888....110 millions of dollars.		1892... 146 millions of dollars.	
1889....123 " "		1893....157 " "	
1890....120 " "		1894....172 " "	
1891....131 " "		1895....200 " "	

Discoveries of new fields — *e.g.* in South Africa — have co-operated in this increase.

181. There is a further fact which adds to the intensity of the rent motive behind the demand for currency. Currency is the most exchangeable, the most generally desired, of all commodities. For this reason one dollar of it is commonly more desirable than one dollar's worth of any one of all the commodities for which it can be exchanged. This is because the receiver of currency has commonly no definite idea of the thing in kind or quantity into which he will ultimately convert his currency; his number of different options is, in itself, an element of desirability.   *The option feature.*

The importance of this option feature is generally not sufficiently recognized. Currency is received in its aspect of general purchasing power, the question of application being ordinarily left to the future. The length of time which elapses between receipt and outlay depends in part upon the character of the individual and his peculiar circumstances, in part upon the industrial and financial conditions of the times. The disposition toward early outlay is at one time especially marked, while at another time the relative advantages of delay are highly esteemed and even exaggerated. This feature of currency will later become of interest in our examination of commercial crises.

182. Note, also, that the advantages of exchange are possible to the individual only to the extent that he has both the desire and the opportunity to turn the goods in his control into other goods. Those things which he prefers to part with upon the terms of the market form but a small portion of his belongings. Thus only a small part of the wealth of the world stands at any given time as demand for currency. The reasons   *Does quantity of wealth measure demand for currency?*

which determined the buyer to buy are, for the larger part of his possessions, reasons which also determine him to retain. The advantages possible to him at any one time through exchange are readily exhausted. His demand for currency is measured by those goods simply which he wishes to exchange for others. So much currency as he has in hand measures his demand, present *or future*, for market commodities.

183. We are now in position to discuss rapidity of circulation. It is commonly stated that increased rapidity of circulation works in parallel manner with an increased volume of currency, thus resulting in a lower exchange value for each currency unit. But obviously in the absence of credit sales, all exchanges would be either barter or cash transactions. An increased rapidity of circulation would in such case mean simply an increased frequency of exchanges, a shorter average period of retention between the time of the receipt of currency and the time of outlay. From this point of view, greater rapidity of circulation is not a cause but an effect of expanding inclination toward trade. Only to the extent that longer average periods of retention make toward a rising power of purchase in the currency unit, and thereby tend to discourage and retire offers of merchandise upon or near the margin, can rapidity of circulation, or lack of it, be regarded in the light of cause rather than of effect.

Rapidity of circulation.

The same reasonings apply to circulating credit.

Suggestive Questions

Would falling prices stop all selling ? Why not ?
What is the ultimate basis of the demand for currency ?
What tendencies make for an increase in the demand for currency ?
Explain how this works out to raise the value of gold.
Is it conceivable that the currency demand for gold should become so acute as to exclude all other uses ?
If other nations should adopt gold as their money, what effect on the value of gold ?
On the production of gold ?
If all nations should demonetize gold, what effect on the value of gold ?

On the production of it?
Would these effects be permanent?
When would the production of gold again reëstablish itself? At what mines first?
Make an estimate of how long the full reëstablishment would take.
What effect on the commodity consumption of gold?
In what sense does cost of production fix the value of gold?
Is this process of quick or slow accomplishment? Why?
If no more gold could be found, what would fix its market value in the future?
What would limit its possible rise in value?

DIFFERENT KINDS OF CURRENCY

First National Bank, Charles City (Iowa), 1894

Loans and discounts .	$237,600 40	Capital stock paid in .	$50,000 00
Overdrafts	385 36		
U. S. bonds to secure circulation . . .	12,500 00	Surplus fund . . .	10,000 00
Due from other National Banks . . .	32,713 04	Undivided profits less current expenses and taxes paid . .	16,533 70
Furniture and fixtures,	1,000 00		
Due from State Banks and bankers . . .	782 52	National Bank notes outstanding . . .	5,760 00
Due from approved reserve agents . . .	24,888 90		
Checks and other cash items	1,649 79	Individual deposits .	255,887 94
Bills of other National Banks	7,972 00		
Fractional currency .	93 63		
Specie	10,035 50		
Legal tender notes .	8,000 00		
Redemption fund with U. S. Treasurer .	562 50		
Total	$338,181 64	Total	$338,181 64

The foregoing is the report of a typical country bank in the fall of 1894. A careful analysis should be made of this report. Notice that the bank has of capital, surplus funds, and undivided profits, about $76,000 invested, and has with it upon deposit $255,887.94.

SUGGESTIVE QUESTIONS

Show what has become of these moneys.
How much in notes or overdrafts is due the bank from borrowers?
How much has been loaned to other banks by way of deposits?
How much may this bank be called upon to pay on any day?
What are its immediate resources for this purpose?
How much cash has it on hand?
How much of this is gold or silver?
How much of its resources are in the form of demand rights against other banks?
What has the bank, in fact, to show for this depositors' money?
Do you know what the item "circulation" means?
How are national bank notes secured?
In what payable?
Get one of these notes and see what the bank agrees to do.
Is it probable that all depositors will call for their money at one time?
What would happen if they did?
Would there be much profit in banking if for every dollar left at the bank the bank must keep a dollar on hand?

(The student should re-read Sections 102-104.)

184. Attention must now be directed to the fact that the circulating medium is composed of different elements. The *Money and currency distinguished.* student may have been puzzled by the use in one place of the term "money" and in another of the term "currency." Money and currency are not equivalent terms. Currency includes all forms of exchange media; money is but one form of currency. We speak of coin, greenbacks, and the like as money. But the *The rôle of credit.* larger part of business is transacted through credit substitutes for these, — through drafts, bills of exchange, negotiable notes, and the check and bookkeeping devices of deposit banking. In their origin, it is probably true that all currencies were composed solely of commodities with a well-defined utility for other than currency purposes. But with the development of society, the use of substitutes has increased. The bank customer thinks of his deposit in the bank as money, and it really serves him all the purposes of money. It was explained in Section 104 how the right to have the money when desired is as good as the actual possession of it, and is as readily and as serviceably transferred. When the bank customer wants to pay a bill he checks against his account. The receiver of the check places it in the bank and gets credit for it, the drawer is charged with it, and the transaction is finished, no money having been transferred. These deposit accounts in banks commonly aggregate several times the cash resources of the banks. These cash resources also are largely made up of deposit claims against other banks. London, for example, is the clearing centre not only for a large part of the business of England, but also for a considerable portion of the business of the world. International interest payments and the transactions of foreign exchange are effected by drafts on London. Balances between London banks are settled, not in money, but in checks and bookkeeping at the Bank of England. It results that the enormous business of the London banks, aggregating daily hundreds of millions of dollars, requires the transfer of only a fraction of one per cent in money. It becomes intelligible that the English people are able to handle their business affairs upon less than twenty dollars per capita of money, while France employs over forty dollars per capita, though at the same time doing a much smaller per capita of business. In fact, one rarely comes across a bank in French cities — deposit banking is almost unpractised, checks unknown in ordinary affairs, and the Paris clearing-house, the only one in France, itself scantily patronized. Working people keep their salaries in their pockets; peasants their savings in their stockings; and each merchant serves as his own banker.

185. Not only have business men invented methods of convenience in doing business which in effect are creations of currency, but governments and banking institutions have made large issues of forms of money known as greenbacks, bank-notes, and the like. These forms _{Government issues.}

of paper money will, for most purposes of discussion, be included within the term "fiat money," although the name applies with accuracy only to irredeemable legal tender government issues. We have seen that all these substitute forms of currency perform the functions of bullion currency — coin — in effecting exchanges, and therefore operate in this respect as **Measure function remains with currency of ultimate payment.** would an actual increase in the supply of the commodity used as money. Note however with especial care that credit currency cannot serve as a measure of value. Nor in fact does any fiat currency preserving an actual redeemability in the money commodity serve as a value measure. The measure function rests with those forms of currency only, in which liquidation is ultimately to be made, or in which payment may be enforced.

186. The value of the basal commodity, or commodities, may be seriously depressed by so large a use of substitutes as to set free from currency uses a considerable portion of the currency commodity. The effect on the market value of the commodity from the use of substitutes is like that of a new supply of the commodity itself. A fall in value becomes necessary if a market is to be found for all. So, a sharp rise may be caused at any time by the concentration of currency demand upon the currency commodity, to the exclusion in a large degree of substitutes. But it still remains true that, however fluctuating may be the measure of value, this measure is furnished by the basal commodity. This principle will, however, be made clearer in the succeeding discussion.

Suggestive Questions

When a merchant deposits in the bank, say $1000, is all of this usually in actual money? In what else?

Suppose you have $1000 to your credit — on deposit as it is called — at the bank, is this money really there?

How much is at the bank to answer for your $1000?

When you wanted to pay a bill, would you probably draw money or make a check?

How could the merchant make the check serve him as money without ever seeing the real money for it?

What is a clearing-house?

CHAPTER XVII

GRESHAM'S LAW

The Cheaper Money Displaces the Dearer

187. Gold serves human purposes not in one, but in many ways. Thus, if the supply of it is increased for any reason, the increase will divide itself among many uses. A part only will go to increase the volume of currency. Likewise, were gold the basal and only commodity used for currency, and were the entire increase in the supply of it coined as money, a share of this increase would flow out from currency into purely commodity uses. This result would come about from the fact that any increase in the volume of currency units must be attended by a corresponding fall in the purchasing power of the unit, this purchasing power being determined by the relation between the number of units and the volume of exchanges to be effected. Double the currency, and it will require two units to purchase what one would purchase before. In view of this tendency to fall, a considerable part of the coined gold becomes more desirable for commodity uses than for purchasing commodities.

The proposition then holds for gold, as for any other form of currency, that doubling the volume halves the purchasing power; but it is to be remembered that to coin gold is not necessarily to fix it in currency uses. Not all of the gold forced into currency is safe to stay there. Coinage of gold sets other gold free. Inflow causes outflow — though, as we shall see, not an equivalent outflow. But, however great may be the entire gold output necessary in order finally to double the currency volume, when once the doubling has taken place the value of the unit must have fallen to correspond. This, of course, assumes that gold is the only currency aside from credit, and assumes, as well, what will later be proved, that the volume of credit, relatively to other currency, tends to preserve a constant proportion thereto, irrespective of the amount of such other currency. (Section 212.)

It is worth remarking, that increases in the volume of coined money do not in fact come about by deliberate attempts at inflation; inflation of a freely coined metal is indeed almost a paradox. The supply of gold for currency is drawn from the general market supply, both coin and commodity uses expanding naturally and simultaneously with expanding supplies of metal. But were it otherwise, — were the entire product first coined as money, — the result would be the same. As gold flowed in, other gold would flow out, only a share of the increase continuing to serve as currency.

In later pages we shall have occasion to note that in case an increase of currency, for example by increased gold production, takes its beginning in any one country, the first effect is an increase in the local volume of currency, necessarily attended by a rise in prices. Imports tend toward increase, and gold goes abroad for payment purely as an industrial product, though possibly drawn mostly from the volume of circulating coin. In the country of its destination, the effects are those which we have just examined as characteristic of all increases in the volume of currency.

Suggestive Questions

Suppose the government to issue a large sum of legal tender paper money, would this make a dollar easier to get?

What effect, then, on the amount of commodities which a dollar would purchase?

Can you have a money in which getting is easier, that is, in which you sell at higher prices, without also paying higher prices when you buy?

What effect would a decrease in the exchange power of gold as money have on its use as plate and gilding and ornament?

Suppose your gold would get you a high-grade bicycle or would make into a gold watchcase ; how if the gold fell so that your choice lay between a second-grade wheel and the gold watchcase ?

GRESHAM'S LAW — *Continued*

188. Because of the power given under the law to fiat currency, equally with the basal commodity, of discharging indebtedness, of serving as a liquidator of credit, currency of this sort is to be conceived for most purposes as a portion of the commodity currency. So long as the fiat issue contains of itself a number of units insufficient at the established purchasing power to supply the needs of exchange, the currency commodity will in some measure circulate side by side with the fiat units, and the fiat units and the commodity units will be of equal value. (Proof of this proposition must be postponed to later pages. Sections 193–202.) But it is to be noted that the displacement in any degree of commodity units by fiat units is possible only upon parallel terms with displacements by credit substitutes. Some part of the commodity currency becomes superfluous as currency, unless accompanied by a depreciation of the unit; the unit therefore depreciates till the demand for non-currency uses has effected a new adjustment of values — the value of the fiat units remaining equal to the value of the commodity units, but the value of the commodity units falling on account of the larger supply at hand for non-currency purposes.

<small>Effects of fiat money.</small>

Put in this fashion the foregoing statement is not readily intelligible. The case is one of that class where a force sets into action partially counteracting tendencies. There is the old example of water pouring from one receptacle into another and coming to a stop, in part from the lowering of the level in the first receptacle, in part from the rising level in the other. So one may stop selling hats, in part from the approach toward exhaustion in his own supply, in part from the constantly greater difficulty in finding a profitable market. So, in our currency case, assume that we start with a billion of coin units, and that now a billion of fiat units be added. The value of the unit must be halved if all the coin units remain in the currency. But at any appreciable fall, coin flows out into industrial uses in response to the larger demand made possible by lowered values. The tendency toward fall, as coin, is in some measure counteracted by the absorption of the bullion for industrial uses. Yet some fall must have taken place in order to attract the larger market demand. The fiat issues have operated in effect as would an increased supply of bullion. Bullion as money and bullion as market commodity have both fallen, and fiat units, being in value merely representative of commodity units, have necessarily followed in the fall.

We may then say that any expansion of the currency, whether by fiat or credit additions, tends, other things being equal, to the depreciation of the unit. Should the fiat issue contain of itself more than sufficient units to supply the demand for exchange purposes, the commodity units would be entirely displaced from the currency by fiat units, and the value of the fiat units would adjust itself by depreciation to the demand. This is an application of Gresham's law that the cheaper money displaces the dearer, or, as it is more commonly put, that bad money chases good.

SUGGESTIVE QUESTIONS

Would an increased use of silver as money set free any gold for commodity uses? Why?

How would the value of gold as commodity be affected?

How would its purchasing power as money be affected?

Would its purchasing power as money fall unless its value as commodity fell also? Why?

Is the purchasing power of gold as money given to it by the fact that it is stamped by the government?

Does its purchasing power result in any degree from the fact that it is used as money?

May its use as money be effective in this regard though the government stamp is not effective?

Is it true that the stamped coin is worth exactly the value of its contained bullion?

If the stamp does no more than certify the weight and fineness, who pays for the stamping?

What is seigniorage?

GRESHAM'S LAW — *Continued*

189. All displacements of currency by fiat or credit substitutes must, as we have just seen, result in depreciation in the purchasing power of the unit — or prevent appreciation — even if the displacement be incomplete, and commodity units and fiat or credit units continue to circulate side by side at equality of purchasing power. It is only by way of depreciation as currency that an outflow of commodity units from currency uses becomes possible. This outflow tends to counteract the depreciation of the commodity as currency, but makes toward depreciation of the commodity as commodity. The outflow continues until the value of the commodity as currency equals the value of the commodity as commodity. So, while it is true that a cheaper currency displaces a dearer, it is not true that for every cheaper unit supplied there is the displacement of a better unit. The usual statement of Gresham's law requires qualification in this respect. If the currency commodity is one the demand for which, for non-currency uses, would be largely expanded by a very slight fall in value, it will result that the number of cheaper units supplied will be nearly equalled by the number of dearer units displaced. If, on the other hand, the utility of the commodity for other than currency purposes is slight, or the demand for it inelastic, the displacement will be small relatively to the number of new units supplied, and the depreciation of the currency unit will be relatively great.

Does unit displace unit?

Here, again, illustration is necessary.

Suppose, in the first instance, that the original currency contains no marketable elements, that it is, for example, all fiat. Doubling the amount will simply halve the value of the unit; if, on the other hand, the original currency is of such a character that any very slight fall will open up a large market demand, the issue of the fiat currency will push nearly the entire body of commodity units into non-currency uses. Almost as many commodity units will be displaced as there were fiat units injected, and the value of the unit will therefore have changed but in slight degree.

Our proposition stands then as follows: The larger and wider the non-currency demand for the currency commodity, the smaller the price fluctuations from fiat additions or from the discovery of new sources of supply.

The use of algebraic processes in the determination of this point of new adjustment will be found helpful as illustrating the operation of this currency law. For this purpose there must be assumed a definite and uniform rate of elasticity in the commodity demand and in the demand for currency — the volume of business to be transacted must be taken as a constant. Let this volume be represented by 1000. Any increase or decrease in the number of currency units must then be offset by a corresponding decrease or increase in the purchasing power of the unit — the total efficiency of the currency never varying from this 1000. The number of units before the expansion takes place must, therefore, be taken to be, for example, 1000 in gold. Assume now that 100 fiat units are issued, and that the industrial demand for gold is capable of absorbing new marketings of it on terms of a fall of one per cent for each 25 units thrown upon the market. It is required to determine how many gold units will be displaced from the currency by this issue of 100 fiat units. Evidently, since the value of the units must depreciate, there must be enough more of them so that the new value multiplied by the new quantity will give 1000 exchange power.

$1000 =$ Currency requirement (demand for business).

$1000 =$ Original volume.

$100 =$ Fiat issue.

$x =$ Net increase in volume.

$1000 + x =$ Total as increased.

25 of gold sold on the market causes 1 per cent fall.

1 of gold sold on the market causes $\frac{1}{25}$ fall $= \frac{1}{2500}$.

$100 - x =$ amount of gold displaced from currency (marketed).

(1) $$1 - \frac{100 - x}{2500} = \text{new unit value.}$$
$$\left(1000 + x\right)\left(1 - \frac{100 - x}{2500}\right) = 1000.$$
$$\left(1000 + x\right)\left(\frac{2400 + x}{2500}\right) = 1000.$$
$$2{,}400{,}000 + 3400x + x^2 = 2{,}500{,}000.$$
$$x^2 + 3400x = 100{,}000.$$
$$x^2 + 3400x + (1700)^2 = 100{,}000 + (1700)^2.$$
$$x + 1700 = \sqrt{100{,}000 + 2{,}890{,}000}.$$
$$x + 1700 = 1729.16.$$
$$x = 29.16.$$

(1) $$1 - \frac{100 - x}{2500} = \frac{2400 + x}{2500}.$$
$$\frac{2400 + x}{2500} = .971664, \text{ new unit value.}$$
$$.971664 \times 1029.16 = 909.99+.$$

The student will do well to set himself new problems for solution, changing the conditions.

CHAPTER XVIII

INTERNATIONAL TRADE AND CURRENCY

If by an increase in the volume of currency prices are raised, what effect will this have on imports? On exports?

If we were to expand our currency by greenbacks or silver, what effect would this have on exports? Imports? Our holdings of gold? Foreign holdings of gold?

If we exported but did not import, what effect on the volume of our currency? On prices here? On prices abroad?

190. But the foregoing is only one of the applications of Gresham's law. Thus far we have failed to allow for differences in the monetary systems of different countries. Our discussion has proceeded upon the tacit assumption that the world's currency is homogeneous, and that fiat or credit expansions in one country exert no peculiar influence at the point of expansion. And in large degree it is true that the great commercial nations of the world form one commercial community and employ one established international currency. But it is true, also, that in each country there exists a considerable volume of currency which is not of international character, but is a substitute therefor, and is adapted to domestic circulation only. Balances in international trade must be settled in the international currency commodity. If in any country for any reason there comes about a level of prices higher **Expansion and balance of trade.** than rules in other countries, there must result both a lessened exportation of merchandise and an increased importation. A resulting adverse balance of trade necessitates a shipment of the international currency. It is evident, then, that the tendency indicated in Gresham's law may

manifest itself in two ways, — first, by retirement of the currency commodity for domestic non-currency uses; second, by export to other countries. The domestic retirement is caused directly by depreciation of the currency unit. The foreign outflow follows an adverse balance of trade resulting from a raised level of domestic prices. It is worth calling to mind in this place that stocks and securities of international standing take in some measure the place of gold or commodities in filling adverse balances.

Let it be supposed, in illustration of international movements of currency, that the money circulation of the United States is 1,500,000,000, and that of Europe 10,000,000,000, which figures are probably not far from correct. Suppose, also, our billion and a half of money to be all of international character, namely, gold. If, now, an attempt be made to double our money volume by the issue of a billion and a half of fiat units, it is evident that prices must by appreciation adapt themselves to the level made possible by a larger volume of currency. This rise in prices must discourage exports and stimulate imports. That which was formerly sold for 90 in Europe and 100 here, now being worth say 110 here, would be more largely imported; what was formerly at 90 here and 100 in Europe, now being worth 100 here, would cease to be exported. So long as our gold continued to circulate as money, the unfavourable trade balance would be settled in exported gold. When international prices had reached their new level, the case would stand as follows: the aggregate currency of Europe and America would have increased from 11,500,000,000 to 13,000,000,000; a general advance of 11.3 per cent in prices would have taken place; our currency would have increased from 1,500,000,000 to 1,500,000,000 × 1.113 = 1,669,500,000, — 169,500,000 of this being gold, and the remainder of the gold having left to swell the circulation of Europe.

An issue of two billions of fiat by us would give the following outcome:

All our gold would have departed for Europe.

Rise in prices in Europe of 15%.

Our need for money on this new gold basis, 1,725,000,000.
Our actual circulation, 2,000,000,000.
Gold at premium of 15.9%.
Rise in prices as reckoned in paper money, 33%.

191. And there is a third manner in which Gresham's law may make itself manifest. If the commodity added to domestic currency is itself the subject of international trade, but is not a commodity used for international currency, there will ordinarily occur, in case of a favourable balance of trade, an inflow of the substitute commodity, while adverse balances must be settled in the international commodity. This inflow of the commodity used as a local substitute is evidently not possible in cases where the local substitute cannot be procured from foreign sources, as, for example, fiat or local credit substitutes (greenbacks, bank-notes, checks, etc.).

192. Bearing in mind that if the volume of currency at any point is in excess relatively to established prices and the needs of business, this excess must, if the currency contain a commodity element, tend toward disappearance either for domestic non-currency uses or for foreign export, the futility and danger of any local effort toward an increased currency becomes evident. Attempts of this sort can attain their purpose only in proportion as the currency of the world is expanded, unless the currency of the nation attempting expansion loses the total of its commodity elements — *e.g.* gold — and becomes entirely a non-international currency — *e.g.* fiat.

The futility of local attempts at inflation.

We shall shortly consider the bearing of this fact upon the question of silver coinage. It is also important to note the argument as it touches the protective tariff question. Until this stage of the currency discussion was reached, it was impossible to develop what is, in fact, an altogether unanswerable argument against the protective tariff system, so far as it is directed towards selling without buying. The meaning of the economic axiom should be now clear that selling depends on buying, and that imports and exports tend to offset each other.

INTERNATIONAL TRADE AND CURRENCY

SUGGESTIVE QUESTIONS

What tendencies would arise to put an end to an export of gold resulting from higher prices?

What effect would foreign prices feel?

How is it true that nations cannot buy unless they sell? Or sell unless they buy?

What has this to do with the tariff question?

Is it true of nations that division of labour is possible only on terms of possible exchange of products?

Give the different workings of Gresham's law; do you yet see any bearing on the silver question?

In commodity currency where does supply come from?

What would measure value if the legislature fixed the supply, for example in paper?

Would paper or commodity currency best adapt itself to demand?

Suppose the portion of the pyramid above the line to represent that portion of the commodity used as currency; below the line the commodity uses outside of currency; in which case would changes in supply work the larger change in the value of the currency unit?

CHAPTER XIX

IRREDEEMABLE CURRENCY

Would paper money be good for anything if all the money were paper: (*a*) If the government promised to pay? (*b*) If the paper were merely made legal tender?
Can value be given to anything by legislative enactment?
Would any demand exist for legal tender irredeemable paper? For what purpose?
If it could be made to perform the functions of money, would it have utility?
If also the supply were limited, could it have value?
What are the requisites of value?
Is there any intrinsic value?

193. That government issues of paper money may be made to circulate and to perform the money function is a familiar fact in business affairs. The American people are accustomed to many different forms of paper money; there is probably no modern nation of considerable size and importance which has not, directly through the government, or indirectly by imperial or private banks, made large use of paper currencies. National bank notes circulate in the United States to the amount of about 200,000,000 dollars, — one-eighth part of our entire money circulation. There were in circulation October 1, 1894, over 260,000,000 of greenbacks, United States promises to pay. The gold coin in circulation at the same date was 500,000,000. Under our present financial system, all forms of paper money are redeemable in gold, either by legal enactment or pursuant to the established policy of the government. Not only is it an important matter theoretically, but it is a question of acute

Paper currency a familiar fact.

political interest to determine whether paper currencies circulate solely by reason of their redeemability, or may circulate without redeemability, and only by virtue of their legal tender power. Note that we are not, at present, set to examine into the expediency of irredeemable paper issues, but only into their theoretical possibility. One large political party asserts that money is of government creation, that the national stamp and the legal tender attribute are the only essentials, and that it is both possible and desirable that the government should furnish from its printing presses the circulating medium. The reply is commonly to characterize these proposals as nonsense, — as attempts at a miracle. The following words from Comptroller Eckels summarize the views of most conservative financiers: "Embedded in the minds of many of our people is the illusive theory that something can be created out of nothing, — and that governments are invested with a power denied to individuals, of making that something out of nothing." Mr. Lyman Gage states the position tersely, as follows: "There is, in truth, only one real money, — metallic coin." *[margin: What makes them circulate?]*

If, however, irredeemable paper currency is possible and the inflationists are right thus far, we need to remember that it is an exceedingly dangerous thing to attack an error where it is strong. There is no evidence like this of the tenability of associated untruths. It is important not to deny too much.

194. We have already had occasion to condemn the notion of intrinsic value. Utility is merely the power of satisfying a human need. Utility is applicability, appropriateness. Whatever serves a human requirement bears value if limited in quantity. The currency need is for an exchange medium. That which serves this need has utility, socially and individually, and lacks no essential of value, if at the same time it is scarce. Utility can be added to anything if the power to serve can be attached to it. There is, then, nothing formidable in the miracle argument pure and simple. The real question remains, however, none the less difficult. *[margin: Intrinsic value is nonsense.]*

It is important that the argument up to this point be clearly understood. The value of the circulating medium, like the value of all other subjects of exchange, is primarily dependent upon the equation of demand and supply, and is only secondarily dependent on sacrifices of production as bearing on the supply factor in the equation. If production is impossible or exceeds in sacrifice the conditions of demand, costs or sacrifices of production are irrelevant. The volume of currency remaining constant, currency values fluctuate with fluctuations in demand. Demand is not measured by the total volume of wealth or commodities, but by the volume seeking change into currency, whether as a step toward an immediate exchange of commodities, or as an effort to obtain currency for purposes of hoarding, or for the purpose of effecting a liquidation of liabilities. The advantages accruing to exchangers, the quantities termed producers' and consumers' rents, are the motive force behind the demand for currency. The demand is made up (1) by the offer of goods against currency by way of immediate sale, or (2) by promise of future goods against present currency (future sale), or (3) by offer of future currency against present currency (borrowing). Appreciation or depreciation, whether believed to be temporary or permanent, can affect this demand volume only to the extent that the sellers' rent is believed thereby to be cancelled and the advantages of exchange therefore destroyed.

Summary.

195. Our foregoing discussions of fiat and credit factors in the currency have proceeded upon the assumption that the introduction of these factors will not seriously modify the demand for circulating media. The correctness of this assumption must now be examined. For this purpose we shall consider separately the different elements which make up the demand for currency — (1) for purposes of immediate reëxchange into commodities; (2) for purposes of retention awaiting a later application; (3) for purposes of debt liquidation; (4) in some small degree, for purposes of holding for so long a time as to merit the name of hoarding.

Would fiat inflation retire the demand for currency?

The demand for hoarding is commonly inconsiderable in modern societies on account of the facilities for loaning at rates of interest which are in themselves an object. The demand for purposes of mediate or immediate exchange cannot be diminished, unless the aggregate social product is lessened, or division of labour is rendered less complete, or in some degree a return to the system of barter takes place. The demand for purposes of debt liquidation is not constant in volume, but is certain to exist as long as indebtedness continues to be created. *for hoarding?*

It is unquestionable that disturbances from currency causes are possible in industry to such a degree as seriously to lessen the aggregate social production. This condition of disturbed exchanges must, however, if long continued, ultimately result in an industrial order characterized by a smaller sum of exchanges; in other words, there must result a less division of labour or an increase of barter. There is certainly no sufficient reason to believe that permanent inactivity for any part of the industrial system would follow a change in currency methods. The disadvantages of barter already outlined are so great as to make it altogether improbable that society would or could, in large degree and permanently, revert to that system. Nor could a permanent decrease in division of labour be expected. Producers' (sellers') and consumers' (purchasers') rents are quantities of such importance that some form of currency is certain to circulate, even if of a most fluctuating and unsatisfactory character. If a demand for fiat currency may be assumed to have once existed, there is no fact other than changes in legislation which would give to fiat currency an extremely fluctuating character. And it seems clear that if any sort of currency exists, the advantages of division of labour cannot for the aggregate of society be lessened. *Would not cause decrease of product or increase of barter.*

It is, however, possible that so great liability to fluctuation should characterize any form of currency, or so great distrust of it should exist, as very seriously to decrease the demand for short- *Fiats not likely to be used as standard of deferred payment.*

time holdings or for hoarding, and, to a still greater degree, to limit its use as a standard of value for deferred payments.

196. We may profitably resume our conclusions up to this point. The use of a suspected or fluctuating currency will not permanently influence the organization of industry in the direction of a less extended division of labour, or of a more extended system of barter or of lower productive activity. Some form of currency, public or private, bullion or fiat, will circulate to an extent to permit of exchanges. But we have as yet seen no reason to believe that some form of private or bullion currency might not be adopted in place of fiat issues. So far as hoarding and loaning are concerned, fiat issues would probably not be employed. But the every-day business of exchange and the holding of currency for short periods would not be interfered with by fiat currency, if only it should circulate at all at any value, and the fluctuations from day to day were so small as to be unimportant.

<small>Intermediate summary.</small>

What course any people would take with reference to depreciated fiat issues, *if depreciation should occur*, is conjectural. California held to payments in gold during the years when gold was at a premium; the gold measure was commonly agreed upon for deferred payments. But our inquiry is merely whether an irredeemable issue would of necessity suffer depreciation.

<small>If depreciation occurs, fiats may be excluded from general business.</small>

197. There is no *a priori* method of determining how large an issue, if any, of fiat currency could be made without apprehensions arising, sufficient to induce the use of some sort of commodity currency as a standard of deferred payments. But until credit methods ceased, or commodity payments were generally agreed upon, fiat currency would circulate. That credit operations should cease is improbable, if not out of the question. A commodity standard of deferred payments would, however, almost certainly appear if depreciation of the fiat issues had set in, and might appear in any case.

<small>Credits will continue with fiats excluded as standard of payment.</small>

But the mere fact that a commodity currency was adopted for deferred payments would not necessitate a depreciation of the fiat currency units relatively to the commodity units. So long as the number of fiat units remained insufficient at the established purchasing power of the unit to supply the demand for currency, so long commodity units would circulate.

198. But would the fiat units preserve their parity with the commodity units? It has been assumed that the mere fact that some commodity units remained in circulation would maintain the parity of the legal tender paper issues. Evidently enough depreciation would accompany the entire disappearance of the commodity units in the degree that the issue of fiat currency was excessive. But so long as commodity units remained in circulation, would the power given to the fiat units equally with the commodity units of discharging indebtedness preserve the market parity?

Is it not possible, or even probable, that the fiat units would be refused at a parity in daily trade, as we have admitted that they might be excluded from use for hoarding or for deferred payment purposes? If the circulating quality of fiat currency depends solely upon its debt-discharging power, how make certain that debts would continue to be created, unless upon provision for commodity payment? In short, how make certain that the demand for fiat currency would maintain itself? Certainly as a psychological question one side is as easy of assertion as the other. Would depreciation cause further depreciation?

199. We have seen in preceding sections that value for currency purposes and value for non-currency purposes exhibit no necessary inter-relation if only the supply of currency be limited. The volume of currency must serve for the business to be transacted, and will do so at no matter how great appreciation. The possibility of seigniorage charges is explicable only upon this principle; the stamped coin has a value which the mere bullion has not. Quantity and not material important.
It is upon the same principle, also, that we must explain the fact that, in the history of English coinage, the currency was never depreciated in the same proportion that it was debased.

(Ricardo.) The theoretical possibility of the profits of seigniorage covering the entire currency value is indicated by these facts.

200. It is doubtless conceivable that through well-founded fear or unreasoning prejudice men should in private affairs refuse to give time in business transactions, **Taxation maintains demand.** unless a commodity payment were agreed upon, or a moral or legal guaranty of redeemability were believed to be recognized by the government. But it is to be recalled that where a full legal tender power is given to fiat currency, the government in its tax collections is compelled to support the market parity, so long as limited fiat issues render this possible. Government yearly creates in its favour a large volume of indebtedness under the form of general or local taxes. In the United States this yearly aggregate of taxes probably exceeds the entire volume of governmental or quasi-governmental currency. As long as a fiat dollar will pay taxes equally with a bullion dollar, so long the fiat currency will retain its circulating characteristic, and depreciation will manifest itself only when, through over-issue of fiat units, every commodity unit, gold for example, is worth more as commodity than as currency; in other words, until the least valuable use for non-currency purposes of any part of the commodity currency is greater than its value when employed as currency. Should this condition of over-issue be reached, the currency would consist entirely of fiat units, and exchanges would take place through them, though a commodity measure might still be employed for deferred payments, and hoarding might be mostly confined to certain kinds of bullion.

201. The correctness of these conclusions is sufficiently attested by history. Fiat issues do circulate. If fiat can give any value, it can by a stricter limit give full value. England has in the past illustrated the truth of this. The legal tender power sustains in a measure the value of currency. Argentine, Italy, Austria, and Russia are recent instances. The United States furnished an example during the period before specie resumption.

The case of the United States must, however, suggest the action of other influences, if the fluctuations in currency values following the changing fortunes of the war of the Rebellion are to be explained. These fluc- *Influence of speculation on fiats.* tuations were far too marked and too rapid to be accounted for solely by changed relations between the volume of business and the volume of currency. Faith in the continued legal existence of the government was a fluctuating quantity, as was also faith in the power or disposition of the government to make ultimate redemption. Hence resulted, at one time, great increases in the volume of hoarding and investing demand, and at another time, great increases of supply through panic-stricken marketings of previously acquired holdings. In short, to the ordinary working of currency laws must be added in cases of this sort all the influences of active and far-sighted speculation.

It remains to add that while we have conceded the theoretical possibility that, for purposes of hoarding or value-measuring, a private or bullion currency might displace fiat issues, and while we must concede that this substitution would probably take place so far as the standard of deferred payments was concerned, yet, for purposes of current market measures the tendency is well-nigh irresistible for that currency which is used as the exchange medium to serve also as a value measure — since, historically and theoretically, the measure function is purely subordinate and derivative.

202. The foregoing discussion should in no sense be taken to justify, for practical purposes or in any case, the issue of inconvertible paper money. There is always dan- *Irredeemable* ger of paper issues being carried to excess, and *currency never* if the safeguard of redeemability is removed, no *advisable.* sufficient provision against excess remains. So long as excess is not reached, redeemability exists in fact, and therefore no harm can attach to the recognition of legal redeemability.

Walker states the case admirably: "Lest I should be misunderstood, let me say that it is my firm belief that the issue of inconvertible paper money is never a sound measure of finance, no matter what the stress of the National exigency may be; I believe it to be as surely a mistaken policy as the resort of an athlete to the brandy bottle. It means mischief always. If there is ever a time when a nation needs its full collective vigour with a steady pulse, a calm outlook, a steady hand, a brain undisturbed by the fumes of this alcohol of commerce, — paper money, — it is when called to do battle for its life with superior force. It is to my mind the highest proof of the supreme intellectual greatness of Napoleon that, during twenty years of continuous war, he never was driven to this desperate and delusive resort. I hold any man to be something less than a statesman in the full sense of that word who, under any stress of fiscal exigency, supports or submits to a measure for the issue of paper money not convertible at the instant on demand without conditions into coin money. The political arguments by which such measures are always supported on the outbreak of war, seem to me the veriest trash, due half to ignorance and half to cowardice." — *Advanced Course*, Sec. 214 n.

BIMETALLISM

203. Whether the currency of the commercial world is tending toward appreciation or toward depreciation in unit value is a question of considerable difficulty. With increasing population, expanding production, and extending division of labour, the demand for currency is rapidly becoming greater. But this demand is in a large degree supplied by the growing use of credit substitutes as currency. Were it not for this currency function of credit, the average of prices would tend inevitably toward fall, unless a larger use were made of fiat currency, or unless the marginal sacrifices of precious metal production should, through discovery or invention, be reduced as rapidly as the marginal sacrifices in the average of other products, due regard being had to the proportions in which different commodities and services enter into the average consumption.

<small>Is the currency unit appreciating?</small>

But as an estimate of actual tendencies, our question needs examination from the point of view of statistics. Expanding production and falling commodity prices are necessarily accompanied by increase in the value of services. With commodity values tending toward fall, and service values tending toward rise, the statistical answer cannot be more than a loosely approximate one. In theoretical aspects this subject was sufficiently covered in Sections 162–166, and will be examined as a current question in Section 317.

There can be no doubt that a tendency toward rising currency value is a thing to be avoided if possible. There is a widespread conviction that such a tendency exists at present, and it is for the most part on this ground that bimetallism is earnestly advocated. Bimetallism is to be understood as a currency system resting upon a double commodity measure of value, gold and silver for example, both commodities being freely coined at the established coinage ratio, and each having, equally with the other, legal tender power for the payment of debts.

204. The application of the principles discussed in Sections 190, 191, to what we may term national bimetallism is sufficiently obvious. The outcome must be at best a system of monometallism, alternating from one to the other currency commodity, accordingly as the relative market values may fluctuate. *National bimetallism equals monometallism.* Any agreement on the part of the State to redeem either metal in the other, at the established coinage ratio, could result in nothing but loss and failure to the government undertaking the burden. This would amount to a standing offer by the government to submit to loss at every market fluctuation in the relative values of the currency commodities. That no one government could sufficiently control the demand to prevent this fluctuation was sufficiently shown in Sections 191, 192.

205. But however clear the case may be against national bimetallism, the question is an altogether different one for international bimetallism. We have seen that no displacement of one currency commodity by another can take place

without some tendency toward depreciation of the currency unit, and some tendency toward depreciation for non-currency purposes of the same material used as commodity. If silver drives gold from the currency, it is because by the inflow of silver the unit of currency is depreciated to such a degree that the gold employed as currency is rendered more valuable in other markets than in the currency market. But the increase of supply in the non-currency market tends to lower values in that market, and to counteract the tendency toward outflow from currency uses. Gold cannot entirely disappear from the currency of any people, unless the supply of silver is sufficiently large to permit the last unit of silver inflow to be of less value than the last unit of gold outflow. Speculative departures in relative values in view of possible future contingencies are to be allowed for in these adjustments of value. Note, also, that just as by the increase of supply in gold for commodity purposes gold tends toward fall, so the increased market for silver for currency purposes and the resulting decrease in supply for commodity uses must tend to force upward the market value of silver.

International is practicable.

206. It is then evident that were a sufficiently large number of governments committed to the use of gold and silver at a fixed ratio of value, the relative market values could for a long time be maintained through the compensatory action above outlined, and that for such time as the market parity was maintained, fluctuations in the value of the currency unit would in a large measure be controlled. But it is still true that were the coinage ratio extremely wide of the normal cost-of-production ratio, this parity might be extremely short-lived, or even unattainable at the outset. And it is true that an increase in the volume of one of the metals at a constantly falling market value is possible in any case to such a degree as finally to disturb the relative values of the two metals; that is to say, it is possible that either metal might ultimately be entirely displaced by the other, — the compensatory working of international bimetal-

Parity might be short-lived.

lism thus conducting finally to international monometallism. Whether or not this outcome could reasonably be anticipated is not a question of theory. A careful study of present and future conditions of supply, and of probable modifications of demand in reference to both metals, would be necessary to justify even a conjecture upon this point. But it is safe to assert, as matter of theory, that international bimetallism, if entered into in good faith and pursued consistently, might be salutary while in operation and without catastrophe in any possible outcome; and if finally conducting to monometallism, would raise no theoretical difficulties to reëstablishment at a new ratio of values between the metals.

Would failure be disastrous?

SUGGESTIVE QUESTIONS

Would free coinage at 16 to 1 increase the amount of money ?
What effect on prices ? On use of gold in arts ? On foreign trade ?
On export of gold ? On foreign prices ? On market value of gold ?

Under international bimetallism, what effects in these same directions?

How would these effects be modified were the coinage ratio 25 or 30 to 1?

The yearly product of gold is about 150,000,000 ; of silver (coinage value), 200,000,000 ; our money volume, 1,500,000,000 ; European volume, 10,000,000,000 ; world supply of gold coined or obtainable for present coinage, 4,000,000,000 ; world's supply of silver, 4,000,000,000.

With conditions as above could the United States alone maintain parity at 16 to 1 ? Or for a long time at any ratio — probably ?

What are the advantages of international bimetallism ? (Jevons, *Money*, pp. 136-147, will be found helpful on this point.)

If gold has appreciated, who have been injured?

Is it possible to have a money in which what you sell shall be dear and what you buy cheap ?

At 200,000,000 annual production of silver, how long would it take silver to displace the gold, thus disturbing the parity ?

Would any depreciation of the unit occur before the parity was disturbed ?

Make as reasonable assumptions as possible and apply to them the principles illustrated in the algebraic method, Section 189.

Why fix the ratio at 16 to 1?

Would this ratio greatly stimulate silver production ?

How about 25 to 1?

Does international bimetallism depend for success on finding one particular ratio?

Would the last stages of change from international bimetallism to monometallism present any especially noticeable features? Would the change be gradual or sudden?

CHAPTER XX

COMMERCIAL CRISES

What sort of years generally precede panic times, as to (a) prices? (b) wages? (c) speculation?

What sort as to (a) the creation of capital? (b) building of houses? (c) construction of factories? or (d) of railroads?

Have the people been mostly at work or have large numbers been unemployed?

Has the social product been large?

How about savings?

If prices have been high and business large, what must have been true as to volume of currency?

Has the volume of money increased?

Are flush times times of relatively large precious metal production?

Or times of unusually marked tendency toward coinage of accumulated stocks of precious metals?

How did these high prices become possible?

207. We have already seen that a large share of modern business is transacted through the intermediary not of money, but of substitutes for money — through different forms of circulating credit, or through the book-keeping devices of deposit banks and clearing-houses. In local trade checks supply a large part of the currency demand. Drafts and bills are the media of debt payment, not only between city and city, but between country and country. Only balances are paid in money, and the clearing-house greatly reduces this latter employment. Bank balances in London are paid by bookkeeping in the Bank of England. It is evident that all exchanges completed without the use of

The use of credit as currency.

money stand with relation to the demand for money as if they had not taken place. Not only this, but more rapid transportation has shortened the time of employment of money in the payment of balances. These influences together have worked powerfully to lessen, if not to cancel, the tendency toward appreciation in the currency unit due to enlarged demand for exchange media. The customer pays the retail trader by check. The retailer pays the wholesaler by draft. Railways and telegraphs have almost cancelled the element of distance in bookkeeping and payment relations between communities. Negotiable notes, bills of exchange, open accounts of debt and credit, all contribute to the economy of money. The credit system is widespread, thoroughly organized, delicately adjusted, swift, effective, and complicated. It is carefully protected by guaranty organizations, by great trust companies, by all-powerful and all-inquisitorial mercantile reporting and collection agencies. In addition to these, there are the investment companies, the savings banks, and the insurance companies, all of which are intermediaries for the gathering and distributing of credit. Their business is to guard the credit system with extreme watchfulness in protection of their legal guaranties. Thus the credit system resting upon infinitely intricate relations between manufacturers, jobbers, wholesalers, retailers, and consumers, has for superstructure the many-storied fabric of deposit and discount banking, of stock investment and collateral borrowing, of savings and insurance investment, and of trust and mortgage guaranty companies. There are even companies to guarantee the validity of titles and the good faith of employés.

208. Not all of these credit devices serve as economies in the use of money. Where items in open account offset each other, the economy is manifest. Where credit circulates, the economy is manifest. But the mere granting of credit, awaiting a later settlement, does not lessen, in the outcome, the demand for money, but merely postpones it. Credit must be used by transfer in payment of indebtedness before it works as substitute

There is a currency and a non-currency form to credit

for money. Nevertheless, this non-currency element in credit is none the less credit, and in the making up of disaster is as important as any other. For, carefully inspected and supported as is this credit system, it is the sheerest card-house. Its contrivances for watchfulness and safety are its most shifty and unstable features. No fire-trap could be more skilfully planned for purposes of destruction, with heavy supports and girders of spontaneously combustible tinder wood. The whole thing is as explosive and volcanic as if earthquakes were built into it for walls. *equally dangerous.*

209. The period preceding a financial crisis is commonly a period of seemingly great prosperity. There is a popular impression that such prosperity is a mere seeming, and that panic is a phenomenon of necessary collapse. It would be going too far to claim that no bubbles are formed in the course of business expansion, or that these bubbles are not sources of financial danger; but, speaking generally, the popular impression is a mistaken one. The years preceding panic constitute a period of great industrial activity and of great productiveness. Wage-earners have been well employed; the industries of distribution have been in smooth and successful operation. At the close of the period it will be found that the wage-earning classes have rarely been as well housed, as well clothed, or as well fed. They are exceptionally well supplied with the smaller conveniences and comforts of life. Measured by their own standard, the labourers are prosperous in pleasant homes and large personal belongings. In the aggregate, they represent a large total of material wealth. It will be found true of the farmer that his farm was never under better cultivation, or his herds larger, his buildings more substantial or in better repair, or his home better furnished. Likewise of the manufacturer and the merchant; never were there larger stocks or more warehouses bursting with merchandise. Never were factories daily pouring forth more goods. Turning to general conditions, it will be found that these prosperous years have rebuilt cities in brick, interlaced states and even continents with railroads, dotted the *Ante-panic years are prosperous.*

prairies with farm houses, beautified them with fields of grain, and made them bountiful with herds. The period has been one of widespread plenty, of remarkable industrial activity and efficiency, of boundless energy and hope. It is strange, it is even impossible, that extensive building operations should, in themselves, result in houseless exposure; that overflowing granaries and fattening herds should foster hunger, or that warehouses of cloths should be the sufficient cause of nakedness. It is doubtless true that these meshes of railroads, these cities of brick and marble, these immense factories and fattening herds, are largely the outcome of reckless hope and borrowed capital; yet it all counts the world as wealth; it is here. That the capital is borrowed chips nothing from this fact.

210. The elements of danger are not to be found in the industrial situation, which was never before so prosperous in thorough efficiency and organization. The difficulty is financial.

Where is the difficulty?

We have seen that the volume of exchanges is the measure of the demand for currency; double the volume of currency, and you double prices. To halve the currency is to lower prices in the same ratio. These propositions are unquestionable; they hardly reach the dignity of principles; they are mere mathematics. Yet, strangely enough, as applied to the facts of industry they are seemingly untrue. Prices almost uniformly rise with increasing activity in business, and fall with failing business. This is seemingly to say that the value of currency falls with an increased demand, and rises with a failure of demand.

The explanation is found in the fact that, with expanding business, the currency also expands, and, commonly, to a degree more than proportionate to the demand for it. This increase takes place not ordinarily in the legal tender element, but in the credit element. Reviving credit always characterizes reviving business. Under existing systems, credit furnishes for currency the only element of ready adaptability. It furnishes, for ordinary conditions, the guaranty of steady market prices. It avoids an enormous application of human energies to the production of commodity currency. Without it, great expanding business operations would carry with them their own veto in falling prices and vanishing profits.

But these advantages are purchased at the risk of enormous dangers. The commercial crisis marks the period when money takes on abnormal scarcity and abnormal value from the fact that substitute media — credit currency — contract in volume. The very height of the credit fabric measures the disaster of its fall. It is at the full tide of prosperity that the danger is greatest. If, then, for any reason, whether of extravagance at some point, or of over-production in some industries, or of failure of harvests in some districts, or of over-speculation, or even of business prosperity carried to the point of over-stringency in the loan market, there sets in a contraction of credit, trouble begins. The debtor can pay only by calling in turn upon his debtor. The pressure for payment increases in almost geometrical progression. Not only does credit largely disappear from circulation, but the burden of liquidating existing indebtedness is thrown upon the legal tender and unsuspected elements of the currency. Panic-stricken marketings of commodities, and panic-stricken or speculative withdrawals of money from the channels of business further complicate the situation. Endless ruin and disaster follow; prices tumble; this is panic: when even the rich seem poor; when business is stagnant; exchanges are suspended; labourers are unemployed and in want. Immediately preceding it were the headlong rush and exultant activity of prosperity, — when all men were hard at work, though doubtless over-confident, and possibly over-venturesome. And now follows the destruction of wealth. In the course of ample credit, things had arranged themselves in the hands of those who knew best how to use them. Now ensues an enforced redistribution. In the outcome one man finds himself with two houses, and can use but one; or with two horses, and needs but one; and with endless steam engines, and trumpery, and stocks in trade of which he wants nothing. He can only let the property grow old or rot or rust. The wheels of the factory stand still; industry has dropped its tools: and all

278   OUTLINES OF ECONOMIC THEORY

this, not because there was too little wealth, or too much, but because what there was was badly arranged to withstand a flurry in credit.

211. It is clear enough that panic is an ebb in credit, and that in proportion as the intermixture of credit in currency is large, is the disaster great. Whatever may be the ameliorations possible, the gravity of the case is not to be questioned. Here is the most noticeably weak point in the modern competitive system. Anything which shall offer a reasonable hope of displacing credit from its enormous development in modern business can hardly be other than a good fortune. The money of ultimate redemption is too small for the credit fabric built upon it. It is like a cone resting on its vertex. This delicate and unstable equilibrium is a condition constantly fraught with danger.

Advantages, disadvantages, and remedies.

Doubtless for so long as credit works, it affords desirable economies in the use of bullion currency and, in some measure, steadies prices. England succeeds at most times in managing a much larger per capita volume of business than does France, and at a much lower per capita of bullion currency. But periodically, England suffers acutely from the commercial crisis, while France is relatively exempt. The losses far outweigh the gains.

That which most naturally suggests itself as remedy, is to enlarge the currency basis,— to assume that more money of ultimate redemption is needed — therefore start the printing presses or coin silver. But remember that it is the shape of the pyramid, and not the size of it, which is matter of concern. Unless there is found to be some tendency in silver coinage, or in any other form of inflation, to lessen the volume of credit relative to money, the inflation argument fails.

Is expansion a remedy?

212. There is no such tendency. Silver expansion, or any other expansion, would result in a proportional rise in prices. The degree in which credit circulates depends upon the methods of business and the organization of industry, and not upon the kind of money. So long as

Silver coinage.

manufacturers find it advantageous to borrow capital, so long as wholesalers take credit from manufacturers, retailers from wholesalers, customers from retailers, and all deposit their funds in banks and pay through checks and bookkeeping, so long must the intermixture of credit remain an element of danger. In truth, the very bulkiness of silver would, in itself, tend somewhat to increase the inducements to deposit methods.

Nor is there any great hope that these credit methods will cease because of their dangers. The advantages and convenience to the individual business man are too pronounced. Here, again, individual interests are not parallel with the general interest. No one business man could afford to stop unless all should stop, and each would gain by violating the rule intended for all. The remedy, if any is possible, lies in the discovery of a currency practicably flexible in time of need. This problem will afford the subject for a later chapter. It is possible, however, that something of ebb and flow in commercial affairs — of that which in philosophic phrase is termed rhythm — is inseparable from the conduct of business, so long, at least, as the industrial organization retains its speculative features. In this view, the question is to some extent a psychological one.

Suggestive Questions

Would it prevent panic if money were all gold ? Or diamonds ? Or if the commodity currency were doubled in volume ?

Would a large money volume prevent the use of credit ?

Do you see any way to prevent the granting of credit, or the use of credit as currency ?

Do you see any way of increasing the amount of legal tender or of credit currency at the acute period of panic ?

CHAPTER XXI

TARIFFS, TAXES, AND PRICES

(Teachers may well omit this chapter)

213. An analysis of the bearing of tariffs and other taxes on prices is a matter of extreme complexity. Roscher explains, **First effects of restriction of trade.** in part, the fall of prices in late years by the tariff barriers established between different countries. This he illustrates by supposing the extreme case that each community should erect prohibitive barriers against all imports. A fall in the prices of those products formerly produced for export would result, and a rise in the prices of products previously obtained through importation. And he seems to regard it as clear that the tendency toward fall would preponderate (*System*, Book III. c. 5; Sec. 139 n. 11). It is unquestionable that these two tendencies would be developed, but it is not so clear upon which side the balance would rest. A lessened aggregate production of utility would result, and a lessened dividend for each community. An increase, then, instead of a decrease in prices would take place, if the decrease in the social dividend were not accompanied by a diminished circulating medium. In the case of a community producing the currency commodity we should expect to find a rise in prices, by reason of the export of this commodity being prevented. If, on the other hand, the case be one of a community importing its currency commodity, the conclusions are not so ready. The final effect would unquestionably be a fall in prices; but the first effect might well be a diminished social product without material modification in the volume of currency. A rise in prices of

commodities formerly imported,— other than the currency commodity,— and a fall in the prices of those commodities formerly produced for export, would be expected. The closing of the sources of currency supply would make itself felt but slowly in the general tendencies of prices. Until this effect should become marked, the case would be one of diminished aggregate production, and substantially undiminished currency. A higher average of prices would be a necessary accompaniment.

The final effect of prohibitive barriers upon the average of prices in different communities, considered in the aggregate, is altogether conjectural, until the effect upon the production of the currency commodity has been determined. *Final effects.* We may assume that the first effect would be an average rise in prices, this rise being especially marked in the communities producing the currency commodity. Where, as under existing conditions, the production of the currency commodity is confined to a few communities, the final effect must be an average fall in prices consequent upon the necessary change of a large portion of productive energies from the production of the currency commodity to the production of other commodities.

214. But turning to conditions as they exist, we find that trade barriers are partial instead of prohibitive. It is by no means clear that existing barriers do in fact cause a realignment of marginal sacrifices or appreciably affect the total production of the currency commodity relatively to the other commodities, or so far impede the interflow of the currency commodity between communities as to modify by this means the average level of prices. And if the production and circulation of the currency commodity are in an appreciable degree modified, it seems probable that the tendency from this cause toward lower prices is more than offset by the tendency toward higher prices consequent upon a diminished world-production of utility.

215. We have considered the effects of taxation on values. We have now to recall that price is an expression of the value

of the currency commodity. No tax on the production of the currency commodity will then modify prices unless it work a rearrangement in the proportions of productive energies applied to other commodities. Imposition of a tax upon the production of all commodities other than the currency commodity would, in some measure, diminish the production and consumption of the taxed commodities. (See Section 156.) The tendency, then, of such taxation would appear to be toward a larger production of the currency commodity at a lower market value of the currency commodity, and at higher prices of the taxed commodities.

Taxes on precious metal production.

The tendency toward larger production of the currency commodity would, however, be less marked than at first thought seems probable. The revenues collected by taxation are commonly expended either in compensations to government employés, or in payment of interest on the public debt. In either case, the result is a subtraction of productive energies from the creation of exchangeable goods. To this extent exchanges are lessened, and the demand for the currency commodity for currency purposes thereby decreased. A tendency toward higher prices, that is to say, toward a lower value for the currency commodity, results.

Thus we may conclude that a system of taxation bearing upon all commodities other than the currency commodity would tend in two ways toward higher prices (lower value of currency), first, by diverting a proportionally greater quantity of productive energies to the production of the currency commodity; second, by reducing the demand for currency purposes of the currency commodity, thereby diminishing its total production and probably permitting a lower marginal sacrifice in production.

216. A general tax upon the production of commodities, inclusive of the currency commodity, would tend in some, though in smaller degree, toward a readjustment of values.

There are differences in the measure in which a demand for different commodities is retired by increase in price. An equal rate of taxation upon all commodities must therefore inevitably disturb the established application of productive energies. It is not clear in what degree an increase in the value of gold would retire the demand for gold for non-currency uses. We may, however, assume that this retirement would not be exceptionally great or small. But general taxes exercise upon the currency commodity an indirect effect, which other commodities do not experience. Taxation of other commodities tends directly to reduce the demand for these commodities. This reduction of demand is, in itself, an indirect reduction in the demand for the currency commodity, and therefore tends toward a rise in prices.

217. We have now to remark that none of the conclusions reached in the last four sections are trustworthy for other than theoretical purposes, since there is one class of utilities which commonly, and in large degree inevitably, escape taxation; these are the utilities indicated under the term "services." A system of taxation which should so bear upon profits, wages, rent, and interest as to cause no readjustment in the applications of productive energies, would involve no changes in market values. Whether or not such a system would be an ideal one, we do not at present need to discuss, since it is evidently outside the reach of human ingenuity. But, in fact, the goods termed "services," and the wage-earnings of labourers occupied in the production of these goods, are commonly unburdened by taxation. Utilities of this class are important items in the expenditures of the average man. Taxation which does not directly bear upon this class of goods must, of necessity, result in relative increase of production and consumption in these lines.

Services must be held in mind.

POLITICAL ECONOMY AS AN ART

(Re-read Section 3)

CHAPTER XXII

THE COMPETITIVE SYSTEM

218. If one will carefully examine a map of the world, he will be struck with the fact that most of the great cities, and especially the cities of the New World, are located at points of advantage for water transportation. There is not a great city on the Western Continent which does not lie upon ocean, lake, or river. And yet the western cities have in the main been built since the era of the railroad, bringing with it the fall in relative importance of water transportation. In the Old World, on the contrary, where almost all cities were planted in the days of water transportation alone, one yet finds large cities like Berlin and Paris located at large distance from any practicable waterway. It is true that cases of this sort are rare, but it is strange that they should have been less rare before the days of the railroad than since. It is true that St. Louis makes small use of the Mississippi. Kansas City and Omaha have no important water traffic. The river boat is mostly a matter of the past. The cities, nevertheless, have somehow grown by navigable streams.

The new importance of transportation.

The explanation is in the fact that the question of transportation has become the all-important one in the trade and commerce of this century. Up to the time of the application of steam to land transportation, the world knew only two sorts of great cities, — the political city, and the trade city by the water-side. The political city was seldom of great size unless, at the same time, a trade centre; this latter it could not be, unless ships could anchor in front of it. The inland city was of necessity the trade centre for but a small territory; and so it is instructive to note the development of the populations of Berlin and Paris since the era of steam transportation.

Berlin in 1817	contained	. . . . .	188,000	inhabitants.
" 1844	"	. . . . .	311,000	"
" 1871	"	. . . . .	825,000	"
" 1890	"	. . . . .	1,300,000	"
Paris in 1806	"	. . . . .	580,000	"
" 1817	"	. . . . .	714,000	"
" 1836	"	. . . . .	909,000	"
" 1856	"	. . . . .	1,174,000	"
" 1872	"	. . . . .	1,852,000	"
" 1890	"	. . . . .	2,800,000	"

Large numbers of men cannot live in one city unless that city can sell and buy over a wide range of territory. With steam there came advantages for the clustering of allied industries, by reason of the opportunity to procure trained workmen, to obtain the necessary materials and supplies, to buy in large quantities and at need, and to sell to other manufacturers direct or to wealthy and widely connected distributing merchants. The larger market made possible the larger production at one centre. This large production, and the applications of steam to industry, made the giant factory possible. Close competition over wide fields; the disappearance of the small employer, of the workshop, and of hand industry; the rise of the great factory, with its impersonal relations between employer and workmen — are the salient facts of the new industrial era.

219. All this was inevitable; steam brought it, and the progress of discovery and invention have served but to emphasize it. How much of good or ill has come with the change is difficult to determine. The antagonisms between employer and employé have mostly come of it. When employers worked

Steam is the cause. Are the effects good?

side by side with their artisans and apprentices, there was room for more of neighbourliness and sympathy, with less of actual clash in interests and greatly less of apparent clash. With but half a dozen or a dozen men in a shop, the gulf of separation between employer and employé was as narrow a quantity economically as it was socially. It was reasonably within the hope of any apprentice to become a master. In the nineteenth century system, it is inevitable that 499 out of every 500 industrial workers shall be underlings. The places of leadership are few.

When many artisans worked independently and the processes were hand processes and the workshop manned with scarcely ten workmen, each artisan was commonly master of the entire art and mystery of his occupation, instead of, as now, the specialized performer of some half-dozen movements or the facile attendant upon some great machine.

As producers and consumers have moved more widely apart, the personal relations of trust and honour have decayed, prices and not makers have come to rule, processes have multiplied for adulteration and scamping, and advertising has developed into the science of lying by newspaper.

It is easy to subtract something from the strength of these facts. It may be that there are more than sufficient advantages in the age of steam to outweigh the losses of change. How much, for example, steam should be credited for the establishment of international division of labour, for the peaceful tendencies of international intercourse, in what degree we shall consider modern industrial development to have set aside, with imperial wars and bickerings, the kings and their trumpetings, to make way for the people and popular government — how much modern life owes of its fulness to the new industrial influences making for science and culture and wealth — we may not readily estimate.

If the labourers have swung wide of their employers socially, they have multiplied and strengthened the ties of association with each other. If greater divergence of interests has seemed to result between employers and employés, it is a mere seeming, which must pass away with better intellectual grasp of the more complex modern conditions. If the workman no longer needs to be a master in all branches of his trade, he has been freed from long apprenticeships and profitless acquirements. The automatic working of his machine and the simplicity of his short processes, leave him as free as is the leisure man for thought and reflection. If the workman has lost in the factory something of independence and hopefulness, he enjoys as one member of society his gain in the greater efficiency of labour,— his share of a larger social dividend,— and there always remain to him, on the terms of his old remuneration, his separate bench and last.

220. Had the labourer the opportunity to choose between the lower wages and the limited life of the eighteenth century on the one hand, and the wages and opportunities of the nineteenth on the other, the choice would not be found a ready one; for there are some aspects of the case which we have not yet examined.

Commercial crises mostly peculiar to the era of steam.

Let it be assumed that the higher wages are an important advance in well-being, despite the larger needs and higher social requirements to which the labourer is now subjected. How about the uncertainties, the chancefulness of employment — the risk of want of work and the possibility of starvation which the modern system fosters? The commercial crisis is mostly a product of steam, also; it is, at all events, an incident to the intricate and highly organized societies of the modern era— to the wide application of division of labour. Interdependence is the law of specialization. Each community not only suffers its own ills, but vibrates in sympathy with the disasters of all associated communities. In the matter of fires, it is well to have tinder-boxes at goodly distances from each other.

The most acute of all the evils of the present social organization is this of irregularity and uncertainty of employment. Cure the disease of panics, and the labourer will not greatly quarrel with his lot. The employer is equally powerless; but the employer need not beg or starve. The commercial crisis means the wholesale loss of hope, independence, and self-respect; the wholesale creation of beggars, wanderers, thieves, and criminals.

All this is serious enough, and yet there is more to be said. It may well give us pause before the tendencies of modern civilization. All this, with the more which might be said, and is commonly said, in attack upon the present social order, is interesting and profitable in an effort fully to understand the present conditions. But admitting for a moment the ill comparison of the present with the past, nothing much seems to follow from it. We cannot go back. The railroad and the steamship, the science and the knowledge, the credit system and the machines, are here to stay. Thus in placing the present industrial order on trial for its continuance, it need form no part of the indictment that it is worse than some one or all of the systems which have preceded it. The question lies not between what was and what is, but between what is and what may be.

THE ECONOMIC HARMONIES

221. One gets no great distance into economic discussion in its practical aspects, without encountering what the participants in the discussion call the social question. It is perhaps not worth while to inquire too closely into the meaning of this term. Those who use it could commonly do little more in the way of definition than to repeat it. It means different things to different people. In a general way, however, it is the question of what is the matter — with more or less definite reference to some one or other scheme of remedy.

The fact, however, that with most earnest and reflective men the conviction grows that there is a social question — whatever
There is a social question. the term may mean, or however obscure or various may be its meanings — is in itself a startling fact. The doctrines of political economy no longer ring with confident assurance. Long asserting that

whatever is, is right, has seemed to put in issue whether what is not, is necessarily wrong; whether there is any hope of progress for the race; whether optimism best rests in satisfaction with what is, or in confidence of what is to come. The economists of the first half of the century were engaged in the study of societies emerging from centuries of kingship, of government by classes, of stupid and unjust legislation. It was clear enough that the progress of society lay in the breaking down of legal barriers and limitations, in the sweeping away of the privileges of caste and class, and in the development of popular institutions under the form of local and individual initiative. The time was one of growth and advance. A wealth of achievement justified the advocates of industrial liberty as theorists and honoured them as prophets. The era was a series of object lessons in the blessings of untrammelled individual activities and in the dangers of over-legislation and paternalism. The benefits of increased freedom argued for the wider abolition of regulation, and the régime of liberty came to stand as the ideal toward which civilization seemed to tend. For most cases, it was manifest that what individuals and peoples chiefly need is to be let alone; that that part of human ill is small which kings or parliaments can cure. In the full flood of hope, economists argued learnedly that the good of each is always and inevitably bound up with the good of all; that in the marvellous divine order of things, selfishness of motive works out in altruism of results; that social ill-adjustments are due to too little liberty, too much meddling, or to ill-informed estimates by the individual of his own interests. Bastiat, for example, proclaimed with all the resources of his marvellous ingenuity and eloquence that "All legitimate interests are harmonious," and pointed out that, this once proved, nothing remained but to enlighten the people in their freedom — that the future could not lie with restraint, but with liberty informed with knowledge.

The early optimism.

222. It is hard to determine how much this school of thinking owed to pure idealism in ethics, how much to the

teachings of experience in purely economic lines. It does not come easily to the reverent mind to believe that the best interests of any can antagonize the interests of all, if only it be possible to the individual to appreciate things in their ultimate meanings and their long effects. Somehow each of us meets the faith in him that, could he see things far-sightedly and clearly, self-love and fellow-love would find themselves reconciled in the moral code as it daily enacts itself in the human conscience. The right of the neighbour can hardly be wrong to us; the claims of sympathy and the demands of duty not only express our obligations to our fellow-beings, but sum up in highest and truest sense our own well-being. Somehow the right thing must be the best thing for each of us; it cannot do our neighbour wrong, it must be best for him as for us.

Largely an ethical conception.

This, then, was Bastiat's first principle — a brave and noble faith — that all true interests must harmonize; any clash must be a mere seeming, or somewhere real interests have been misconceived. Notice, however, that Bastiat did not say that all interests are harmonious, that all selfish activities make for the common good, but that all legitimate interests are harmonious — which is as much as to say that all *justifiable* selfishness works for the common good — no great discovery, after all, since all selfishness which makes for the common good is by that very fact justifiable. Subjected to strict analysis also, to say that all self-seeking within the limits of good morals must profit the general well-being does not advance the argument, since the very test of right action is in this, that it shall result in no harm to the general well-being.

So, again, to say that only right action can be consistent with the best interests of the actor holds only when one assumes that no outside advantage can balance the inner ill which comes from violation of the dictates of conscience. Dishonesty is not necessarily bad policy, if measured merely in outside results. The doctrine of the economic harmonies, if of any weight for practical purposes, must be interpreted to assert the coincidence of individual and social interest without reference to the purely personal meanings of right action simply as such. Our question is whether it is possible that a human being intellectually perfect, but lacking in the tendernesses, aspirations, and repugnances of conscience, should ever find it to his interest to do his fellow-man an injustice — to steal from his employer, cheat his creditor, overcharge his clients, oppress his employés, weave shoddy into his fabrics, enter into combinations for buying and trusts for selling. It is idle to say that, if he does these things, others will, also. Possibly enough — and so they will if he does not; and even did his lack of restraint lead them to follow, the monopolist is only in slight degree robbed of his profit, or the thief of his plunder, by the fact that other men ply the same trades.

This laissez-faire (don't interfere) school, these advocates of liberty, claim too much, even were it not true that in human shortsightedness men constantly fail to see their true interests to be parallel with the general interests, when, in fact, they are so. Perfect liberty of action will be a practicable system, when men shall have come to possess that acute sympathy for others — that fine regard for the well-being of one's fellows — which makes an injury to another an echoing injury to each, and when the intellectual powers have been developed to the position of an adequate aid and guide for the conscience.

LAISSEZ-FAIRE

We find ourselves confronted by the sweeping doctrine that the sole function of an ideal government, in relation to industry, is simply to leave it alone. This view, in some minds, seems to be partly supported by a curious confusion of thought; the absence of governmental interference being assumed for simplicity's sake in the hypothetical reasoning, by which the value of products and services are deductively determined, is at the same time vaguely regarded as a conclusion established by such reasonings. — SIDGWICK, *Principles*, p. 399.

Now, I beg you to remark the strange assumptions that underlie this reasoning. Human interests are naturally harmonious; therefore we have only to leave people free, and social harmony must result; as if it were an obvious thing that people know their interests in the sense in which they coincide with the interests of others, and that knowing them they must follow them ; as if there were no such things in the world as passion, prejudice, custom, *esprit de corps*, class interest, to draw people aside from the pursuit of their interests in the largest and highest sense. Here is a fatal flaw on the very threshold of Bastiat's argument ; and it is a flaw which no follower of Bastiat has repaired, — which, for my part, I believe to be irreparable. Nothing is easier than to show that people follow their interest, in the sense in which they understand their interests. But between this and following their interests in the sense in which it is coincident with that of other people, a chasm yawns. That chasm in the argument of the laissez-faire school has never been bridged. The advocates of the doctrine shut their eyes and leap over it.

— CAIRNES.

The modern era has undoubtedly given new openings for dishonesty in trade. The advance of knowledge has discovered new ways of making things appear other than they are, and has rendered possible many new forms of adulteration. The producer is now far removed from the ultimate consumer ; and his wrong-doings are not visited with the prompt and sharp punishment which falls on the head of a person who, being bound to live and die in his native village, plays a dishonest trick on one of his neighbours. — MARSHALL, *Ec. of Ind.*, p. 7.

Thus, for instance, there is no reason why, even in a community of most perfect men, a few wealthy land-owners, fond of solitude, scenery, or sport, should not find their interests in keeping from cultivation large tracts of land naturally fit for the plough or for pasture ; or why large capitalists generally should not prefer to live on the interest of their capital, without producing personally any utilities whatever.

— SIDGWICK, *Principles*, p. 404.

In the first place, then, as you will anticipate, the doctrine, laissez-faire laissez-aller, is impracticable in cases where the present situation is directly traceable to the action of that government or administration which has been permitted or encouraged to commit the mischief. No question is indeed more difficult in the whole range of the ethics of social life than the modern doctrine of vested interests. It is obvious that if you were to extend the principles which some persons have laid down, we must persist, even in the near prospect of national ruin, in continuing in what we have once allowed. If Charles II., for example, had given the son of Louisa Querouaille, the French prostitute and spy, the whole revenue of the town, we should be obliged to go on paying the proceeds to the Duke of Richmond. If it be true that the bounty and the corn laws, as many contended, were as much the inheritance of the English land-owner as his acres were, no reforms could have been permitted. If, on the other hand, maintenance out of the rates were, as was alleged, the absolute right of the British labourer, in consideration of his having been ousted, without a compensation, from his commonable rights in the land, occupiers would have been bound to keep paupers until they became paupers themselves.

. . . The strength of socialism is the injustice of government: it is weakened by every act of equity, and becomes an extinct or at least dormant force when all rights are respected.

— ROGERS, *Ec. Int. of Hist.*, pp. 251, 252.

LAISSEZ-FAIRE AS AN ETHICAL SYSTEM

223. Underlying all the opposition to socialism as an economic scheme, there is probably an element of antagonism resting in purely ethical conceptions. The purpose of our study is mostly to examine the bearings of economic principles upon questions of political and social interest. It is, however, not the less, but the more necessary to survey our field of investigation carefully, and to mark off the limits of the purely ethical side of the inquiry. We must, if possible, guard our path from occasions for digression, by setting aside from our discussion those aspects of the question upon which political economy can throw no helpful light.

The individualist holds one opinion in a fashion almost deserving the dignity of a great moral idea. He distrusts all schemes for social amelioration containing in them any element of force. How they may fail, or when, he may not see; but, no matter how fair the outlook, he is convinced that they will somewhere fail as applied to the complex conditions of society. Human nature is, as he thinks, somehow safe to baffle them.

This is in essence the opinion, perhaps rather the feeling, of a great body of liberal and earnest thinkers, — that the socialistic idea, after all possible has been said in favour of it, must yet remain as a system inherently weak because fundamentally in denial of the ultimate principles of the moral code. Somewhere, then, they think a latent flaw — some leak — must surely develop itself in any scheme of social reorganization whose first principles violate the sanctity of individual rights.

This ethical side of individualism has, in its compactness and simplicity, an appealing quality to the reason. Each man's rights over his neighbour are asserted to flow from his own right to liberty, to security, and to the enjoyment of his property. From these absolute rights must be derived all rights of enforcement. When the first meeting of men took place in the primeval forest, these questions of right first took on a relative aspect. Either man might have said to the other, I want nothing of you; leave me alone. I will not molest you. I will go my way in safety unmolested by you. The world is wide for both of us; go you your ways. This first man's just claims to control the second must have been limited to mere rights of enforcement — to the use of such methods as should be reasonably necessary to make the primary rights effective.

That the world has become densely populated changes in no manner these ethical relations, but merely makes their application and adjustment more complex and difficult. Some paring down of claims to property and liberty must take place, in order that the largest aggregate of liberty and initiative shall be preserved. It is in this process of adjustment of conflicting claims, and in maintenance and protection of such adjustments as are established, that the province of legislation and the purpose of government are found. The rights of society are the aggregate of individual rights. All powers of enforcement are the summed-up powers of the individual members. If no member has other than a self-protecting jurisdiction over his neighbour, society, organized as a state, must fail of possessing other than protective functions.

224. It is worth noticing, however, that to admit the necessity of a government of any sort involves the assumption that human interests, as conceived by human beings, are not in strict harmony. Nor for practical purposes is it sufficient to reply that men misconceive their own interests, since in any case it

But this is anarchy.

remains true that entire liberty must fall short of the best possible adjustment of social interests. Again, this system of individualism, reared upon strict ethical conceptions, fails to justify the State in even its minimum of activity — really denies all justification for a government of any sort. *As an ethical doctrine*, it leads logically and inevitably to anarchism. The individualist condemns higher education at public expense as a misappropriation of funds; public railroads, waterworks, telegraphs, as an unwarranted coercion of individuals into a business venture. These things are said to fall within the exclusive sphere of consent and contract. They are not protection to anybody in his ultimate rights. No one has the right to be educated or transported, or to have his property or his thought transported, or his thirst slaked, at my expense. These things are rather transfers of benefits. If I interfere with another's rights, he may properly coerce me. He must not compel me to minister to his well-being. No one need misunderstand this distinction — nothing could be clearer. So when X asks me to restrict my freedom or to contribute from my pocket-book for the benefit of his woollen mill, I am disposed to refuse, and if he gets the legislature to command it, I pay under protest. If I am told that this is for my benefit also, I reply either that I do not believe it, or that, in any case, that is my business and not another's. Nobody has been authorized by me to tax me for my benefit.

The difficulty with all this, however, is that the case is exactly the same with all the functions of government. When X asks that Y should not injure him and takes measures to prevent it, I approve; but when X by himself or through the government requests me to contribute to the process, I urge the strict parallel for my purposes of X's woollen mill with X's head. If he values either, let him protect it.

This is sheer anarchism — the denial of all right of taxation — the reduction of government to a system of voluntary coöperation.

And here we have in hand the material for some important definitions. The consistent anarchist carries individualism to the extreme of perfect liberty, advocating voluntary coöperation or nothing. The socialist is the complete antithesis, the advocate of a general system of compulsory coöperation. Democratic and Republican schools are found within these two extremes — the democrat tending toward the individualist idea, the republican toward the enlarged powers of the State. "Socialistic" suggests a verging from the present conditions toward larger state activities. Socialism, as a system, contemplates all productive and distributive processes as functions of the State.

Some definitions.

225. The opinion grows among students of these questions, that the limitations of state activity must be established upon grounds of utility — upon considerations of expediency — and not at all, or at all events not fundamentally, on grounds of abstract moral right. That form of government which strikes us as ideal — as consistent with absolute ethical standards — would not fit the imperfect mental and moral conditions of the present. That government is fit for us — best under the circumstances, relatively right — which we are fit for. Primitive societies would go to wreck under republican institutions. Whether or not abstract moral ideas are more than generalizations of expediency fixed in the human mind from a long race history, — our moral concepts being merely the summary of past-proved utilities to the race, — at all events, no philosophy of morals can ignore the fact that whatever forces or sanctions may underlie moral notions, only those conceptions which have served the well-being of the race have tended to survive. Those peoples holding notions antagonistic to race welfare have tended toward disappearance. The persisting dictates of conscience are, then, the inbred register of those ideas which, pursuant to the very nature of right action, have proved themselves of benefit to the race. They furnish safe guides for human conduct, in so far as the circumstances at hand do not present novel conditions and new questions. In any given case and for any particular question, it is vastly improbable that a new moral measure, or a new ethical con-

A priori method fruitless.

ception, is safe, or will ever become consistent with human well-being. Nevertheless, it is equally true that moral intuitions, the dictates of conscience, have been subject to change in the past and will in the future change in some measure for some lines of human conduct. Those moral ideas, for example, on which the very existence of a warlike tribe depends — ideas which must then bé registered in the average conscience of the people — are not suited to the conditions of an industrial society, and would tend to work not merely the disruption of the society, but the destruction of the race. As societies advance, moral conceptions undergo modification. As the necessities of our civilization change, the moral code must change to necessary correspondence — change, however, for the most part, by expansion and extension of those ideas now generally held as moral and apparently definitely and intricately interwoven with the well-being of society.

Upon this abstract notion of justice, and upon different interpretations and extensions of it, rests most of the ethical opposition to socialism. But it must be recognized as possible, — it is not *prima facie* probable — that our present idea of justice, and particularly our extensions of it by logic and analogy, may in the development of the race undergo important modifications. That for present necessities the dictates of conscience are to be regarded as registered rules deduced from the past for the well-being of the race, does not imply that the future well-being of the race will of necessity be associated with these rules. And yet, when there is found a moral conception as firmly established as is this of justice, as clearly upon the increase in definiteness and breadth of application, and as fundamental to social existence in all highly developed societies, we must admit the probability that larger applications of it will accompany further social progress, and we must assent to the improbability that any system repugnant to this conception will prove for any long period of time to be of advantage to civilization.

226. On the other hand, it must be borne in mind that the extension of state activities in the direction of socialism

does not, in fact, strike the average human conscience as a question of morals in any sense. To regard the case as a moral one is mostly peculiar to those who, proceeding from cases in which the conscience dictate is clear for all men, have reasoned thereon by analysis and comparison. Morality is not in origin, or largely in mental processes, a matter of analogy or reason. Proposals which do not offend the general moral consensus must be hesitatingly condemned, even if to the view of the trained intellect they appear to be inconsistent with logical and analogical extensions of abstract moral ideas.

As the outcome of this phase of the discussion, we may conclude that the ethical line of approach is neither very helpful nor altogether trustworthy; that the justification for government is neither to be sought nor found in abstract moral conceptions, but in the necessities of race existence in view of conditions as they are; and that by the moral test socialism does not stand condemned, although fairly subject to an unfavourable presumption. Any particular measure tending toward enlarged state activities is not to be condemned upon that ground alone, but is to be examined upon its merits as a question of expediency entirely apart from questions of tendency.

We may, at the same time, as does for himself the writer, retain our faith in the general tendencies of liberty as against restraint; our trust in individual initiative, in local government, in decentralization, and in strict constitutional construction; our belief that there is danger of too much rather than of too little government, and our conviction that in all cases of doubt, opinion should incline toward non-interference.

HISTORICAL ASPECTS

227. Still arguing about the edges of socialism, we find ourselves at these intermediate conclusions,— that it does not greatly matter to the argument that the conditions of one or

three hundred years ago may have been more fortunate than those of the present; that laissez-faire, either as a scheme for practical government, or as a system of ethical theory, will not serve in rigid and consistent applications; but that for purposes of presumption and prophecy, the ideal of liberty has some indefinite value.

We may go somewhat farther than this in mere presumptive condemnation of socialism. While we are not able to follow the individualist in his *a priori* condemnations of restraint and in his idealistic assertions of human perfectibility, we yet must believe that, as long as men live together in society, they are likely to become better adapted to social conditions. As mere matter of correspondence to environment, the high moral requirements which the present social organization makes, if it is to run smoothly, will tend in larger degree to be fulfilled as the present organization continues. A presumption, therefore, exists against any system which seems to run counter to the main currents of civilization, and to be destined to abandonment at some, though possibly a distant time, in the forward movement of humanity. Nevertheless, as a temporary expedient, it may well be that the system of socialism is best for the present emergency. *The ideal society.*

228. Turning from these ethical aspects of socialism, some perplexing questions of historical development present themselves. The socialist is convinced that the streams of tendency are with him. Humanity has met a new set of conditions during the last hundred years. Steam in the factory and steam for transportation on land and sea, together with the developments of this century in the science and technique of industry, have, in bringing the great cities, the great factories, and the great employers, brought in their train, as one further stage of development, the monopolies, the trusts, the pools, the world-wide tendency toward world-wide combination. Four men together are said to be in practical control of the railroads of the United States, which are nearly half the railroads of the world. Competition is destroying competition; com- *Tendencies in history.* *One side.*

bination is the inevitable outcome. Monopoly profits turned in part toward sinking funds for cut-throat competition, have already destroyed the very fibre of the present industrial organization. If the government will not absorb the monopolies, the outcome will not be very different in the absorption by the monopolies of the government.

Not only this, but the growing strength of law and order and organization in the world, the constant reaching out of the State toward new industrial fields — the railroads and telegraphs in Europe, the postal service over almost the entire world, banking interests in large measure, and the coining function generally — present themselves to the socialist as tendencies in his favour. More than all this, the tendency of democracy toward extension of the powers and functions of the State is so marked as to have roused the apprehensions of far-sighted opponents of socialism. All Europe, even England, is striving against the rising tide of state insurance, state charities, state savings banks, state regulation of the trades, state supervision of shops and factories, state arbitration by compulsion, state tenement houses. The socialist rightly perceives, in the development of political power among the masses, his best hope of triumph. If socialism comes, it will come ushered in by democracy.

229. The individualist, on the other hand, finds something of an argument for his side of the case. Indeed, one always finds facts enough for his own side to make a respectable argument, if he carefully leaves out all that is inconvenient. It is called to mind that the history of civilization is the story of the decay of tyranny and the growth of liberty, of the breaking up of military despotisms and the substitution of free commonwealths of industry, of the change from kingship to manhood suffrage and representative government. The individualist argues, also, that under the régime of free contract and individual initiative, the world has progressed beyond parallel at any other time; that under the stimulus of private interest, have resulted a long series of the most glorious triumphs of human

The other side.

thought and energy; that these have come about in human societies very nearly in proportion to the degree in which individualism has been developed; and that not only have these achievements covered those departments of activity most closely connected with personal interests,— for example, the applications of science to industry and to methods of organization in business,— but have also, and in nearly equal degree, extended themselves into the realms of philosophy and art and abstract science. In fact, one touches no levels of lower achievement in passing from the most practical of human concerns to subjects like biology and psychology. There are no evidences of paralysis in literature, sociology, or speculation. The forces of individualism seem in no wise exhausted in the fields of higher education, religion, and philanthropy, or even in the earnest scientific examination of the claims of socialism. These last one hundred years of liberty have been at once the very flowering and fruiting time of human history. The student of it is even inclined to wonder how long this marvellous rush of things can last, and whether when it ceases it may not indeed be socialism which is to follow as a close of a wonderful era — coming like the dead leaves after harvest, or as the gathering ashes over waning fires. The earnest observer is inclined to give more than the expected weight to the argument of the individualist, and to query whether civilization has not grown top-heavy in material and intellectual progress; to believe that a period of comparative lethargy is necessary in which the race shall gather new forces and shall develop morally to the level of the new requirements.

In truth, the socialist himself, no matter how bitter his criticism of the present order, will hardly deny that his system would be impracticable and unendurable did it not follow after the present society, its accomplishment in science and invention, its organization of industry, its lessons of experience. If, now, the State shall come to own the telegraph, the steamboat, the electric motor, the loom, the railroad, it is yet reasonably certain that under state control these things would never have come into existence. Socialism may prove an excellent thing after the period of advancement has passed, when the progressive energies of competition have spent themselves and the time of harvest has come, but it will remain true that under no other than a system of liberty and free contract could this progress have been possible.

Upon the assumption of a general tendency in civilization toward development, socialism seems therefore possible only as a temporary condition. Otherwise than as temporary, it must stand in antagonism to the forward movement of the race.

It is not, however, safely to be assumed that society will continue to progress along the line upon which progress has already taken place; or, indeed, that the next social epoch will be a distinctly progressive one.

SOCIALISM

When Louis Blanc and Mably rely upon the sentiment of honour instead of personal interest as the spur of production and the rein of consumption, and in respect to effectiveness instance the army code of honour, they forget, among other things, the thirty cases of capital punishment provided in the military code. . . . Were all burdens and pleasures of life equally distributed under strict communism, and distributed equally in line with the concepts of the masses, men like Thaer, Arkwright, and others, who now in library and laboratory produce food for hundreds of thousands, would produce with mattock and shovel at the highest enough for three or four men only. . . . General and equal popular education as the communists demand it would practically work out at this merely — that no one would attain to the higher scientific development. . . . "In place of the current competition to produce the most and the best possible there would come about under socialism a competition as to who could produce least and worst." (BASTIAT.) . . . When the first Virginia settlers in 1611 abandoned the system of communistic labour and joint-stock methods, it came about immediately that in one day there was as much accomplished as before in a week, three labourers producing as much as thirty did before. Even in New England among strong men accustomed to labour, who had made so great sacrifices in the interest of their faith, communism was attended with continual famine; this changed only in 1623, when private property was established. — ROSCHER, translated from *System der Volkswirtschaft*, Book II., *passim*.

As to the attitude of socialistic thought toward the more important sides of civilization, Roscher recalls the decree of September, 1793, by which the garden of the Tuileries was ordered changed to a potato field, and notes that later Hebert obtained a decree whereby under pain of death all parks were to be changed into potato fields. Babeuf declared all science and art to be evil; no one ought to learn more than reading, writing, and ciphering, and a little geography of France. It is intelligible that Bismarck should have pronounced socialism "Ein von inappellablen Demagogen regiertes Zuchthaus." — Roscher, Book II. c. 81, 82.

In truth, I regard it unfortunately as very conceivable that the future may bring us important tendencies toward the level of current German socialism, — not so much along democratic as along imperial lines through greatly increased taxation, police organization, and centralization, and especially through increased state activities. . . . Moreover, experience teaches that for the most part very poor and uncouth stages of social development practise in greater or less degree common ownership of property. — Roscher, Book II. c. 84.

ECONOMIC ARGUMENT

230. We are now ready to approach the different schemes for social remedy in their more purely economic aspects. It will, however, conduce to the saving of time still to apply ourselves more particularly to the examination of socialism.

However antagonistic socialism and anarchism may be on their positive sides, they join issue in fierce attack upon the present social order. We shall find that in their affirmative aspects, in definite tangible recommendations, in the detail of their proposals, neither socialism nor anarchism has as yet much to offer. The normal development and adjustment of things is expected to provide a new scheme of organization after the old is once done away.

There is, however, this much of definiteness in positive socialism: its new organization is expected to establish itself through a gradual extension and multiplication of the activities of the State substantially as we now know it. No cataclysm is wished or expected, no breach in orderly development and continuity. Your modern socialist is an evolutionist.

In an earlier aspect of the discussion, the question was raised, but not answered, whether the developments of the last hundred years have worked to the advantage of the labouring classes. It seems clear that with the increased productive efficiency of labour, wages have largely increased and the level of comfort has risen. That this gain is in no part offset by other tendencies, we need not claim. Whether the development of things has been fortunate or unfortunate, competition cannot justify itself by pointing to progress achieved under it, — if there has been any, — without showing that this progress has been due to the competitive system. Compulsory coöperation does not make out its case till it has shown itself better adapted to conditions as they will and must exist.

Has the nineteenth century been well for men?

Likewise when the socialists assert that the outlook for the future is a dismal one, that the doctrines of the established political economy point to disaster, the truth of the assertion need not, for present purposes, be examined. The reply is by way of a question — What of it? Will socialism serve better? If, as the necessary outcome of the tendencies toward reproduction, the world is definitely set toward over-population, nothing in particular follows. Is the danger less under the collectivist's scheme? There are restraints more or less effective in the competitive system; how does the other system compare? If the Ricardian doctrine of rent compels the conclusion that over-population means hunger, the question remains whether under socialism over-population can mean something else. The competitive system is not responsible for these sociological and agricultural facts, nor is the economist who announces them chargeable with them. Our business is to compare competing systems in the light of economic laws. The competitive system is on trial in comparison with other systems and not as an ideal type of organization.

What of it?

For this purpose of comparison, then, it will be profitable to consider the objections urged against the present organization of society, and to inquire what remedy therefor is offered by the socialistic scheme as against the solutions possible under the existing system.

These objections will be considered under the three heads of Production, Distribution, and Consumption.

COMPETITIVE PRODUCTION CRITICISED

(See Section 147)

231. That there are considerable wastes in competition is not open to question. The stimulus of private interest works out in a vast amount of crime and disorder which necessitates, in policemen, courts, juries, sheriffs, and lawyers, the expenditure of important social energies. *The wastes of competition.* Likewise, in purely private affairs the expense of preventive methods against ill-faith and dishonesty is a weighty matter. Outlays of this sort would be relatively small in the collectivist system.

There are large wastes of energy in competitive attempts to give to cheapness the outside gloss of value. Shoddy in cloth, paper in-soles in shoes, clay in soap, marl in sugar, not only waste the energy of putting them in, but largely destroy the usefulness of the honest share of the product. Socially speaking, all this cheapness is excessively dear.

There is a similar compound of waste with something worse than waste, in the enormous outlay for newspaper puffing and lying. The entire system, also, of marketing through agents and commercial travellers has in it large elements of waste. The excessive multiplication of middlemen, generally, falls under the same head. No doubt, however, some share of this outlay is socially productive. (See Section 101.)

232. In many industries, also, competition does not make toward cheapness either apparent or real, but conduces directly and inevitably to wastes of energy. These are, for the most part, cases falling under the law of increasing returns, where, with expanding production, the cost decreases per unit of out-

put. In these cases, combination of some sort is an ultimate certainty, unless made legally impossible. But commonly combination does not occur until large expenditures have been made in unnecessary competing investments. One city water plant, one gas plant, one tramway company, are all that are needed in most cities, and all that are possible if the minimum of productive cost is to be attained. Parallel lines of railroad work in many cases not merely a loss of capital, but compel permanently high outlays for transportation and high transportation charges. It continually happens that several railroads divide the traffic which might equally readily, and much more economically, be handled by one. Socially speaking, there is no escape under the present system from these evils, otherwise than as in some degree combination may transform them into another sort of evil — which will be discussed under the head of Distribution.

Wastes as related to industries of increasing returns.

The carelessness of employers in matters of light, ventilation, and sanitation must also be regarded as productive losses, by reason of the permanent injuries which are entailed upon the productive powers of the labourers. For similar reasons, the mental, moral, and physical evils of child labour, and in some degrees of women's labour, must be considered under this head.

The present system is also responsible for hordes of human beings living by their wits or their worthlessness — social make-nothings, paupers, vagabonds, speculators of useless types, prostitutes.

233. Parallel with these are the respectable do-nothings, the leisure rich, the inheritors of wealth, the coupon-cutters. Within this class of respectable make-nothings must be reckoned, also, the valets and waiting-maids, the out-riders, hostlers, servants, and flunkeys, whose energies never work out in any utility for which the world has any real need. (But see Sections 250, 251.)

And in a background of misery stand the unemployed, with whom, as misery, we are not at present concerned, but only as waste. Never an inconsiderable class, they swell in times of industrial depression to an enormous army.

COMPETITIVE DISTRIBUTION CRITICISED

234. Recalling that the subject of distribution concerns the forces which apportion the social dividend into wages, profits, rent, and interest, we have to inquire whether the competitive system works out to justice in this regard. What are its tendencies?

The evils falling under this head are not largely in the line of waste. Such leaks of energy as are due to the multiplication of middlemen, jobbers, wholesalers, agents, commercial travellers, and numberless retailers, fall, as we have seen, under the head of production. These men are not in theory distributors, but producers. But there are, clearly enough, too many of them.

It was shown in Section 153 that little can be accomplished by wage-earners toward decreasing the share of the capitalists in production. Nor have we yet seen good reason in justice why this decrease should be attempted. In truth, there appears to be no good reason to believe that, could this decrease be accomplished, any benefit would accrue to the wage-earner therefrom. (Section 127.)

The objections to the landlord's share of the social product seem to be well founded, to the extent that this share is derived from the unearned increment element in land values. This subject will be discussed more fully in later pages. (Sections 282, 283.)

The wage-earner's quarrel is, however, mainly against the employer, the imprenditor, and concerns the distributive share called profits.

Are imprenditors' profits out of proportion to their services? (See Section 127.)

Can wage-earners other than in individual cases greatly suffer from injustice at the employer's hands?

Does competition generally protect the wage-earner in this respect? (See Section 128.)

Who profit mostly, imprenditors or consumers, from unjust treatment of wage-earners? (See Section 128.)

Does any one, in the long run, profit from the different methods of scamping? (See Section 128.)

235. Criticisms of the distributive system are better founded as applied to monopolies. We have seen that monopolies result from conditions in which competition involves large wastes. Where these wastes come to an end, the bad distribution of monopolies begins.

The profits of speculators also fall within the topic of distribution. What part of these are indefensible? (See Sections 134–136.)

In what degree are they attributable to a bad land system, or to stock operations within the industries which naturally tend toward monopoly?

Are the profits of middlemen, merchants, wholesalers, etc., defensible in any degree? (See Section 101.) Are they overlarge?

COMPETITIVE CONSUMPTION CRITICISED

236. Consumption is merely one phase of demand — the most important phase — and as such is at the very foundation of all economic reasonings. Political Economy, as an art, can hardly go deeply into its subject-matter, human welfare, without attempting to fix, so far as is possible, the relations of wealth consumption to human well-being. In a later chapter, something like a full examination of this topic will be attempted. For present purposes, however, we shall merely note what seems, under this head, the most effective line of attack on the present social order; namely, the entirely artificial nature of much of its demand for wealth. Under a system of practical equality in the division of product, the present enormous outlays of energy devoted to the competition

of display would find no place. How important a matter these are must be postponed for later examination.

237. The great total of consumption in vicious, or wasteful and health-injuring lines requires mention here. It is a serious question, however, whether with our present imperfect knowledge of physical and mental hygiene, and with the impossibility, in the nature of the case, of our ever becoming certain that there is no more to know, it is desirable to attempt control over the individual in these respects, otherwise than as his action may bear in direct and considerable fashion upon the well-being of his fellows. It is well to keep in mind, however, that any form of protection, if judged to be expedient, may as properly be extended over the interests of future generations, as of contemporaries. On the other hand, it must be remembered that liberty as a developmental force by virtue of the responsibility which it imposes upon the individual, and as the first condition to the effective working out of the law of the survival of the fittest, has in itself a value to offset many an admitted evil. *Sumptuary legislation.*

SOCIALISM AS A REMEDIAL SCHEME

238. Before proceeding to a detailed examination of the various problems suggested in the preceding sections, it will be well to consider, in broad lines, the merits of socialism as a remedy for these evils.

Would it enlarge the social dividend? Undoubtedly in some degree the protective duties of the State would be lightened by the disappearance in a large measure of the temptations to evil associated with private interests. On the other hand, the multiplication of purely administrative offices would be great. *Would it enlarge the dividend?*

The wastes of adulteration and scamping would mostly be avoided, but trades-unionism and well-considered legislation should be sufficient to control these under the present system.

The outlays for middlemen, agents, and advertising are not entirely wastes at present — perhaps not even mostly wastes. That goods could be sold at lower prices without them is not final, if they must be sold at less convenience in time or place. Centralized merchandising is not an unmixed advantage, as is proved by the fact that the small shop maintains its existence under the present system. Yet in large measure it is true that the competition of middlemen is a strife for customers rather than for lower prices. In the degree that the case is a serious one in this aspect, voluntary coöperative merchandising, as at present applied, appears to offer a complete remedy.

The wastes from the subdivision of industries which could better be centralized, and from the multiplication of lines of transportation, must be admitted. If, however, these evils could be avoided under state socialism, this fact would justify precisely this degree of socialism under the present system, but not the socialistic system entire. We shall see later that, even in these cases, state operation does not appear to be the only practicable remedy.

The army of loafers, rich and poor, are not necessary products of the competitive system, but are in large measure the result of a vicious system of landholding, of an extremely individualistic view of rights of inheritance, of a lax and unscientific administration of both public and private charities. These questions will come up later for extended treatment. The leisure classes, also, have some important economic functions commonly disregarded. (See Sections 250, 251.)

There remain for consideration the wastes of productive energy attending financial crises. Not only from the point of view of production alone, but as well from other points of view yet to be considered, we are constrained to admit that if the commerical crisis is beyond remedy within the present system, there can be little danger of society finding itself worse off in any probable change. Indeed, it may be asserted that, in the view of the average wage-earner, if there were no commercial crisis with its uncertainties, its injustices, its hunger, its temptations and

Crises.

humiliations for men and women, there would be no social question.

239. To resume, socialism, as a system of production, must be admitted to possess important advantages over the present system, so far as concerns natural monopolies and some of the immoralities of production. It could do something to limit the undesirable multiplication of middlemen. It would put an end to commercial crises. *Resumé.*

On the other hand, it would paralyze the motive powers of production by removing the stimulus of personal interest — by destroying all relation between remuneration and product, between compensation and effort.

Not so evident, but equally important, is the fact that under socialism, religion, art, poetry, literature, science, philosophy, and speculation would become state activities, or would perish; and as between disappearance and state control, there could be no great choice. These things are economic products — commodities under the form of services. The socialistic conception of wealth is sheer materialism. (See Section 20.)

Again, even restricting the notion of wealth to material products, it must be called to mind that the industrial effectiveness of labour is largely dependent upon the aid of science. If socialism in its economy of energies is of doubtful advantage at present, it would with passing time become increasingly bad.

Socialism would introduce an era of individual irresponsibility, and of state tyranny in matters of thought and faith. It would result in intellectual and moral lethargy — a vegetable humanity.

As a scheme for distribution, socialism would do away with the imprenditor — the captain of industry — the brain centre of enterprise. This can hardly be proposed in the interests of maximum production. The employer holds his place by virtue of his service to the wage-earner. (See Section 127.)

It may, however, be true that society could well forego some measure of product in aid of a better distribution of product.

Under the head of Consumption, we shall find some ground for assenting to this proposition in the abstract. Still it is not clear that the present system allows to the imprenditor rewards out of proportion to his services, or that the tendency of profits is such as to justify uneasiness. (Section 127.) Income taxation deserves examination in this regard. To the extent that employers are able by injustice or oppression to profit at the expense of wage-earners, the development of trades-unionism ought, in different ways, — later to be examined, — to offer a remedy. At all events, the sufferings of wage-earners under free contract are probably not greater than would be those under officialism with its possibilities in oppression and favouritism.

As concerns consumption, socialism seems to offer a sufficient remedy for the wastes of product which go with the competitions of display. These evils are far-reaching, even appalling, and it is not clear that the present social order has in it any remedy. (See Sections 259–274.)

In the lack of speculative adjustments of supply to social requirements, socialism is at some disadvantage. A system of exchange of day's labour for day's labour would not serve for this case. Yet some practicable modification could probably be found with regard to cereal products, and, if necessary, the State might hold even the supply of an entire year in reserve.

240. Early failures of socialism do not of necessity argue its ultimate impracticability, but merely that success is not possible on crudely experimental lines. There is a science in socialism if there is an art.

Confusion in terminology.

Nor, indeed, have all the efforts toward social amelioration called socialistic, rightly borne the name. The brave band of philanthropists who, under the lead of Kingsley and Maurice in England, devoted themselves forty years ago to the spread of self-help, coöperation, and labourer's initiative, called themselves socialists. They were individualists in methods — advocates of voluntary association. So at present there is a body of earnest, high-purposed effort, which insists on confusing terminologies by calling itself Christian-socialistic. Socialism is something else.

241. There are defects enough in our present social order — grounds for discontent and dissatisfaction — evils which the socialists believe their plan to avoid. Nevertheless the central fact in the competitive system, the free struggle for competitive profits, is the central point in the socialistic attack upon it. *Profits are subject of controversy.* The wage-earner asserts that he fails of obtaining his fair share of the social dividend. He does not receive as much as he produces. Lay aside the question of waste, lay aside the query whether socialism would better apply the social energies, the present system is denounced as unjust in not properly apportioning rewards to services, in somehow tricking the labourer — exploiting him, as he puts it — for the gain of some one else.

Observe, however, that the attack is not greatly upon the rent share of the product. Rents are inevitable, though possibly the State should appropriate a larger share of them. (See Sections 282, 283.) This, however, is possible by taxation or by some method outside socialism. Nor is the contest largely upon the question of interest. Interest also is unavoidable. As long as wealth aids in production, its use will be attended with the right to compensation. Interest is remunerative of real services.

242. The socialistic quarrel is with the employer — the imprenditor — upon the justifiability of profits. The question remains, then, whether these are too large. Is the profit system just? Are profits received at the expense of employés? Do profits correspond to services rendered?

On the side of the socialist, it is urged that labour alone is creative of wealth. Capital itself commands remuneration only in its character of stored-up labour. If all product is the result of labour, the remuneration should absorb it all. There is no room for profit. *Is labour alone productive?*

This is true enough, but true only when the term "labour" is made sufficiently inclusive and is rightly understood. There are different sorts of labour. No man has raised more corn than the chemist, or woven more cloth than the inventor. The employer is a labourer as well as is the operator at the loom. Under socialism, there must be overseers, planners, managers, directors, captains. In war, the generals as well as the privates are soldiers. The victories are due to both.

Wage-earners enlist with the imprenditor, because of his ability to procure from them larger services, and to provide for them a larger recompense than they could obtain under their own management. (Section 127.)

Profits, when large, fall to the employer by the commonplace fact that peculiarly large ability brings peculiarly large returns, the amount of the profit being chiefly determined by the degree in which any imprenditor is able to reduce his expenses of production below those of the marginal employer. (Section 127.) Even the marginal employer is able to pay labourers at above their productive ability when working for themselves. Labourers receive, by reason of the competition of their employers, approximately the amount by which they add to product.

Any system of economy which attempts to dispense with high managerial ability will suffer correspondingly in social dividend. Wherever labourers can succeed without an employer, the system of coöperative production stands open to them. (Section 127.)

The evils associated with the relation of employer and employé are numerous enough and serious enough. So far as these evils consist in injustice by the employer toward individual employés, trades-unionism should suffice for a remedy. Trade-unions and the law together should suffice to prevent adulteration and scamping. (Section 153.) Monopoly, so far as it is socially injurious, rests largely upon cut-throat competition. The remedy is a problem well within the machinery of legislatures and courts. The compensations for risk are justified by the very fact of the risk. Speculative profits flow from social

Is socialism necessary as a remedy?

service, though intermixed with gains from dishonest methods. Land speculation should meet through taxation all necessary discouragement.

The discussion has probably proceeded far enough to indicate that, in the view of the writer, the social question is not strictly one question, but rather a congeries of questions. No one thing is the matter with society, and no one device will suffice for a remedy. In this attitude will be approached the various methods of social amelioration.

COÖPERATION AND PROFIT-SHARING

243. Much that has been said of socialism will apply to coöperation, so far as coöperation is a method of distribution of the social dividend. The terms "coöperation" and "coöperative distribution" are liable to misconception. *Definitions.* Coöperative production and coöperative merchandising must be accurately discriminated. That coöperation is a vast success in England and Scotland is certain, but coöperation mostly confined to merchandising.

There are undoubtedly great wastes in the system of middlemen, in extensive advertising, including in large part the rent of palatial locations, in the dear cheapnesses of gloss and shoddy, and in bad debts. *Advantages of coöperation.* The coöperative societies of England and Scotland embrace a membership of nearly a million and a half, representing a consuming population of probably five millions of people. These societies have succeeded in cancelling the wastes above mentioned. The local societies, mostly doing business on a cash basis, are relieved of the necessity of advertising and of losses from bad accounts. Goods of honest quality only are bought and sold. These local societies are banded together coöperatively, in great central wholesale houses, conducted similarly to the retail societies. Both wholesale and retail societies sell at ordinary market prices in competition with ordinary dealers, and distribute the profits annually to members in proportion to the purchases made. The system operates primarily as a reduction in prices, and secondarily as an automatic savings institution. Its success has been enormous and progressive. Coöperative merchandising is no longer an experiment.

244. Distribution, as an economic term, means something altogether different. It points to the method of distributing the dividend and not of expending the quotient.

What about distribution? The problems of distribution refer to the forces and tendencies manifest in the apportionment of wages, profits, rent, and interest. Coöperation, as it bears upon production, meets difficulties similar to those examined under socialism. How dispense with the manager? How substitute for his far-sighted authoritative direction the collective, many-minded stupidity and inexperience of the workingmen? This problem may be solved sometime with increasing ability among the masses. Sometime also positions as industrial managers may afford openings as a half-philanthropic profession to those among the rich who seek a life of usefulness. Thus far coöperative production has registered few successes.

Clearly enough, it offers advantages in enlisting the earnest, watchful interest of the labourer, and in the economy of material and machinery which it fosters. In some

Coöperative production. industries it may prove practicable; but even at its best, it is unlikely to occupy more than a subordinate position in any condition of society. Social students may wish well to the institution, in view of the fact that, with its spread, many of the fallacies current among workingmen, both in politics and industry, will tend to disappear with repeated illustration that wages flow from product. In fact, coöperation is in many ways educational.

245. In one other respect, also, coöperative distribution has great value as supplementary to competitive distribution. In ultimate analysis, demand and supply are merely

different aspects of supply, different products seeking exchange with each other. Coöperation is well adapted in times of distress to preserving demand and supply in condition of effective adjustment for purposes of exchange. The poverty of hard times is the equivalent of low production following upon the out-of-joint condition of exchanges. Division of labour is only in part effective, and the substitute system of barter establishes itself slowly and inadequately. This condition of faulty adjustment finds its cause in currency disturbances. Clearly if coöperation were general, money might be dispensed with, as in socialism. With a widely extended system of coöperation also, coöperators might, without great discomfort, forego, during the period of emergency, the use of circulating media. *Amelioration of panics.*

In this connection there opens up a promising field of usefulness for trades-unions. A system of emergency workshops between which exchanges should take place by the crude appliances of barter, the terms of exchange being determined by the price levels of the general market, would go far to mitigate the sufferings from lockouts and strikes, and would largely disarm the famished competition of the out-of-works. The Salvation Army at present makes partial application of this principle.

PROFIT-SHARING

246. Accepting the principle that wages flow from product, it follows that in proportion as competition among employers is effective, wages tend to increase with advancing product. Competition is, in fact, a sort of automatic profit-sharer. Labourers, however, rarely appreciate this; and in truth competition seldom acts swiftly or perfectly enough to make it completely true. To the extent that it is true, employers can have no reasonable objection to profit-sharing. To the extent that it fails of *Competition tends to protect wage-earners.*

truth, profit-sharing is due to labourers as a mere matter of justice, on condition, however, that they will live up to it, that is, will accept a necessary fall in wages cheerfully and loyally, allowing some part of their accrued profits from prosperous times to stand as a guaranty fund for their fidelity in less favourable weather. Wages, as they rise slowly, fall slowly. It will later be considered whether some of the most serious aspects of commercial crises do not find their explanation in this fact.

247. Profit-sharing is thus at best a system of wages-supplement, intended to conform, as nearly as practicable, to conditions as they would exist under perfect competition. Profit-sharing rests, as matter of theory, upon the just and normal tendency of wages to correspond to profits. (Section 65.) It follows, then, that if there is in profit-sharing of itself some tendency toward an increase of product, wages may advance consistently with the advancing profits of employers. In fact, the motive of employers in proposing profit-sharing is rarely one of philanthropy or love of justice, but merely an offer of somewhat enlarged wages in consideration of considerably enlarged product — a mere device in wage-paying. This is possible through the heightened energy and care and economy of the employés resulting from their clearer view of the fact that, as producers, their interests are parallel with the interests of their employers. In fact, many economic complications will come untangled with the better appreciation of this principle.

A wage-paying device.

In the light of the foregoing discussion, the advantages and disadvantages of the ownership by employés of stock in incorporated industries will readily be estimated.

NOTES

The difference between the product of interested labour and that of labour which is careless and lazy is always noticeable; but in a whale fishery it is exceptionally great. An eager search, a zealous pursuit, and a resolute attack are secured only by the stimulus of a personal interest

in the result. Superintendence by owners is impossible, unless the captain be a proprietor ; and, if he is so, the plan becomes to that extent coöperative. Even though the captain were the sole owner, his best efforts would not insure a profitable voyage, unless a heartier obedience could be secured than is usually seen on ships. Moreover, payment by the day might interest the crew in unduly prolonging the voyage. Profit-sharing has, therefore, driven the wage system from this industry.
— CLARK, *Phil. of Wealth*, p. 184.

STATE AND MUNICIPAL OWNERSHIP

248. The measure in which it may prove desirable for society as a whole to operate industries under government monopoly, depends largely on how far these industries tend to become private monopolies otherwise. Wherever competition is attended with considerable wastes, combination tends to establish itself. With railroads, for example, multiplication of lines and division of traffic make for increased cost of service, whatever may be the effect on the charge at which these services are rendered. The tendency, therefore, toward combination is a strong one. *Natural monopolies.*

Over and above these wastes, private ownership of transportation interests is accompanied by the familiar evils of traffic discrimination and by the infinite ingenuity of dishonesty for personal gain.

249. Governmental intervention of some sort in transportation industries is unavoidable, not in granting corporate existence, — for this is merely the recognition of a partnership, — but in the delegation of the power of eminent domain, without which projected railroad improvements would go to wreck upon the greed of private ownership. Intervention seems indispensable likewise for the control of dishonesty and the prevention of discrimination. Whether something more radical than intervention should be undertaken, is more questionable — as a matter, however, of expediency or necessity, and not as a *Intervention of some sort necessary.*

question of abstract principle. Comparing state ownership in the continental states of Europe with private ownership in England and America, either in cost of service or in efficiency of service, experience thus far argues strongly in favour of private ownership. Such improvements, indeed, as have been made under a state ownership have been mostly borrowed from railroads managed under individual ownership. Not only this, but as long as private ownership in land, with its attendant speculation, continues, state ownership of transportation industries must lead to infinite demoralization in politics. On the other hand, there are in the present system great dangers in something the same direction by lobby and bribery.

If possible, the advantages of private enterprise should be preserved in combination with the helpful tendencies of state control. Rigorous supervision, together with progressive taxation on profits and dividends, should be sufficient for this case. The French people have proceeded upon the plan of granting franchises for long terms of years with a reversion to the State of the franchises and property at the end of the term. Possibly state ownership of roadbeds would be advantageous, the property being leased by competitive bids for operation by private corporations.

Practical intervention.

With regard to natural monopolies in municipal affairs, as, for example, tramways, gas, electric light, and water companies, the choice seems to lie between municipal operation pure and simple, progressive taxation on profits, and competitive leasing. It is certainly indefensible that these valuable franchises should be transferred without compensation and in perpetuity to private interests.

THE SOCIAL FUNCTION OF THE RICH

250. Riches are largely relative. The desire for inequality is an important force among the motives of wealth production. Were all equally rich or equally poor, both the joy of wealth

and the sting of poverty would mostly disappear from life. Mere leadership and the possession of power are things which human nature prizes. No inconsiderable share of our wealth owes its attractiveness to the fact that others admire us or envy us. The mansion on the hill is desirable, not so much for the view which it commands of the squalid huts below, as for the view which the squalid indwellers have of the mansion on the hill. **Riches partly relative.**

These uses of wealth outside the range of ordinary consumption have already been referred to, and are at the foundation of some of the most perplexing problems of social life. Yet no small part of the charm of rural scenery and of the beauty which makes city life endurable has its origin in mere ostentation. The rich are not able even in this respect entirely to monopolize their wealth.

In truth, no man can in his own right and for his own benefit consume a very considerable portion of riches. This is partial consolation socially for those cases in which large fortunes fall to their possessors otherwise than as the reward for productive activity. The profits of land speculation, in almost their entirety, and in considerable degree the profits of other speculation, correspond to no social service. But the inventors, the manufacturers, the projectors and organizers of the great industries, the new methods and the new systems, hold their fortunes by good title of services rendered.

The consuming capacity of the individual is in many directions strictly limited. The rich can eat no more abundantly than the comfortably poor. Opportunities for pure waste are mostly confined to expenditures for servants, attendants, and flunkies. Rich men are commonly busy men of simple tastes. Extravagance is due to other members of the family. But whether directly or by the aid of the family, it is impossible for the very rich to consume their wealth. They must place it at the service of society as the condition of its preservation and of its dividend-paying capacity. Vanderbilt's steamships and railroads are not used or consumed by him, but by society. Factories **Limits on consumption.**

ultimately profit consumers rather than proprietors. Waste by the rich is doubtless an evil, but as mere waste a no very considerable evil. Distributed *per capita* among the wage-earners or the poor it would count for little.

251. The evils of great fortunes are rather political or social than economic. This is strikingly shown in Mr. Charles Booth's lately published work on the people of London. It is reassuring to note that out of the five million people in the rich city of London only sixty thousand all told, men, women, and children, enjoy the luxury of an establishment with as many as four servants. "With less than half of these is the number of servants greater than that of those they serve."

Evils mostly non-economic.

There are, however, some important and helpful social functions performed by the rich which are in danger of escaping attention. The first and the most obvious service is that of aiding in the accumulation and capitalization of wealth. It is also to be noted that the reserve force for meeting commercial depression and famine is in a large measure afforded by the savings of the rich and by the possible reduction in their superfluous consumption. The second helpful function is, perhaps, the more important. It is certainly the less obvious.

Benefits.

The case is stated admirably in the following quotation from Sidgwick: —

> There are, in fact, several distinct practical questions suggested by the connexion which history shews between the development of culture and the existence of a rich and leisured class in a community of human beings. We may (1) balance the additional happiness gained to the lives of the few rich by culture, against the additional happiness that might be enjoyed by the poor if wealth were more equally distributed; or (2) we may consider how far whatever happiness is derived from culture by the many poor depends at any given time on the maintenance of a higher kind of culture among the few rich; or (3) we may endeavour to forecast the prospective addition to happiness when culture shall have become more diffused, which would be endangered by any injury to its present development among the limited class who now have any considerable

share in it. From each of these distinct points of view, arguments of a certain force may be drawn in favour of the present inequality in distribution of wealth.

I refer to what may be comprehensively though vaguely designated as the function of maintaining and developing knowledge and culture. I distinguish knowledge from culture, though the latter notion would naturally include the former, because of the peculiar economic importance of the progress of science, as the source of inventions that increase the efficiency of labour. This progress in past ages has been largely due to the unremunerated intellectual activity, assisted by liberal expenditure, of rich and leisured persons. At the same time it is of course conceivable that the development of knowledge should be adequately carried on — as it is chiefly in Germany at the present time — by persons salaried and provided with instruments at the public expense. And the connexion between scientific discoveries and technical inventions is now so firmly established in the popular mind, that probably even a government controlled by persons of small incomes would not refuse the funds requisite for the support of the study of physical science in universities, academies, etc. The case is different with such knowledge as has no obvious, practical utility, and is therefore only likely to be valued by persons susceptible to the gratifications of disinterested curiosity. Such knowledge must be ranked, as a source of elevated and refined gratification, along with literature, art, intellectual conversation, and the contemplation of natural beauty. The capacities for deriving enjoyment from these sources constitute what we call culture; they are generally regarded by persons possessed of them as supplying a most important element in the happiness of life; while at the same time, so far as we can judge from past experience, it is only in a society of comparatively rich and leisured persons that these capacities — and, still more, the faculties of producing excellent works in literature and art — are likely to be developed and transmitted in any high degree.

There seems, therefore, to be a serious danger that a thoroughgoing equalization of wealth, among the members of a modern civilized community, would have a tendency to check the growth of culture in the community. The amount of loss to human happiness that is to be apprehended from this effect is difficult to estimate; especially since those who estimate it most highly would probably refuse to allow the question to be decided by a mere consideration of the actual amount of happiness that culture has hitherto given. They have a conviction for which they could not give an empirical justification that a diffusion of culture may be expected in the future which has no parallel in the past; and that any social changes which cripple its development, however beneficent they may be in other respects, may involve a loss to humanity in the aggregate which, if we look sufficiently far forward, seems quite immeasurable in extent. — *Principles*, p. 524.

Note in passing that by so much as weight is given to this argument is socialism condemned. There is, however, another aspect of the case which deserves examination. (See Sections 264–274.)

POPULATION

252. The law of decreasing returns as related to population indicates merely that the time has already come or will one day come when the food supply of the world must be obtained with increasing difficulty.

Decreasing returns.

Progressive development in the art and science of agriculture may for a long time counteract this tendency, but seemingly cannot in the outcome overbalance it. It is indeed possible that chemistry may sometime solve the problem of food production without recourse to agricultural methods. The secret once learned, the nitrogen in the air of the back yard and the ton of coal in the bin may furnish food for an ordinary family for a year. But assuming the necessity of a constant increase in the proportion of human energies applied to the production of food and of raw materials, it does not therefore follow that the lot of the race must grow increasingly harsh. The law of increasing returns is valid so far as it rests upon the possibilities of human development in the production of wealth. This tendency toward increasing returns may more than offset tendencies characteristic of land as a productive agent toward decrease. Indeed, this seems certain in the non-agricultural industries and possible even in the agricultural.

At all events, it would be a gross error to suppose that to double the population would halve the average distributive share in the social dividend. Why? (Section 92.)

253. The tendency with advancing civilization toward a lower rate of reproduction has already been remarked. (Sec-

tions 96, 97.) In view of this fact and of the evidence thereof furnished in the statistical tables already examined, the dictum of an English publicist that the future dominion of the world will rest with three races —the English, the Russian, and the Chinese, —is intelligible. *Lower birth-rate.* With Russia's yearly increase of a million and a half in numbers, with the spread of its populations over Russian Asia, and with its warlike imperial traditions, one understands the nightmare of dread which rests over western Europe. When Russia has perfected its Siberian railway system and has established its back-door *Russia.* basis of supplies in the civilization and workshops of America, its populations may again stir themselves to roll westward as once before two thousand years ago. A German said to me a few years since, "Germany has no longer any fear of France; we tremble for what may come from the east."

254. The contest of civilization against the hordes of Asia will hardly be one of arms, but a struggle for survival in the business of living. When western gunboats have foolishly broken down the barriers of *Asia.* exclusion about the Chinese, and have forced upon Asia the arts and sciences of western civilization, the Caucasian will find himself engaged in industrial death-grapple with a people of marvellous industrial efficiency, of swarming reproductive fertility, and of ability through centuries of poverty to thrive upon the minimum requirements of existence. The west has small interest to disturb the Asiatic hive. When the Chinese begin to pour out over the world, there will remain to the western races but one resource, that of crossing with the Chinese if they will consent to cross. On other terms western civilization may endure, but the western races hardly will. Viewed in this aspect, the value to the world of English civilization and of the colonizing and reproductive energies of the English-speaking people can hardly be exaggerated. From their little island in the North Sea twenty millions of people have in a hundred years subdued to English institutions two continents almost entire, and a large portion of two more,

while English stations and smaller English colonies are scattered over all the seas. The English language is now spoken as mother tongue by one hundred and twenty millions of people, and is the alternate language of three hundred millions more.

255. Some perplexing questions present themselves as to the relations of birth-rates and standards of comfort to race progress — questions which must for the most part await a wider knowledge for their answer.

Even with such modifications to the law of decreasing returns as have already been proposed, there are ominous suggestions in the tendencies of rent and population. Malthus, a hundred years ago, sounded the warning that over-population and poverty are fast linked together. We have seen some reason to question the universal validity of the Malthusian forecast. There are certainly some conditions in some types of civilization in which the tendency toward increase of numbers is not manifest. However, it seems clear enough that taking humanity as a whole, with the strong reproductive tendencies of the lower races, the Malthusian prophecy is essentially a correct one.

Standard of living and birth-rate.

Adopting in substance these conclusions, Herbert Spencer has constructed thereupon an argument of altogether un-Malthusian hopefulness. Let it be admitted that the race is unavoidably set toward poverty; it is precisely upon this condition and upon this condition only that its highest development is possible. According to this reasoning humanity will profit by the struggle for existence as have all other forms of life. The argument, in fact, goes farther. In modern society success in the struggle for existence mostly turns upon moral and intellectual qualities, rather than upon physical strength or physical endurance. Natural selection will tend to the elevation of the race average, through the constant elimination by death of those specimens of the race least adapted morally and intellectually to the strenuous conditions of the struggle. The necessarily increasing drain of nervous energy must moderate the strength of the

Herbert Spencer.

reproductive instinct, and will coöperate with hunger and disease in weeding out the over-productive and the improvident specimens of the race. The strongest forces for human improvement must therefore await the race discipline of poverty.

256. This is a skilful flank movement. If poverty is in truth inevitable, this new theory interprets it reassuringly. Moreover, as we have already seen, the evidence from lower forms of life lends strong support to the Spencerian interpretation.

There are, however, some characteristics peculiar to the human family which fit awkwardly into this doctrine. Roscher remarks, "The greater number and the longer continuance of his wants, are amongst the most striking differences between man and the brute. While the lower animals have no wants but necessities, and while their aggregate wants, even in the longest series of generations, admit of no qualitative increase, the circle of man's wants is susceptible of indefinite extension. And, indeed, every advance in culture made by man finds expression in an increase in the number and in the keenness of his rational wants." *Criticism.*

The accuracy of this observation is unquestionable. All forms of vegetable life and the non-human orders of animal life increase in number to the limits of subsistence. The limit of requirement does not change. Man develops new needs, new tastes, new desires, as well as a new intensity in each. That in any case higher standards of requirement have established themselves is proof that humanity has not in this case reproduced to the utmost possible limit. It costs care and money to raise children. Increased production of wealth may therefore expend itself in more rapid multiplication, or in service to higher *per capita* requirements. But the two lines of expenditure are distinct and antagonistic. Rising standards of life discourage procreation.

Not only this, but lower standards appear as clearly to encourage procreation. Nor are analogies for this case wanting among the lower forms of life. It is the knurly apple that has the most seeds, the lower orders of animal life which reproduce in swarms. With the higher orders the period of gestation is longer, the number brought forth at a birth is less. So with humanity, low standards of living mean hopelessness, carelessness, ignorance, and improvidence. The highest birth-rate is commonly found among criminals and paupers.

It seems inevitable that with those plants of which only one seed in a thousand comes to maturity, there should be an abundant production of seed, or that where of the young fish not one in a hundred escapes its enemies, the hatch should be a large one. This high birth-rate is the necessary condition to race survival, a necessary correlative of a high death-rate. Outside the human races, also, a high birth-rate involves a high death-rate, as does a high death-rate a high birth-rate. With an inelastic standard of life, increase in numbers cancels any advantage from easier conditions of existence.

257. But with an elastic standard of living, an entirely new problem is presented. Plentiful food no longer means, of necessity, a more rapid rate of multiplication, but, possibly enough, better houses and food, or better clothing, or more recreation, or more competitive show. A lower birth-rate, reaching even to absolute loss in numbers, may result.

If, on the other hand, diminished means of subsistence mean not so much a higher death-rate as a higher birth-rate with a falling standard of life, increased population making for poverty, and greater poverty for more rapid increase of population, until the minimum requirements of existence characteristic of brute life are reached, there is no great hope for humanity through the discipline of poverty.

In truth, there is small basis for expecting poverty or disease or crime to cancel itself by excess of death-rate over birth-rate.

Again, fortunately or otherwise, human sympathies introduce into the problem a new element. Men would be other than they are, were they wanting in this characteristic of sympathy. The criminal, the pauper, and the invalid will not be allowed to perish even were there likelihood of their disappearance in the absence of aid. But it is better to attempt to cure in the conviction that multiplication will take place anyway, than to abandon disease and vice in the hope that they will perish without offspring. Questions of methods are, however, matters of much greater difficulty.

258. Our discussion has been carried far enough to indicate the perplexities of the question. The author has small light to throw on the problems he has suggested. The following propositions, however, are hazarded, with no very strong confidence in their helpfulness or tenability.

Hope of race improvement, by the weeding out of material at the lower margin, as well as apprehension of deterioration from the relative infertility of the upper classes, are both without sufficient basis. So long as society does not crystallize into hard lines of caste and class, intermarriages may be depended upon to preserve any nation substantially homogeneous. *A process of adjustment.* To those who have sufficiently considered the bearing of the suggestive questions and arithmetical problems following Chapter VIII., it will be clear that in view of the essentially similar forces of heredity uniting in each one of us, there is small room for pronounced or important dissimilarities in nature or capacity, other than such as two or three generations can create or cancel. We are all of us more truly children of the race than children of our immediate parents. In conditions of life as complex as are those of the present, with fitness for survival a matter of so many and varied aspects, and in combinations so numerous, the law of the survival of the fittest can have no great share in the tendencies of race development. If the race shall ever become better adapted to the requirements of a higher life, it will be for the most part by that process known in biology as adjustment of structure to function — the progressive effects of use toward growth, and of disuse toward decay — the law which is broadly stated for everyday life in the expression, "practice makes perfect."

FASHION

259. We have just discussed the standard of living in its relation to birth and death rates. But the topic is a far wider one than this. In another aspect it is the whole subject of the consumption of wealth. Economics is, on one side, the study of wants manifested as demand, and working out through production into supply of commodities. On the other side, it is an examination of the different applications of wealth to human requirements and of the relation of these applications to the wealth-producing efficiency and the general well-being of men.

The task before us is one of no small difficulty. All the machinery and all the processes of economic life trace their energies back to this fact of consumption. All the purposes of production look forward to this fact as their goal. Man is the centre. The economic cycle begins in desire and ends in satisfaction. Having, therefore, examined consumption in its aspect of demand as economic energy, we have now to examine it more especially in its aspect as motive. We are set to investigate the ultimate values of wealth to men.

260. Evidently the subject goes wider than mere economics. As all sciences are one in service to the conduct of life, it necessarily follows that all problems of human life appeal for aid to many sciences. The consumption of wealth is inextricably interwoven with the most perplexing questions of living. It includes, indeed, the whole science of living and dying. It is therefore intelligible that political economy has no light of its own with which to walk this labyrinth. Appeal must be made to physiology and biology, as well as to ethics and religion, for aid in the solution of these problems. What, for example, is the test, or what are the tests, of right living? In what aspects is life worth living, and why and when? What things in human nature are best to be fed and what best starved? Is this merely a question of individual well-being, or has

Subject wider than economics.

An ethical question.

the neighbour a part in the estimate? How many neighbours? what neighbours? Does the inquiry cover one life, or more? Are unborn generations our neighbours for this purpose? And what, indeed, is another's good to me? Why should any man be sympathetic — brother-loving? Are sympathies and tendencies matters of choice and motive, or are they fixed human attributes, parts of our organization, as far beyond our power to create or cancel as are our appetites or tastes, or our bodily constitution? Are these things mere characteristics, as weight belongs to matter or impenetrability to stones?

At any rate, selfishness, self-care, self-respect, self-reverence, have their place also. Where is the line of adjustment — the boundary of reconciliation between one's well-being and one's duty or interest in regard to his neighbour? How harmonize egoism and altruism? These problems are all hidden in the science of wealth consumption. Political economy alone will not furnish the solutions.

261. Let it be temporarily assumed that the ultimate ethical test is in the conformity of all activity to what Ward has termed "the organization of happiness." This seems a safe enough test, since if happiness is not the ultimate fact in human well-being, yet somehow highest happiness must flow from highest well-being. By reason of this parallelism, therefore, happiness may in incomplete and imperfect fashion serve to summarize the purposes of human endeavour. But even here we are not greatly helped, since it still remains to determine whose happiness shall be taken into computation and in what measure. How far does it rationally bear upon my manner of life that my descendants, or the race in general, are therein concerned? What are your duties to your neighbour? How shall you reconcile these claims with the adverse claims of others? And in what estimate shall be measured his happiness against the happiness of others, if in the widening circles of heredity his well-being may seem to conflict with that of others yet to be?

It must be taken as fundamental to all ethical discussion

that the well-being of the human race is the ultimate test of right action. Should this proposition fail to commend itself as axiomatic, reference to Section 225 must suffice for argument, merely adding, however, that in the degree that the breadth and the power of the sympathetic faculty shall enlarge, will this abstract principle tend more and more to become a working emotional fact in the human mind — an instinctive moral guide. "It can be shown that in the last analysis egoism and altruism are one, that altruism is only an indirect or mediate form of egoism in which the motive is sympathy, *i.e.* a kind of feeling which results from a contemplation of suffering in others, and which is strong in proportion as the organization is delicate and refined. For this reason, and not because it is of a distinct nature, is altruism a far higher and nobler, though thus far, a much less powerful sentiment than egoism." — WARD, *Dynamic Sociology*, Vol. I. p. 15.

<small>Egoism and altruism.</small>

262. The capacity for expansion of human needs and desires is the key to many fortunate tendencies in social life. It is the elastic spring which constantly pushes men upward to new efforts and new acquirements in industry, in art, and in science. New effort means new power. Mind and body develop with the activity drawn from new desires. Did each new achievement in production and thought bring with it no correspondingly larger task, but only larger ability for an equal task, progress would carry with it its own veto in progressive stagnation. Human history excellently illustrates this truth. Civilization has not maintained itself in the places of its beginnings, but has moved to colder climates. With the human race in possession of something more than barbaric skill, the problem of tropical existence, so far as the primary needs are concerned, is over easy of solution. All food requirements are too readily provided for. The climate discourages any exercise of energy unless in face of an acute need. There are no such needs. Neither human standards nor human powers tend toward development in these conditions.

<small>Expansiveness of desires. Advantages.</small>

In the temperate zones the necessities of comfortable existence are to be had only on terms of such effort as to conduce to human development. The remunerations of effort are not over large, but are yet sufficient to induce effort where the putting forth of it is not extremely irksome. Yet evidently there was a time when the warmer climates offered more favourable conditions for the race, in view of the powers then possessed by it. Something more than bare necessities is requisite if civilization is to make a beginning — some surplus of time and strength after mere existence is provided for. But when human powers had developed so that men could and did avoid that measure of effort necessary to growth, progress ceased.

It is worth remembering also that no high civilization has yet established itself in the frigid or semi-frigid zones. That necessary something above the minimum of existence is impossible there, for other than highly developed races. These decline the attempt. The Icelanders abandoned Greenland after a century or two of struggle and are now abandoning Iceland. Where, however, human perseverance was sufficient for the case, the outcome would probably be the failure of civilization, inasmuch as the compensations for effort are so meagre that energy would probably give place to languor, and effort adapt itself to the minimum standard of life. With sufficiently acute desires, humanity will one day probably become able to maintain civilization in tropic climates.

263. For races, therefore, as for individuals, burdens should be apportioned to strength. Nor is there much choice between the excess and the defect. For example, the athlete is as likely to suffer from over-training as is the scholar from under-training. Exercise may be carried too far for muscle as well as discipline for brain. A cold bath is a helpful stimulus to the system able to set up the necessary reaction. Tasks accomplished make strength, — abandoned, weakness. Exposure hardens where it does not injure. The same rule holds in the moral world. Temptation strengthens, but each human being may well pray to be delivered from too much.

Successfully resisted, it toughens moral fibre; succumbed to, it works disintegration.

The doctrine, therefore, of some currency among economists, that every rise in the standard of living is fortunate, and every new line of consumption, unless affirmatively injurious in itself, a benefit, must be taken as of something less than universal validity. Only that sort or that degree of consumption can be justified which in the getting or in the using makes for human well-being.

264. It is difficult to estimate how much the actions and thoughts of each of us are influenced by the standards and opinions of others. The world is in the main ruled by something else than laws. The good faith of business has another basis. Such laws as exist rather rest on the general good faith than the good faith on the laws. We buy not upon our confidence in the public weigher or examiner; we sell with scant reliance upon the collector or the sheriff; we sleep with faith in something else than the night police. The standards of all furnish standards for each. The faculty of sympathy, of which we have spoken, exhibits itself now in pity, in charity, or in self-sacrifice, again as an intense interest in the respect and approval of our neighbours. These customs of right living, borrowed by each from each, are the foundations of social safety. Here health is as catching as disease. The morality of the best of us is in a large degree conventional,— made up from others' opinions, supported by our respect for others, imitated from the habits of others, reflected from men's interest and kinship for each other. There is no safety for you or me but in this mutual support in right living. Conscience mostly shines by the light of what others think of us.

Yet not all aspects of custom and convention and neighbour interest are equally commendable. Within this field of inquiry are to be examined the economics of ostentation — the laws of show — the theory of appearing and seeming and being seen.

265. If one looks for the most noticeable characteristic of that condition of social temper commonly described as the

social question, he will find it in discontent. We need not immediately inquire for the cause. Indeed it has several times been suggested that the social question is not in truth one question, but a congeries of questions — a multitude of evils; the remedy, a series of minor ameliorations. In human affairs there is seldom any sole cause for anything. *Disadvantages.*

And yet, commonly, we fail to appreciate the significance of this nineteenth century unrest. Nihilism in Russia, socialism in Germany, communism in France, coal and railroad wars in England, riot in London, mob in Brooklyn, pillage and arson in Chicago, rebellion in Colorado, pitched battles with government troops in the coal fields of Illinois and the iron districts of Pennsylvania, — and yet all these things have lost the dramatic character of the unusual. They have become commonplace, they cease to interest us, and in this lies their greatest significance. Nor, indeed, are these symptoms of discontent confined to the wage-earners or the poor. Literature and art manifest all the signs of the same disease. Romanticism idolizes the past; idealism reaches toward the future; realism mocks the present. There is no literature of content in the world to-day. Optimism, even, is in essence discontent with the present. *Is civilization sound?*

266. It is at first thought odd that unrest should especially mark the nineteenth century. The world is rich and growing richer, and wise and growing wiser. Never before would a day's labour bring so many dollars, or a dollar buy so much. Never did men work so hard, or their work return them so much. Science has revolutionized the arts of production. It has made levers for us of the powers of nature. San Francisco is now nearer to New York than was Boston a hundred years ago. The telegraph has annihilated space for the passage of thought. You and I shall yet talk in whispers with London. Knowledge multiplies so that each year's product of it is a life-work for him who would follow it all; and somehow also through the *The achievements.*

wonderful interdependence of each science with every other, and of the arts of industry with the science of industry, all this new knowledge counts us in some way for the business of everyday life. There is no man who has grown more corn than the chemist. Machinery is in one sense a tool and in another a harness for the forces of nature — a multiplier of human powers. The railway and the steamship have made the great cities and the great factories possible. The farmer at one end of the world and the artisan at the other have come into helpful relations of give and take, into unconscious but effective coöperation. The warehouses of all the world groan with the products of all the world's climates and of the talents of all the world's races. All things cheapen as measured in the sacrifice of human effort. We have conquered nature and we have conquered knowledge ; we have opened new continents with their fresh soils and new resources, and we have advanced upon them with new knowledge and new appliances. Man grows in will and skill, and nature widens in opportunities and helpfulness. From this new adjustment of the two factors in production, man and environment, a larger, wealthier life is open to us, and it ought to be a greatly happier life. And yet we ask ourselves what does it all profit? Pass rapidly over in thought the question whether with all our centuries of achievement we are so greatly better off than were the Greeks without. Is the greater rush and push of life a good thing in itself? In the stress of it is there found a compensation to make the effort worth the taking? What does it mean that the insane asylums yearly build larger for minds unstrung by tension? How about the multiplication of suicides? Likewise our prison populations are not disappearing as the good things of life become cheaper, but theft somehow grows out of plenty.

The failure.

There is a grim paradox in civilization somewhere. Wherein do we fail, or waste, or misuse? How is it that with all our opportunities, our harvests somehow do not altogether shield us from hunger or our looms from tatters? What does it mean that as science grows and wealth multiplies the cry of poverty swells louder and louder, and that discontent has become the fixed malady of our civilization?

267. We are in face again of the old question of the standard of living. That which was once relative comfort has become privation — privation absolutely, in view of our higher standards of desire, privation relatively, in view of higher levels of comfort and luxury about us. If, on the one hand, expanding powers of satisfaction are to be regarded as a human gain, on the other hand, desires without the power of satisfaction must be counted for a misfortune. Thus what might be absolute gain in the absence of increased requirements by society, may be very truly a loss. Without the ability to satisfy it, a new need is a misfortune.

We inevitably make our well-being largely relative. With an increasing industrial product there have arisen new needs and desires. The causes which have made greater consumption possible have themselves made greater consumption necessary, — in some part because we have individually become adapted to different standards, for the most part because society about us has set for us a different level. The cloth which once went with elegance is now the badge of poverty. The plainer and simpler would answer our purpose equally well were there no richer or more striking with which to make comparison — no outside standard with which we must comply. Thus our silks serve us no purpose which our homespuns might not serve; our palaces are not greatly better than our huts. Splendour, no matter how much labour it has cost, is not splendour when it has become general. All may as well stand still as run in an equal race. When things are measured by comparisons and averages, scramble and scrabble count for nothing but exhaustion. Thus material progress in the way in which we use it, — material progress so far as it is directed to competitive show, — cancels itself in a strife for precedence. There is no share of gain in it for any one, which does not stand for discontent and heartache for some one else.

The explanation.

All ostentation is waste from the point of view of

society as a whole. For the poor, it aggravates their poverty.

268. Fashion takes its beginning in obsequiousness — in the attempt to propitiate a superior by imitation. Flunkyism still stands for something in the case, but a stronger force is now the dominant one — the desire to assert equality by similarity. But the chase after fashion is a chase for the end of a rainbow. The desire to be inimitable, to be distinguished and peculiar in glitter, is as strong with the leaders as is the disposition of the lesser people for imitation. The latter succeed and the leaders change. Worth spends all his time in devising new styles which shall minister to the demand for inequality and set again the great mob off the scent. It is clearly enough impossible, as the world goes, that the wealthy ladies should wear the same pattern that the servant girl may also get and will be sure to get if they buy it.

Derivation of fashion.

269. We need to see this thing very clearly. The rich in carelessness of their responsibilities, the poor in their foolishness of imitation, are dissipating modern progress in a general and therefore fruitless ministry to vanity. In the increase of wealth the rich get more numerous and more wealthy, the dividing gulf of discontent grows wider and deeper, and fashion flaunts itself more widely. In our false standards of well-being — our improvidence in the competitions of display — we not only waste the product of our own energy by an automatic method of cancellation by averages, but in wasting our own share of product we at the same time make our neighbour's share poor and mean and insufficient. We rob ourselves and yet filch from him. Poverty, though relative, is as real as ever before, since artificial but none the less imperative needs leave as little as ever to spare for primary necessities. There is no cure for it but in rational standards of well-being. So long as by the expenditure of one in empty magnificence another is compelled in stupid fear of stupid criticism to waste the raw material of his welfare, material progress must prove a delusion, and the

The results.

old doom stand unrepealed — the poor ye shall have always with you.

Our labour helps us to live only on condition that its result is a life-giving, life-developing product. Wealth is well-being only as it furthers human welfare. If the attractiveness of diamonds is all in their rarity, diamonds are a delusion and diamond worshippers fools. Were diamonds abundant and coal scarce, we should burn diamonds and worship coal. Half the shops upon our streets sell nothing but the commodity, display.

The first law of ostentation is, then, this — that all ostentation is waste; the second law, that the luxury of the rich not merely causes but is the poverty of the poor.

270. Political economists have something to answer for in this regard. Of all the problems awaiting solution under the competitive system, and of all the arguments proposed in favour of socialism, this of fashion is the most weighty. If the waste and envy and exhaustion of display can be avoided only by compulsory equality of wealth, social welfare must be found in compulsory equality. Whether or not the economists can study them, there are better things in life than wealth. However market values fail to indicate them, the differences are great in the kinds of wealth and their uses. There is a deal of wealth in the world worse than none, a deal more not better than none. Yet all of it costs humanity in thought, strength, energy, leisure, pleasure. *The gospel of work.* The point was long since passed when more burdens were needed for the mere gain of exercise. Work also is good for us only so far as it is good for us. Enough develops us, expands us in health and strength and power of thinking. Too much is a strife for vain things to the outcome of weariness. Wealth is not the motive of life, and man a mere machine for its production. Man and manhood are the centre of all science, and political economy but one department in the art of living. If race welfare is indeed the test of right action, there is something not merely infinitely foolish but infinitely wicked in the rush of toadyism. The children

of America are ceasing to be born because children cost money, and because with all the demand for finery the fathers' income is insufficient for the children, while with all the demands of society for attention and strength, the mothers have no will to be mothers. From 1870 to 1890 the average of American families fell from 5.9 to 4.9.

271. There is possible room here for exaggeration. Wealth is a good thing rightly used. There is no occasion to deride riches or comfort. Asceticism is as false a scheme of living as is imitation. The day of anchorites and pious dirty mendicants is past. Let men get what is worth while out of life, but be sure that what they get is worth while. True welfare is not in what others think, or abiding pleasure in their admiration, or sorrow in their criticism. This is very simple. Each must live his own life and his own needs. Whatever does no good when it is gained, is not worth getting. One cannot satisfy his hunger through another's eating. The standards or opinions of others are not our evil or our good. Remember also that that which is futility to one stands for envy and poverty to another. Pleasure is good, the things of comfort, and luxury, and art, and thought, and beauty are good, but only on condition that one needs them and enjoys them for himself and for their service to him, and not as reflected from some one's else desires or as prescribed by another's standards?

<small>Uses for wealth.</small>

272. The rich have also their responsibility here and their duty. Wealth and culture have a social service in their saving influence toward higher standards of thought and life, and away from the raging materialism of modern society. Expenditure of wealth in ostentation demoralizes, disturbs, and degrades. And note that the distinction is world-wide between luxury and ostentation. That which the rich desire for itself and not as the badge of precedence or the target for silly envy, they may well have — but only on condition that they rather hide than flaunt it. Society is greatly in need of object lessons in plain living and high thinking.

<small>Responsibility of the rich.</small>

273. The purely economic aspects of fashion need not detain us long. It is a fallacy to suppose that the wastes of the rich are necessary for the employment of the poor. The consumption of the rich determines whether the labourer shall produce this or that, and not whether he shall produce at all. If the rich refrain in some measure from consumption, their savings profit society under the form of capital in the production of a larger social dividend.

Does fashion employ the poor?

But the changing demands of vanity stand to society for more than mere waste and overwork. They corrupt art; they confuse and disturb the organization of industry.

First, they corrupt art; no beautiful fashion, if once attained, is safe to stay. If grace and simplicity come as fashions, they go as fashions. The greed of novelty leaves the beautiful behind as antiquated, to be succeeded by the ugliness of hoops and humps and wings. From champagne to plumes of slaughtered birds, from skunk skins to jewelry, there is nothing permanent but novelty, no custom but change. And note that as soon as nothing in art which is good can abide, there will be nothing really good. The great artists, if they work, must work for all time — for the centuries, not the seasons. When the best work can have but a butterfly life, there will be no best work.

Effects on art.

Fashion demoralizes industry and fosters starvation. Warehouses are filled with commodities to supply a demand which has vanished, or to forestall a demand which never appears. Disaster and ruin result. A novelty strikes the popular fancy; there follow immense profits, intense production, multiplied factories, prosperous allied industries, growing cities, inflocking labourers, investment, and speculation. Fashion grows cold when the commodity becomes cheap and plenty; then failure, closed factories, cancelled capital, collapsed boom, idleness, hunger, and riot. Almost all industrial centres know something of this experience. All over the world there are Nottinghams regretting a banished lace industry. The foe of industrial

Effects on trade.

peace is ebb and flow, change and uncertainty. Fashion in commodities is parent to business gambling, great fortunes, great losses, feverish activity, feverish lassitude, fluctuation, and bankruptcy.

274. But all of this was better said hundreds of years ago.

"He that loveth silver shall not be satisfied with silver, nor he that loveth abundance with increase; this also is vanity.

"The sleep of the labouring man is sweet, whether he eat little or much, but the abundance of the rich will not suffer him to sleep.

"There is a sore evil which I have seen under the sun, namely, riches kept for the owners thereof to their hurt.

"But those riches perish by evil travail, and what profit hath he that laboured for the wind?

"There is an evil which I have seen under the sun, and it is common among men:

"A man to whom God hath given riches, wealth, and honour, so that he wanteth nothing for his soul of all that he desireth, yet God giveth him not power to eat thereof, but a stranger eateth it: this is vanity, and it is an evil disease.

"Seeing there be many things that increase vanity, what is man the better?

"For who knoweth what is good for man in this life, all the days of his vain life which he spendeth as a shadow?"

NOTES

It matters far less for the future greatness of a nation what is the sum of its wealth to-day, than what are the habits of its people in the daily consumption of that wealth; to what uses these means are devoted.
— WALKER, *Adv. Course*, Sec. 382.

The ultimate foundations of political economy lie deeper than the strata on which existing systems have been reared. The point of divergence between the present science and the true science lies farther back than ordinary inquiries extend. . . . Knowledge of men is the beginning of this science; knowledge of the social organism of which men are members is the middle and the end of it. Individual desires are molecular forces in the general life of society, and to them all phenomena of wealth must be ultimately traced. It is by a deeper analysis than has been dreamed of in our philosophy, that we may hope to attain that higher insight, that knowledge first of man, and then of humanity, which is the basis of true economics. — CLARK, *Phil. of Wealth*, p. 54.

Wants on the margin of actual possession are the active incentives to effort. Civilized man struggles no longer for existence, but for progressive comfort and enjoyment. Progress has limits, and many wants must remain forever unsatisfied. By a kindly provision of human nature such wants are generally quiescent. Other wants near to the border line of actual possession must be active, with a prospect of satisfaction by effort, if happiness is to be attained. It is the want of things which lie far above the line of necessities, and the consumption of which would be classed as unproductive, which is the constant motive power in industrial progress. The comforts to be enjoyed to-morrow set in action the muscular energy gained by the food consumed to-day. It is the so-called unproductive consumption which, if soul forces be recognized, is productive of wealth. — CLARK, *Phil. of Wealth*, 54.

A distinction must be drawn between the motives which incite man to seek wealth; they are of two different kinds, and correspond to two aspects under which the idea of wealth is presented. Men seek wealth, both to satisfy their wants and to mark themselves off from their fellows; they are urged in the former direction by the desire for well-being, in the latter by the desire for inequality. . . . It is the desire for inequality, or, if you will, what comes exactly to the same thing, the desire to rise above the common level, which is the ceaseless goad of man's natural idleness. — GIDE, *Political Economy*, p. 32.

And now the world will have to pause a little and take up that other side of the problem, and in right earnest strive for some solution of that. For it has become pressing. What is the use of your spun shirts? They hang there by the million unsalable; and here by the million are diligent bare backs that can get no hold upon them. Shirts are useful for covering human backs; useless otherwise, an unbearable mockery otherwise. . . . The wages of every noble work do yet lie in Heaven or else nowhere. At bottom dost thou need any reward? Was it thy aim and life purpose to be filled with good things for thy heroism, — to have a life of pomp and ease, and be what men call "happy" in this world, or in any other world? I answer for thee, deliberately, No. The whole spiritual secret of the new epoch lies in this, that thou canst answer for thyself with thy whole clearness of head and heart, deliberately, No. My brother, the brave man has to give his life away. Give it. I advise thee. Thou dost not expect to sell thy life in an adequate manner? Give it like a royal heart; let the price be nothing; thou *hast* then, in a very certain sense, got all for it. — CARLYLE (England), *Past and Present*.

Franklin remarks that our eyes, although very useful, require nothing more for themselves than a pair of spectacles, an outlay which ought not greatly to disarrange our finances; it is the eyes of others that ruin us. If all the world were blind excepting myself, I should have need neither of fine raiment, nor of palaces, nor of extravagant furnishings.
— Letter dated at Passy, July 26, 1784, to Benjamin Vaughan.

P. What riches give us let us then enquire;
Meat, fire, and clothes. *B*. What more? *P*. Meat, fine clothes, and fire. — POPE.

TAXATION

275. The different rules proposed for the imposition of taxes were shortly examined in Section 155. It was there suggested that an approximately ideal system would probably recognize in each of these different rules some element of validity.

There are a few generally admitted principles. Taxes should be such as not to require a large cost of collection relative to receipts. As far as possible, premiums upon dishonesty should be avoided. Collection should take place as near as practicable to the point of consumption, in order to avoid the payment by the consumer of interest and profits upon the tax payment.

There is great difficulty, however, in fixing upon any just and practicable system of taxation, so far as refers to the basis of it. That taxation of some sort is unavoidable follows from the fact that for humanity, in its present stage, the right to tax and the right to exist are one. The objections to taxation proportioned to wealth, omitting to take account of the uses to which that wealth is put, whether to charity and philanthropy or to vice

Different systems.

and luxury, are sufficiently evident. It is also clear that taxation upon any of the implements of production, as for example factories, lines of transportation, etc., largely fall on consumers. There is danger, also, that taxation proportioned to wealth simply, should tend to the discouragement of capitalized savings, in the degree that the tax is not shifted to consumers. Taxes on interest receipts mostly shift. (Section 157.)

276. By reason of this shifting process taxes on interest work out in extreme injustice. Commonly, indeed, the very people intended to be favoured are most burdened. A possessor of five thousand dollars **Double taxation.** in property, owing four thousand dollars, is worth, in fact, but one thousand dollars, and yet pays taxes not only upon his five thousand dollars' worth of property, but in some part upon the indebtedness against it. Recalling to mind that for every credit there is a debit, and that cancellation of this credit relationship would work no change in the aggregate of social wealth, taxation upon interest is seen to be in effect double taxation upon wealth.

Taxation proportioned to the benefits derived from government would largely exempt the very people best able to pay, — those best able to dispense with the aid or protection of the State. The millionaire is not benefited a thousandfold more than the humble householder. The pauper is greatly benefited, and yet pays nothing. Taxation necessarily avoids the very poor, else that which is taken under the form of tax must be returned as public charity.

Taxation according to ability to pay would require careful examination of the properties owned, whether income paying or other, and as well would require careful account of the family and social obligations recognized and fulfilled by the contributor. The father of a large family does not stand for this purpose upon a level with the bachelor.

277. And yet on the whole the scheme of taxation according to ability to bear the tax, recommends itself as the best approximation to fairness and practicability. Burdens are

thereby apportioned to strength. Upon this line of reasoning the income tax is commonly regarded as the ideal tax, to the extent that it can be made practicable in operation. A progressively higher rate of taxation is commonly advised with increasing income. Here again the difficulty presents itself of making allowances for the different uses to which incomes are put. One who has a large family to support and educate, or who applies a large proportion of his yearly receipts to the support of philanthropy or charity, has a strong case for corresponding exemptions, could these exemptions be made practicable.

Faculty tax.

278. Proceeding, however, upon the basis of income — of tax on faculty, a rational and practicable system is within reach.

Let it be recalled that all taxes are, in ultimate incidence, taxes on consumption (Section 159); that no one gets any benefit of his wealth, otherwise than in the mere power and pride of possession, till he comes to use it; and that taxes upon luxuries and vices are particularly to be favoured as involving the minimum of interference with both liberty and well-being. (Section 160.)

If, now, all taxes were drawn from that portion of income which goes for the consumption of the contributor, no philanthropist would stand under penalty for his charities. There is no occasion to tax savings as long as they are represented by factories, or until they are turned by the owner to his own benefit. Seed at the time of planting is best exempt. Wait for the harvest. If the owner of wealth is taxed prior to the time of consumption, he is taxed for that which has not yet served him, and may never come to service. This tax, also, is certain in some measure to shift.

Tax on expenditure.

279. Incomes, then, should be taxed not by the measure of receipts, but by the measure of expenditure, — not by income, but by outgo. This principle has been put into successful operation by the French. The dangers of perjury, the premiums on dishonesty, and the general impracticability

which have attended all attempts at income taxation in England and America, as well as the injustices and the shifting which mark income taxation when proportioned to receipts, are all avoided by adjusting the tax levy upon the basis of the outside indicia of expenditure; for example, upon the rental value of the home, the amount of furniture, the number of servants and horses. Undoubtedly the system requires skill in the selection of leading facts and in the apportionment of their relative weight, but amounts in outcome to a tax on that portion of income expended for personal uses.

Clearly, however, this system is not ideal if no allowance is made for the exemption of incomes at or below the mark of strict requirements, or if no provision is made for progressive burdens upon larger incomes. These modifications provided for, this form of income tax burdens the wealthy in proportion to their ability to bear the burden. Nor is it to be condemned thereby for injustice, in view of the fact that society as a whole furnishes the organization and the civilization in which alone great wealth becomes possible.

280. If, however, the rich are to be taxed in the measure of their capacity, so ought also the poor. Whatever is spent for vice or for luxury in any stratum of society, is by that fact proved not indispensable. Here is opportunity to tax the poor to their benefit, or, at all events, to no great injury or burden. *Taxes on the poor.* All of these taxes may be avoided by abstention from consumption. Should taxation of this sort seem to savour too much of paternalism and of sumptuary legislation, — if it is objected that there is too great room here for mistaken, extreme, or dogmatic measures, — the answer is that the State must follow what light it has. Taxes must be collected. They fall of necessity upon one sort or another of consumption. The State is bound to collect its revenues with as little harm as possible.

281. There remains yet one method of taxation ideal in fairness and in freedom from oppressive character — the tax on future unearned increments in land values. (Section 282.)

Probably, also, a high rate of taxation on successions and

inheritances will be found to furnish large resources to the State. No valid objection appears to this sort of taxation from any point of view. From various points of view its advantages are great.

Taxation upon monopolies will best be treated under another head.

Under our form of government income taxes should probably be collected by the national government, as should also vice and luxury taxes, as far as they are levied under the form of tariff or of taxes on production.

State and local taxes.

Inheritance and land taxation and all forms of taxation upon consumption, by license methods, are probably best placed with state and local governments.

It is worth noting as a matter of experience that taxation upon personal property is impossible, consistently with justice, and commonly fails for the most part of enforcement. In almost all communities, and especially in the newer communities, land taxation affords nearly the entire revenue. Unfortunately, however, no distinction is made between land and improvements.

THE SINGLE TAX

282. Refute the proposition that inasmuch as all food products and all raw materials are obtained from the land, therefore land is the source of all wealth. (Section 67.)

What have modelling, fashioning, transporting, etc., to do with it?

How many factors in production are there? Would interest be possible without the reproductive forces of nature? Is opportunity more truly primary than activity? Is land more truly than man the primary condition to wealth?

Is control over the industrial product more readily exercised through ownership of land than through ownership of capital or of labour-capacity?

Suppose all land-owners could combine; what factor in production would then be in control? Can land-owners combine effectively? Why?

Suppose all labourers could combine; would they be equally at advantage? Which sort of combination would be more easily made?

Refute the arguments (1) that all improvements in transportation tend to increase rents, (2) that all improvements in agricultural arts and processes tend in the same direction. (Section 79.)

It is true, however, is it not, that all cheapening of manufactured products operates as an increase in the purchasing power of rents?

283. Whether land should be owned individually or socially is a question of expediency to be determined by the general interest of humanity.

It is clear enough that state ownership of land, in the form either of state cultivation or state landlordism, is open to all the objections applicable to socialistic production. As far as state landlordism is concerned, all the objections apply which apply to the landlord-and-tenant relation generally. The best administration of land requires ownership in the cultivator, otherwise the interests of the tenant are adverse to permanent improvements and in favour of the misuse of the land, in aid of immediate returns. The tenant can hardly be expected to improve or fertilize for the benefit of the landlord or of a later tenant. *Objections to state cultivation.*

Opponents of private profits from increasing land values do not, however, advocate state landlordism, but only such high taxation as shall preserve to society the major part of the increase, but shall yet leave all the forces of individualism in working condition.

Careful examination of the different arguments in favour of the land tax ought to convince the student that, overlaid by a deal of sophistry, there is a sub-stratum of hard fact in the single-tax proposition. The evils of speculative ownership and unearned profits are unquestionable, but are greatly exaggerated. The system of private ownership has long existed, and labourers' wages, capitalists' interest, manufacturers' profits, are now represented by landed investments. If society sees fit to secure to itself by progressive taxation future advances in land values, it will therein be wise. Wholesale appropriation of accrued values is wholesale robbery.

THE EIGHT-HOUR DAY

284. Recalling that wages, though fixed by the adjustment of supply and demand, are determined by the productivity of labour, as the measure of demand and of the maximum ability to pay wages,— that therefore wages must be drawn from product, and that competition measures interest and profit from the level of marginal services, — it is clear that the effect of the eight-hour day on wages must be determined by its effect on the social dividend. All attempts to obtain high wages by making labour scarce, or its aggregate product small, rest upon sheer fallacy, unless the restriction be limited to one industry and that industry be one in which the monopoly principle may be applied. (Section 154.) Even here not employers but consumers must finally pay the costs of the artificial rise. Employers pay wages as fixed by the selling price of their products. Shorter hours and relatively high compensation for labourers would quickly recruit the ranks of wage-earners at the expense of agricultural or other labourers.

A question of product.

The question thus remains twofold: (1) Will the aggregate production be lessened by the change to an eight-hour day? (2) If so, is the change desirable?

285. (1) Clearly enough, as a question of maximum product, a twenty-hour working day would not be desirable. Indeed in most industries a twelve-hour day is probably undesirable as compared with ten hours. As clearly, this shortening process may go too far. That sixteen was an improvement on twenty, or ten on twelve, does not conclusively recommend

the eight-hour day as against the ten. Much depends upon the industry, much also upon the national characteristics of the labourers. Probably, in the average, productiveness would fall with a change to eight hours.

(2) Is this necessarily an ill? Is leisure good for anything? On what conditions? How about health and content? Would five ten-hour days per week or six eight-hour days be preferable, (1) as question of product, (2) as question of the health and pleasure of life?

APPRENTICES

286. Attempts on the part of labour unions to limit the number of apprentices for the purpose of holding up wages, may be successful in any one industry. Bearing in mind, however, that wages in the average must fall with falling social dividend, it follows that for wage-earners as a whole no method of reducing or cancelling the effectiveness of labour can conduce to higher average wages. The general interests of society cannot profit through preventing wage-earners from becoming skilled workmen. The profits, indeed, which accrue to the labourers in one industry by this process of restriction, must be largely cancelled as other industries come to practise the same methods. (Section 154 and notes.)

THE SWEATING SYSTEM

287. What fixes the wages of employés in sweatshops? (Section 122.)

Do the employers make unusually large profits or is competition probably fully active among them?

Do the merchants make large profits in the handling of goods from sweatshops, or is the margin one of close competition?

With as many dozen shirts to sell, is it possible to maintain higher prices and yet sell all the shirts? How arrange to get higher prices per shirt? What must be the effect on the labourers if only as many shirts are sold as can be sold at high prices?

What effect (1) on employers, (2) on labourers, if wages are increased without increasing the price of products?

Is the purchaser of sweatshop products doing a benefit or an injury to the employés? What if the shirts could not be sold?

288. The conditions of bad sanitation, bad water, bad food, ignorance, vice, disease, and crime characteristic of the sweatshop are well known. Merchants find it convenient and profitable to let the making up of fabrics to the lowest bidder. These successful bidders, the sweaters, undertake to find the necessary labourers. The work, undertaken at starvation figures, must be placed among people compelled to work at starvation wages. The fabrics are therefore distributed for making up among the ignorant and vicious in quarters of cities foul with stench, filth, and disease. The labour is performed in garrets and cellars or in sick-rooms among sufferers with all sorts of contagious ills, where the uncompleted garment may serve as the pillow or cover of fever, cholera, or smallpox. On the counters of the great wholesale or retail establishments these sweated garments furnish the material for great bargain sales or attractive trade discounts.

Description.

The notion exists among many people that the only thing necessary to cure this great evil is for the State to prohibit letting or receiving work at these low figures. It remains, however, to ask what these ignorant and inferior workers will do if prevented from earning these small wages. Were something better open to them, it would be unnecessary to prohibit this line of employment. Or again, it is urged that purchasers should refuse to buy garments made at starvation wages. How would these starved labourers be better off? Unless their product can be sold for little, it cannot be sold at all. (Section 122.)

289. It may be, however, that as a measure of public health, the State should attempt supervision and regulation of the sweatshops. It probably is true that the inmates might in many cases do better paying work if they could find it, and would often find it if they were aware in a general way of its existence, or if they were not wanting in energy and self-direction. Something is possible here through charity and education. But in any event the remedy will have to begin at the labourers. Uninformed denunciation of the system, or of the merchant, or of the intermediate employer will do little good; nor will the corresponding schemes of remedy serve. For this class of labourers the choice is between sweatshops and something worse.

LABOUR OF WOMEN AND CHILDREN

290. Courts and lawyers have established the rule that in case a parent is shown to be affirmatively unfit to care for a child, a guardian may be appointed in his place. Merely as a matter of protection to the child, in some cases it becomes justifiable to limit or suspend the usual authority of the parent.

The labour of children in shops or factories is injurious both positively and negatively, — positively in weakness and stunted growth from over-arduous tasks, negatively in loss of opportunity to prepare for the more important tasks of later life. These conditions of disadvantage tend to reproduce themselves. When the child-labourer matures, he in turn finds himself unable to give his children proper care and education. Thus in justice to the unborn children as well as to the living, some sort of restriction upon child labour is desirable. If parents are unable under present conditions properly to prepare their children to live, there is the clearer necessity that the next generation be not worse equipped.

General considerations, therefore, favour state interference in these matters. Any rule must, however, be very flexible in application. Parents or even whole families are in some cases in considerable measure dependent upon the services of children, where state aid could not be recommended and would not be received. The self-respect which goes with independence is a valuable quantity. Authority should exist to handle these cases after their exceptional character; otherwise the protection of children may work out at tyranny for both parents and children.

291. The labour of women stands economically and socially upon other grounds. Where women's labour in shops or factories is necessary to a wholesome plane of living, it is doubtless to be regretted. But that it is to be regretted makes it none the less necessary. Especially for married women are the effects bad in lower physical tone, and in neglect of important home duties.

Women.

Whether in any case a woman's labour is necessary is probably best left to her own decision or that of her family. There is small occasion for the State to interfere otherwise than, as for other labourers, to prescribe conditions of good sanitation, light, heat, and safety. These latter matters are not well left to normal adjustment. Competition without regulation works out in this regard in higher wages for recklessness and higher profits for inhumanity.

There may well be regret for the necessity of wage-earning by women; but the active opposition to it rests upon the pernicious fallacy already many times remarked, that the competition of women reduces the wages of men by an amount equal to the wages of the women and possibly by more. It is assumed that wages are a fixed quantity and the social dividend inelastic, instead of depending upon the effectiveness of productive forces. If women's labour adds to the social product, it necessarily adds to the aggregate of wage receipts. Obviously, however, if the competition of women centres in some one or some few industries, the wage level therein may be seriously lowered and, conceivably, the wage aggregate decreased. (Section 142.)

THE UNEMPLOYED

292. In the background there still remains the problem of the unemployed — the most important practically and perhaps the most difficult theoretically of all the problems of economic science. Theory and fact here seem somehow out of harmony. It is easy to argue that the consuming power of society is unlimited in comparison with its productive abilities; that so long as there are desires yet unfulfilled, there can be no failure in the demand for labour; and that employment must somewhere await the out-of-works, the difficulty being merely to bring the demand and the labourer together. It is easy, also, to assert that the unemployed lack employment by their own fault, and that would they accept the opportunities which offer at the wages which offer, the solution would be easy. And it is doubtless true that a large proportion of the beggars, the tramps, the patrons of night shelters and free soup counters, who whine their eagerness to work, could work be found for them, are lying. But imagine yourself in a great city, even in prosperous times, seeking employment. Ask yourself to whom you would apply. It helps little that the demand is there if you cannot find it. The very employer seeking further help will probably not accept you; he does not know you. Who are you? what are your credentials? why are you not already at work? He can wait — you cannot. He seeks a contented, steadfast, trustworthy servant. You may be all this, but he does not know it. For his purposes, therefore, you are not all this. He needs more than an efficient worker, more also than a trustworthy worker; he needs one whom he knows to be both efficient and trustworthy.

Normal non-employment.

All these adjustments of supply to demand take time. An employé losing his place and finding another within thirty days may count himself fortunate beyond the average. The intermediate period is to be charged up to friction, lost motion, in the interplay of demand and supply. This loss quantity is never a small one. Consider the transformations constantly occurring in modern industry, — new inventions, new processes, new factories, changing demands of time and season, new fashions, new centres of trade, bankruptcies, retirements, restrictions of output, new schedules of tariff, speculations, booms, strikes, and lockouts, a very kaleidoscope of change, — and one begins to appreciate the causes which lie back of disturbances in employment. Give each change its time for completion, for the fitting of each industrial block to its new niche, and the phenomena of non-employment are seen to be inevitable. The best-disciplined regiments require time for reforming after ranks are broken. The streets are thronged with people, by the mere going to and fro from one place of business to another ; for several hours of the day the ways are filled with passers to and from their meals.

There is, then, a normal and, in a certain sense, healthful volume of non-employment. We have already had occasion to note that periods of crisis and depression aggravate this condition to one of veritable disease. So far, however, as non-employment is connected with currency phenomena, discussions of remedies must be deferred to a later chapter.

293. Even were seekers of employment informed of the various opportunities for employment, and did questions of fitness and proof of fitness present no difficulties, there would still be a great measure of immobility in labour, resulting in non-employment. Men dislike changes of home even if they are able to make them, and are often unable to make them even if disposed. When, for example, the lace factories of Nottingham close for lack of demand, it is small help to the operative that in Glasgow or in Dublin there is employment in ship-building or iron-working. Assume for the time being the ability to change from loom to forge. Assume, also, the knowledge of the opportunity and the disposition to embrace it. But the workman cannot move his cottage. It is, indeed, common enough that he is unable to undertake the expense of moving his family and personal belongings. And always the risk of misfortune or failure

Inertia of labour.

is menaced by new surroundings, strange people, and new methods.

Nor have we yet done with the important influences recruiting the army of the unemployed. The leading characteristic of the modern industrial system is the division of labour. As has already been remarked, this principle applies not only to individuals, but in large degree to communities, states, and nations. In sociology as well as in biology, specialization of function involves interdependence. In complicated machinery, when one wheel fails to turn, all stand still. In our present society production depends upon exchange. The agriculturist employs the mechanic and *vice versa*, — the steppes of Russia, the workshops of Germany. So if the American Northwest ceases to produce, and in default of production ceases to buy, the industrial centres experience a partial paralysis. A crop failure in several states, chiefly agricultural, works some measure of non-employment in those manufacturing centres with which the barter of commerce commonly takes place. At the best, the manufacturer must reach out to new and difficult markets of low profit-paying quality. Shut out by trade restrictions from the world's currents and price levels, the process is necessarily slow and painful. For the agricultural states the case is evidently still worse.

<small>Effect of division of labour.</small>

<small>Crop failures.</small>

In short, there comes about a condition of want, of acute necessity, which yet affords no demand for present labour, but rather for immediate purposes a diminished demand. Ultimately, we must remember, product furnishes demand for product. The Northwest will not demand hats or shoes until it can produce wheat or meat. The manufacturing states must do their exchanging with such agricultural producers as have produced. Low prices, therefore, tend to follow for the products of the factory. Possibly enough, also, slow or hard collections in the districts of crop failure may permanently embarrass some centres of production. At all events, the condition is one of abnormally low social product accompanied for a time, not by correspondingly large outlay of productive energies, but by a reduced outlay. The world acutely needs more grain and meat. What of it? It must wait until another year. This larger requirement will mean increased activity when next year comes; it means stagnation now. Agricultural production is mostly periodic. Were the question one of hats or shoes, a disproportion of product to wants would bring about a stimulus to production. Not so with the industries of agriculture. When these fail in product, it is an empty mouthing of generalities to assert the adequacy of employment as the necessary corollary of hunger. Months must pass before agriculture will renew its opportunities of employment. Other industries are over-manned at present, in view of the abnormally restricted market. Even did they offer possible employment, they are so far away as to be practically inaccessible. That agriculture is prospering on the other side the equator helps the agriculturist on this side not at all, and the manufacturer not much.

294. Recurring conditions of non-employment are thus inevitable in society as at present organized. But the difficulty is not fairly to be ascribed to the manner of organization. It results from the uncertainties of climate and the periodic nature of agricultural production. These failures of product could not be avoided under any circumstances. Systems can differ only in their manner of distributing the disaster. Socialism is clearly enough better adapted for this distribution than is the competitive form of society. It is, indeed, possible that socialism would fail in precisely the other direction — in an over-ready and therefore over-wasteful distribution and consumption of a food supply insufficient at the best. (Sections 135, 236.) The best amelioration possible under the present system is to be found in the postponement of all works of national or municipal improvement to seasons of labour stagnation. Work performed by men who would otherwise be idle costs society nothing. It is saved energy. There is no excuse for public work in times of brisk employment unless the need is immediate and acute.

Remedies.

In times of lax employment the choice lies between public enterprise, public charity, and suffering. The public should borrow for public work in times of depression and pay in times of prosperity. Bonds payable after a short period at the public option should be regarded as an emergency resort. Public finances in easy times should always be conducted with this in view.

Doubtless states have gone too far in providing employment for the out-of-works. But there is a certain amount of public improvement which is inevitable. For the purposes of the present argument, the choice is merely as to the time at which public work shall be attempted, and to which payment shall be postponed. That amount of work which must in any case be performed should be performed at the period of lowest social cost.

295. The bearing of the competition of the unemployed upon the wages of labourers in general deserves examination at this point. Seekers of employment readily make concessions. Why does not this place the employé at the mercy of the employer? <small>Out-of-works and wages.</small> What stands in the way of enormous employers' profits? What maintains the wage share at a fair distributive portion? Shortly, the employers' indisposition to hire a poor labourer, and the consciousness of his inability long to retain a good one at inadequate wages. The employer acts in view of the competition of other employers. This applies as well to unskilled labour; and it is to be held in mind, also, that there are all degrees of worth and worthlessness in unskilled labour. The history of industrial enterprises and the proportion of failures therein prove that, with occasional glaring exceptions, competition is active and effective in the labour market as in other markets.

In times of depression, employed wage-earners may seem to suffer from the fierce competition of the unemployed. Wages are, in truth, forced down nominally — possibly also in some localities really. Yet these periods are not periods of great employers' profits, but just the contrary. With falling prices of products, nominal wages must fall, or the employer be forced to restrict his product or to discontinue production. In the interest, then, of the maximum social product, which is ultimately the interest of the wage-earner, wages must fall to a level permitting the maximum utilization of all the productive energies of society. This aspect of the case, will, however, receive full discussion in Sections 300, 301.

CURRENCY

296. The commercial panic has been several times referred to as the most noticeably weak point in the present industrial system.

No society organized on lines of division of labour and competition can function successfully without a medium of exchange and measure of value. (Section 168.) It is idle to look for the disuse of credit methods in business (Section 212); and, as we have seen, the tendency is always strong to use the medium of exchange as a measure of value, not only for cash or short time exchanges, but as well for the long time exchanges called deferred payments. (Section 201.) Cash and credit transactions shade off into each other practically as well as theoretically.

297. We saw in Sections 163, 164, that the injustices which attend a fluctuating standard of deferred payments, could be avoided by the use of the multiple or commodity standard, payment being still made in currency, but the amount of currency being determined by reference to statistical tables. It is quite another question whether the paralysis of business, both of production and of exchange, which follows upon the commercial crisis, could be avoided by granting debtor or creditor the right to have the terms of payment determined in this manner. Actual commodity payment would be both unjust and impracticable. The debtor could rarely make it, and the creditor rarely conven-

Multiple standard.

iently receive it. Payment in symbols would remain necessary. The stringency for money currency in place of credit currency would still be possible and probable. Forced liquidation would still occur, and such cases of insolvency as came to light would complicate business conditions, and compel the readjustment of property holdings. Insolvencies due to the mere appreciation of currency would, however, in considerable degree be avoided by the very fact of decreased fluctuation.

298. The evils of panics, it must be remembered, are due to the fact that in a society organized upon lines of division of labour, production depends upon the possibility of exchange. When the mechanism of exchange is dislocated, factories close, production lessens, and wage-earners are subjected to acute suffering. Society is thrown back upon the system of barter or upon the necessity of adjusting its volume of exchanges to a lower volume of currency. This is possible only through fall in prices. This fall in prices pushes some debtors into insolvency, and where these debtors are at the same time employers of labour, locks the doors of enterprise. In this view the multiple standard becomes important, not merely in the interests of justice, but as a palliative of industrial stagnation. *Stagnation results from division of labour.*

It is too much to expect, however, that any amelioration in currency methods will fully counteract the fluctuating tendencies of credit, or will prevent the alternation of periods of expansion with periods of liquidation. A wavelike movement in prices is unavoidable where credit serves as currency, though the roll may become less marked and the trough less deep. No substitute currency will inflow automatically or can be practically supplied till a need has manifested itself. Falling prices must be the evidence of this need. After the ebb in credit and the process of liquidation have commenced, the most that can be done is to make the process as easy and as free from disaster as possible. So far as the evil results are not due to the discovery of insolvency in business, they are due to the effect on production and exchange of a fall in prices. Men who could pay their debts at the old price level become insolvent by the fall. Men who could borrow for their business needs now find it impossible. Men with currency in hand exercise the option of retention (Section 181), rather than immediately to invest or expend; currency is thus practically withdrawn from circulation. Lenders of currency are timid and withdraw their holdings from circulation. Prices tend toward further fall. This discourages the production of commodities by employers. Men are discharged. Not producing, they cannot buy of producers in other industries. Still other men are thereupon thrown out of employment.

299. Thus far the case is not difficult of analysis. But there are some difficult underlying questions. Debts and credits add nothing to the wealth of the world, nor do they subtract. Doubling or halving cannot affect the social aggregate of wealth but simply its arrangement in point of ownership. A general fall in prices is equivalent to an increase of indebtedness. The injury to the general well-being cannot therefore be explained by enlarged indebtedness, otherwise than as the change in conditions works out to change the aggregate production and consumption of society.

Why so severe — so enduring.

All societies organized upon lines of division of labour are very sensitive to derangement, from the fact that with them production is conditioned on exchange, and that reduced production in one direction tends to cause reduced production elsewhere. Disturbed exchanges may, therefore, be expected to bring about reductions in the social dividend, as well as inequality and injustice in distribution. The hard times which follow panic are explained by reduced production lowering consumption and reduced consumption reacting to lower production.

Therefore for the understanding of commercial depressions it is not sufficient merely to explain the closing of factories through business reverses, but also to explain why they do not open. Why is the condition of depression so enduring? With numbers of labourers wanting food, and numbers of farmers wanting manufactures, why does each side fail to produce for lack of the opportunity to sell? Why do these wants fail to meet? How explain the long-enduring inability of supply to exchange with supply?

300. The explanation is found in the imprenditor system, and for the most part in the relation of employer with employé. The imprenditor buys raw materials and employs labourers for the purpose of making profits. He is a mere intermediate. If he is unable in marketing his products to make his receipts exceed his outlays, he withdraws from production, however social interests may thereby suffer. *Explanation.*

In the fall of prices following a panic not all commodities fall with equal rapidity. Goods from foreign sources, for example, may nearly or quite hold their old level of prices. Other products are perhaps produced under conditions more or less approaching monopoly; others again may be well sustained in price, through speculative holdings by the producers or through restriction of product. The imprenditor must produce in view of market prices. Prices are his master. If his productive outlays are too high, he must withdraw from business. There is, however, for most employers one resource and one only — that of reducing wages. A small reduction may possibly be sufficient. But here is precisely the kernel of the difficulty. Even were raw materials for all industries falling regularly and equally, the imprenditor would still be compelled by lower prices of product to reduce the wages paid. As a practical fact, this is a difficult matter. Labourers resist angrily and persistently. They do not understand the necessity of the reduction — they believe that they have merely to stand firm. To prevent a strike or a long continuance of strained relations, the employer often finds it not less profitable and much more comfortable to close his shop. In times of depression profits are scant enough at the best. *The wage question.*

Inertia is a fact which must be reckoned with. Wages rise slowly and when fall is inevitable fall slowly and with painful struggle. Public opinion concurs with difficulties in business to impel the factory owner to quit the contest. Competition among wage-seekers does not protect him. If the industry requires skilled labour, he cannot readily reman his factory — the unemployed even are loath to present themselves for the vacant places. Ostracism is visited upon them if they do, and they are even prevented by force.

301. Were it possible for prices to fall evenly all along the line, and for wages to be forced to fall in conformity with prices, the depression following upon panic would be unimportant and of short duration. But (1) as long as indebtedness does not fall as measured in money units, there is tremendous resistance — in many cases a struggle for very financial existence — against sale and liquidation at the ruling level of prices. Even were this difficulty avoided, as will be shown to be possible, there would still remain (2) the inequalities already mentioned in the fall of commodities generally. This, however, is not a very considerable matter. (3) The difficulty of accurately adjusting wage-payments to market prices still remains. Capital, labour, and employer must coöperate in production. If with any employer labourers insist upon all, or more than all, of the product, production must cease. The marginal principle applies here in an important manner. Those employers hardest pushed by the demands of employés, or those least able or least disposed to continue production on narrow margins, close the doors of their factories. A resulting increase in the competition of wage-earners for employment reduces in some measure the pressure upon the remaining employers.

Wages.

This analysis points to large advantages in the commodity standard of payments, especially as applied to attempts to fix upon a basis of agreement between employers and employés.

302. The currency problem, as restated, is then to prevent a reduction in the social dividend by preserving from disaster the mechanism of exchange. Such remedy as is possible under the competitive system must be found in the discovery of a currency system

The direction of remedy.

practically flexible in time of need — a method by which legal tender or unsuspected currency can be made to take the place of ordinary credit when this will not perform its function.

We shall be better able to estimate what is possible in this direction, after having examined some of the problems relating directly to paper currencies.

It is to be deduced from the discussions in Sections 193-202 that paper money should never be issued, even under stress of emergency, to such an extent as to exclude from currency uses, either for foreign export or for domestic commodity uses, the bullion portion of the currency, or to such an extent that, as a mere matter of numbers, the paper units cannot, by virtue solely of their legal tender power, hold their parity with bullion.

303. The economy of wealth possible by use of paper money is now as generally admitted as the method is generally practised. Several questions, however, present themselves in this connection. (1) Is the circulation of government issues possible without redeemability? (2) Is it ever advisable? (3) Ought the government ever to do more than merely to regulate and supervise paper issues? (4) If the issue function is left with banks, what measure of supervision and regulation is necessary?

Questions (1) and (2) were sufficiently discussed in Sections 193-202. Whether paper issues should be left exclusively to private enterprise, or in what degree if not exclusively, are more difficult questions. In favour of issues exclusively by banks, it is urged that, inasmuch as these rest upon bank credit, the government is released from the strain of this liability. Interconvertibility — parity — would be guaranteed by the very system. All banks must fulfil this primary obligation as a condition to their existence. As soon as over-issue should approach, there would be increasing difficulty in keeping the paper money in circulation. Redemption would be demanded, and this fact would prevent the loss of parity between paper and bullion. *Bank vs. government issues.*

304. On the other hand, it is urged that there is no reason

for denying to the State the right of paper issues unless private interests are likely to perform the service better. The money function is one of purely social importance. Not only this, but the economies of wealth worked by paper issues, depend upon the manner of social organization and the established commercial and industrial methods. These economies are distinctly social economies. Good reason should be shown before turning them over to the conduct and profit of private interests. At best, government must superintend and regulate in any event, and in this degree at least become responsible. Deposit banking might possibly enough be left entirely without supervision, but the right of bank-note issues can hardly be exempt from state regulation. Otherwise the thing would be almost certain to be overdone, and might be made the occasion for deliberate and extended dishonesty. The experience of America in wild-cat banking furnishes an excellent illustration. The issue of money must in any event be so limited as to partake of monopoly features. Why turn it into private instead of public monopoly? Why restrict the function of government to the fixing of standards and to certifying the weight and fineness of the bullion presented to it for coinage?

305. In which system lies the greater danger of over-issue? It must be admitted that the State has been found prone to excess in this direction, and it is perhaps true that the danger of excess is especially great under popular suffrage. On the other hand, if banks are unrestricted, the danger is equally great, indeed greater. The larger profit would come with the greater recklessness. Nor would it be a safeguard that all banks were held to strict terms of redemption. The call for redemption, following from a plethora of currency issues, would not be felt by those banks alone which had exceeded reasonable limits. Gold would be called for by holders of paper without regard to the bank of origin, unless indeed there were different ratings of value upon the issues of different banks, — a condition which could hardly be admitted as probable by advocates of bank issues.

306. Not only this, but deposit banking is essentially a brokerage of credit, the bank serving as an intermediate and guarantor between lenders and borrowers. (Section 184.) In times of credit contraction, a severe strain is placed upon the bank, the borrowing customer calling shrilly for more accommodation, and the depositing customer very possibly making demand for his deposit. In this pressure for legal tender currency, it is often impossible for a bank to retain enough of it to maintain cash payments to depositors. It follows, then, that bank-note currency is of fluctuating volume and value, unless some scheme of guaranty by government or some method of government control is adopted. Even then there is no certainty that redeemability in bullion can be maintained, even by banks ultimately solvent. This fact has been several times demonstrated in the history of United States banking. (Sumner's *History of American Currency, passim.*) To preserve, therefore, the financial system from serious disaster at critical times, some form of governmental intervention seems to be necessary. At present all bank bills are secured by deposit of United States bonds, and are therefore not subject to distrust. Possibly a scheme *Intervention necessary.* of coöperative guaranty would effect this equally well, as is proposed under the famous Baltimore plan. It needs be clearly understood, however, that while now in times of crisis banks fail from inability to pay their depositors, they are not now subjected to the necessity of cashing their own bills, nor are their gold reserves the reservoir from which gold for foreign shipment is necessarily drawn. Whenever for any reason a shipment of gold now becomes necessary, United States notes can be presented at the United States Treasury and the gold demanded. Retire this greenback volume, and this strain would be thrown on the banks, in proportion as their note circulation should have become considerable. Some authority then would have to be lodged in the banks to make larger issues in times of their own distress, or of distress of the public. This is practicable only upon the assumption that they have not already used this privilege to its limits. But panics com-

monly occur as the result of inflation. In any system in which inflation is at all times possible, there will be small reserve power for panic necessities.

307. But if, in fact, these objections can be met, it still remains true that the currency issuing function is a source of large profits and ought not to be turned over to private institutions gratuitously. Society merely claims its own in appropriating the gains possible under this system.

We still seek a system which shall reserve for times of emergency a large measure of safe elasticity, and which after the stress has passed shall automatically contract to its normal volume. Otherwise, in preventing a disastrous fall in prices from disappearing credit, there will later result a disastrous rise in prices when credit flows back into currency channels. That which was originally a corrective of contraction will operate as direct expansion.

Methods followed by imperial banks in Europe offer a suggestion. In times of panic in London the Bank of England has several times, under the sanction of the ministry, made large illegal issues of paper awaiting parliamentary approval. Ordinarily, however, the mere announcement of authority to issue has sufficed to control the panic, without the necessity of actual issues. But in Germany the imperial bank is authorized at all times to enlarge its issues on terms of paying to the State so high a tax or fine as to insure the retirement of issues when the stress is passed. This method is not as readily practicable under a system like that of the United States, wanting any great central banking institution and wanting, also, any one banking centre of preëminent importance, but, on the contrary, made up of thousands of separate and independent banking institutions. However, the New York banks in the crisis of 1893 followed, by purely voluntary association, in the issue through the clearing-house of the famous clearing-house receipts, the principles here advocated. But to be broadly effective all banks in reserve cities should be compelled to carry a certain proportion of their capital in government

Interconvertible bonds.

obligations bearing a low rate of interest, and should be entitled to receive upon demand from the United States Treasury, upon the deposit of these securities, approximately their par value, paying, however, to the government a rate of interest so high as to insure the retirement of the emergency issues when the exceptional demand was over.

FREE COINAGE OF SILVER IN AMERICA

308. A few propositions may now be taken as established.

(1) The volume of exchanges furnishes the normal demand for currency.

(2) Increase in the supply of currency, whether by coin, greenbacks, or credit, tends to depreciate the unit, that is, to raise prices.

(3) The value of the unit, if made of coin, ultimately equals its marginal cost of production; that is to say, free coinage finally fixes the value of the unit at the value of the contained bullion (seigniorage is unimportant for this purpose).

(4) If two metals are to circulate side by side, they must maintain exact market parity at the coinage ratio, else but one will circulate, and that the cheaper.

(5) The use of gold as currency tends to enhance its market value, and has thereby greatly increased the amount produced.

(6) Demonetization, partial or complete, of gold would, temporarily at least, lower its value and discourage production, till the over-supply had drained away. Ultimately its value would again come to coincide with its marginal cost of production.

(7) The remonetization of silver would tend to raise its value and to stimulate its production, with the final outcome that the purchasing power of the unit would fix itself at the cost-of-production mark.

(8) It is then possible that the free coinage of silver at any reasonable ratio should bring about a parity between gold and silver. If this ratio did not approximately correspond to the normal cost-of-production ratio, it would be short-lived in proportion as it was wide of this mark.

Would silver coinage by the Caucasian nations at the ratio of 16 to 1 bring about either a temporary or a permanent parity?

309. The total quantity of gold in actual circulation among the Caucasian peoples is about three and one-half billions of dollars. Bearing in mind the fact that an inflow of silver would not displace gold, unit for unit, because of the concurrent tendency of gold toward fall, it is evident that there is not in the world sufficient uncoined silver to displace all the gold. Parity would therefore result, attended by some measure of increase in the number of currency units. Recalling that the present output of silver, estimated at the ratio of 16 to 1, is over two hundred millions annually, and that this ratio vastly overvalues silver as measured by its cost of production, it is questionable whether this parity could long endure. An enormous stimulus would be given to silver production. Its inflow into currency uses would bring about a marked tendency toward rising prices. But even with a product of four hundred millions per year, several years would elapse before the parity would be disturbed.

International ratio of 16 to 1.

310. Attempting now a forecast of the results of free silver coinage limited to the United States, we find something less than a half billion of gold in our present circulation. The stores of uncoined silver in the world would probably be sufficient immediately to overwhelm the parity. It would at best be destined to so short a life as to drive gold from circulation by speculative influences, thereby bringing about so sharp a contraction as to precipitate a panic. Were, however, the uncoined silver insufficient to break the parity, it is well to remember that the Bank of France alone com-

National ratio of 16 to 1.

monly carries sufficient silver to supply half our entire coinage need, and the French people still more, if only permission could be obtained from the French government to sell us this silver for our gold, and to substitute in its reserves gold for silver, covering its apparent bookkeeping loss by paper issues. Five years later it could unload its gold and repurchase silver with a net gain, at our expense, of from two hundred to two hundred and fifty millions of dollars. In any event, our parity could endure but shortly. After the spasm of contraction due to the speculative disappearance of gold had passed, our prices would move upward and our gold, no longer required or used as currency, would flow abroad as a commodity export, in payment of adverse trade balances.

311. After the disasters of a change from the gold to the silver standard are measured, there remain for consideration (1) the question of the justice of the change, (2) the inquiry whether we should be any better off with a new silver standard than now with the gold standard.

First, as to the justice of the change. We may admit, though it is not altogether clear, that the gold dollar has greatly appreciated in purchasing power within the past twenty years. Measured by the prices *Justice.* of 1896, this seems reasonably certain. But remember that not panic but normal prices furnish the just basis of estimate, since panics are not at all peculiar to the gold basis. We may also admit — and this is probably the fact — that had we followed the course of silver as our standard rather than gold, a less unjust standard of deferred payments would have been afforded. But in fact we did not do so, and seemingly from the outlook of twenty years ago would not have been justified in making the attempt. But these possibilities and probabilities are not much to the point. They are mere retrospect. Business has adjusted itself to conditions as we have established them, and not to conditions as they might have been. An appreciating standard of value is an injustice to debtors, in the measure only that appreciation has taken place during the term of the indebtedness. Suppose that your grocer has just purchased a bill of goods in Chicago and has borrowed the money from a banker to pay for the goods. If, when the note matures at the bank, he presents himself and requests that in justice his note be scaled down in proporti n to the appreciation which the dollar has undergone in the past twenty years, the bank will doubtless manifest the intense unreasonableness and rapacity said to be characteristic of the money power. Should the grocer reply that he was merely insisting upon a rule just to debtors in general, and incidentally working to his particular advantage, it would be necessary to examine the grounds on which this general rule was advocated.

312. If any appreciation has taken place, some injustice has resulted. But the question is one of comparison. Where the balance of justice lies is not a difficult matter to determine. The question is whether the volume of indebtedness is for the most part long time or short time. The debts of wholesalers to manufacturers, of retailers to wholesalers, of customers to retailers, of retailers and business men to banks, of banks to their depositors, are all short time relations, or ought to be. At all events, no one should ask for a reduction of his debts on the ground that he has defaulted in payment at maturity. Even with municipal, state, and government bonds, and long time real estate mortgages, it is well to remember that transfers are constantly taking place. The last holder has himself invested money in payment of all the appreciation which had taken place before the time of purchase. It would be hard on him to make him responsible for all the appreciation which had accrued before his title was acquired. Why limit the time for which he is to be plundered to twenty years? Why not begin with the Christian era?

313. It will be well to inquire upon whom the hardships of a cheaper standard of payment would chiefly fall. We are apt to assume that creditors are rich and debtors poor. But people who know how to use wealth often borrow of people who do not know as well. This is one way in which rich people get rich and keep rich. Bankers commonly show a preference for loaning their money to rich people and for bor-

rowing it of the poor or middle classes. Savings-bank accumulations are derived from the same source. Insurance-company assets commonly belong to the same middle and poor classes. Manufacturers and wholesalers are great borrowers, while banks and trust companies reckon large numbers of poor people among their stockholders as well as among their depositors. For every Rothschild there are millions of savings-bank customers.

314. Whether gold or silver will furnish the fairer standard of value for the future is impossible to decide. It is hard to foresee the developments in mining and discovery which will bear upon production; perhaps even more difficult than it was in 1873. Great stores of gold have lately been discovered in Africa and Colorado. The influence of this is evident in the tables of gold production which will shortly be given. That there are less pounds of gold than silver produced per year does not greatly signify. There are more pounds of spring poems than of classic lyrics, but the whole stock of spring poems could be bought the more cheaply.

315. When once the change from the gold to the silver standard had taken place, it is not clear that silver would be greatly inferior to gold as the basal money commodity. The process of change would be attended with panic, followed by rising prices and ending with still another and more severe panic. South America and Asia hold by the silver standard. There is no ground to believe that silver would be more subject to fluctuation in value than will gold. The greater weight of silver in proportion to its value would, however, increase the expense of shipment and thereby raise the cost of exchange. Also it is to be remembered that our trade is for the most part with nations which use the gold standard. The fluctuations of gold and silver relative to each other would, in considerable measure, increase the hazards of business and would thereby result in a higher cost in transactions of international trade. *What of the change when made?*

316. The following table excellently illustrates many of the principles established in our discussion of currency:—

OUTLINES OF ECONOMIC THEORY

Year.	Ratio of World's Product. Silver to Gold.	Commercial Ratio of Values.	World's Product of Gold.	World's Product of Silver. Coinage Value.	Per Capita Effective Money.
1852	4.87	15.59	...	...	...
1853	4.16	15.33	...	...	...
1854	5.08	15.33	...	...	...
1855	4.79	15.38	...	...	...
1856	4.40	15.38	...	...	...
1857	4.87	15.27	...	...	...
1858	5.21	15.38	...	...	...
1859	5.22	15.19	...	...	...
1860	5.46	15.29	...	...	...
1861	5.96	15.50	...	...	...
1862	6.70	15.35	...	...	...
1863	7.28	15.37	...	...	...
1864	7.17	15.37	...	...	...
1865	6.85	15.44	...	...	...
1866	7.20	15.43	...	...	...
1867	7.77	15.57	...	...	...
1868	8.23	15.39	...	...	...
1869	8.50	15.60	...	...	...
1870	9.05	15.57	...	...	...
1871	10.99	15.57	...	...	...
1872	12.68	15.63	...	...	...
1873	13.61	15.92	113 [1]	94 [1]	20.57
1874	12.60	16.17	105	96	21.09
1875	13.19	16.52	103	90	19.95
1876	13.51	17.94	110	97	19.14
1877	11.36	17.20	114	81	18.98
1878	12.77	17.94	119	95	19.83
1879	14.11	18.55	107	89	20.16
1880	14.53	18.06	106	97	23.05
1881	15.83	18.15	103	102	25.59
1882	18.05	18.19	103	112	26.04
1883	19.32	18.48	95	115	26.40
1884	16.59	18.56	102	111	25.88
1885	18.16	18.92	108	118	26.11
1886	17.47	20.04	106	121	25.88
1887	18.79	21.02	106	124	26.40
1888	20.42	21.59	110	141	26.66
1889	20.64	22.18	123	162	25.46
1890	22.98	21.33	120	174	25.33
1891	23.04	19.83	131	186	24.55
1892	...	22.07	146	196	25.10
1893	...	24.57	157	208	24.19
1894	...	...	172	...	...

[1] Quantities are given in millions.

These figures are mostly taken from the tables compiled by Maurice L. Muhleman, cashier of the United States Sub-treasury in New York.

317. The following table throws light upon the mooted question as to the tendencies of the gold dollar in purchasing power during the last fifty years. These tables apply solely to European prices, but in a general way are valid for America. Comparing 1850 with 1890, no great appreciation has taken place. Prices have, however, considerably fallen, that is to say, the purchasing power of gold has increased since 1873: —

Years.	Sauerbeck. 44 articles.	Sootbeer and Heintz. 141 articles.	Kral. 265 articles.
1847–1850	100	100	100
1851–1860	116	116	114
1861–1870	124	123	110
1871–1875	128	133	122
1876–1880	110	123	112
1881–1883	103	122	109
1884	94	114	101
1885–1891	87	105	101

The unsatisfactory character of all tables of this sort was pointed out in Section 164. In a general way, however, the facts are probably correctly represented. According to these tables, the appreciation of gold has mostly taken place since 1885. To say that through improved machinery and improved processes the fall in prices may be explained, does not deny the fall.

The following table, compiled by Miss S. McLean Hardy, gives the movements of prices in America since 1860. The estimates are based upon 232 articles of merchandise, 100 being used as the index number for 1860: —

1860......100	1875......127.6	1885......93
1865......216.8	1879...... 96.6	1890......92.3
1870......142.3	1880......106.9	1891......92.2

It is evident that in America also the purchasing power of gold has increased since 1873. The table of market values of silver, as compared with gold, indicates that silver has fallen somewhat more rapidly than have other commodities in the average.

Note in column (2), page 374, that the silver product in 1852 was less than five times the weight of the gold product. In 1891 the annual product of silver was twenty-three times that of gold. The relative fall of silver is mostly explained by this fact.

Note that at no time prior to 1874–1875, did silver become so cheap as to be worth less than one-sixteenth as much per ounce as gold. Until this time arrived, silver could not be coined on the 16 to 1 ratio. It had not, in fact, been coined in America since about 1834, otherwise than as token money.

While France maintained the free coinage of both metals, it held to the ratio of $15\frac{1}{2}$ to 1. The discoveries of gold in California and Australia tended to raise the price of silver relatively to gold. As will be seen by the table, silver stood from 1853 to 1867 so high relatively to gold that it was not coined in France till 1867. It was then coined enormously. The ratio of $15\frac{1}{2}$ to 1 in France did not prevent a further fall, and after a few years had passed the United States could have coined it at 16 to 1, had its mints remained open to it.

Note that the production of silver has enormously increased during the last twenty years, though upon a constantly falling market.

THE END.

INDEX

(References are to Sections)

Ability. See Taxation.
Abstinence and Interest. See Interest.
Agriculture. See Land and Rent.
Alcoholic Drinks. See Taxation.
Anarchy, Argument for, stated, 223, 224.
Apprentices. See Trades-unions.
Average Man does not exist, 121.

Bagehot, Walter, 118 n., 128 n.
Banks, Statements, 183.
    Issues *vs.* Government Issues. See Currency.
Barter, 168.
Bastiat, Frederic, 128 n., 140 n.
Bimetallism, 203-206, 308-316.
    National, is impossible, 204.
    International, is possible, 205.
    See Currency.
Birth-rate. See Population.
Boehm-Bawerk, Eugene V., 44 n., 55 n., 60 n., 114, 115 n., 119 n., 140 n.
Booth, Charles, 251.
Bounties, 161.
Brassey, Thomas, 98.
Brentano, Lujo, 128 n.

Cairnes, John, 25 n., 135, 139, 221 n.
Capital: Creation of, 106, 107.
    Defined, 100.
    Different Points of View, 100, 101.
    Intellectual, 8, 9, 10, 15, 100.
    See Interest.
Carlyle, Thomas, 274 n.
Child Labour, 290.
Clark, J. B., 23 n., 44 n., 128 n., 136 n., 217 n., 274 n.

Clearing-house, 184.
Coin. See Currency.
Coinage. See Currency.
Collectivism. See Socialism.
Combinations. See Monopoly.
Commercial Crises. See Crises.
Communism. See Socialism.
Competitive System: Analyzed and Criticised, 147, 218-220.
    The Harmonies, 147, 221-223.
    The Dangers, 128.
    Production, 231-233.
    Distribution, 234, 235.
    Consumption, 236.
Consumers' Quasi-rent, 39.
Consumption, 236, 259-274.
    Related to Birth-rate. See Population. See Demand.
Coöperation, 243-246.
Corners. See Speculation.
Cost of Production: a Question of Sacrifice, 47, 48.
    Usual Statement, 52.
    Usual Statement criticised, 53.
    Demand the Ultimate Force, 54.
    Cost and Wages, 56-58.
    Cost and Interest, 59, 60.
    Cost and Rent, 82-86.
    Which is Cause, and which Effect? 83-90.
Courcelle-Seneuil, J. C., 7 n., 23 n., 28 n., 55 n., 136 n., 140 n.
Credit: Its Functions, 170, 184.
    Relation to Capitalization, 104-107.
    Dangers. See Crises.
Crises, 207, 298-300.
    Remedies, 302-307.

INDEX

Cultivation, Margin of. See Rent.
Currency: Is Paper Money Wealth? 103.
  Defective, as Standard of Payment, 161.
  Standard should follow Utility, 162.
  Allowance for Standard of Life, 165.
  A Mere Medium, 167.
  Necessary Qualities, 169.
  Credit one aspect of Exchange, 170.
  Fluctuations in Volume of Exchange, 171.
  Exchange and Division of Labour interdependent, 172, 179, 182, 194.
  Volume, how fixed, 175–178.
  Quasi-rents and Currency, 179.
  The Option Feature, 181.
  Rapidity of Circulation, 183.
  Credit serves as Currency, 104, 170, 184.
  Government Issues, 185.
  Gresham's Law, 186–192.
  Fiat Money, 185, 193–200.
  Quantity and not Material important, 199.
  Importance of Taxation, 200.
  Importance of Speculation, 201.
  See Bimetallism.
  See Crises.
  Silver Question, 212, 308–317.
  Multiple Standard, 297.
  Free Banking, 303–307.
  Interconvertible Bonds, 307.

Decreasing Returns: Diminishing Returns. See Returns.
Deferred Payments. See Currency.
Demand: Is Primary Fact in Economics, 88–90.
  Elasticity of, 79, 88–90.
  How related to Rent. See Rent.
  Explains Cost and Value, 54.
Desire. See Demand.
Distribution: Distinguished from Merchandising, 240, 243.
  Tendencies, 130, 131.
  Analysis, 123–127.
  Primarily a Question of Product, 129.

Distribution: Competitive System of. See Competition.
Division of Labour, International. See International Trade.
  Relation to Currency. See Currency.
  Aids Production, 23 n., 137, 140 n.

Economics, Scope of, 1, 2.
  Definition of, 1.
  As Science and as Art, 2, 9, 34.
  Basis, 25–28.
Economic Laws, Nature of, 3, 4.
  Factors in, 5–7.
  Motive in, 24, 28.
  Harmonies. See Competition.
Education, Advantages, 7, 23 n.
Eight-hour Day, 284.
Eminent Domain. See Railroads.
Employer. See Imprenditor.
Entrepreneur. See Imprenditor.
Environment. See Man and Ethics, Test in, 223, 224, 260, 261.
Exchange: Is Productive, 37.
  Relation to Currency. See Currency.
  Expansion, 211.
  See Currency.
Export Duty, 143.

Fashion, 133, 259–274.
Franklin, Benjamin, 140 n., 274 n.
Free Banking. See Currency.
Free Silver. See Currency.
Free Trade. See International Trade.
Freewill and Scientific Law, 7.
Freight. See Transportation.

Garnier, Joseph, 99 n.
George, Henry. See Taxation of Land.
Giddings, F. H., 131 n.
Gide, Charles, 44 n., 131 n., 274 n.
Government, Justification for. See Laissez-faire.
  Functions of. See Laissez-faire.
Gratuity, Relation to Value, 67.

Harmonies. See Competition.

Import Duty. See International Trade.
Imports. See International Trade.

INDEX

Imprenditor, 127, 128.
   Injustice from, 128.
   Profits of, 127.
   Relation to Wage-earner, 127.
   Point of Socialistic Attack, 241, 242.
Improvements. See Land.
Income Tax. See Taxation.
Inertia of Labour and Capital, 140.
Intellect. See Capital.
Interest, Definition, 112.
   Source of, 109–112, 114.
   Determination, 117.
   Tendencies, 130.
   Imperfect Competition, 115.
   Abstinence, 59.
   See Risk.
International Trade, 137–146.
   As Division of Labour, 137.
   Quasi-rents in, 139.
   Inertia of Labour and Capital, 140.
   Monopoly Conditions, 140–142.
   Infant Industries, 145.
   Tax on Foreigners, 144.
   Effects on Rents, 146.
   Prices and Currency Movements, 190–192.

Jevons, Stanley, 28 n., 44 n., 55 n., 60 n., 168.

King's, Gregory, Law, 79, 142 n.

Labour. See Wages.
   Has value, how? 50. See Value.
   Unions. See Trades-unions.
Laissez-faire examined, 223.
Land, Fertility, 73.
   Diminishing Returns, 68.
   Improvements, 84.
   Tax on. See Taxation.
   See Rent.
Loans. See Interest.

Machinery. See Rent. See Wages.
Malthus. See Population.
Man, the Centre of Economics, 10, 91.
   And Environment, 5–7, 28.
   What is Productive, 61.
   Average, 121.
Margin of Cultivation. See Rent.
Marginal Utility. See Utility.

Marshall, Alfred, 32, 44 n., 55 n., 60 n., 68, 68 n., 73, 81 n., 128 n., 136 n., 160 n., 221 n.
Mill, J. S., 136.
Modern Era. See Competition.
Monometallism. See Currency and Bimetallism.
Money. See Currency.
Monopolies, 147–152.
   Buyers, 152.
   Sellers, 149.
   Labourers. See Trades-unions.
   Causes, 142, 148.
   Evils, 149.
   See Municipal Ownership.
Morality, Advantages, 15, 23 n.
Multiple Standard, 297.
Municipal Ownership, 248, 249.

Nature. See Man and Environment.
Needs. See Demand.
Normal Value. See Value.

Panics. See Crises.
Paper Money. See Currency.
Political Economy: Its Scope, 1.
   Definition, 1, 2.
   Attitude as a Science, 2.
   Attitude as an Art, 2.
   Character of its Laws, 3, 4.
   Basis, 15.
   Motive, 14–16.
Population, 92–99, 252–258.
   And Rent, 68–69.
   And Labour-cost, 92.
   Malthusian Law, 94–97.
   Standard of Life and Birth-rate, 252–260, 262, 263. See Fashion.
Porter, Robert, 99 n.
Price. See Cost of Production.
Prices, Retail, 133.
Production, is Creation of Utility, 61.
   See Cost of Production.
Profits: Defined, 61, 62.
   Tendencies, 131.
   Fixation, 127.
   Absolute and Relative, 63.
   Distinguished from Wages, 64.
   See Risk.
   See Imprenditor.
Profit-sharing, 247.
Protection. See International Trade.

380   INDEX

Quasi-rent, 39, 40, 76.
    In Interest, 117.
    Is Part of Profits, 117.

Railroads, 248, 249.
    Discriminations, 249.
    State Control, 249.
    State Ownership, 249.
Rent of Land, 67–81.
    Ricardian Theory stated, 68–70.
    Ricardian Theory modified, 72, 73.
    Demand, 79, 80.
    Urban Land, 80.
    Relation to Price. See Cost of Production.
    Diminishing Returns, 68.
    Margin of Cultivation, 70, 73, 75.
    Unearned Increment, 73, 81.
    Methods, Machinery and Transportation, 79, 80.
Retail Prices, 133.
Returns, 252.
    Decreasing, 68.
    Increasing, 132.
Revenue. See Taxation.
Ricardo. See Rent.
Rich, Social Function of; 250, 251.
Risk, and Profit, 66, 134.
    And Interest, 115, 119.
    See Speculation.
Rogers, Thorold, 60 n., 66 n., 99 n., 142 n., 222 n.
Roscher, Wilhelm, 44 n., 55 n., 228 n.

Sacrifice. See Cost. See Motive.
Salaries. See Wages.
Say, Leon, 44 n.
Science, Growth of, 14, 15.
    As Capital, 23 n.
Selfishness, 15.
Senior, N. W., 44 n., 99 n.
Services, 12.
    In Standard of Living, 164.
Sidgwick, Henry, 23 n., 81 n., 104, 119 n., 128 n., 131 n., 136 n., 160 n., 226 n., 251.
Silver. See Currency.
Sismondi, J. C., 28 n.
Smith, Adam, 7 n.
Socialism, 218–242.
    Ethical Argument, 223–226.
    Historical Argument, 227, 228.

Socialism: Economic Argument, 229.
    See Competition.
Speculation, 134–136.
    In Land, 136. See Taxation.
    See Risk.
    Corners, 136.
Spencer, Herbert, 255.
Standard of Life. See Population.
    See Demand.
Standard of Payments. See Currency.
Steam, New Era, 218.
Strikes. See Labour-unions.
Successions. See Taxation.
Sumptuary Laws, 237. See Taxation.
Survival of the Fittest. See Population.

Tariff, Effect on Prices, 213–216.
    See International Trade.
Taxation, 155–161.
    Incidence, 155–160.
    Income, 278.
    Expenditure, 278–280.
    Luxury, 159, 161 n.
    Vice, 159, 160.
    Land, 81, 159, 282, 283, 146.
    Inheritance, 279.
    Progressive, 249, 279.
    Paupers, 280.
    Direct and Indirect, 161 n.
    Double, 276.
    Faculty, 277.
Trades-unions, 153, 154, 241, 245.
    Conditions of Success, 153.
    Effects, 153, 284, 285.
    Apprentices, 286.
Transportation: Is Productive, 36, 101.
    Modern Importance, 218.
    Incidence of Cost, 128.
    See International Trade.
    See Taxation.
    See Railroads.
    See Monopolies.
    See Municipal Ownership.
Trusts. See Monopolies.
Turgot, Anne R., 119 n.

Undertaker. See Imprenditor.
Unearned Increment. See Taxation on Land.
Unemployed, 292–295, 300.
Unions. See Trades-unions.

INDEX

Utility, Defined, 8.
   Morally considered, 9.
   An Outside Fact, 10.
   Antagonism with Value, 34.
   Marginal, 30, 31, 39, 40.

Value: Defined, 32, 37.
   Fixation, 38.
   Value and Cost. See Cost of Production.
   Antagonism with Utility, 34.
   Equals Marginal Utility, 36, 41.
   Normal, 91.
   Relation to Labour, 46–51, 120.
   Intrinsic, 15, 194.
Vice. See Taxation.
   See Consumption.

Wages: Defined, 61.
   Real and Nominal, 66 n.
   Fixation, 56–58, 121, 122.

Wages: Tendencies, 131.
   Of Women, 122, 291.
   Relation to Rent, 146.
   A Result from Value, 121, 122.
   Eight-hour Day, 284, 285.
   Relation to Cost of Production, 55–60.
   Sweating, 287–289.
   Children, 290.
   Unemployed, 292–295, 300, 301.
Walker, F. A., 99 n., 131, 202, 274 n.
Ward, Lester A., 261.
Wealth: Defined, 10, 18.
   Different Points of View, 19–21, 19 n.
   Materiality, 13.
   Growth of, 14.
   A Question of Correspondence, 22.
   Not always due to Labour, 23.
Women, Labour, 291.
   See Wages.